Leadership Theories
and Case Studies

Leadership Theories and Case Studies:

An Epidemiological Perspective

By

Garry Wade McGiboney

Cambridge
Scholars
Publishing

Leadership Theories and Case Studies: An Epidemiological Perspective

By Garry Wade McGiboney

This book first published 2018

Cambridge Scholars Publishing

Lady Stephenson Library, Newcastle upon Tyne, NE6 2PA, UK

British Library Cataloguing in Publication Data
A catalogue record for this book is available from the British Library

ISBN (10): 1-5275-0937-0
ISBN (13): 978-1-5275-0937-5

This book is dedicated to my son,
Matthew McGiboney, BBA.

Other Books by Garry Wade McGiboney

TABLE OF CONTENTS

Introduction 1

Chapter One.. 7
Leaders and Boards

Chapter Two 29
Selecting a Leader

Chapter Three 62
Successful Leadership Transition

Chapter Four.. 75
Leadership Styles and Traits

Chapter Five 101
Building a Strong Executive Team

Chapter Six 117
Hiring the Right People

Chapter Seven.. 129
Motivation and Change

Chapter Eight.. 144
Safety and Workplace Climate

Chapter Nine.. 161
Strategic Planning that Matters

Chapter Ten 180
External and Internal Evaluations

Chapter Eleven 194
Data-Influenced Decisions

Table of Contents

Chapter Twelve 210
Leadership and Criticism

Chapter Thirteen 222
Preparing for and Handling Bad News

Chapter Fourteen 236
Preparing and Responding to a Crisis

Chapter Fifteen 263
Rumors Management and Control

Notes on Theories and Models 286

Identifying Leadership Style 309

Additional Leadership Self-Assessment Instruments 321

References 323

Biography 343

Index 344

INTRODUCTION

In her book *Bad Leadership*,[1] Barbara Kellerman identified several types of leadership that could be considered destructive: incompetent, rigid, intemperate (lack of control), callous, corrupt, insular, indifferent, and evil (vindictive). Rising to a level of incompetence is not readily apparent to some leaders because a few of them are oblivious to their own shortcomings or they are in a state of denial about their own level of ability and are blinded by their ambition. Also, an incompetent leader is often unaware of his own circumstances because of the grip of his ego. Ryan Holiday wrote,

> *Ego is the enemy of what you want and of what you have: Of mastering a craft. Of real creative insight. Of working well with others. Of building loyalty and support. Of longevity. Of repeating and retaining your success. It repulses advantages and opportunities. It's a magnet for enemies and errors. It is Scylla and Charybdis.* [2]

Some leaders view rigidity and stubbornness as an asset and as a leadership function. Sometimes this type of leadership comes with the encouragement (intentionally or unintentionally) of the organization in which the leader works. It is an extension of the military model of leadership and is reinforced typically at the beginning of a leader's time at the helm of an organization as a clear message to everyone that "a new sheriff is in town." This type of leader is determined to be the boss and everyone must follow blindly or leave immediately. Any employee that disagrees with the rigid leader is branded a trouble maker and is considered disloyal to the organization. This type of "bad" leadership has many elements to it.

In the field of epidemiology, the word "determinants" is used to describe those elements that are causal factors in determining an outcome or

---

[1] Barbara Kellerman, *Bad Leadership*, (Harvard Business Review Press, 2014).

[2] Ryan Holiday, *Ego is the Enemy*, (Portfolio, 2016). Note: *Scylla* and *Charybdis* are monsters in Greek mythology and are in Homer's *Odyssey*, Book XII–the comment "It is Scylla and Charybdis" is in reference to being caught between two irrepressible monsters.

circumstances, such as the determinants of a disease.[3] It is important to note that determinants are not random–they occur in patterns and for a reason. The negative determinants that come from a leader who has a callous disregard for employees or who is ego-based and detached from employees or who cannot make decisions or who makes reckless decisions are often the same leaders that lack self-control, but the lack of self-control is not necessarily manifest in verbal outburst or overtly aggressive behavior. Instead, many destructive and ineffective leaders contrive to embarrass, control, demean and discourage employees in a variety of ways: through other employees, through sarcasm in front of others, by marginalizing the duties of employees or by demoting employees.[4] There are many examples of how these destructive traits take leaders to a point where self-importance causes the demise of an organization and the destruction of the leader's influence if not his career, as he spirals into a pattern of leadership corruption that leads to insularity and isolation and even to what Kellerman calls "evil."[5]

An article in *Psychology Today* titled *"A Toxic Leader Manifesto"* by Alan Goldman describes the role and outcome of destructive leadership and how that type of leadership style creates a negative workplace climate.[6] Goldman challenges toxic leaders in a sarcastic tone. If a leader is determined to be destructive; if that seems to be the only way to lead an organization, Goldman wants, with tongue-in-cheek, to make sure that type of leader does it "correctly." Although Goldman is approaching the topic in a sarcastic manner, there are many essential and meaningful points to gain from his "manifesto" because it adroitly characterizes all that is wrong with a toxic leader.

It is essential to bypass dialogue and question and answers; the leader must attack, deflate or discard employees who are identified as lacking in any way or who dare challenge the leader; bullying must be cultivated and perfected; the leader must yell at and demean employees who fall short, error or are deemed annoying; the leader must stifle any workplace conversation that questions the leader; all attacks against employees must be brought forth into public forums for all to witness; it is mandatory to yell at employees in an effort to promote fear, humiliation and sufficient loss of face; when criticizing

---

[3] *Principles of Epidemiology in Public Health Practice- Third Edition*, (Centers for Disease Control and Prevention, 2010):
https://www.cdc.gov/ophss/ csels/dsepd/ss1978 /lesson1/section1.
[4] Jack Welch, *Winning*, (Harper Collins Publishing, 2005).
[5] Barbara Kellerman, *Bad Leadership*, (Harvard Business Review, 2014).
[6] Alan Goldman, "A Toxic CEO Manifesto," *Psychology Today*, July 2011.

employees the leader must carry this forth harshly and publicly without any opportunity for the offending employee to respond, and the destructive leader must remember that civilized and substantive feedback is his mortal enemy.[7]

Additional research on destructive leadership can be found in Lipman-Blumen's book, *The Allure of Toxic Leaders*, which addresses why employees follow the toxic or destructive leader-typically from a basic need to survive.[8] Employee compliance gives the leader the false impression that he is a good leader and virtually everything he does is appropriate; therefore, the leader believes that his leadership style is effective in the organization. He sees employees being compliant; he sees employees implementing his policies without question, and he hears no criticism of his leadership style or any feedback from his staff that suggests the conditions in the workplace are negative.

Many times, the internal negative determinants of an organization are hidden by a temporary boost in productivity or the illusion of productivity. In this scenario, the board assumes that the new leader is really "shaking things up" and, consequently, improvement, success, and prestige cannot be far away. Lipman-Blumen found that some employees think a strong, dominating, overbearing, cruel leader is attractive and necessary. Typically, employees who fall into this category are those that had little respect for the previous leader and think a new "ass-kicking" leader will bring back past glory. However, there are employees with so little self-respect and self-confidence that they think they deserve someone that is cruel and insensitive.[9] And, of course, there are employees who think being an insensitive and bullying leader fits their style of management, so they view the totalitarian leader as a role model.

It seems that a destructive leader would be easy to identify and dismiss; therefore, it is puzzling why so many destructive leaders exist and it is equally interesting why so many continue in leadership roles for years in organizations before their brand of caustic and negative leadership negatively impacts the organization. However, it makes sense when we look at the profile of many such leaders.

The destructive leaders can be smart, strategic, manipulative, skilled, observant, instinctive, perceptive, articulate, and very persuasive. These are skills that many successful leaders possess, so it is not surprising that

---

[7] Ibid.
[8] Jean Lipman-Blumen, *The Allure of Toxic CEOs*, (Oxford University Press. 2006).
[9] K.R. Harrison, *Victors and Victims*, (Authentic Publishers, 2014).

destructive leaders continue to find work at significant levels of influence and control in organizations. The boards that select this type of leader are naturally very defensive about their selection and are quick to point out the qualities of the leader that first made the person attractive for the position. This is called *cognitive dissonance*–a decision is considered correct even in the face of opposing facts because it must be justified.[10] This is a vague and weak excuse, for seldom does a destructive leader first show signs of venomous behavior when he becomes the leader of an organization. There is usually a telling work history of the leader that some boards ignore or perversely thought were the types of behavior and attitude needed in the organization.

The powerfully negative impact of destructive leadership and the determinants that shape the leadership style can eventually reduce profits, weaken effectiveness, dampen the competitive edge, stifle innovation and improvements, disrupt the strategic plan, negatively impact the workforce, and drive organizational purpose into the ground. Studies by the Harvard School of Business estimate the cost of a failed executive leader at anywhere between $1 million to $2.7 million, depending on the size of the organization.[11] Regardless of the size or type of organization, few can afford for its leadership to fail.

Destructive leadership takes a significant toll on morale and productivity. Studies show that over 40 percent of American employees classify their jobs as stressful and 75 percent of employees said the most stressful part of their job is the behavior and attitude of their immediate supervisor.[12] Studies also indicate that many employees would prefer a more conducive, healthy, and positive working environment over a higher salary.[13] These same studies point to workplace climate as a reflection of leadership.[14]

Destructive leadership behavior in non-profit organizations negatively impacts donations, reduces the volunteer workforce, and causes a reduction in services to the community. Negative and ineffectual leadership in businesses, educational organizations, such as private and public schools and colleges, and other organizations is equally devastating. Careers are destroyed and the

---

[10] Leon Festinger, *A Theory of Cognitive Dissonance*, (Stanford University Press, 1962).
[11] Pamela Mendels, "The Real Cost of Firing a CEO," *Chief Executive*, April 1, 2013.
[12] National Institute for Occupational Safety and Health, Publication #99-101, 1999.
[13] Demet Leblebici, "Impact of Workplace Quality on Employees Productivity," *Journal of Business, Economics and Finance Survey*, Volume 1, Issue 1, 2012.
[14] Ibid.

collective negative impact on the community of stakeholders is negative and far-reaching.

A conundrum is that the elements of good leadership and destructive leadership are so closely aligned that it is not simple to discern the two. This coupled with the dearth of people qualified to be effective leaders creates a near crisis in some organizations. However, the negative impact can be controlled and managed when components of destructive leadership are revealed in organizations by descriptions of behavior and the consequences of such behavior, as well as clearly delineated examples of non-productive leadership versus productive leadership. That is the purpose of this book.

Descriptions of leaders and their behaviors are central to better understanding why boards cannot misstep when choosing a leader and why leaders must understand their role in organizational leadership and leadership accountability.[15] Furthermore, this book includes research and case studies that offer valuable tools and lessons for leaders.

Many people and students of leadership look at examples in the business world and in business-related articles and books to glean information about good leadership to more easily recognize flawed leadership, but seldom will business leaders and non-education entities look at examples of flawed leadership in education and non-profit settings as a learning tool. This book offers lessons for anyone interested in leadership by exploring multiple types of organizations.

But there is something else to offer here, too. Any discussion about the determinants of destructive leadership would not be complete without also including what works. Destructive leaders, boards, and organizations are not necessarily lost causes. There are "antidotes" to the poison of destructive leadership. Sometimes the antidote is disproportionate to the number of determinants to counteract the effects; for example, it takes a steady and long-term "dose" of *servant leadership*[16] to counteract the destructive effects and aftereffects of dictatorial leadership.[17]

The case studies in this book of leadership and governance, including both destructive and effective leadership, come from several sources. There are 500 references and over 50 case studies analyzed to illustrate leadership

---

[15] Kelly Hannum, Jennifer W. Martineau, and Claire Reinelt. *The Handbook of Leadership Development Evaluation*, (Jossey-Bass Publishers. 2006).

[16] Robert Greenleaf, *Servant Leadership: A Journey into the Nature of Legitimate Power and Greatness*, (Paulist Publishing, 2002).

[17] Ibid.

points. Some of the case studies are troubling and some are reassuring. Some case studies are puzzling but they are all revealing.

The message should become clear when reading this book that boards and leaders should be held accountable for allowing a destructive workplace climate to contaminate what otherwise could or should be a healthy organization. Of course, there are well-functioning organizations with effective leadership and governance; however, research shows that half of the people currently new in leadership positions, at least in the western culture, will fail.[18] They fail primarily due their inability or unwillingness to build and maintain a productive team, a positive work climate, and a leadership style that encourages and motivates employees. However, it does not have to be that way.[19]

In this book, the word "determinant" is used frequently. It is a concept that no other book on leadership uses. The word and concept come from the field of epidemiology. Epidemiologists work from two basic principles: (1) all diseases have determinants and (2) diseases do not occur randomly.[20] In other words, there are always causes for diseases and there are patterns that reveal how a disease spreads, which holds the key to how it can be prevented and treated. Effective and ineffective leadership can be viewed the same way because there are always determinants and those impacts are not randomly distributed; the impacts are uniformly and deeply spread throughout an organization. Epidemiologists look for treatments, also, by matching the determinants to the disease. Like the epidemiologists, this book not only identifies determinants, such as arrogance, it also provides research-based "antidotes" to the determinants at the end of each chapter.

At the end of each chapter, there is a list of key terms and concepts, discussion items, and lessons learned highlights. At the end of the book is a section on leadership and motivation theories and models, as well as a section that provides leadership style surveys and assessments that can help readers identify their leadership style while also becoming aware of what changes in leadership style can improve the workplace. The reference section includes numerous citations and advanced reading suggestions.

---

[18] Jacquelyn Smith. "Commons Reasons Half of All New Executives Fail," *Business Insider*, March 2, 2015.
[19] Ibid.
[20] R. Bonita, R. Beaglehole, and T. Kjellstrom, *Basic Epidemiology–2nd Edition,* (World Health Organization, 2006).

CHAPTER ONE

LEADERS AND BOARDS

"The trouble with the world is that the stupid are cocksure and the intelligent are full of doubt."

-Bertrand Russell[1]

Determinants: The role and duties of board members in every organization is important. Board members should not become involved in the daily operations of the organization. Board members that interfere with the daily operations of an organization have a detrimental effect on the entire organization, from top to bottom and inside and outside the organization. Leadership from the board that is self-focused, narrowed-minded, self-serving and that sacrifices the best overall interests of the organization at the altar of self-indulgence is a potently destructive force. That type of leadership from the board can be destructive to an organization's efficiency, reputation, and ability to hire and retain quality leaders and employees. Also, boards that interfere with the daily operations of an organization are prone to select leaders that do not encourage and nurture creative and independent thinkers. An organization's leadership that capitulates at all costs to the board sacrifices his effectiveness and loses the confidence and trust of employees and others. This double dose of negative determinants jeopardizes the future of the organization by leading to decisions that may cost the organization in untold ways for many years. Yet, board members can be the foundational strength of an organization.

Boards must limit its operational intrusions and the leader must have the courage to say no to the board leaders, and they, in turn, must trust his judgment and respect the purpose of the organization. Obviously, board members should be active partners with the leader and bring insight, experience, and suggestions to the leader but not in a manner that forces action. Forcing a leader to act can threaten the level of trust in the

---

[1] Nicholas Griffin, Ed, *The Cambridge Companion to Bertrand Russell*, (Cambridge University Press, 2003).

organization. On the other hand, a disruptive or an inactive or overly deliberate and cautionary leader can force a board to become involved in the operations of the organization to fill the vacuum of leadership.

Leaders and Boards–Interactions

It is a simple but unfortunate truth that many citizens, employees, stakeholders, and investors are not aware of the decisions made by boards and organization leaders until or unless negative events reach the news media or sudden decisions are made inside the organization that comes as a surprise to everyone. Even in organizations where investors, clients, and citizens have a key role to play they remain almost completely and totally disengaged. The level of disengagement is highest with boards that oversee organizations providing services to communities. This is disturbing when one considers that most boards, such as boards of public education and local governments in the United States, are elected.

Citizens could have more of a voice in public policy and local services if they participated in the local board election process. Many citizens cannot name their own board representatives whether it is their school board members, county commissioners, or city council members.

According to the Civic Index for Quality Public Education (Civic Index), a non-profit entity,

In more than 90 percent of the nation's public school districts, elected boards serve as governing bodies and provide leadership in support of education. District boards are often the smallest and most localized elected bodies of our country's governing structures. Unfortunately, the public often overlooks its local board activities and elections while paying more attention to state and national elected officials. Board meetings are often under-attended or seem to be controlled by a few vocal individuals or interest groups. Board members themselves are often doubtful of the public's desire to become involved and informed about issues. In the high-pressure situations common to boards, it is often easier to decide than to reach out to the public and obtain their views before voting. Moreover, in our fast-paced society, members of the public often fail to make the effort to get involved in board issues [2]

According to Fredrick Hess, most governmental boards are composed of five to eight elected members.[3] Many board members are employed full-time

---

[2] *Civic Index for Quality Public Education*, (Public Education Network, 2008).
[3] Fredrick Hess, "The Role of the Local Board." *Center for Public Governance*, 2002.

in a business or some other type of organization, but only a few have a professional background. Individual board members work on average 25 hours per month on board tasks.

In a survey by the Iowa Boards Association (ISBA), the results indicated that only 10 percent of registered voters participated in board election races.[4] According to the ISBA, the percentage had dropped to six percent in some communities. The Civic Index found that 48 percent of citizens could not name one member of the local boards that make decisions that impact citizens, businesses, and others. This is an incredibly low percentage and in large part explains why many board members disagree with each other and often show little interest in working together because there is virtually no accountability for their behavior, leadership, or effectiveness and few people are present to witness the behavior. Consequently, an increasing number of organizational leaders have conflicts with their boards.[5] It should also me noted that employees of non-profit agencies and businesses could not name any members of their respective boards either.[6]

Board members themselves complain that board meetings are generally unproductive since the few people who attend the meetings do not have the larger best interests of the community at heart; instead, the few that do attend board meetings usually advocate for narrow, self-interest topics.

According to the Civic Index, boards, such as education boards, report little public involvement.

While these individuals control the education of all the children in a community and can impact other aspects of the community, research and policy analysis of the way schools are run tells us that the public is uninvolved in keeping boards responsible for their decisions and actions. In fact, public participation has been described as disorganized and occasional.[7]

Hess also found that when boards focus on their mission and adopt the strategies of working together, action planning, and evaluation, the results are positive – outcomes improve as does the fiscal management of the organization.[8] Too often, however, boards do not function that way.

---

[4] *Local Board Voter Participation Survey*, (Iowa Boards Association. 2007).
[5] Kent Weeks, *Boards: Duties, Responsibilities, Decision-Making, and Legal Basis for Local Board Powers*, (State University Press, 2000).
[6] Ibid.
[7] *Local Board Voter Participation Survey*, (Iowa Boards Association, 2007).
[8] Frederick Hess, *The Role of the Local Board*, (Center for Public Education. 2002.)

Case Study #1

A school district in Georgia, United States of America, lost its accreditation because of the behavior of board members and not because of low student academic performance, mediocre teacher or administrator performance, nor was it due to financial issues. The school district lost accreditation because of the outrageous behavior and actions of the board members. The board members tried to force the superintendent to make personnel decisions that favored friends and relatives; they were frequently disrespectful to each other and to the superintendent in public sessions, and they went into schools and intimidated principals and teachers.

The Southern Association of Colleges and Schools (SACS – also referred to as AdvancEd), an accrediting agency approved by the United States Department of Education, previously warned the school district's board members about their unprofessional behavior. In fact, the school district was put on probation by SACS several years before losing accreditation for the same type of misbehavior. After a few years on probation, the school district was removed from probation status. New board members were elected (with a 10 percent voter turnout); however, within just a few years the same problems were cited again by SACS. Citizens and the professional community began to question the power and influence of SACS because the behavior of the board did not change; in fact, the board became even more dysfunctional, even after SACS issued warnings and provided governance training and other interventions. At the same time, SACS officials began to question how seriously the citizens and community leaders wanted the board to improve because the same members were re-elected.

When SACS finally pulled the school district's accreditation due to the behavior of the board members, the community was incredulous. The loss of accreditation had a profoundly negative impact on students graduating from a non-accredited school district, which impaired the students' chances for college acceptance and college scholarships. Also, the loss of accreditation negatively impacted local businesses and property values. However, during the decade of poor board governance, local business leaders made no effort to improve the conditions or influence the board nor did they become involved in the election of board members.

The Role of Boards

Business boards, non-profit boards, and other institution boards often make the same mistakes, with the most common getting entangled with personnel issues.

Ellis Carter writes about non-profit board members that interfere with the day-to-day operations of organizations, which causes disruptions and confusion with functions and employees.

For a nonprofit organization with paid staff, once board members demand keys to the organization's offices and start making direct demands on staff members that report to the chief executive, the board has crossed the line. The board's key duties are to provide oversight and strategic direction, not to meddle in the organization's day to day affairs. Board members who cross this line are undermining the authority of the chief executive to their own detriment and should be prepared to quit their day jobs. Similarly, staff should not invite micromanagement by asking the board to take on day-to-day tasks that the staff should be handling. The size and budget of smaller organizations necessitate some blurring of these lines, but board members and staff should know their roles and attempt to adhere to them as much as possible. [9]

In an article entitled *Boards: Duties, Responsibilities, Decision-Making and Legal Basis for Local Board Powers,* Kent Weeks writes about how board members confuse their role as policy makers and disrupt administrative operational decision making.

A regular criticism of local boards is the tendency of board members to confuse monitoring of key outcomes and executive performance with prescribing how to manage the components of the system. A study conducted in West Virginia found that boards spent 3 percent of their time on policy development and as much as 54 percent of their time on administrative matters. A study of fifty-five randomly selected boards indicated that financial and personnel issues were among the most frequent areas of decision-making, displacing deliberations on policy by a significant margin. The local board has a vital role in providing leadership, serving as a forum for citizen input relevant to public interests, and inculcating the beliefs, behaviors, and symbolic representations that define the organizational culture of the organization. In this role, the board's responsibilities include adopting a

---

[9] Ellis Carter. "Top Ten Non-Profit Governance Mistakes." *Charity Lawyer,* September 12, 2009: charitylawyerblog.com/2009/09/12/top-ten-non-profit-governance-mistakes /#ixzz4K9x8oqJc.

unifying vision and mission, soliciting and balancing the participation and input of members of the community, and advocating on behalf of the needs at the local, state, and national levels. Consistent with this leadership responsibility, the local board should emphasize the standard of continuous improvement for its own operations as well as that of the community as a whole and undertake to evaluate its performance and improve upon that performance.[10]

The United States of America national report *Facing the Challenge: The Report of the Twentieth Century Task Force on School Governance* recommended that boards focus on their role as policy makers instead of trying to be management committees:

Clear delineation of roles and responsibilities between the board and the CEO, clearly stated expectations, continuous sharing of information, and open, honest communication among all parties nurture a positive relationship between board members and their respective CEO. [11]

Boards must trust the organization's leader and leadership team to make administrative decisions that are best for the organization.

Boards often select leaders for short-term reasons and not with the future in mind, and many of the board members do not understand how the organization operates daily; therefore, they do not understand that running an organization is a complex task that can be negatively impacted by board behavior and the selection of a leader that does not meet the needs of the organization.

In some cases, board members previously worked in the same organization or in a similar organization; therefore, they may think they know how the organization operates or should operate and what the leader should do to make the organization run effectively. But the reality is that once a person is removed from the daily operations of an organization it all changes very quickly and the perspective is from a different angle, so while previous experience can be beneficial, it does not equate to the board member possessing more knowledge of management than the organization's leader, and it certainly is no reason or excuse for interfering with the daily operations of the organization.

---

[10] Kent Weeks, *Boards: Duties, Responsibilities, Decision-Making, and Legal Basis for Local Board Powers*, (State University Press. 2000).

[11] Jacqueline Danzberger, *Facing the Challenge: The Report of the Twentieth Century Task Force on School Governance*, (Brookings Institute. 2002).

In diverse types of organizations, there are examples of board interference. In a widely publicized case reported in the *St. Louis Business Journal*, a member of a bank board resigned, complaining that the chairman of the bank's board constantly and consistently interfered with the CEO and managers of the bank. After resigning from the board, he wrote:

> *The present management staff does not have the ability to run the bank under the conditions set forth by the chairman of the board. The board will not allow the management to run the bank.*[12]

The chairman of the board had previous banking experience and thought he knew more about operating a bank than the leader the board hired to run the bank.

In another example, a board member of a private school insisted on major renovations including a six-classroom addition to the elementary section of the private school even though the school was experiencing declining enrollment. The school director and other members of the board capitulated to the board member's demands, so dollars went toward the unnecessary renovations of the school. This decision cost hundreds of thousands of dollars, damaged morale, and eroded community and employee confidence in leadership because the additional rooms were not used for students; instead, they became storage rooms. Again, the other board members and the school director should have stopped it. More to the point, the parents and other stakeholders should have shown enough interest by selecting more responsible board members and then holding them accountable. This was an example of two elements of poor leadership: bullying behavior and apathy.

Bullying leadership at the governance level not only affects the top management of an organization, it also negatively impacts the entire organization.[13] When leaders give in to board members although they know the decision does not meet the needs of the organization, they have diminished their influence. At the very least the leader should try to persuade the board by doing research, finding the facts, and collating and reporting the facts that clearly show that a decision is best for the organization and clearly explain why contrary decisions are detrimental. Anything less is a display of

---

[12] Greg Edwards, "Truman Bank Board Member Resigns Cites Interference." *St. Louis Business Journal*, September 28, 2011.

[13] Alice G. Walton, "The Dark Side of Leadership." *Forbes*, February 7, 2013.

apathy in the disguise of "keeping the peace," which is an enemy of leadership.[14]

Case Study #2

On nothing more than the whim of one board member, a privately held company purchased a large tract of land for millions of dollars that included an abandoned shopping mall with the idea that the company would relocate to the facility after it was remodeled. The board member thought the large parking lot could be used to park all of the organization's vehicles in one place for logistical benefits, security, and maintenance purposes. The CEO of the company was against the purchase of the property for several reasons, but he did not create a counterproposal nor did he speak out against the purchase, much to the frustration of his executive team. His apathetic response was grounded in fear of the board and his own indecisive leadership style. He adopted the philosophy that "everything will work out on its own." According to Nayer, leaders become indecisive for a variety of reasons but primarily because,

1. *The leader is a perfectionist who will not decide until every possible piece of data is gathered;*
2. *The leader is paralyzed by uncertainty; or*
3. *The leader prefers the safety of the status quo – go along to get along.*[15]

The building was in such bad repair it would cost over $400,000 to renovate it. Also, upon closer inspection, it was determined that the huge parking area would have to be repaved to handle the weight of the vehicles, which included heavy equipment. The building was purchased and at the time of the publication of this book, it sits unused and deteriorating. The surrounding property has gone to seed. That decision cost almost three million dollars of company assets because one board member insisted that it be purchased, the CEO capitulated and showed no leadership, and no other board member objected. The board and the CEO made lethal mistakes related to poor leadership: they did not plan; they let one board member dominant; they

---

[14] Grady Bogue, *The Enemies of Leadership*, (Phi Delta Kappa International Press, 1985).

[15] Vineet Hayar, "Managing Three Types of Bad Bosses." *Harvard Business Review*, December 1, 2014.

misspent assets; they did not do their homework, and they neglected due diligence and sound leadership and stewardship principles.[16]

Case Study #3

A non-profit agency that provided essential services to its community was considering expanding its outreach program. To do so, it needed a larger facility. The organization's CEO received permission from the board to develop the expansion concept further. The CEO and his management staff spent considerable time researching all possible pros and cons of the expansion and received many hours of pro bono work from attorneys, real estate agents, architects, accountants, and other professionals. A thorough expansion plan was developed that included the site of the proposed facility, a service map of the projected expanded service area, the reallocation plan of existing staff, an implementation timeline, and a cost-benefit analysis. Everything seemed to be going well during the presentation to the board. However, one board member asked the CEO if he considered vacant buildings in the board member's neighborhood. The CEO replied that the management staff with the assistance of several volunteer professionals considered several buildings and the one being recommended was the best choice. Despite all evidence to the contrary, the board member objected. He insisted on knowing in more detail why the buildings in his neighborhood were rejected. During a board meeting, he said the new facility should be placed in his neighborhood. Showing weak leadership and no skills at negotiation or mediation, the leader and the remaining members of the board invested $15,000 more in another feasibility study, even though the previous study showed that no buildings in that area of the community would fit the needs and intentions of the non-profit. The follow-up feasibility study results were the same. So, because of one self-serving board member, the non-profit wasted thousands of dollars.[17]

Influencing

John Jantsch, the author of *The Commitment Engine*, referred to dysfunctional leadership as *"disconnected influence."*[18] This is when the

---

[16] Pat Curry, "Ten Lethal Mistakes." 2015, *Bankrate.com.*

[17] Holly Hall, "Feasibility Studies for Capital Campaigns Are a Waste of Money." *The Chronicle of Philanthropy*, March 17, 2015.

[18] John Jantsch, *The Commitment Engine*, (Penguin Group, 2012).

influence is focused on a board member getting what he wants at the expense of what is best for the organization. A board member suffering from disconnected influence views almost everyone, including fellow board members, as either adversaries or allies and uses what Jantsch refers to as "*conditional compliance.*" This is when the outcomes make him look good and satisfy his egocentric needs. This type of board member takes adversarial positions personally and only focuses on the short-term, regardless of what the long-term impact may be. Contrast this to the healthier and more productive "*connected influencer.*" The connected influencer tries to influence in a positive manner for overall better results for the organization.[19] Jantsch says that the connected influencer is a board member who views other people as collaborators, regardless of whether they disagree with him or not. If there is a disagreement, he will try to better understand why someone disagrees with him. Also, he "*strives to gain sustained commitment and communications.*"[20] The power of a connected influencer board member is her ability to persuade without pushing. Therefore, her influence is more profound because it is meaningful and not at the expense of other board members or the organization's leadership.[21]

Leadership and governance must co-exist and there is no time to waste. As Jantsch points out, board members who insist on "pushing" their point of view without listening to or considering other points of view have a flawed and failed strategy that certainly will not benefit the organization. Jantsch says this approach is deeply flawed.

Pressing your case too much instead of striving to understand your counterpart's point of view and perspective is not good for the organization.[22]

The behavior of boards and the failure of an organization's leader to make tough decisions and stand by them is not an exercise in petty politics that impact only a few people. It is a seriously negative determinant that impacts the entire organization.

---

[19] Ibid.
[20] Ibid.
[21] Ibid.
[22] Ibid.

Case Study #4[23]

One year an internationally known commercial development company purchased large parcels of land to build a shopping area with plans to include apartments, condominiums, houses, office building, and a park. It was slated to be a "Live, Work, Play" community. The only remaining parcel of land the company needed was owned by the local school district. The parcel of land was in a strategically important section of the proposed development. The project could not proceed without that parcel of land. An old high school building that housed a non-traditional high school, a small performing arts school and a teacher training center was on the section of property the development company needed to begin the project. Also, there was a 40-year-old high school football stadium in bad repair behind the school building.

The board, school district CEO, local businesses and property owners were in favor of the purchase. However, two local board members who lived in the area were worried about traffic problems. The developer's plans would have relieved traffic in the area, but the two board members spoke out against selling the property. They never said anything about what was best for the entire school district, the business in the area, and what the long-term plan was for the property, or even what was best for students and the neighborhood. However, the two local board members pressed hard to refuse the developer's offer on the land. The five other board members supported the purchase but said very little in opposition to the two board members. No one from the business community, the neighborhood, parents, nor other board members tried diligently to influence the dissenting board members. The developers offered $64 million. The only portion of the $64 million that would be obligated was for replacement of the stadium, which was about $10 million (purchase of land and the cost of building a stadium). The rest of the money would not be obligated because a new facility for the non-traditional high school and plans for the other program occupants of the building were already approved and funding for construction of the school was available from a special purpose local option sales tax (SPLOST), which is used to avoid bond debts.[24]

Because the school district owned the last essential piece of property to complete the site plan, the school district could have received several million

---

[23] Garry W. McGiboney, *Leadership Lessons for Leaders and Governing Boards*, (Anaphora Literary Press, 2014).

[24] Carla Parker, "School District Officials Discuss What to Do with Briarcliff Property." *The Champion Newspaper*, September 27, 2013.

more dollars for the sale of the land had they continued to negotiate with the developers, but that did not occur. With resistance from only two of seven local board members who refused to see the value to the school district overall and in the long term the possibility of funding a new regional stadium to replace the dilapidated one and the availability of money that could have been used for other essential projects to help students was forever lost.[25] Fast forward a few years to find the same school district struggling with its budget because of the declining economy, reduced local revenues, and education cuts at the state level.[26] Instead of $54 million in the bank, assuming $10 million would have been spent on a new stadium, for the first time in the school district's 80 year history employees were laid off and the operating reserve was down to just a few million, enough to operate the school district for one day in an emergency.[27] Additionally, the school building on the site of the property had to be abandoned because of the poor condition of the building and the school district's lack of resources to remodel or maintain the building. The detrimental determinants of the two self-serving board members coupled with the failure of the CEO and the other board members to press forward to do what was best for the school district damaged the school district for decades.

The Negative Effects of Boards

In an article by Lisa Iannucci, she describes the disruption caused in a community neighborhood association through the voice of a board member who was demoralized by the behavior of a fellow board member, which is an example of how board behavior can jeopardize the mission of an organization regardless of its mission or size.

> There are the WIIFMs (What's in it for me) and the Idiots. The WIIFMs get on the boards because they have an ax to grind or a pet issue they want to promote. The Idiots either get roped into it by some well-meaning family member or neighbor, or they think they know everything and know nothing. To be good board members they must be able to set aside their personal biases and ambitions, be willing to learn and listen, and think about the good

[25] Patti Casey, "Sembler Property Offer Considered." *GoDeKalb.com.*
[26] Will Frampton, "DeKalb County Schools Face Even Deeper Cuts." *CBS46 News*, [written transcript], July 11, 2012.
[27] Ibid.

of the whole community and organization. Many folks find that very difficult.[28]

Iannucci strongly suggests that the other board members

...have a talk with difficult board members, explaining to them what it is they are doing wrong. If there is a bad board member and it affects your situation it may worth trying to win him over.[29]

The Pros and Cons of the "Business Model"

Many local board members and the public accept the premise that all the ills of every organization would be or could be remedied if they would only adopt the "business leadership model." Of course, this is reference to the western culture business model. Board members are particularly outspoken about the value of operating organizations like a business.[30] It is a popular notion. But should school districts or non-profits or for that matter any organization really operate like a business? Should all businesses operate the same? Should a background or experience in the business world be a qualifying requirement of prospective board members and organizational leaders? What does it mean to run an organization like a business?

Many board members with a business background readily agree that organizations should be run like a business. It certainly is an opinion that is shared by board members and leaders of many organizations, but those that advocate so ferociously for this focus on the business model should be cautious about forcing it on organizations and fellow board members without describing and defining exactly what that declaration means.[31] It is a crucial point because the business model may not suit every organization. Forcing an organization to adopt a business model is outside of the responsibility of board members because it is dictating the operational functions of the organization but unfortunately, it is not uncommon.

Since many board members believe that all organizations should operate like a business, let's take a closer look at what that really means. According to *Forbes*, eight out of every 10 new businesses fail within the first 18

---

[28] Lisa Iannucci, *Dealing with Difficult Board Members*, (The Cooperator, 2008).
[29] Ibid.
[30] Mohan Sivaloganathan, "Why and How You Should Run Your Non-Profit Like a For-Profit Organization," *FC Leadership*, January 2015.
[31] Dan Ehrenkrantz, "Why You Should Run Your Business Like a Non-Profit," *Forbes,* September 2014.

months.[32] That is an average of 15,000 business failures per year in the United States.[33]

Which company business model do board members want organizations to adopt? The overgeneralizations about running all organizations like a business run up against the data and facts. Instead of relying solely on a business model, boards and leaders should first consider what is best for the organization and how their behavior and decision-making can benefit the organization. The strategic plan should be an operational plan that remains true to the purpose and nature of the organization instead of being forced into a model that may not be suitable.

Case Study #5

In a small community with a long tradition of art appreciation, a board managed the policies of the local arts council. Over the course of many years, the reputation of the community's appreciation of the arts grew statewide. For decades, the arts council thrived and the community benefitted greatly from the business, industry, and education that developed through local pride in the arts.

One year a new member of the board became disenfranchised with the director of the arts council because he did not include the board member's art piece in the annual art exhibit. The director assured the board member that the artwork was judged to be good by the advisory committee that selected art for the art exhibit, but many other art pieces were superior to that piece of artwork. For decades, the selection of art for the annual exhibits by the advisory committee was sacrosanct. The thought of interference in the selection process by a board member of the arts council was unthinkable. The new board member was selected by his peers primarily because of his financial standing in the community, not because he had a history of supporting the arts. In fact, he had shown very little interest in the community's arts endeavors and exhibits before joining the board. This was widely known by many others on the board and by the director; yet, he was added to the board. It became obvious soon after his appointment that the board and the director had sacrificed its purpose and commitment to the arts for the status of and possible financial contributions from the new board

---

[32] Eric T. Wagner, "Five Reasons Eight Out of 10 Businesses Fail," *Forbes,* September 2013.
[33] "United States Bureau of Labor Statistics. Annual Report – 2014." *United States Government.* Usgov.documents.org.

member. It was also obvious that the new board member was not committed to the arts and he had no respect for the long-standing process of selecting art for the annual exhibit. After the director explained the process of selecting art for the exhibit and the critical role of the advisory committee, the new board member was unmoved. He insisted that his artwork is included in the exhibit. The director informally and formally addressed the issue with the other board members. Rather than maintaining its integrity and focus on the traditional process of artwork selection; instead of standing strong against one board member's inappropriate demands; instead of appreciating and respecting the authority and responsibility of the director's position and key role in the council and community; instead of standing on its own principles, all of that was compromised and the questionable artwork was included in the exhibit. This unfortunate and ill-advised decision by the board and director created chaos. Other board members began to question the art show selections by the advisory committee and each one began to name their own favorite art pieces. Over a brief period, the selection process broke down completely; the quality of the art exhibit declined; the trust of the director diminished, and the once broad community support of the arts council started to erode. The director was removed and without a succession plan for the leadership position, a director was selected that was unqualified for the position and who was told by the board that he was not to operate independently of the board. In other words, the board made it clear that they would run the organization.[34] Years later that once proud and prestigious arts council became a shell of its former existence, and its decline started with one board member who put himself over the best interests of the organization and was supported by a board and leader that failed to carry out its duties and responsibilities when they abandoned the organization's purpose and traditions. Once the trust was eroded and the focus of the organization shifted from its mission to individual self-interests, the core of the organization was damaged from the inside out. The purpose of leadership was lost. But more importantly, sustainability of the effectiveness of the organization suffered.

Antidotes: There are many examples, almost too many to note, where sustainability was lost and an organization faltered because of conflicts between a board and leadership of the organization. In every story told in this chapter, the goals and the effectiveness of each organization were compromised and the organization's ability to sustain good, effective programs was weakened substantially.

---

[34] Ron Auster, *Small Non-Profit Organization Case Studies*, (Astor Publishing, 2013).

In Stephen Covey's book *The Speed of Trust*, he states that an effective leader must have the trust of everyone in the organization. The failure to act in the best interests of the organization comes from a lack of trust and over self-indulgence from the leader at the CEO level and at the board level.[35] Covey asks the question: "Do people trust their boss?" If the trust of leadership is diminished it reverberates across the organization. In the book *The Twelve Absolutes of Leadership*, Gary Burnison suggests that the lack of trust and the forfeiture of leadership develop when an organization loses its purpose.[36] That purpose is compromised when the trust and integrity of the leader and the board have diminished due to role confusion and the failure to remain true to the purpose of the organization.

In this chapter, there are examples of board members replacing the purpose of the organization with their own agendas and ambitions. This is most likely to occur when the leader of the organization abdicates his role to please board members, which compromises the functions of the organization. The antidote to this type of determinant is an absolute, unbreakable devotion and commitment to the organization's purpose. Burnison writes:

> *To be a leader is to be passionate about purpose, authentically and genuinely. Leaders make purpose their North Star and continually lead the organization toward it. Embody purpose–people will watch you and follow your lead; shape and continually deliver the message about purpose; walk the talk of purpose in everything you do–if you don't, the purpose is just the slogan du jour; be grounded in purpose over time.[37]*

Board members and leaders must maintain the purpose of the organization and protect it because the insidious effects of even the smallest slippage away from the organization's purpose can ruin it. Boards must also understand their role as leaders. Carlo Corsi listed several effective components of board leadership.

> *The effective functioning of a board depends on a number of factors, including the mix of knowledge and experience among the directors, the quality of information they receive and their ability to operate as a team. The chairman's role is pivotal in managing the group dynamic, playing to the board's strengths and maintaining regular contact with organizational directors between meetings. High-functioning boards rotate meetings around*

---

[35] Stephen Covey, *The Speed of Trust*, (Simon and Schuster, 2008).
[36] Gary Burnison, *The Twelve Absolutes of Leadership*, (McGraw-Hill Education Publishing, 2012).
[37] Ibid.

locations. Directors are invited to attend all committee meetings and are free to ask questions, however difficult. Boards not only evaluate the performance of the CEO but take the formal assessment of their own work seriously and use the findings to develop—and hold themselves to—objectives for improvement. Transparency and trust prevail.[38]

An effective board should take the time for self-evaluation, using the role of the board and the mission of the organization as cornerstone indicators of effectiveness. The effective board member stays focused on the purpose of the organization. Each board member's role is protecting and encouraging the purpose of the organization. Effective boards can put their organization at a distinct advantage. This is evident in the way they address strategy-from the formation of the organization's strategic plan to implementation of the strategic plan. The conventional delineation of responsibility focuses on the CEO and his executive team being responsible for the strategic plans with input or suggestions from the board. The strategic plans are fine-tuned and then executed by the CEO and her team. This also provides a means of assessing the CEO's performance against a set of agreed-upon objectives.[39]

The distinction is clear–an organization's leader and his executive team create the strategy and execute the strategy. The board offers support and holds the leadership accountable, but board members are not involved in the operational components of the organization. When the roles of the board and the leader are unclear or are reversed, this threatens the operations of the organization.

Managing Risk–a Board Function?

Since the start of the most recent economic crisis, boards are urgently rethinking their approach to risk oversight. Outside of financial services, where risk committees are well established, responsibility for risk still tends to lie with the audit committee, where most time is spent on financial risk. Now, however, the risk is defined in broader terms, encompassing not just financial matters, but also areas such as safety, the environment, information technology security, industrial relations, workplace climate, and corporate reputation. Boards should determine whether they have the optimal structure

---

[38] Carlo Corsi, Guilherme Dale, Julie Hembrock Daum, John Mumm, and Willi Schoppen, *Five Things Board Directors Should Be Thinking About*, (Point of View, 2010).

[39] Crispin Gregoire, "The Role of Boards in Fostering Accountability." *The International Journal of Not for Profit Law*, Volume 2, Issue 3, March 2000.

for overseeing risk, including whether there is a clear delineation of risk management responsibilities between the board and the executive team. Boards should review plans for risk management and evaluate the leader's ability to carrying out and manage the risk. They should tailor their participation and committee structure to the sensitivity and vulnerability of their organization's risk factors. When speaking about how businesses responded to the fiscal crisis in 2008, Carol Stephenson said that leaders that created a work culture of risk awareness and freedom to express concerns were the ones that survived.

> *The good leaders welcome different opinions and points of views. Because of this, they are aware of potential risks and have the ability to make more informed and inevitably wiser decisions. Our research about the global financial meltdown showed that receptiveness to diverse viewpoints and opinions often defined the cultures of companies that survived the crisis and continue to thrive.* [40]

Stephenson found that leaders who created either intimidating or insensitive workplace climates did not respond well to the fiscal crisis because there was no motivation or incentive for employees to share in risk management.

> *Policies and procedures for predicting, evaluating and managing risk are important. But if leaders don't ask the right questions, if they don't seek out a diversity of opinions and perspectives, and if they don't act with integrity, these rules won't make any difference. And when that happens, the blame for the damaging consequences rests solely with leadership.* [41]

The importance of risk management cannot be overstated. Some experts report that this is the primary reason for increasing board participation in the operations of the organization; it's an effort to minimize risks.[42]

The accounting firm of Ernest & Young[43] offers a list of important questions for leaders and boards that can guide appropriate considerations of risk and may be used to determine the role of a board regarding risks.[44]

---

[40] Carol Stephenson, "The Role of Leadership in Managing Risk," *The Ivey Business Journal*, December 2010.

[41] Ibid.

[42] *"The Critical Role of the Board in Effective Risk Oversight."* (Ernest & Young 2015).

[43] Ernest & Young is an international company that focuses on assurance, tax, transaction, and advisory services.

[44] Ernest & Young Corporate manual, 2015.

1. *Do we have the right balance between strategic and compliance risks?*
2. *Are we doing our best to expect the unexpected?*
3. *Is our board fully cognizant of the benefits, implications, and potential risks?*
4. *Are we doing enough to validate that our risk management reflects our stated values?*

Contrary to what some board members think, board interference and persuasion could make financial and other risks higher and more pervasive. It is a matter of trust between the leader of the organization and the board and the appropriate roles of each. Financial risk concerns are becoming an excuse for some boards to virtually take control of organizations, in the name of reduced risks. The leader cannot let this happen for several reasons, but primarily because the board members do not have the operational insight or expertise to run the organization and because the mission and purpose of the organization can be compromised when the roles of the board and the leader are confused, which increases risks factors.

Sustainability

Ultimately, it is sustainability that is the measure of success. There are organizations and businesses that found short-term success but do not exist now; for example, the *Fortune 500* list.[45] *Fortune* magazine annually lists the top 500 successful businesses in the world. In the 1980s it took five years for one-third of the *Fortune 500* to be replaced; in the 1970s it took a decade to replace the *Fortune 500*, but prior to the 1970s it took two decades.[46] Jim Collins, author of *Built to Last*, notes that only 71 companies on the original 1955 *Fortune 500* list are there today.[47]

Sustainability should be a major concern to board members and leaders, which means, for example, that constant changes in an organization's leadership because of the failure of the board to select effective leaders and/or its failure to work effectively with leadership jeopardizes the sustainability of the organization. It can be a challenge to get boards and leaders of organizations to understand and accept the necessity to work together and set aside their petty grievances with each other.

---

[45] Dane Stangler and Sam Arbesman, "What Does Fortune 500 Turnover Mean?" *Kaufman Foundation*, 2012.
[46] Jim Collins, *Built to Last*, (Harper Business Essentials, 1994).
[47] Ibid.

Organizational leadership from the board and the CEO that focuses on self-interest has no real goal or plan for sustainability and therefore focuses only on short-term outcomes. They may articulate long-term goals and lofty plans to give the impression that innovation and sustainability are important attributes, but they are not. They desire to make a flashy impression at the expense of substance and sustainability based on a nearsighted and ego driven plan.

No organization's strategic plan will function effectively in a workplace climate where board interference and leader indifference results in short-term operations at the expense of long-term positive outcomes of sustainability. Nor will it be effective if the organization's leadership fails to communicate frequently with employees, which is an essential element of sustainability.

Some organizations understand that sustainability is too important to depend on the interactions between the board and the leader, so they created "*sustainability managers*."[48] Sustainability managers work with the organization's leader and the board to point out how decisions and the behavior of board members may impact the future of the organization. The sustainability managers also provide guidance for boards and leaders in matters that enhance positive results and sustainable outcomes. The sustainability managers are excellent at risk management because they are skilled at identifying possible risks and growing risks, and they feel unafraid to share their concerns with both the board and the leader.

Chapter One Key Words and Concepts

Accreditation
Perfectionist
Ambiguity
Status Quo
Reallocation
Cost-Benefit Analysis
Disconnected Influence
Connected Influencer
Special Purpose Local Option Sales Tax
WIIFM
Speed of Trust
Forfeiture of Leadership
Strategic Plan

---

[48] Steven Cohen. *Sustainability Management*, (Columbia University Press, 2011).

Risk Oversight
Compliance Risks
Made to Stick
Built to Last
Sustainability Managers

Chapter One Discussion Items

Case Study #1: Should the accrediting agency change its purpose? What could the accrediting agency do to encourage school districts to focus more on the academic achievement and hold them accountable for student outcomes?

Case Study #2: Why did the CEO succumb to the wishes of one board member? Could and should the CEO have responded in a different way to the pressure of the board member? What is the leadership role of the CEO and board in controversial situations?

Case Study #3: Should the CEO have consented to another feasibility study for one board member for a new facility? Was that a reasonable request from one board member? What is the leadership role of other board members when one board member makes demands of the CEO?

Case Study #4: Should the majority of the board called for a vote on the sale of the land to the developer and let the board's vote represent the board? Could the CEO offer more advice or information to the board regarding the advantages of the purchase? What could the CEO and board do to prevent a small segment of the board from dominating decisions?

Case Study #5: Why did the board sacrifice its mission and tradition to add a board member with different values and goals? Why didn't the board support the director and the traditions of the organization? What were leadership functions absent in how the director and members of the board handled the situation?

Chapter One Lessons Learned

Boards must limit its operational intrusions and the leader must have the courage to say no to the board leaders, and they, in turn, must trust his judgment and respect the purpose of the organization.

Hess also found that when boards focus on their mission and adopt the strategies of working together, action planning, and evaluation, the results are positive – outcomes improve as does the fiscal management of the organization.

Boards must trust the organization's leader and leadership team to make administrative decisions that are best for the organization.

When leaders give in to board members although they know the decision does not meet the needs of the organization, they have diminished their influence.

The connected influencer tries to influence in a positive manner for overall better results for the organization.

The strategic plan should be an operational plan that remains true to the purpose and nature of the organization instead of being forced into a model that may not be suitable.

If the trust of leadership is diminished it reverberates across the organization.

When the roles of the board and the leader are unclear or are reversed, this threatens the operations of the organization.

The distinction is clear – an organization's leader and his executive team create the strategy and execute the strategy. The board offers support and holds the leadership accountable.

CHAPTER TWO

SELECTING A LEADER

The first responsibility of a leader is to define reality and the last is to say thank you. In between the leader is a servant.

-*Max Dupree*[1]

Determinants: The selection of a leader based on personal agendas of the board or on perceived short-term needs of the organization can decimate critical components of the organization. This is especially toxic when the leadership style of the new leader is laissez-faire or totalitarian because no organization can survive or thrive under either type of leadership. The laissez-faire leader is often controlled by the board, thus, decisions such as personnel decisions are driven more by the leader's need to please the board than by the needs of the organization. The totalitarian leader, on the other hand, tries to control everything and ends up controlling very little. This situation becomes even more disruptive when critical decisions must be made in times of crises. Without the right type of leader - one who has effective communication skills, understands the value of trust, develops strong support staff and seeks independence from the board - a once successful or promising organization can decline rapidly and irreversibly.

Selecting a Leader

There are many different types of leadership found in the literature on management from Robert Greenleaf's *Servant Leadership* [2] style to George Patton's *Military Leadership* [3] style and every type in between, but there are basically three leadership styles, with some crossover, that seem to be central

---

[1] Max Dupree, *Leadership is An Art*, (Crown Business Publisher, 2004).
[2] Robert Greenleaf. *Servant Leadership*, (Paulist Press, 1977 and 2002). Some of Greenleaf's servant leader elements were influenced by Hermann Hesse's book *Journey to the East*, (Samuel von Fischer, 1932).
[3] Alan Axelrod, *Patton on Leadership*, (Palgrave MacMillan Books, 2007).

to the *circular pattern* of leadership selection used by boards in many organizations: benevolent, laissez-faire, and totalitarian. The circular pattern describes how boards select a certain type of leader and then shift to a different type of leader until coming full circle back to the same type of leader previously determined unworkable for the organization.

The cycle may start at any of the leadership styles. For example, an organization with a benevolent leader often moves to the laissez-faire leader to maintain the status quo and moves to the totalitarian leader before cycling back to the benevolent leader and so on. This occurs most often when the board falls into the trap of selecting a leader based not on qualifications for the long-term, but instead on perceived short-term needs of the organization, the biases of board members, and the misconception that the board should be involved in the operational decision-making of the organization. These misguided perceptions can derail the opportunity to select an effective leader.

Jack Welch, in the article *5 Types of Directors Who Don't Deliver*, labeled the type of board member that wants to dictate how an organization operates as "The Meddler."

> ...*meddlers get all mucked up in operational details. They seem oblivious to the fact that board members are there for their wisdom, sound counsel, and judgment, not the day-to-day running of the business.* [4]

The Meddler seeks the support of other board members to select a leader that can be manipulated by the board in order to facilitate more input in the daily operations of the organization.

Often, the different leadership styles follow each other in a peculiar dance of roving leadership styles and inconsistent expectations of boards. The shift in leadership style preferences has as much to do with the purposes and intent of the board and the idiosyncrasies of each board member at the time of the selection than anything else. In other words, circumstances on the board mixed with individual agendas and the condition of the organization often determine what type of leader is selected by the board instead of the qualities of the individual for sustainability and the long-term needs of the organization.

Board members have their own preferences about the type of personality necessary to successfully lead the organization – more so than a leader's skill set. This makes sense if:

---

[4] Jack and Suzy Welch, "5 Types of Directors Who Don't Deliver," 2015, *Linkedin.com*.

1. *The personality type is a good match for the mission and purpose of the organization;*
2. *The personality type is grounded in a positive attitude toward subordinates coupled with superb communication skills;*
3. *The personality type is not one that is perceived as the perfect match because it mirrors the personality of board members who expect the leader to act as they do; and*
4. *The personality type cannot be easily dominated by the board.*

If a leader is viewed by the board as a dictator, a totalitarian (bully)[5] who intimidates the board, employees, and maybe even clients or service providers, the board will grow tired of that leadership style because it generates complaints from clients and employees. A board will also become burdened by the complaints from others who find the behavior of the totalitarian leader worrisome and disrespectful. However, many times the leader was selected by a board that was fully aware of the leader's aggressive style. They wanted him "to shake things up; take the organization beyond the status quo." This happens in several organizations, including the business world. It is the rare circumstance where a board does not have some indication about the leadership style of a newly hired leader. They know what they are getting.

When a totalitarian leader has been selected, typically the board wants a mover and shaker-someone who is not afraid to make changes. A fleeting time later when the board dismisses him, it seldom selects someone of the same leadership style. Instead, the board will most likely select a benevolent, servant-type leader to replace a bully.[6]

The benevolent leader is rare. He possesses three essential elements of an effective leader: he is internal, external, and focused. A very common misconception about a benevolent leader is the notion that he is a saint or has impressive but easily definable traits. That is not the case. Benevolent leaders vary in types of personalities, strengths, and weaknesses – some are introverts and some are extroverts. But they possess a soulful heart for people and they are laser-focused on finding and defining what is best for the organization from the inside and out.

A benevolent leader is hired to make peace, to solve problems with a wise and steady hand, to restore morale and good relations, to calm things down so

---

[5] Chris Meyers, "Why Bullies Make Bad Leaders." *Forbes*, April 1, 2016.
[6] "Benevolent leader:" used in this discourse has many of the qualities of the *Servant Leader*, as described by Robert Greenleaf, in addition to a more practical and practiced skill set that embraces unconventional tactics for problem-solving.

the organization can focus again on its mission and purpose.[7] Many times, this type of leader inherits a dysfunctional organization. The board expects the benevolent leader to be all things to all people and bring purpose back to the organization.

The benevolent leader will look to develop an inclusive vision and mission for the organization and will want to communicate with and support employees, clients, and the board. The benevolent leader will have a good sense of humanity and humility so she will know how to interact with people of all backgrounds in diverse types of situations.

As the philosopher, Sun Tzu wrote:

When one treats people with benevolence, justice, and righteousness, and reposed in them, the army will be united in mind and all will be happy to serve their leader.[8]

The benevolent leader is just as comfortable meeting with leaders, politicians, and benefactors as he is meeting with employees, customers, service providers, citizens, and others that communicate at various levels and in diverse ways. She understands and embraces the value of social capital, collaboration, motivation, and interaction. Yet, the benevolent leader is smart enough to know that tough decisions must be made and someone must be the bearer of tough news sometimes, but the messenger will not necessarily be the benevolent leader. Oftentimes, a benevolent leader will select a tough financial officer, a tough human resources officer, and a tough number two person in command (chief of staff, for example) to handle those duties. This is not avoidance behavior; instead, it is a wise delegation of responsibilities. By doing it this way the benevolent leader is taking on the issue without being controlled by the issue. He is doing his job under tough circumstances by utilizing the talents and expertise of his executive team that he has carefully selected. This is a leadership function.

The collective wisdom of others helps identify and isolate the significant issues and open ideas for solutions. Therein the leader will have a quicker and fuller understanding of the issues and the ramifications of actions or lack of actions based on the recommendations or findings of his team. Of course, if a crisis demands immediate action, the benevolent leader is strong enough to

---

[7] R. Likert, *The Human Organization: Its Management and Value*, (McGraw-Hill, 1967).
[8] Eric Jackson, "Sun Tzu's 31 Best Pieces of Leadership Advice," *Forbes*, May 23, 2014.

make those decisions [this is addressed in the chapters on handling bad news and crisis preparation and response].

The benevolent leader has what Robert Greenleaf calls "*Servant Leadership*" qualities. Greenleaf describes the servant leader:

> *It begins with the natural feeling that one wants to serve, to serve first. Then conscious choice brings one to aspire to lead. The difference manifests itself in the care taken by the servant--first to make sure that other people's highest priority needs are being served.*[9]

The benevolent leader knows how to blend respect for others with the realities of day-to-day leadership and challenges of leading the operations of an organization. In this regard, the benevolent leader, much to the surprise of others, can be shrewd.

Benevolent leaders tend to last longer than other types of leaders because often they follow a short tenure totalitarian leader who created a tense workplace climate and because their leadership style serves the organization well. Consequently, the benevolent leader is given more time in her role because she is generally well-liked by virtually everyone. The "likeability factor" also buys more time for her. There is no guarantee, of course, that a benevolent leader is always a long-term successful leader, but this type of leadership style has better odds for success than most other types. Benevolent leaders are typically successful because the nature of their leadership style is a good match with the needs and challenges of many organizations and because the leader identifies and maximizes the talent pool in the organization.[10]

The benevolent leader leads by example of a positive approach to leadership, by encouragement, by motivation, by focusing on the needs of clients that the organization serves. If the leader must get tough in certain situations, it means more because it is a stark contrast to the leader's typical behavior, which translates into a powerful message. If a leader is a tyrant most of the time and gets upset even for good reason, his tyrannical response does not generate the reaction he wants because it does not signal anything different.

The benevolent leader also can build and maintain a formidable team. He recognizes the needs of the organization at many levels and consequently selects team members that will meet those needs [see the chapters on team

---

[9] Robert Greenleaf, *Servant Leadership: A Journey into the Nature of Legitimate Power and Greatness*, (Paulist Publishing, 2002).

[10] Kenneth Blanchard, *The Servant Leader*, (Thomas Nelson Publishing, 2003).

building and hiring the right person for the job]. It does not mean that the benevolent leader will not ever make an appointment that is political. Politics is part of any organization, but he will not select a team member based solely on that reason and certainly will not sacrifice the good of the organization with a politically-based selection.

The benevolent leader is not intimidated by intelligent employees and is not threatened by team members that do not always agree with him. In fact, he seeks to surround himself with the best and the brightest. In Marcus Buckingham's book, *The One Thing You Need to Know*, he writes:

> *Some managers claim that they don't have the time to select the right person for the team. I have openings now, they say, and these openings must be filled. Good managers know the folly of this approach. They know that, when it comes to building the right team, time is nonnegotiable. You will spend the time. The only question is where you will spend it: on the front end, carefully selecting the right person, or on the back end, desperately trying to transform the person into who you wished he was in the first place.* [11]

Organizational leaders have a thankless job. It is a job that many people do not understand and or care much about until something happens that draws media attention or impacts them or someone they know. According to Cooper, Fuserilli, and Carella, the public perception of organizational leadership positions is that of a job so daunting that only a few individuals desire to pursue the challenge.[12]

The average tenure of a leader in non-profit settings and businesses is not long. According to Steve Denning, chief financial officers last about six years.[13] Based on research by The Center for Association Leadership the average tenure of non-profit chief executive officers is less than four years.[14]

In many cases, the length of time a leader can maintain her job is related to her ability or inability to work with and satisfy board members. Too often if a leader stands up to board members who are out of line with their governing role on issues that are essential to the organization, she is labeled uncooperative.

---

[11] Marcus Buckingham, *The One Thing You Need to Know*, (The Free Press, 2005).
[12] B.S. Cooper, L.D. Fusarelli, and V.A. Carella, "Career Crisis in the Superintendency? National Survey Results," *The American Association of School Administrators*, 2002.
[13] Steve Denning, "Seven Lessons Every CFO Must Learn," *Forbes*, January 2013.
[14] Eileen Morgan Johnson, *Succession Planning for Non-Profit Leaders*, (The Center for Association Leadership, 2007.)

A cooperative relationship between the leader and the board should be the number one quality board members look for in hiring and a leader; at least that is what most board members claim. If, however, a leader gives in to board member's whims, the same board may be quick to label him as weak and insufficiently suited for the job. Many leaders and their boards have this complex issue that creates an awkward dance in governance.

When the Board and Leaders Clash

There are few things more distracting to an organization at all levels than when an organization's leader and the board are locked in one battle after another with each other. If conflicts are routinely resolved that can be a manifestation of a working relationship, but if the conflicts are unresolved and spill over into the operations of the organization then everyone loses. The causalities of these conflicts are the employees, clients, volunteers, and others who matter the most to the organization.

While research cited by the Civic Index shows that most of the time board members vote to approve items brought to the board by leaders of public organizations, businesses, and non-profits[15] that does not include personnel issues or budget issues, which, of course, are critical to the operation of the organization. Several boards address personnel, real estate, and budget issues in executive sessions (closed sessions). The research also does not include the pressure some board members exert on leaders about operational matters–the day-to-day operations of the organization. This is a critical distraction because the daily operation of any organization can be very complicated– providing services or materials each day to clients; maintaining order and cleanliness in facilities; taking inventory and processing countless purchase orders; answering dozens or hundreds of phone calls, emails and letters; addressing personnel and stakeholder issues; maintaining financial records and transactions, and much more, and that is on a good day. If something unforeseen happens, all operations functions can be further stressed. The responsibilities are multi-faceted, so the last thing a leader and his staff needs is an interfering board member. Therefore, how the board interacts with the leader is crucial, so crucial that the relationship can and frequently does impact the vision, mission, performance, morale, and operations and

---

[15] "Civic Index for Quality Public Education, 2008 Annual Report" – developed by the Public Education Network (PEN). PEN was a network of local education funds community based organizations in high-poverty school districts.

effectiveness of the organization. This tenuous relationship depends on a lot of factors.

One of the main factors related directly to the quality of the board and leader relationship is communications. Many studies of various organizations indicate that the lack of communications is a major obstacle to a positive relationship. A study by Young, Peterson, and Short found that communication skills relate directly to the quality of the leader and board relationship which in turn influences decision-making more than any other factor.[16]

In his seminal book, *The Twelve Absolutes of Leadership*, Gary Burnison lists communication as one of the essential leadership functions. In fact, the effectiveness of an organization's leader at all levels of influence on employees, clients, and board members depends significantly on his communications ability and acumen as well as his willingness to take the additional step of identifying successful means of communications.

Communication is where leadership lives and breathes. In good times, people look to the leader for validation and in tough times they look to the leader for assurance. This is accomplished through communications.[17]

Methods of Communications

Most of the studies, research, and articles on communications focus on timing, technique, process, and accuracy, but some of the more recent books written by successful CEOs point out the importance of, among other devices, humor as a communication method, because communication can be enhanced with the insertion of a well-timed bit of humor. One interesting contrast in the use of humor in communications at the leadership level comes from the same company with two distinctively different communication styles.

For years, the iconic leader of IBM was Thomas Watson, Jr., the son of the legendary founder of IBM. Watson, Jr. was an enormously successful leader who made IBM an economic power and a business giant. He was didactic in his communication style and serious-minded with little if any

---

[16] Michelle Young, George J. Petersen, and Paula Scott, "The Complexity of Substantive Reform: A Call for Interdepen-dence Among Key Stakeholders," *Educational Administration Quarterly*, vol. 38 no. 2, (April 2002): doi: 10.1177 /00131 61X02382003.

[17] Gary Burnison, *The Twelve Absolutes of Leadership*, (McGraw-Hill, 2012).

humor or emotion in his written communications method. At times he was too emotional and aggressive when communicating verbally.[18] Contrast that communication style with another IBM CEO, Edward Gerstner, who was also very successful. When he took over the helm at IBM the giant company was bleeding money and had a bleak future. There was even support within IBM and with stockholders to break the company up into several small businesses.[19] Gerstner managed to pull IBM from the brink of being dismantled and returned IBM to its former glory and profitability. In his memoir *Elephants Can Dance,* Gerstner points out the importance of communications and he states that humor is a very important component of effective leadership–an element of communications that is often overlooked. Of course, the timing and circumstances must be right and the humor must be relevant and in good taste, but he noted that humor can create a positive workplace climate and is a very effective communications device.[20]

It is interesting to note that in Watson Jr.'s memoir, *Father, Son and Co.*, he frequently points to the importance of communications with his executive staff, executive board, line and sales staff, media, and IBM clients. But at one point in his book, Watson Jr. laments about his failure or reluctance to show his humorous side more often at work and more importantly at home. He felt that he could have improved workplace climate and his home climate if he had not taken everything so seriously all the time.[21]

President Dwight Eisenhower, known for his stellar military career before he was elected President, often surprised people with his delightful sense of humor and his timing for humor. Regarding the importance of humor, Eisenhower stated,

A sense of humor can be an immense help...a sense of humor is a part of the art of leadership, of getting along with people, of getting things done.[22]

---

[18] Thomas Watson, Jr., *Father, Son, and Company*, (Bantum Books, 1991.)
[19] G. Anandalingam and Henry C. Lucas, Jr., *Beware the Winner's Curse,* (Oxford University Press, 2004).
[20] Edward Gerstner, *Elephants Can Dance*, (Harper Collings, 2003.)
[21] Thomas Watson, Jr., *Father, Son, and Company*, (Bantum Books, 1991.)
[22] Jacquelyn Smith, "10 Reasons Why Humor is a Key to Success at Work," *Forbes*, May 3, 2013.

Communications Skills

Highly effective leaders possess what Kowalski refers to as *expert communication skills* that range from analytic communications to humorous communications with the ability to pivot based on the situation.[23] An effective leader can shift easily from talking in personal and caring tones with a client to talking to a corporate CEO or to an irate board member. This type of leader also recognizes that each board member has his or her own unique means of communication, which requires a leader to possess a wide range of communication methods and skills.

Too many leaders do not communicate directly with their board members on a regular basis, which is a mistake and a missed opportunity. An effective leader will develop a routine of talking with board members often. He will arrange daily or weekly contact with board members. When board members feel like they are respected and can rely on information from the leader, it takes the stress off everyone in the organization during challenging times when tough decisions must be made because the leader and the board members know and trust each other and have shared information all along.

One large longitudinal study found that over 60 percent of leaders spend only three hours or less per week in direct communication with board members.[24] The survey participants also admitted that more time spent on communications with board members would have reduced tensions and created a more productive working relationship. Other studies of organizations found the same thing - failure on part of the leader to communicate with board members on a regular basis created tension.[25] A leader who does not communicate with the board except during board meetings can expect to experience difficult board meetings and maybe even confrontational board meetings. Many leaders find that board members interfere less with the operational side of the organization if the leader communicates with the board members on a regular basis with pertinent information.

---

[23] Theodore Kowalski, *Effective Communication for District and School Administrators 2nd Edition*, (Rowman and Littlefield, 2015).

[24] Thomas Glass, Lars Bjork, and Cryss Brunner, *The 2000 Study of the American Public School Superintendent,* (American Association of School Administrators, 2000).

[25] Tom Wajnert and Stephen A. Miles, "Advice to the New CEO: How to Handle Your Board," *Forbes*, November 12, 2009.

According to General Colin Powell, former Secretary of State, it is through communications that trust is built between and among people in an organization.[26] The successful leader knows that the number of conflicts and the number of confrontations during board meetings is diminished if he communicates with the board members *before* the board meetings. This gives him the opportunity to gauge the opinion of the board members about certain agenda items before he takes those items to the board meeting. But a successful leader, of course, sees his leadership purpose as much more than communications. He tries to create an *organizational judgment*, much like that discussed in Davenport and Manville's study on judgment calls:

> *The role of the leader in creating organizational judgment is often first about reframing decisions as indeed not their own exclusively. But great leaders also work to ensure that the processes and mindsets of more distributed, problem-solving approaches key to judgment are in place and part of the norms of doing business in their enterprise.* [27]

Regarding communications, sometimes leaders may need to mediate or break up disagreements and misunderstandings between and among board members. That is part of the communication function of a leader with a board, maybe an unwritten part, but an important part nevertheless. It is also an illustration of how disrespectful board members can be to each other and how difficult managing can be for an organization's leader when he is caught between feuding board members.

In a study by Jason Grissom, he found boards that utilize professional decision-making practices and whose members share a common vision for their work through frequent communications and interactions, experience internal conflicts at substantially lower rates.[28] He also found that boards that monitor their own behavior, namely, the behavior and attitude of each board member, were more successful in their role of supporting each other, the leader and the organization.[29]

---

[26] Colin Powell, *It Worked for Me: In Life and Leadership*, (Harper Perennial, 2014).

[27] Thomas Davenport, Brook Manville, and Laurence Prusak, *Judgment Call: Twelve Stories of Big Decisions and the Teams That Got Them Right*, (Harvard Business Press Books, 2012).

[28] Jason Grissom, "The determinants of conflict on boards in public organizations," *The Journal of Public Administration Theory and Research*, (April 2009): doi: 10.1093/ jopart/mup043.

[29] Ibid.

The interaction of board members can be a tenuous situation. I was in a closed board executive session one afternoon that spiraled out of control. I was there only for answering questions about an employee discipline case. The board chair reviewed the relevant issues of the case and another board member asked for clarification. The board chair in a condescending manner answered, "I'll make it easy for you." This caused the board member who asked the question to lose his temper. Rising from his chair as his temper flared, he said, "I'm goddamn sick and tired of you treating me like I'm something under your fingernails. You think you're so wonderful and so smart. Well, you may be smart but you're a bastard and I'm not going to put up with it anymore." He moved quickly around the table and was heading for the board chair with pure rage in his eyes. Before anyone else could react, he was near the board chairman. I was close so I stepped in front of the angry board member while the target of his anger was backing up and trying to calm him down. I did not touch him but I darted in front of his every effort to get past me and at the board chair. The CEO quickly took charge. He took the board chair and the angry board member out of the room together. I was not privy to all the communications that took place after that incident, but by the time the next public board meeting was held two weeks later both the board chair and the angry board member talked to each other in respectful tones. This is what happened. After the incident, the CEO talked at length to both and helped them work out their issues with each other. They both trusted the CEO because he communicated with the board members frequently. The incident was forgotten. The bad feelings mended. The work of the board continued and all due to the communication skills of the CEO.[30] The board's ability to select an effective leader with a thorough understanding of his role as a communicator served the board well in many ways.

In *Elizabeth I–CEO: Strategic Lessons from the Leader Who Built an Empire*, Alan Axelrod wrote, "Effective leadership is still largely a matter of communications."[31] Boards must take the time to look for communications qualities and skills when selecting a new leader, and they should look for evidence of effective communications skills in the prospective leader's history.

Another key factor in the relationship between an organization's leader and the board is how they react to tough decisions, which includes, of course, effective internal and external communications. In an article written by Debra

---

[30] Author's notes, 2003.

[31] Alan Axelrod, *Elizabeth I, CEO: Strategic Lessons from the CEO who Built an Empire*, (Prentice Hall Press, 2000).

Nussbaum, Dr. Mary Stansky, who was retiring as the superintendent of the Gloucester City Public Schools after nine years in the job, said that she had a mostly good relationship with her board members in Gloucester City but tough decisions challenged that relationship. She said,

> *Now, as soon as you make a decision a board doesn't like, you're out."* She said. *"A lot of people come onto boards with personal agendas. Sometimes you have to make decisions that aren't popular. A lot of it is politicking. No matter what you do, it is wrong, and a lot is driven by politics. My blood pressure medicine has quadrupled since I started this job.*[32]

An example of tension building during difficult decision-making comes from Hewlett-Packard. The board of Hewlett-Packard seems to fire CEOs on a regular basis, particularly CEOs that disagree with them when tough decisions must be made. Hewlett-Packard is currently on its fifth CEO in seven years.[33]

From his research, Glenn Llopis lists five critical components of making tough decisions by leaders that are central to effective communications with the board.

These five components can also shape how boards receive or accept decisions.[34]

1. *Make no decision before its time. Clay Mathile, former owner of the Iams Company and now founder of Aileron believes that this is the key for any leaders. "If you don't make those decisions that you don't have to make, invariably, there's additional information that comes, there's more information, better information, better data."* Deciding later may lead to a more informed one and thus is more likely to be accepted and trusted by a board and employees. This is sometimes difficult for board members to accept, particularly to ones who are impatient and intense and who consequently want all problems resolved immediately, which is exacerbated if the leader has not communicated effectively and often with the board prior to challenging times.

---

[32] Debra Nussbaum, "Calling All Superintendents," *New York Times*, September 4, 2007.
[33] List of Hewlett-Packard Executive Leadership, Wikipedia, 2015: https://en.wikipedia.org/wiki/List_of_Hewlett-Packard_ exe-cutive _leadership.
[34] Glenn Llopis, "The Most Successful CEOs Do 15 Things," *Forbes*, February 8, 2014.

2. *Accept that this is not an easy decision and there are seldom "exact right" answers. Stop searching and doubting and exercising repeated second-guessing.* There is only a "current" right decision, based on the information that is available now. It is important to convey this to the board before such situations occur and certainly while they are occurring.

3. *Deciding with heart or head? The leader must admit if he or his employees are making decisions based on emotion or the facts. While it is not necessarily bad to make a decision based on emotions, this needs to be clear and the rational sensible and relevant.* When leaders make a decision out of anger with a board member it seldom stands the test of reason and good sense, especially if the decision serves no purpose or is contrary to what is best for the organization.

4. *Make the decision after careful consideration, but then do not waver. Commit to one path and take action. Wavering will almost guarantee that the desired outcome is not accomplished.* Boards want and demand decisive leadership from the leader, but they may encourage the leader to reconsider his decision if it goes contrary to the board's wishes. The leader must examine his decision and if it is the right decision at the right time based on the circumstances, he must be committed to that decision and stand by it. Boards, employees, and the public have doubts about leaders that waiver and constantly change decisions. When this happens many times, the board and employees begin losing trust and confidence in the leader.

5. *When a definitive action is taken, learn from the result and then plan the next move. Success is typically a series of patient interim steps, not giant wild leaps. Often boards expect a new leader to take those wild leaps because the board wants everything to change immediately; they want all the problems to be addressed at the same time with positive outcomes.* Organizational change and decision-making are complex. Systematic change comes from a series of connected, related, mindful, and thoughtful decisions with the long-term in mind. Short-term solutions often create even more serious long-term problems. A leader can condition the board to this type of decision making by communicating with the board on a regular basis, particularly when the decisions are tough.

The interaction and relationship of a leader and the board can be hampered by the leader's attitude toward the board. Glass, Bjork, and Brunner found that 30 percent of organizational leaders, for example, believe their board members are unqualified.[35] Though there may be some truth in this description of the qualifications of some board members, it is a dangerous and counterproductive view by a leader. It may shape the leader's decisions and communications on prominent issues with the board, and more specifically his communications with them may be condescending. Whether the leader believes that the board members are qualified or not, he must work with them, communicate with them, and remain united during tough times. Many facets of the relationship between an organization's leader and the board are dynamic and complex but often it circles back to how leaders are selected by boards in the first place.

On the *Opportunity Knocks* job website,[36] which lists non-profit sector jobs, almost every executive level job description includes most of the same traits as other organizations. As reported by *The Balance*,[37] the most common traits are:

1. ***Communication****: Communication is about more than the basics of sharing ideas, or sharing information. For leaders, communication is the most fundamental skill he or she can possess when it comes to leading an organization. Leaders should effectively communicate with board members, individuals, and with groups.*

2. ***Nonverbal Communication****: Being a good communicator means transcending written and verbal communication. An excellent communicator will convey a sense of openness and non-judgment, even when they're not saying anything. Body language and general countenance can sometimes convey even more than words.*

3. ***Coaching****: Managing people means supporting subordinates. The means not only enabling them to do their jobs well but also helping them to move forward in their careers. Whatever the work is, adopting a coaching mindset is an integral part of being a good leader.*

4. ***Directing Others****: Giving direction doesn't come naturally to every leader, but it's an integral aspect of a leadership job. Leaders should be able to clearly and effectively formulate directions for others, and then articulate them in such a way as to convey them effectively.*

---

[35] Thomas Glass, Lars Bjork, and Cryss Brunner, *The 2000 Study of the American Public School Superintendent,* (American Association of School Administrators, 2000).

[36] *Opportunity Knocks, Inc.* is a non-profit organization dedicated to enhancing the capacity of individuals with disabilities to live, work and participates as active members of their communities: http://www.idealist.org/viewnon profit/ SJdtnsn 6tpw4/.

[37] *The Balance*, 2016, https://www.thebalance.com/leadership-skills-list-2063 757.

5. **Relationship Building**: *Along with communicating and coaching, relationship building can make or break a leader. A good leader will value relationships, and will actively work to build one-on-one associations as well as fostering healthy relationships among the community.*

Selecting the Wrong Leader

Why is the longevity of organizational leaders so short-lived? Certainly, the candidates for the leadership positions are not all misrepresenting themselves. That may occur, but infrequently. The capricious nature of leader selection has more to do with the *expectation of the situation.* Too often leaders are not selected based on qualifications; instead, they are selected based on the board's opinion of the immediate problems facing the organization. Boards try to match a skill, personality, history or experience of the prospective leader to its perception of the ills and needs of the organization instead of considering the candidate's overall and long-term potential.[38] This ill-fated practice frequently applies to almost every type of organization.

A new leader is very susceptible to pressure from board members primarily because she wants to keep her new job; consequently, situations between the board members and the new leader can become awkward. For example, organizational leaders, especially leaders new to the organization, who succumb to pressure from boards to hire family members, friends, or relatives seldom last very long. Their short tenure is due to loss of respect by employees and the board but also because of the amount of time spent, as Buckingham says in his book, *One Thing You Need to Know*, desperately trying to train incompetent employees to help the organization, which seldom works. Then there is the cost of training someone to eventually replace that person or the cost of engaging another employee to "carry" the incompetent but politically connected employee.[39] When that type of employee becomes a liability for the organization, it is virtually impossible to terminate him or transfer him to another job or location. This situation can have a negative impact on staff morale and productivity.

---

[38] David A. Katz, Wachtell, Lipton, Rosen & Katz, "Advice for Boards in CEO Selection and Succession Planning," *Harvard Law Forum on Corporate Governance and Financial Regulation*, June 11, 2012: corpgov.law.harvard. edu/2012/06/11/advice-for-boards-in-ceo-selection-and-succession-planning/.

[39] Marcus Buckingham, *One Thing You Need to Know*, (Simon and Schuster, 2005).

Case Study #1[40]

An organization was led by a competent and quintessential bureaucrat. He was selected as the CEO by the board because they respected his tenacity and strong will. The CEO's leadership style was clearly an autocratic "by-the-book" style. He was very bright but very temperamental and irascible. The board knew about his traits when they hired him.

What the board soon discovered was that he invited confrontation when it was not necessary. He even managed to get into a public fight with the board over what should have been a win-win situation-a large budget reserve.

At a board meeting, one of the board members asked the CEO what he planned to do with the substantial amount of money in the reserve. Instead of explaining the importance and necessity of a budget reserve during economically tough times-to help the organization face any type of financial shortfall or react to an unforeseen circumstance, the CEO instead made the statement, "You're not going to tell me to use up the reserve and you're certainly are not going to tell me how to use that money." He should have and could have told the board that the amount of money seemed large for a budget reserve, but the budget reserve amount equaled to the organization's operating costs of only one month. It was very prudent of the CEO to manage the organization's budget so frugally and thoughtfully. Had he explained the budget reserve that way, instead of responding in a condescending manner, the issue would have ended then and there. In reaction to his arrogant and condescending comment, the board members turned against him very quickly. They had each heard complaints about the leader's derogatory demeanor toward just about everyone and they were growing very tired of it. Even though he was a good steward of the budget and a very intelligent person, he did not delegate authority, did not have any interest in building a team, had poor communication skills and had no interest in anything associated with *servant leadership*. Additionally, he had no respect for the board members and avoided communicating with them at all costs. The board wanted him to use some of the budget reserves so that services could be expanded. However, the CEO said he would not be told how to spend the reserve and to spend the money for the sole purpose of temporarily expanding services would come back to haunt the organization during complicated economic times. Instead of focusing on that point he fought the board over its efforts to tell him what to do. The issue became a personal one, not what was

---

[40] Malcolm Flagerty, *Once Upon a Failed Success*, (Provider Independent Press, 1981).

best for the organization. It became one of the many power struggles and communication breakdowns between the board and the CEO. The CEO failed to understand that the issue shifted to his behavior and lack of leadership skills, even though the financial points he raised were legitimate. How he communicated was not effective. About this topic, Sydney Harris wrote:

> *The two words information and communication are often used interchangeably, but they signify quite different things. Information is giving out; communication is getting through.* [41]

John Maxwell refers to this as the difference between "*communicating and connecting.*"[42] A leader must *connect* with his board members. According to Maxwell,

> *Connecting is the ability to identify with people and relate to them in a way that increases your influence with them.* [43]

In this case, the CEO's message did not connect. The leader's message was not getting through to the board members because of his arrogant, condescending communication style. Soon, the abrasive CEO was fired by the board and replaced with a beloved and successful benevolent leader.

A few years later when the local economy took a downward shift and revenues declined, the board realized that even though the former CEO was a difficult and arrogant leader he was right about the budget reserve and the negative impact of temporarily expanding services, but he failed to convey that critical message in an effective way during a crucial time for the organization – he failed to *connect* with the board.

In this case study, the arrogant CEO was followed by a quintessential benevolent leader. The board wanted someone to quiet the turmoil and work with them and the staff and community in a more collaborative manner. The person they selected was such a masterful leader that he was CEO for several years and could have continued ad infinitum if retirement had not looked so much more attractive to him than the problems of a large organization.

As do many dominating and controlling leaders, the previous CEO consolidated power so that virtually every decision came from his office. He never delegated any decision-making authority. He controlled or tried to

---

[41] Sydney J. Harris. AZQuotes.com, *Wind and Fly* (LTD, 2016): http://www. azquotes.com/author /6311-Sydney _J_Harris.
[42] John Maxwell, *Everyone Communicates, Few Connect*, (Thomas Nelson, 2010).
[43] Ibid.

control every aspect of the decision-making process and ridiculed anyone who expressed an opposite opinion, which is precisely why the board hired him. However, their shortsighted plans for the organization led to the selection of a leader who would not and could not be successful long term.

The leader intimidated employees so much that no one tried to influence his opinion and no one survived any effort to exert influence on his decisions. As indicated by the story of the battle over the budget reserve, he showed virtually no respect for the board or his own employees. His style and talent combined to produce an efficiently run organization for a time when he was its CEO, but he had difficulty adjusting to change and challenges to his authority and for that reason, the efficiencies weakened after a few years and he was terminated. Leadership effectiveness is often measured by inspiration and seldom by domination, just like success is measured over the long-term and not short-term.

When the new CEO took over he wanted to deregulate the decision-making process by delegating authority and placing decision-making closer to the daily operations of the organization. He was surprised and baffled to see so much activity around his office and the constant flow of employees coming in his office with questions. It took him a while to figure out that many of his executive employees could not or would not make decisions on their own. He later talked about the blank stare reaction when he asked a veteran executive staff member, "Well, what do you recommend we do?" The staff member did not know what to do or what to recommend because all he had done under the previous totalitarian leader was to carry out orders. He was not expected to think, analyze and offer solutions or an opinion.

The new CEO spent a great deal of time studying the organization. He visited sites and talked to hundreds of people inside and outside of the organization. He met with each board member in formal and informal settings, and he held meetings with the central office staff to discuss issues facing the organization. During his first several months as the CEO, he made no changes of significance at the central office level or elsewhere in the organization. He was very respectful of people and thoughtful about the opinions of others. He knew that changes had to be made but he wanted to be very thoughtful and respectful before, during, and after the changes.

In the book, *Influencer-The Power to Change Anything*, the authors discuss the importance of enlisting employee and board support by taking the time necessary to learn about the social interconnections within an organization, which also shows respect for the employees and the organization's history. If a leader is going to be a significant influencer he must show respect in many ways.

When it comes to creating change, you no longer have to worry about influencing everyone at once. If you preside over a company with 10,000 employees, your job is to find the 500 or so opinion leaders who are the key to everyone else. Spend disproportionate time with them. Listen to their concerns. Build trust with them. Be open to their ideas. Rely on them to share your ideas, and you'll gain a source of influence unlike any other. [44]

The new CEO realized that the central office would have to undergo some significant changes and in what became his trademark he talked individually with board members to explain what he was going to do and why. He showed them courtesy and respect by sharing his thoughts and plans but he was not asking them for permission to make operational and personnel changes. He made that clear to a few of them who initially misinterpreted his intent.

After working with the previous arrogant and disrespectful leader, the board members were enamored with the new CEO who respectfully and clearly communicated with them on a regular basis. He met with the central office staff he inherited from his predecessor's regime. He told them that his leadership style dictated a change in everyone's approach to his or her job. He did not "clean house" and start replacing them and he did not threaten to replace them, which is exactly what some new leaders would do and was what the board expected the new CEO to do.

In Clemens and Mayer's extraordinary book on leadership, *The Classic Touch*, they focus on change at the leadership level through the ideas of the famous Edmund Burke, the 18th-century British statesman, parliamentary orator, and theorist of leadership. Burke warned against trashing all traditions of an organization and creating a clean slate of processes and people at the expense of time-honored traditions. He believed that some of the traditions in an organization have immense value. Burke said, "They are the storehouse of the organization's collective wisdom."[45] Burke said that a new leader who does not recognize the value of tradition and fails to take the time necessary to sort out which traditions are essential can easily destroy the good aspects of the organization's traditions, and once destroyed he may not be able to rebuild them. Burke said that a leader can the thoughtful and deliberate when making changes.

---

[44] Kerry Patterson, Joseph Grenny, David Maxfield, Ron McMillian, and Al Switzler, *Influencer: The Power to Change Anything*, (McGraw-Hill, 1987).

[45] John Clemens and Douglas Meyer, *The Classic Touch*, (McGraw-Hill, 1987).

Any effort to change the organization, therefore, should be implemented slowly, a little at a time; and always carefully, so that the changes agree with its history and its tradition.[46]

This approach is the long-term strategy of sustainability. Overreactions such as dramatic, traumatic changes seldom work and rarely lasts in organizations, according to Burke.

The new leader listened and observed and he told his staff that he trusted them to make decisions and to make good decisions. That is the only way he said he could determine the value of their contributions to the organization and if their efforts were important to the long-term mission of the organization. He also expected them to keep him abreast of operations and issues, and he encouraged them to be proactive and innovative–to look for creative solutions and anticipate what may become a problem. He wanted them to think. Also, he wanted them to be innovative. He wanted them to be leaders, decision-makers, and instruments of creative thought and influence.

This transfer of decision-making from the leader to employees for purposes of efficiency was met with wide skepticism and genuine angst. Some of the central office staff could not handle making decisions. They did not know how to be responsible for making decisions. They were adept at gathering information that would guide the decision-making process, but they became catatonic when asked what they thought. Consequently, some employees retired, some moved to other jobs, and a few made the conversion.

Changing the Culture and Climate

When Louis Gerstner took over IBM at a time that many experts did not think it would survive he found a status quo culture where employees continued to hang onto to the successes of the distinct past and had very little confidence in their abilities.

Many used hierarchy as a crutch and were reluctant to take personal responsibility for outcomes. Instead of grabbing available resources and authority, they waited for the boss to tell them what to do; they delegated up. In the end, my deepest culture-change goal was to induce IBMers to believe in themselves again–to believe that they had the ability to be innovative and make decisions.[47]

---

[46] Ibid.
[47] Edward Gerstner, *Elephants Can Dance*, (Harper Collins, 2003).

The CEO in the case study was smart and intuitive enough to know which central office employees could work efficiently during his administration and he was wise enough to know that those who could not adjust would make their own decision to leave or retire. He did not force anyone out, but under his steady and thoughtful ways central office staffing and operations changed and became more effective, which prevented bureaucratic stalemates that could have hampered the organization. He also knew that even the most inept central office employees had supporters, so it was important not to embarrass them and thereafter have enemies that could be the genesis of destructive rumors and other problems.

The CEO found that the ways of his predecessor had negatively impacted the flow of decision-making and problem-solving. What appeared at times to be efficiency was more control processes than actual efficiency–compliance dominated to the point of stifling creativity, innovation, and problem-solving. The board was very astute in the selection of the CEO who was communicative, patient, intuitive, and smart because the turbulent financial times could not have been handled by a tyrant or laissez-faire type leader. Those days were challenged with a declining economy, shortage of resources, and growing competition. Those times called for change, collaboration, innovation and thoughtful decisions to problems, and the CEO rose to the challenge. Not only was the CEO an excellent communicator, he was a trusted communicator; he recognized the importance of trust and he often spoke about trust with the board and with employees. Stephen M.R. Covey refers to the concept of *Speed of Trust*.[48] According to Covey, when trust improves production increases, but this CEO recognized a simple but important fact long before Covey and others wrote about trust–effective communications depends on trust.

It came as a shock when the benevolent leader announced his retirement, but he knew it was time for a change. He had been the CEO for over 15 years. He told the board that he did not want to hang on like an aging King Lear, unwilling to let go. The board started the search for a replacement with the idea in mind to maintain and sustain the leader's vision, mission, and goals. The board was pleased with the work and the progress of the organization, and like many boards in an analogous situation sought a clone of the retiring leader. They wanted to maintain the status quo. Of course, that's not possible. What the board did not recognize was that the retiring CEO kept the organization moving always and the progress made during his

---

[48] Stephen M.R. Covey, *The Speed of Trust*, (Simon and Schuster, 2006).

tenure was due in large part from never standing still or settling for the status quo.

Selecting a Successor

Selecting a new leader is not an easy task for any board, organization, or business. Clemons and Mayer wrote:

> *Picking a successor is rarely easy, and there are no general rules for how this task is to be accomplished. At Exxon, for example, the personnel department uses a forced distribution scoring system to rank potential candidates. Those who make the grade are placed in a waiting line for the next executive vacancy. Even selecting a successor in a family-owned organization is difficult.* [49]

In the case study scenario, it was very unlikely that another benevolent leader would be found during the search, or at least that was the expectation of the board, so they thought the next best thing was a status quo leader–keep things as they are. The prevailing thought was "don't rock the boat." Consequently, an administrator from inside the organization was selected as the next CEO. This is not uncommon in the business world or within other types of organizations. Selecting a successor to a successful leader is one of the most difficult challenges facing boards, and boards are especially concerned when they replace a successful leader because the new leader's performance is clearly seen as a measure of the board's judgment. Consequently, a successor that supports the status quo is frequently selected in those circumstances, which is often a mistake.[50] A status quo leader adopts the laissez-faire leadership style primarily because that is what is expected of him by the board.

The laissez-faire leadership style is described by experts as the "hands-off" style. The leader gives employees as much freedom as possible, relies on existing structures, processes, procedures, and shuns innovation or confrontations. Considerable authority or power is given to the employees and some power shifts to the board during the leadership vacuum.

---

[49] John Clemens and Douglas Meyer, *The Classic Touch*, (McGraw-Hill, 1987).
[50] Henry Doss, "Status Quo Leadership is the Biggest Impediment to Innovation, " *Forbes*, March 28, 2015.

The concept of laissez-faire leadership was first described in 1938 by Lewin, Lippitt, and White.[51]

Laissez-faire leaders are characterized as uninvolved with their followers and members; in fact, laissez-faire leadership is an absence of leadership style. Leaders of this style make no policies or group-related decisions. Instead, group members are responsible for all goals, decisions, and problem-solving. Laissez-faire leaders have very little to no authority within their group organization.[52]

This style of leadership is acceptable and can be productive but only when employees are skilled, experienced, placed in positions that match their talents and motivation and are resourceful, which is a very critical point to remember – laissez-faire leadership only works under very narrow circumstances.[53]

In this case study, the laissez-faire leader who followed the benevolent leader had the necessary skills to be successful and he inherited a talented central office staff, but he followed closely to the whims and wants of the board and he tried diligently to hold onto the existing status of the organization so innovation, creativity, and risk-taking slowed and then stopped. Also, some of his personnel decisions compromised his good intentions. Eventually, he was caught between two worlds with shifting leadership expectations and operational needs. He was expected to follow the success of his predecessor and ensure continued success and progress, but at the same time, he was not confident enough in his own leadership skills, unlike his predecessor, to stand up to the demands of the board and the ever-changing challenges and needs of the organization. That is the reality that a laissez-faire leader faces. Apparently, he was under the impression that his predecessor made decisions based on the board's whims, but that clearly was not the case. Furthermore, the new leader undervalued the contributions and essential roles of talented employees.

Laissez-faire leadership may work in an organization that has strong leadership at the managerial and operational levels and when an organization has strong and talented managers throughout the organizations. But even that is compromised over time primarily because every organization in some way is active, ever changing, with diverse needs growing out of responses to

---

[51] Kurt Lewin, Ronald Lippitt, and Ralph White, "Patterns of Aggressive Behavior," *Journal of Social Psychology*, Vol. 10 (2), January 1939.
[52] Ibid.
[53] Ibid.

challenges. Laissez-faire leadership does not typically handle change, challenges, or crisis situations well.[54]

When Louis Gerstner was selected to bring IBM out of the malaise of financial problems, morale problems, and operational problems, he learned that the internal leadership training program for young executives was one that encouraged and embraced the status quo–they were training laissez-faire leaders.[55] Through the years this philosophy was supported by the board because they were still linked to past successes, so a string of laissez-faire leaders eventually led the company to a philosophy that often accompanies laissez-faire leadership: status quo – hang on to past successes because the processes and decisions associated with success will ensure continued success. The status quo norm gravely damaged the company's financial base and standing in the industry as leaders of innovation.

Laissez-Faire Leaders

It is not unusual for a laissez-faire leader to surround himself with employees that are in good standing with board members and who cling to the past. To the laissez-faire leader, the skill set of the central administration supporting the leader is too often less important than who they know on the board and their link to past successes. He thinks if the organization is coasting along and there appears to be no need for major changes what harm would be caused by strategically placing employees who can have something positive to say to board members about the leader and who can recall past glories? However, this is very disrespectful to competent and experienced employees.[56] When a laissez-faire leader begins losing competent and experienced employees, his leadership style will lead to a collapse of services while the promotion of employees with little experience and few skills acerbates the situation.

To make the situation worse, laissez-faire leaders often criticize employees when things go wrong instead of recognizing their own

---

[54] Anders Skogstad, Stale Einarsen, Torbjorn Torsheim, Merethe Aasland, and Hilde Hetland, "The destructiveness of laissez-faire leadership behavior," *Journal of Occupational Health Psychology*, Vol 12(1), January 2007: http://dx.doi.org/10.10 37/1076-8998.12.1.80.

[55] Edward Gerstner, *Elephants Can Dance*, (Harper Collins, 2003).

[56] Kurt Lewin, Ronald Lippitt, and Ralph White, "Patterns of Aggressive Behavior," *Journal of Social Psychology*, Vol. 10 (2), January 1939.

responsibilities and shortcomings as a leader. Ken Blanchard's *One Minute Manager* research found that,

> *Not supporting, believing in, or championing direct reports was cited as a problem area that can undermine leadership effectiveness.*[57]

Laissez-faire leaders do not understand that there is no such thing as *status quo* in any successful organization. Organizations and all their components are in a constant state of change. Sometimes the change is subtle and sometimes it is dramatic. That is why it is rare for a laissez-faire style to be successful in a leadership position for very long if at all. It should be noted, however, that laissez-faire leaders can change. The primary challenge to them is accepting and recognizing that they are a laisse-faire leader. That self-realization and self-evaluation can be difficult but it is the first step.

Antidotes: In the book *Influencer: The Power to Change Anything* the authors note the attraction of short-term strategies to make short-term progress, which often leads to long-term negative effects.[58] While there is something to be said in positive tones about immediate success to build motivation and morale and to let everyone inside an organization and outside know that a new leader is in place and the board is taking care of business, as Louis Gerstner did when he first joined the troubled IBM. However, there is a dynamic chain of events that spirals to dysfunction when a leader is selected based on short-term needs. The long-term needs of the organization will suffer.

Boards must be very thoughtful about the selection of the organization's next leader and refrain from the overwhelming temptation to select for the short-term or select based on the qualities of the incumbent. It behooves the board to take the time to review its strategic plan; conduct a self-assessment; survey the employees; include the opinions of clients, and conduct a gap analysis to determine the gap between the goals and the outcomes that will need to be addressed by the board and the new leader. This process gives the board a clearer understanding of what it should look for in the next leader.

In addition to the retirement of a leader, there can be internal and external circumstances in an organization environment that require a change in leadership.

---

[57] Ken Blanchard, *One Minute Manager*, (Harper Collins, 1982).
[58] Kerry Patterson, Joseph Grenny, David Maxfield, Ron McMillian, and Al Switzler, *Influencer: The Power to Change Anything*, (McGraw-Hill, 1987).

These factors can be organized into three main groups.[59]

1. *Changes in the environment*. Changes in the external circumstances of an organization require a change in leadership to help the organization adapt to an unfamiliar, rapidly changing environment. There could be changes in technology, competitors, suppliers, buyers, and potential entrants that require significant changes in operations and strategies to meet the new challenges.
2. *Changes in the organization's structure*. Internal circumstances prompted by alliances, joint ventures, or mergers and acquisitions demand changes in the structure of the organization, as well as changes in leadership and operations to rebuild the organization according to these changes and the needs of the organization.
3. *Changes in the operational vision of the organization*. There could be changes in goals, scope, competitive advantage, the logic of an organization that could be prompted by internal or external changes, or simply to change the path of the organization's thinking, positioning, and anticipation about the future of its functions, purpose, goals, attributes, vulnerabilities, and prospects.

---

[59] M. Watkins, *What Should a New Leader Do When Entering into an Existing Team?* (Wikipedia Books, 2003); S.V. Manderscheid, *The First 90 Days*, (Harvard Business School Publishing, 2008); "New Leader Assimilation: An Intervention for Leaders in Transition," in *Advances in Developing Human Resources* (Alexel / Institute of Executive Develop-ment, 2008); Frederick P. and Morgeson, D. S., "Leadership in Teams: A Functional Approach to Understanding Leader-ship Structures and Processes," *Journal of Management* 36, 2010; Ciampa, D., & Watkins, M., *Right from the Start: Taking Charge in a New Leadership Role*, (Harvard Business School Press, 2008); David Koeppel, "Executive Life; A Tough Transition: Friend to Supervisor" *New York Times,* March 16, 2003; Michael Watkins, D. C., "Advice for Vikram Pandit, the New CEO of Citigroup," *Harvard Business Review*, (December 18, 2007): http://blogs.hbr.org/watkins/ 2007/12/ advice_for_ vikram_pandit_the_n_ 1htmlcm_mmc=npv-_-listserv-_-APR_ 2008-_-leadership; Hakala, D., "Promoting from within," *HR World*, August 21, 2008: http://www.hrworld com/ features /promoting-within-082108/; Gilmore, A., "In With the New: Leader Dos and Don'ts," *Talent Management*, April 2008:
http://www. talentmgt.com/newsletters/talentmanagementperspectives/2008 /April /587/index.phpen.

From this thoughtful approach, the board can create attributes that the next leader must possess in order to move the organization toward short-term and long-term goals.

Board members should govern their own behavior in order to make an appropriate selection of new leadership and to understand their own roles and responsibilities. To facilitate this, boards should annually sign an *assurance of governance* that compels each board member to refrain from nepotism and interference in the daily operations of the organization. This could be part of the ethics agreement board members sign. The board's by-laws should be carefully and thoughtfully crafted to include processes, procedures, the election of officers, service time of officers, development of meeting agendas, etc., but the by-laws should also include ethics, decorum, and behavior of the board and respect for leadership and employees. The new leader should also sign an assurance of governance and should review the board's bylaws and the organization's internal policies. This is a commitment on part of the board and the leader to stay true to their distinct roles in the organization.

Contrary to many of the myths and assumptions surrounding the selection of new leaders, James Citrin and Julie Hembrock argue that the process of choosing a leader should begin with a deep understanding of the organization's needs and the kind of person who will both fit into its culture and bring the right experience and skill-set to be effective. Only then should the board seek the person who best matches those organizational needs.[60] This may seem like common sense, yet in practice, this represents a different way of thinking for many organizations.

Contrary to the opinion of many board members, research by LaBelle found that the first hundred days do not comprise a sufficient indication of how a new CEO is doing.[61] The key is communications.

To keep the organization steering in the right direction requires constant and constructive communication between the leader and the board. Open communication links should allow the leader to bring both good news and bad news to the board. In turn, the board needs to listen appropriately and give honest feedback. Change in leadership is hard. Support from the board is imperative. The new leader's personal successes will serve as an

---

[60] James Citrin and Julie Hembrock, *You Need a CEO – Now What?* (Crown Business, 2012).

[61] Antoinette E. LaBelle, *Transition to New Leadership*, (The Bridgespan Group, 2012).

encouragement; the board's recognition of the new leader's results will reinforce and strengthen the process and outcomes. "[62]

Research by the Hay Group and reported by Gilmore found that if a new leader is following a well-liked leader it is important for the new leader to avoid a popularity contest to fit in and be liked by everyone. Gilmore states that the new leader must communicate often through his own self of presence and purpose. A new leader cannot pretend to be something he is not or try to emulate his predecessor. Assuming the role of another leader by acting like that leader never works. Following the vision, mission, and values of a successful predecessor is different than trying to copy the behavior, personality, and personal interaction style of another leader.

Simply put, you need to be yourself and follow your own vision and communicate effectively. In establishing credibility and a loyal following amongst the team it is important that they see you for yourself and not a mold of the previous leader. You have to let them all know that you are not your predecessor, but you have your own talents and motivation.[63]

Gilmore also developed a list of recommendations for new leaders to consider.[64]

1. **Don't step into the old leader's shoes.** *If following a well-liked leader, it is important not to get into a popularity contest; conversely, if a new leader is following a leader that experienced negative feedback throughout his time in the organization, the new leader should not be overly concerned with making the same mistakes. Simply put the new leader needs to be herself and follow her own vision. Establishing credibility and a loyal following amongst the team is important. They need to see the style and personality of the new leader and not a mold of the previous leader.*

2. **Stand up for what you believe in.** *One of the first steps is to let everyone know what the new leader values, what is important to her. Often a new leader has skills, values, and beliefs that others aspire to have and it is essential that those be communicated clearly and often throughout the organization.*

3. **The great pretender.** *All new leaders are going to have knowledge gaps of essential information. This specific information relates to history, processes, procedure, strengths, weakness, etc. that will take the time to*

---

[62] Ibid.

[63] A. Gilmore, "In with the New: CEO Dos and Don'ts," *Talent Management*, April 2008.

[64] Ibid.

learn. It serves no purpose and can be counterproductive if a new leader pretends to know everything about the organization. There is always going to be the fear of being ill-prepared; however, a successful leader will effectively deal with this natural anxiety and start the process of listening and learning.

4. **Listen and learn.** *A new leader should not be consumed with wanting to act in the beginning of the transition. While it will be important for him to share some small successes with the team early on, it is also important to listen with an open mind. This step can help the new leader gather valuable information that may aid him in making future decisions which may have gone unnoticed or overlooked if he is only concerned with acting and making changes in the early stages only for the purpose of trying to impress the board and employees.*

5. **Seek advice.** *This can be the most problematic and difficult trap for a new leader to overcome. After taking over an organization, some leaders fail to reach out to others for advice; instead, they try to solve problems and project an image of self-reliance and control. The reality is that the best leaders are those that can recognize that they do not know everything about the organization and seek out advice to make the most informed decisions possible.*

New leaders pressured by board members to protect the status quo should not fight back initially but should instead ramp up communications with them to "sell" his vision and purpose. The new leader needs to let employees and the board know what he stands for and he needs to communicate that effectively and often. New leaders must recognize and develop key relationships and build networks in the organization and respect some of the rituals of the organization to convey the clear message that he is team-oriented and respectful of the organization's history, traditions, and the work of employees. One of the most effective ways to express confidence in employees is to delegate projects, programs, and decision-making. According to research by Goodyear and Golden, delegation is important to employees trying to adjust to a new leader.

It is important that a new leader conveys trust in the organization from the beginning through delegation. Focused discussion between leaders and followers about successful outcomes, delegation, and accountability mechanisms can result in focused and successful implementation.[65]

---

[65] Martha Goodyear and Cynthia Golder, *Leadership Transitions*, (Professional Development Publishing, 2008).

Chapter Two Key Words and Concepts

Servant Type Leadership
Military Type Leadership
Benevolent Leader
Laissez-Faire Leader
Totalitarian Leader
Circular Pattern of Leadership Selection
Meddler
Lemon Leadership
Bully
Vetting
Social Capital
Delegating
Likeability Factor
Politically-Based Selection
Executive Session
Leadership Communications
Humor as a Communications Tool
Analytical Communications
Organizational Judgement
Incongruity
Expectation of the Situation
Information versus Communication
Communicating versus Connecting
Influencer
Organizational Collective Wisdom
Operational Vision
Assurance of Governance

Chapter Two Discussion Items

Should boards select organizational leaders based on the short-term or long-term needs of the organization? Why?

What type of leader do you think most likely to be successful in organizations? What traits would a successful leader possess? How would success be determined?

Are leadership traits learned? If so, how? If not, how are leadership traits developed? Can a leader change her leadership style?

Are leaders more effective if they remain consistent with their leadership style and traits or should leaders change based on circumstances? What are the advantages and disadvantages of being consistent and being adaptable?

Give examples of the difference between communicating and connecting and explain why the distinction is important to organizations and leaders.

What does Operational Vision mean and how does it apply to an organization's ability to meet the needs of its customers, stakeholders, and employees?

Chapter Two Lessons Learned

Without the right type of leader - one who has effective communication skills, understands the value of trust, develops strong support staff and seeks independence from the board-a once successful or promising organization can decline rapidly and irreversibly.

Circumstances on the board mixed with individual agendas and the condition of the organization often determine what type of leader is selected by the board instead of the qualities of the individual for sustainability and the long-term needs of the organization.

The benevolent leader leads by example of a positive approach to leadership, by encouragement, by motivation, by focusing on the needs of clients that the organization serves.

One of the main factors related directly to the quality of the board and leader relationship is communications.

Too many leaders do not communicate directly with their board members on a regular basis, which is a mistake and a missed opportunity. An effective leader will develop a routine of talking with board members often.

Boards that utilize professional decision-making practices and whose members share a common vision for their work through frequent communications and interactions, experience internal conflicts at substantially lower rates.

When leaders make a decision out of anger with a board member it seldom stands the test of reason and good sense, especially if the decision serves no purpose or is contrary to what is best for the organization.

A new leader is very susceptible to pressure from board members primarily because she wants to keep her new job; consequently, situations between the board members and the new leader can become awkward.

Selecting a successor to a successful leader is one of the most difficult challenges facing boards, and boards are especially concerned when they replace a successful leader because the new leader's performance is clearly seen as a measure of the board's judgment.

Following the vision, mission, and values of a successful predecessor is different than trying to copy the behavior, personality, and personal interaction style of another leader.

CHAPTER THREE

SUCCESSFUL LEADERSHIP TRANSITION

"A new hire at the top of the organization signals to the world that everything is up for grabs – all options for change are on the table."

-*Antoinette LaBelle[1]*

Determinants: A new leader in an organization comes in with lofty expectations and the board has even higher expectations. There are several issues facing a new leader. Many of them relate to communications that can make the transition to new leadership successful or a failure. The failure of a board to prepare the new leader and the existing staff for change that comes with new leadership threatens the success of the transition. The exchanges between a board and the leader of an organization can positively or negatively impact succession planning and the transition to new leadership. The many issues facing the organization, particularly when there is a stressful relationship between the board and the leader and when there is a conflict between and among board members. The breakdown in communication and an unproductive disconnection between expectations and outcomes is detrimental to workplace climate and the mission of the organization. Consequently, the entire organization suffers and the new leader's tenure will be short.

Leadership Transition

Even in the best of times and under positive circumstances, according to an article by Dayton Ogden and John Wood, *Succession Planning: A Board Imperative*, boards need to understand the importance of succession planning, but all too often they just don't do it very well, if at all.[2] Many boards don't

---

[1] Antoinette LaBelle, "Transition to New Leadership: The First 1,000 Days," *The Bridgespan Group,* September 2011.

[2] Dayton Ogden and John Wood, "Succession Planning: A Board Imperative." *Bloomberg Business Week*, March 2008.

give themselves strong marks for planning for a new chief executive officer. According to Ogden and Wood,

> *Even today only about half of public and private corporate boards have CEO succession plans in place, according to a recent survey by the Center for Board Leadership.[3]*

A report from the National Association of Corporate Directors found that only 16 percent of boards had an effective CEO succession plan.[4] Yet, its importance cannot be overstated. The succession planning process must be thoughtful and deliberate and not sabotaged or hijacked by individual board members. According to the Society for Human Resource Management, in an article titled *Succession Planning with Your Board*, the editors wrote:

> *Succession planning is a means for an organization to ensure its continued effective performance through leadership continuity. For an organization to plan for the replacement of key leaders, potential leaders must first be identified and prepared to take on those roles. It is not enough to select people in the organization who seem right for the job. Not only should the experience and duties be considered, but also the personality, the leadership skills, and the readiness for taking on a key leadership role.[5]*

Succession planning and the selection of a new leader is a very difficult process, and it is a very important board function. Everyone seems to agree that succession planning is essential for any organization. If it is not done very effectively during smooth times it can become a severe problem if ineffective succession planning occurs during difficult times. It is another insidious outcome of ineffective board governance behavior.

In an article about leadership transition by Antoinette LaBelle, she reported on a survey of 630 nonprofit leaders throughout the United States that focused on transitioning to new leadership. LaBelle states,

> *A new hire at the top of the organization signals to the world that everything is up for grabs – all options for change are on the table. Prior research on leaders and change tells us that new hires feel a need to make an immediate impact – to both establish credibility and legitimize their hiring…it is of*

---

[3] Ibid.

[4] "Board Composition and Succession Planning," *National Directors of Corporate Directors*, 2012.

[5] Editors, "Succession Planning with Your Board." *Society for Human Resource Management,* Guideline Series 2013.

*interest that few leaders in our study underwent a formal orientation or
onboard programs.* [6]

According to LaBelle, if a new leader is not prepared to understand how
change in leadership will blend with existing conditions of the organization
and the leadership team is not prepared for the change brought by new
leadership–how to adjust to the change while continuing to run the
organization–then the transition will be in jeopardy from the beginning. Too
often, according to LaBelle, boards do very little to prepare for a new leader
or prepare the new leader and existing staff for the transition. In other words,
a succession plan is often not in place. Thus, there is the potential for a
complete breakdown in operations and the possibility that the new leader is
placed into a situation where it will be very difficult to succeed. This is
especially critical during the first few months of a new leader's tenure in the
organization. At the very least each organization should have a short-term
succession plan that includes transition processes.

Michael Watkins, the author of *The First 90 Days*, opines that a new
leader's success or failure is tied to the first 90 days in the position.

*The actions you take during your first three months in a new job at the top
will largely determine whether you succeed or fail. Transitions are periods of
opportunity, a chance to start afresh and to make needed changes in an
organization. But they are also periods of vulnerability because you lack
established working relationships and detailed understanding of your role.* [7]

Other experts do not believe the first 90 days or 100 days determine the
success or failure of a new leader. The difference of opinion is centered on
the presence of or the lack of a succession plan. With a succession plan in
place, the first 90 to 100 days can be predictive, but without a succession
plan, it is difficult for a new leader to be successful or to adequately measure
progress or failure.

Communicating

John Maxwell, the author of *Everyone Communicates Few Connect*, states
that a leader, especially a new leader, is communicating always, whether he

---

[6] Antoinette LaBelle, "Transition to new leadership: The first 1,000 days," *The
Bridgespan Group,* September 2011.
[7] Michael Watkins, *The First 90 Days: Proven Strategies for Getting Up to Speed
Faster and Smarter, Updated and Expanded,* (Harvard Business Press, 2013).

intends to or not.[8] The difference is that new leaders are scrutinized more than existing or experienced leaders. Virtually everything a new leader says or does or does not do communicates something. Maxwell opines that new leaders must connect to increase their influence in every situation.[9]

1. *Connecting* is related to learning about others. Connecting is taking the time to learn about the lives, interests, and talents of others.
2. *Connecting* goes beyond words. Connecting is more than a daily casual greeting. It involves taking time out of a busy schedule to listen, learn, and engage with others in the organization.
3. *Connecting* requires a great deal of energy. Communicating takes time and energy, but connecting takes more time, more energy, and more sincerity, but it's worth the investment.
4. *Connecting* is more skill than natural talent. Some leaders have natural communication talents but that does not mean they effectively connect with people. Connecting requires dedication and talent to develop and cultivate.

These elements can be part of a succession plan so that the board and the leader who is leaving can work with the new leader on these elements. To improve organizational performance requires these elements plus that one essential need the new leader must recognize - the need to improve morale by connecting with employees and the board, which is more likely to occur if the succession plan addresses the issues related to morale. A succession plan would inform the new leader about the level and nature of morale in the organization. This would prevent the new leader from making mistakes that historically may have been a problem for morale.

The classic research study by Jay Hall created a communication and success rubric for new leaders that should be embedded in succession planning and new leader orientation.[10] It is based on a delineation of leadership behavior that is divided into three categories, with each accompanied by a description of the leader's attitude. The three categories are (1) high achievers; (2) average achievers; and (3) low achievers.

Each of these three levels and types of leaders has different opinions about the balance between productivity and respect for employees. In fact,

---

[8] John Maxwell, *Everyone Communicates, Few Connect*, (Thomas Nelson, 2010).
[9] Ibid.
[10] Jay Hall, "To achieve or not: the manager's choice," *California Management Review*, Haas School of Business, University of California, 2014: http://cmr. berkeley.edu/search/article detail. aspx article=5114.

low achievers do not recognize the importance of personal interaction and support of employees.

High Achievers: Care about people and success
Average Achievers: Concentrate on production
Low Achievers: Preoccupied with job security

High Achievers: View subordinates optimistically
Average Achievers: Focus more on their own status
Low Achievers: Show a basic distrust of subordinates

High Achievers: Seek advice from colleagues
Average Achievers: Are reluctant to seek advice
Low Achievers: Do not seek advice

High Achievers: Listen well to others
Average Achievers: Listen only to certain people
Low Achievers: Rely on self, policies, and manuals

Hall stated that a research study of 16,000 managers found that the difference between high achieving managers and low achieving managers, as noted above, illustrates significant differences in temperament, attitude, and behavior, which are each important in the succession process. Hall summarized the research findings in very compelling terms.

The portrait of the high achieving manager which emerges from our study is that of an individual employing an integrative style of management, wherein people are valued just as highly as the accomplishment of production goals wherein candor, openness, sensitivity, and receptivity comprise the rule in interpersonal relationships rather than its exception wherein participative practices are favored over unilaterally directive or lame duck prescriptive measures. From a motivational standpoint, the Achieving Manager needs to find meaning in his or her work and strives to afford such meaning to others. Higher order, constructive incentives are his or her motivational preoccupations, while their less achieving comrades remain mired in fantasies of defense and self-preservation.[11]

---

[11] Ibid.

The Purpose of a Succession Plan

The major purpose of developing a succession plan is rooted in the needs of the organization which should be matched with the experience, expertise, and abilities of the new leader. Perhaps this explains in part the findings by the Alexcel Group and the Institute for Executive Development. They discovered that 68 percent of failed new leaders lacked interpersonal skills; 45 percent lacked leadership skills, and 41 percent failed due to goal conflicts between the leader and the organization[12]. Also, many of the failed leaders came into organizations that did not have a succession and transition plan and unclear expectations of board members. This includes a failure to build an effective and efficient team within the organization [see the chapter on building a strong executive team], which is a succession planning function. Cindy Kraft summarized the study:

Global CEO turnover is approximately 15 percent according to a 2007 study by Booz Allen, a high number. Other studies suggest 40 percent of new leaders fail within the first 18 months. And Aon Consulting reports a 50 percent chance an executive will quit or be fired within his first three years. Ninety-two percent (92 percent) of respondents said it takes 90+ days to reach productivity and 62 percent said over six months. And even after making it through the first 90 days and the first 180 days, a significant percentage of external executive hires are gone within two years. While not as long as with external hires, 72 percent of respondents said internal executives need more than the "first 90 days" to get up to speed, and 25 percent said over six months were needed. Thirty percent of external hires fail to meet expectations in two years and the fail rate of internal senior executive transitions is 20 percent, representing millions of dollars in losses at the executive level.[13]

The study also revealed that 90 percent of new leaders hired outside of the organization said it took more than 90 days to become productive especially if there was no succession and transition plan in place to assist the new leader.

---

[12] John Baldoni, "How to Help New Executives Succeed," *Harvard Business Review*, May 5, 2008; Cindy Kraft, "Executives Transitions Market Study:" http://www.cfocoach.com/2008/06/executive-transitions-market-study. html. Citing research from the Institute of Executive Development http:// strategicedsolutions.org/research/.

[13] Ibid.

A study from the Stanford University Rock Center for Corporate Governance and the Institute of Executive Development found that only 46 percent of businesses have a formal process for developing successor candidates for key executive positions and a transition plan for new leaders. Additionally, only 25 percent have an adequate pool of ready successor CEO candidates at their companies,[14] which is due to the lack of a succession plan and training.

David Larcker, an expert on succession planning and new leadership training and recruitment and a professor at Stanford Graduate School of Business said:

> *These findings are surprising given the importance that strong leadership has on the long-term performance of organizations. The corporate leaders we interviewed all believe that succession and transition planning are vitally important. But the majority do not think that their organizations are doing enough to prepare for eventual changes in leadership, nor are they confident that they have the right practices in place to be sure of identifying the best leaders for tomorrow.* [15]

Antidotes: The transition to new leadership can be an exciting time for the new leader and the organization if there is both a transition and succession plan that is centered on communications, essential management functions, strategic planning, sound decision-making, employee morale, and the development of a strong executive team. It is also critically important that the new leader is oriented to the succession and transition plan, which includes issues within the organization.

Boards should ask each finalist for the leadership position how he plans to make the transition, including how he plans to communicate with employees; how he will handle staffing decisions and appointments, and how he will communicate with the board during the transition period. The questions should become even more specific and focused on these topics when the selection has been narrowed down to a final candidate.

These questions should be centered on all aspects of the transition to new leadership. The board should tell the finalists about the issues facing the organization; only an honest assessment of the organization will prepare the potential leader to address those issues, but the board cannot be divided in its assessment of the organization, where one board member tells one thing

---

[14] Chad Brooks, "Few Companies Prepared to Replace CEO," *Business News Daily*, March 7, 2014.
[15] Ibid.

while undermining the opinion of other board members. This, too, is a vital component of a transition plan.

An assessment of the finalists' communication skills and communication plans may help determine if the finalists have what it will take to make the transition successful. Michael Myatt states,

> *The moral of the story is that [prospective] leaders have to be honest, have a demonstrated track record of success, be excellent communicators, and put an emphasis on serving those they lead, be fluid in approach, be focused, and have a bias for action. If these traits are not possessed by your new leader and leadership team, you will be in for a rocky road ahead.[16]*

The advice of Myatt stands strong for leaders who also must improve morale, which is one of the most overlooked aspects of new leadership because often low morale is an issue for an organization going through a transition. There should be a separate section in the transition plan that addresses morale [see the chapter on motivation].

Louis Gerstner, Jr. was keenly sensitive to the morale of his IBM employees when he took over IBM. He came to his new job when the company was struggling in many ways, but addressing morale was one of his first priorities and thus improving morale became one of his most urgent transition strategies. Gerstner said this to IBM employees:

> *It is not helpful to feel sorry for ourselves. I'm sure our employees don't need any rah-rah speeches. We need leadership at all levels and a sense of direction and momentum, not just from me but from all of us. I don't want to see a lot of prophets of doom around here. I want can-do people looking for excitement.[17]*

Gerstner went on to say that the organization did not have time to focus on who created the problems. He thought organizations could learn from mistakes of the past but not if the leaders focused more on placing blame than learning not to make the same mistakes.

> *We have little time to spend on problem definition. This means let's get to the problems, work the solutions, and do this together. We must focus our efforts on communications, solutions, and actions.[18]*

---

[16] Michael Myatt, "*15 Ways to Identify Bad Leaders,*" *Forbes*, October 2012.

[17] Edward Gerstner, *Elephants Can Dance*, (Harper Collings, 2003.)

[18] Ibid.

Rosabeth Moss Kanter said that leaders, especially new leaders, must energize despondent employees, passive teams, or sluggish organizations. She offered four guiding principles to accomplish this.[19]

1. *Believe in people and their power to make a difference.* Show employees they are worth it by investing in things that matter to them and show sincerity by taking the time to find out want matters to employees.

2. *Direct the energy tied up in negativity (resentment, rivalry, or disrespect) into positive actions.* If employees seem negative, make them nobler by focusing their attention on a bigger cause and giving them a chance to contribute to it. Negativity inevitably leads to rampant rumors and spreading dissatisfaction which compromises the effectiveness of the leader and organization outcomes.

3. *Make initiative possible and desirable.* Try to awaken creative and innovative thinking by opening real opportunities to contribute new ideas. Seek them, find them, fund them, praise them, and provide a support system for them. It is also critically important to provide feedback to employees about their work and ideas.

4. *Start with small wins – things that people can control.* Look for even small successes, promising ideas, and other things that can be praised, especially during a leadership transition period when employees have a high-stress level. While this is important, it must also be sincere, because false praise of mediocrity can portray the new leader as naïve or worse. Also, it is important for even the small successes to be relevant and not linked to some obscure or unimportant task.

When board members interview candidates for the top leadership position, they could conclude the interview by asking the candidates this question, which was suggested by Marcus Buckingham: *"What is the difference between chess and checkers?"*[20] Most leaders will respond that chess is more difficult and requires more strategic thinking. While that is true, the most insightful answer is this: the pieces in checkers move in only two directions while the pieces in chess are different and move in different directions. As Buckingham said,

---

[19] Rosabeth Moss Kanter, *Confidence: How Winning Streaks and Losing Streaks Begin and End,* (Crown Publishing, 2006).

[20] Marcus Buckingham, *The One Thing You Need to Know*, (The Free Press, 2005).

Thus, if you want to excel at the game of chess you have to learn how each piece moves and then incorporate these unique moves into your overall plan. The same is true for the game of leading. Mediocre new leaders play checkers with their people. They assume that their employees will be motivated by the same things and driven by the same goals. [21]

The effective leader understands the fact that employees are different and cannot be managed effectively without taking the time to learn about their strengths and weaknesses. Also, there is a perception that new leaders are more concerned about how they appear to others than about the well-being of employees. If the new leader during the transition period shows that he cares about employees, the transition may go more smoothly.

In his book, *The New Boss: How to Survive the First 100 Days*, Peter Fischer states that successful new leaders understand relationships and the importance of connecting and engaging with employees. They intuitively understand that the culture of an organization is embedded in the attitude of employees. Respecting that is a sign of respect for employees, which aids the development of relationships.

"...recognize and develop key relationships, deal adroitly with hidden rivals and predecessors, build networks in the organization, show that they are team oriented, communicate with senior management on strategy and style of leadership and impart confidence and trust." [22]

Planning or Development?

Organizations too often stagnate in the succession and transition *planning* stage and do not move to the *development* level. Harvard Business Review suggests four steps in the succession and transition process.[23]

1. ***Change the name from Succession Planning to Succession and Transition Development*:** Plans do not develop anyone — only development *experiences* develop people. Many organizations put more effort and attention into the planning process than they do into the development process. Succession and transition planning

---

[21] Ibid.

[22] Peter Fischer, *The New Boss: How to Survive the First 100 Days*, (Kogan Page, 2008).

[23] Marshall Goldsmith, "Efficient Succession Planning," *Harvard Business Review*, May 20, 2009.

processes have lots of work — forms, charts, meetings, due dates, and checklists. They sometimes create a false sense that the planning process is an end rather than a precursor to real development.

2. *Measure outcomes, not process*: This change of emphasis is important for several reasons. First, leaders pay attention to what gets measured and what gets rewarded. If leadership development is not enough of a priority for the company to establish goals and track progress against those goals, it will be difficult to make any succession or transition planning process work effectively. Second, the act of engaging with senior executives to establish these goals will build support for succession and transition planning and ownership for leadership development. Third, these results will help guide future efforts.

3. *Keep it simple*: Sometimes organizations add excessively complex assessment criteria to the succession and transition planning process to improve the quality of the assessment. Some of these criteria are challenging for experts to assess, much less the average employee. It works best for the new leader and the employees to follow a simple and straightforward assessment process.

4. *Stay realistic*: Some succession and transition plans are unrealistic because they are overly ambitious, naïve, unrelated to the needs of the organization, too expensive, or the role of the new leader does not match the job description.

Without a thoughtful transition process as part of a succession plan, an organization can feel the destructive effects and both the leader and the organization will suffer and ultimately fail.[24]

Chapter Three Key Words and Concepts

Succession Planning
Transition Planning
Leadership Transition
Planning and Development
Connecting
High Achievers
Average Achievers

---

[24] Peter Fischer, *The New Boss: How to Survive the First 100 Days*, (Kogan Page, 2008).

Low Achievers
Interpersonal Skills
Internal and External Hires
Morale
Intuition
Negativity
Small Wins
Chess and Checkers Views of Leadership
First 100 Days
Measure Outcomes Not Process
Key Relationships

Chapter Three Discussion Items

What is succession planning and why is it important?

What is the difference between succession planning and transition planning? Give examples of each.

Is it reasonable to expect every employee to be a High Achiever? Why or why not?

Is it reasonable to expect every employee in leadership positions to be High Achievers? Why?

Describe the role of interpersonal skills in planning, development, and operations.

Describe and explain the significance of "Chess and Checkers" views of leadership.

What is the difference between measuring outcomes and processes?

Chapter Three Lessons Learned

The exchanges between a board and the leader of an organization can positively or negatively impact succession planning and the transition to new leadership.

At the very least each organization should have a short-term succession plan that includes transition processes.

With a succession plan in place, the first 90 to 100 days can be predictive, but without a succession plan, it is difficult for a new leader to be successful or to adequately measure progress or failure.

Virtually everything a new leader says or does or does not do communicates something.

The difference between high achieving managers and low achieving managers is based on significant differences in temperament, attitude, and behavior.

The effective leader understands the fact that employees are different and cannot be managed effectively without taking the time to learn about their strengths and weaknesses.

CHAPTER FOUR

LEADERSHIP STYLES AND TRAITS

"It is a disaster when leaders take all the hype about change literally and grab every new management fad that comes down the pike. It is change overload!"

-Jack Welch[1]

Determinants: There are many leadership traits and styles that can be a detriment or enhancement to an organization's success or failure. A leadership style that does not match the needs of an organization, regardless of the good intentions of the leader, usually leads to an unsuccessful experience for both the leader and the organization. An organization can lose precious momentum and subsequent ineffective selection of support staff can jeopardize the future of the organization. The situation can be exacerbated by a board's decision to hire a leader who has leadership traits and a style of leadership based more on the bestowed and perceived power of the position than on influence. The perception of power based mainly on position becomes a negative thread that spins throughout an organization. The leadership styles and traits come with consequences for an organization.

Leadership Traits and Decisions

Case Study #1

A non-profit organization hired a laissez-faire leader to replace a very effective long-term leader who had brought prominence and distinction to the organization. The laissez-faire leader did very little to help the organization respond to internal and external changes. He tried to hold on to his predecessor's programs and strategies and never tried to update anything in the strategies, goals or actions. A general malaise settled over the organization. The laissez-faire leader remained in place for a few years but he

---

[1] Jack Welch, *Winning*, (Harper Collins, 2005).

was basically a figurehead during the last two years of his administration. By then whatever influence he once had was marginalized by his leadership style, the infighting of his staff, the growing control and influence of the board on the operations of the organization, questionable hiring, and promotion practices, and looming budget issues.

With its growing power and influence in the vacuum of leadership created by the laissez-faire leader, the board decided it was time to bring in a firebrand leader to spark the organization back to life. A leader was hired who had a reputation for making drastic changes in organizations in a brief period. He was referred to as a "turn and burn" leader.

Louis Gerstner, Jr. wrote in his book about taking over IBM, that "hired guns" don't always shoot straight and they seldom last very long.[2] Within three months, the new CEO of the non-profit that was once known for its dynamic community presence and leadership had alienated employees, clients, contributors, grantors, service providers, vendors, and even the employee parking lot attendant. The new CEO once handed a towel to the parking lot attendant and instructed him to "wipe the dust off my car, and if you do a decent job, you won't have to wash it." He told a female senior vice president to "fetch me a cup of coffee, and fix it like I like it." At a local Rotary Club dinner where he was invited to give remarks, he talked a full 30 minutes about himself without once mentioning the work of his organization or the Rotary Club.

As an outside accounting firm was completing its annual financial audit, the auditors had questions about the new CEO's travel claims. There was nothing out of the ordinary; the auditors simply asked him for more documentation for some of the travel claims. The CEO was rude, insulting, and accused the auditors of conspiring to embarrass him. He had a negative attitude toward the board, too. He showed little respect for the board members and often blamed them for his failures, which he also did with employees. At one board meeting, a confrontation ensued between the CEO and the chairman of the board. During the confrontation, he reminded the board that they hired him because of his leadership style, and he added that they were being disingenuous by now claiming that his confrontational and high-pressure style of management was unacceptable. He claimed his leadership style was exactly the type of leadership the organization wanted and needed but now the hypocritical board determined that the CEO's leadership style was no longer acceptable. As he continued addressing the board, he became verbally aggressive and pointed to each board member

---

[2] Edward Gerstner, *Elephants Can Dance*, (Harper Collings, 2003.)

saying, "You're the problem. You lack the toughness and the judgment to do this job." Within two days of the outburst, the board fired him. However, he received a sizable compensation package that cost the organization a lot of money.

Case Study #2

There are times when a news media report reminds us of a company or organization that at one time seemed so engrained in the United States culture that no one could imagine life without it. Such is the case when the name of Bethlehem Steel is brought up.

Following the economic Panic of 1857, Bethlehem Steel was formed from a consolidation of several smaller companies that fell victim to the economic disaster. In 1861, the company was fully incorporated as Bethlehem Iron Company and it quickly became prosperous and powerful. The company's phenomenal growth was fueled by the rapidly expanding railroad's need for iron and steel. Also, the building of armor plating for Navy ships became a large market for the company. In 1913, the company expanded its business into shipbuilding. Soon it became one of the world's largest companies. Over the next several decades the company became famous for several projects, including providing steel for the world's first Ferris Wheel, steel for the Golden Gate Bridge, steel for the rapidly growing Navy fleet and ship guns, steel for skyscrapers, and many other projects. During World War II, the company built at least one ship each day, famously fulfilling a promise to President Roosevelt. Post World War II, the company continued to prosper. During its most dynamic growth, it employed over 400,000 people. The respected and successful president of Bethlehem was Eugene Grace. He was the president from 1916 to 1945, and then became Chairman of the Board from 1945 until his retirement in 1957. A few years after his retirement, the company's spiral downward began. His successor was Arthur Homer who had a background in manufacturing but no experience with finance. The board had no succession plan or a transition plan, and little information about Homer's leadership style or his ideas about the future of the company.

Immediately upon accepting the position, Homer insisted on being the highest paid CEO in the world. He also made the decision to build a massive steel plant in 1964 without contracts in hand that would justify such an enormous investment. Consequently, the debt burden dug into the company's operating expenses and ability to meet debt payment timelines. In what was expected to be a boost to the company's financial stability, it bid on construction material for the World Trade Center buildings in New York. The steel production necessary to build the twin towers was predicted to be over 100,000 tons. However, an attitude of arrogance and entitlement at Bethlehem Steel led to a careless, slipshod, and ill-prepared bid for the project. Despite the common perception that Bethlehem Steel would win the bid, the contract went instead to steel mills in Seattle, St. Louis, New York, and Illinois. The investors, architects, and builders of the World Trade Center preferred that the steel come from one source, but they had no choice except to diversify the contracts because it appeared that Bethlehem was not prepared to fulfill the material orders.

The company faced growing competition from other countries, it was not prepared for its aging workforce and increasing pension costs, and it was not nimble enough to make changes to meet market needs and demands. The company lost billions of dollars but due to a strong core of salesmen, the company showed signs of a comeback in the mid-1970s. To fulfill the promise of better days ahead, the board realized that the company needed more than ever a dynamic, creative, and insightful president, so in 1980 it hired Donald Trautlein. The board was impressed by Trautlein's analytical approach; he was a data-driven and no-nonsense type of leader. The board expected Truatlein to get tough and lead Bethlehem Steel back to prosperity and prominence. However, the board failed to ask him how he would accomplish the resurrection of the company.

When Trautlein came to Bethlehem Steel, he felt that he did not have time to be "Mr. Nice Guy." Using the Hersey-Blanchard Leadership Model[3] terminology, his mission was "high task and low relationship" because of the urgency of his mission. However, Trautlein was full bore low relationship and high task all the time. He had the full support of the board who instructed him to make changes and to make changes quickly. He was empowered to be an overbearing, dictatorial leader. Had Trautlein tempered his approach and listened to consultants knowledgeable about the industry as suggested in the Fielder Contingency Theory[4] (the effective manager assesses a situation and the needs of the organization and determines if it is a low task-high relationship situation or a high task-low relationship situation) he may have been successful.

In the *contingency model* of leadership, the leader takes the time to determine the amount of direction (task behavior) and the amount of socio-

---

[3] Paul Hersey and Ken Blanchard, *Management of Organizational Behavior: Utilizing Human Resources 3rd Edition*, (Prentice Hall, 1977).
[4] F.E. Fiedler and Garcia, J. E. Garcia, *New Approaches to Leadership, Cognitive Resources and Organizational Performance*, (John Wiley and Sons, 1987).

emotional support a leader must provide. This is contingent on the level of maturity and ability of the staff and the executive team. The *task behavior model* of leadership is based on how much the leader engages in explaining the duties and responsibilities of employees–telling them what to do, how to do it, when to do it, and where to do it. This requires no or little dialogue. The communications are one way instead of two ways and the expected behavior of employees is compliance instead of innovation. Trautlein's leadership style was task behavior.

Another complicating factor was Trautlein's lack of knowledge about the steel industry or even how steel was made. He never visited any of the steel mills and he showed no interest in learning about steel or meeting with customers or prospective customers. Trautlein was not involved in any company functions or activities nor was he committed to community matters.

After he experienced several failures, Trautlein shifted from making all the decisions to avoiding tough decisions; in fact, he avoided making almost any decisions. Trautlein changed the strategic plan so often that the company's executive leadership team did not know what or how to communicate to the employees. He continued to reach out to expert consultants, but his pride or paranoia caused him to ignore their advice. Over time, it was proven that the advice he received was accurate and could have saved the company had he listened.

In a move that devastated morale throughout the company, Trautlein insisted on and continued to receive large annual pay increases at the same time pay was being cut for all employees and many of them were being laid off. He used the misfortunes of the company to justify laying off top-level executives, but then he replaced them with higher paid lawyers and financial analyst with no experience or knowledge of the steel industry.

In 1986, after six years of driving the company toward failure, he was forced out by the board. His "golden parachute" was millions of dollars. A succession of CEOs tried various methods and ways to bring the company back to profitability but it was too late. The damage was done. The company continued to exist only in name and was finally dissolved permanently in 2007.[5]

---

[5] For a more detailed history of Bethlehem Steel Company's demise, see "The Sinking of Bethlehem Steel," Carol Loomis, Patricia Neering, and Christopher Thaczyk, *Fortune,* April 5, 2004.

Leadership Styles

Case studies like Bethlehem Steel could have ended differently if the behavior of the leader focused on socio-emotional dynamics that provide two-way communications, where the leader listens, facilitates, directs when necessary, clarifies goals, and supports employees.

The key difference and what determines the appropriate leadership style in each situation is decided in large part by the maturity and skill levels of the employees matched with the needs and purpose of the organization.

Stephen M.R. Covey added *trust* to the leadership model, where trust becomes a determinant of the productivity of employees. Covey illustrated his point through a formula:

Strategy (**S**) x Execution (**E**) multiplied by Trust (**T**) equals Results (**R**); therefore, *S x E (T) = R.*[6]

The determinants of maturity, skill, and trust levels of employees dictate the leadership style. For example, low maturity, skill, and trust result in *task-oriented leadership* until those issues are addressed, while *relational leadership* is based on high levels of maturity, skill, and trust. As the maturity level and productivity of the employees improves, the astute leader will become less task-oriented and rely more on the skills and initiative of the employees.

A leadership style that is based primarily on intimidations is contrary to all research on effective management. For example, research by Jim Collins on effective companies reported in his books *Good to Great: Why Some Companies Make the Leap and Others Don't*;[7] *Built to Last,*[8] and *Great by Choice*[9] does not support dictatorial leadership. Collins notes that leadership that focuses on serving, guiding, and supporting employees and boards is much more effective than dictatorial tactics and can be task-oriented as well. Collins wrote,

---

[6] Stephen M.R. Covey, *The Speed of Trust*, (Free Press of Simon and Schuster, 2008 edition)

[7] James Collins, *Good to Great: Why Some Companies Make the Leap and Others Don't*, (Harper Business, 2001).

[8] James Collins and Jerry Porras, *Built to Last 3rd Edition*, (Harper Business, 2004).

[9] James Collins and Morten Hansen, *Great by Choice*, (Harper Business, 2011).

The moment you feel the need to tightly manage someone, you've made a hiring mistake. The best people don't need to be managed. Guided, taught, led–yes. But not tightly managed.[10]

Research conducted by Daniel Goleman on the distinctive styles of leadership found that the *"coercive style"* is the least effective in almost all situations and in all types of settings.[11]

A leader that expects immediate compliance without any expectation of feedback and no regard for employees or clients has compromised the organization's capacity to respond effectively to most situations. It is a destructive style of leadership. Goleman found that effective leaders exhibit a coaching style of management.

The leader shares goals, listens, identifies employees' strengths and weaknesses, encourages, and helps them to improve their performance by building long-term capabilities. [12]

The style of leadership is important at all levels of an organization because it becomes a model for other employees. Employees report that a good, effective, caring, organized, and efficient leader is just as important as a good salary.[13] Mid-level administrators say the same thing about their supervisors as do program managers at the line level.

The effect of leadership style starts at the top and filters down eventually to all levels of an organization and then toward the clients. If a CEO's leadership style is based on intimidation that style of behavior is very likely to be modeled by top management, middle management, and program or line management. Employees that experience a coercive, abrasive leader often believe that that type of leadership is not only expected, it will be rewarded. So, at every level of the organization, it is more likely that the coercive type of leadership is emulated. The negative determinants seep into all elements of the organization.

---

[10] James Collins, *Good to Great: Why Some Companies Make the Leap and Others Don't*, (Harper Business, 2001).

[11] Daniel Goleman, "Leadership That Gets Results," *Harvard Business Review*, March 2000.

[12] Daniel Goleman, Richard Boyatzis, and Annie McKee, *Primal Leadership: Unleashing the Power of Emotional Intelligence*, (Harvard Business Press, 2013).

[13] Victor Lipman, "5 Easy Ways to Motivate and Demotivate Employees," *Forbes*, March 2013.

In a study by the Center for Creative Leadership, it was found that 40 percent of leaders fail within their first 18 months on the job. Of those that failed, 47 percent did not communicate effectively and 21 percent tried too hard to "show who's in charge."[14]

Failed leaders also do not select and hire effective employees. In an article by Rick Piraino on leadership titled *Leadership and Favoritism,* he states that,

> *Favoritism is a leadership and morale killer. It's natural for leaders to have people they enjoy working with more than others, but this can never be justification for special privileges or breakdowns in the consistent application of accountability.*[15]

Every leader in any organization has favorite employees and trusted confidantes, and those individuals may be judged by a different standard; that's only natural and is generally recognized and accepted by others in the organization, but there is a line that cannot be crossed – where the favorite employee's work is so lacking or his behavior is so egregious that it's known to all within the organization and it threatens productivity and morale. Enabling that type of behavior by ignoring it seriously jeopardizes the effectiveness of the leader. Typically, there will not be an overt protest of favoritism by employees, but the diminishing influence of the leader is insidious and persistent. In the long run, the leader and the organization will suffer. The negative impact is multiplied if there is a double standard, especially when the work of other employees is scrutinized while favored employee's work is not. At the deepest level, the casualty is trust. Leaders that are insecure or that are overly dominant are more likely to fall into this pattern. It is a control issue in part and a paranoid-related tendency to tighten the circle around him.

Stephen Covey wrote in his book *The Speed of Trust* that production and quality are directly proportional to the level of trust of leadership by employees.[16] The trust comes from hiring the right employees and providing them with the vision, plan, and resources to do their jobs and then trusting them to get the job done without showing favorites that have a distinct set of

---

[14] As reported in "SHRM Workplace Forecast, The Top Trends of HR Professionals," *Society of Human Resources Management*, May 2013.

[15] Rick Piraino, "Leadership and Favoritism," *Ezine Articles*, December 2008: http://ezinearticles.com/ Leadership and- Favoritism&id.

[16] Stephen M.R. Covey, *The Speed of Trust*, (Free Press of Simon and Schuster, 2008 Edition)

expectations and standards. There obviously must be a level of accountability. Establishing trust through fair treatment of employees does not mean accountability is compromised or minimized. A leader who insists on accountability but has several types and levels of accountability based solely on which employees are closest to him or most loyal will create a workplace climate that is negative and counterproductive.

In the book *The Classic Touch*, the authors speak about a basic failing of many leaders–the failure to encourage their managers to show good manners and courtesy to all employees.[17] From the history of leadership, according to the authors, going back centuries, even during violent times the most effective leaders showed respect for others. Caesar understood the importance of connecting with and trusting his staff as well as the soldiers. He could and would be demanding and did not shy away from correcting his immediate officers, but then he would later talk with them one-on-one or in front of others to point out how important the person's work was to the Roman Empire.

Some leaders are disciples of the *Machiavellian*[18] leadership style, based on the mistaken belief that it is better to be feared than loved because there is more security in fear than in love.[19] Machiavellian leadership in precise terms is "the willingness to utilize manipulative tactics and act amorally and endorse a cynical, untrustworthy view of human nature."[20]

In a recent study of the impact of Machiavellian leadership on employees, the researchers found that the overbearing nature of the leadership style resulted in higher levels of emotional exhaustion among employees. They were trying to cope with the constant stress created by Machiavellian leaders.

We investigated the relationship between Machiavellian leadership and emotional exhaustion. Even more, we investigated an explanatory mechanism of this association by encompassing organizational cynicism as a mediator.

---

[17] John Clemens and Douglas Meyer, *The Classic Touch*, (McGraw-Hill Publishing, 1999).

[18] The term Machiavellianism is "the employment of cunning and duplicity in statecraft or in general conduct". The word comes from the Italian Renaissance government represent-ative and professional writer Niccolò Machiavelli (1469-1527), according to the *Oxford Dictionary*, 2012 Edition.

[19] Anthony Jay, *Management and Machiavelli: A Prescription for Success*, (Prentice-Hall, 1996).

[20] J.J. Dahling; B.G. Whitaker and P.E. Levy P. E., "The Development and Validation of a New Machiavellianism scale." *Journal of Management*, October 2009: 35, 219–257.10.1177/014920 6308318618.

Results showed that Machiavellian leadership has a both direct and indirect,
through organizational cynicism, on employees' emotional exhaustion. [21]

When boards are looking for leaders, they should take the time to learn about a prospective leader's management style and management belief system. Too often board members seem influenced more by ideas, proposed strategic initiatives, and dramatically energetic presentations rather than by what a candidate offers through his fundamental beliefs about leadership, organizational management history, record working and collaborating with employees and stakeholders, and how his work history aligns with the needs of the organization.

Some boards make selections of leaders without contemplating how that leader will implement strategies successfully with employees' full participation. A strategic plan is not that difficult to develop. The difficult part is implementation, managing change, engaging employees, and planning for sustainability, which are based on the leadership style, principles, practices, and priorities of the leaders.

A leader must be cognizant of anything that may distract from the strategic plan and waste good intentions and cause morale issues. The leader must be effective at communicating the strategic plan to those that will implement it at all levels. Some leaders do not know how to or are unwilling to do this effectively or choose not to take the time and effort necessary to involve employees and solicit their support, which undermines and erodes morale and the fabric of the organization's functions and outcomes.

In an article about morale killers, Joey Faucette found that workers agree their jobs are easier and less stressful if leaders treat them well and use the elements of *servant leadership* as the guiding principles of leadership. Servant leadership includes various methods of frequent communications.[22] It is clear from research that when leadership is dysfunctional and dictatorial, motivation and productivity levels plummet. Faucette adds that leadership-caused morale killers are moodiness, cruelty, greed, aloofness, and a focus on negatives.

---

[21] Panagiotis Gkorezis, Eugenia Petridou, and Theodora Krouklidou, Monitoring Editor: Vlad Glăveanu, "The Detrimental Effect of Machiavellian Leadership on Employees' Emotional Exhaustion: Organizational Cynicism as a Mediator," *European Journal of Psychology*, (11), 4, November 2015: doi: 10.5964/ejop.v11i4.988

[22] Joey Faucette, Are You Your Employee's Morale Problem? *Entrepreneur*, August 2011.

I used to count the dandelions in my lawn every spring and try to kill every one of them until my daughter asked if she could pick them and make a bouquet. That's when I stopped looking for dandelions. You should, too, with your businesses. If you keep on asking whether your workers are wasting time on Facebook or stealing office supplies, you will find proof, as surely as I used to find those silly flowers. Instead, look out for your employees doing something right, and tell them every occasionally. It will make their day.[23]

Leaders have varying ideas about motivation. Some think motivation by intimidation is the most effective leadership style while others think motivation is not their responsibility. An effective leader is successful because he motivates people by his example, encouragement, constructive and specific feedback, and through a positive attitude.

In the book *Influencing Up* by Allan Cohen and David Bradford, they cite the example of destructive leadership by the CEO of a *Fortune 500* company, Jeff Kindler.[24] He seemed highly qualified for the job and was brilliant, but his leadership style was contaminated by outrageous behavior toward employees. He was dictatorial, did not want input, was bullying and intimidating, and he showed no respect for employees or stakeholders. Consequently, valued employees left or were demoralized into non-productive behavior. Some of Kindler's good ideas were never developed simply because of his negative leadership style and his disrespect toward and lack of trust of employees. According to Erica Brown, author of *Leadership in the Wilderness*, it is time for a leader to leave when he has no respect for his followers.

One of the greatest threats to leadership is losing faith in those you lead. The gradual breakdown of trust, the anger, and the disappointment chisel away at a leader's energy and eventually lead to paralysis. You cannot lead people you do not believe in because soon they will cease believing in you. If you have arrived at this point, you have betrayed your most fundamental role.[25]

Cohen and Bradford offer advice to leaders who still believe that disrespect for and exerting power over employees is the best leadership method.

---

[23] Ibid.
[24] Allan Cohen and David Bradford, *Influencing Up*, (Wiley Publishing, 2012).
[25] Erica Brown, *Leadership in the Wilderness*, (Maggid Books, 2013).

Some experts will advise you to become totally Machiavellian and seek power for its own sake. From these people, you will hear advice such as don't be afraid to bully, intimidate or use fear if you want to keep your power; you get an advantage from appearing to be tough. Forget focusing on honesty and self-disclosure because they will turn that against you. This is destructive advice that will certainly lead to failure. [26]

The advice to be Machiavellian, according to Cohen and Bradford, is not uncommon and there are many leaders who think being a dictatorial and intimidating leader is the best insulation from insubordination and efforts to take power away. Cohen and Bradford add that research and reviews of effective companies and organizations do not support the use of Machiavellian leadership. They explain that a leader can maintain power and yet influence through relationships.

People often consider power and relationships to be antithetical; they wonder, 'Do I use all my power and ability to coercively push for what I want and risk alienating others, or do I go along for the sake of maintaining the relationship?' However, these two themes are not only compatible; they, in fact, build on each other. The influence approach we use recommends that people build relationships; there are both reciprocity and mutuality despite inequality of power, and taking a 'partner' orientation increases your influence. Making powerful people partners helps determine their response to the approach. Because this partnering approach is founded on a concern for mutual and organizational success, the assumption of the potential partnership is most likely to gain cooperation. [27]

The leader that knows how to maintain a power base and develop relationships through participation and trust is much more likely to implement and manage organizations and change effectively. Louis Gerstner, Jr., the architect of IBM's reemergence said that one of the primary keys to his success was team building and showing respect for employees, but he added that team building does not work if the leader does not listen and actually "build." A leader can create the idea of team building, but it is only a false concept if the leader is not willing to listen to members of his team and select members that will stand up and speak their opinion. Many leaders in organizations don't take the time to listen to executive staff members, other employees, clients, board members, or other stakeholders because they are

[26] Ibid.
[27] Allan Cohen and David Bradford, *Influencing Up*, (Wiley Publishing, 2012).

too enamored with the power of position that drives them to mistreat, ignore, or disrespect employees, the board, and others.

Henry Mintzberg suggests in *The Nature of Managerial Work* that activities of most leaders are "characterized by brevity, variety, and fragmentation."[28] These types of leaders are always on the move and seldom take the time to study, listen, and plan effectively. Mintzberg says that this type of leader's only interaction with his employees is when something is not working effectively. And to this type of leader no situation or issue, no matter how important, can interrupt the leader's busy schedule – a hectic schedule that is supposed to illustrate to everyone how important he is and how hard he is working.

Social Learning Theory and Leadership

In many ways, leadership is linked to social learning theory. There are valuable lessons from Albert Bandura's research for leaders of any organization (Bandura's *Social Foundations of Thought and Action*).[29]

Bandura is the father of social learning theory and the preeminent authority on *influence*. At a time when most leaders and many psychologists thought that the most influential way to change the behavior of people was through direct rewards and punishments, Bandura's research found that observing the behavior of others to learn how they respond to social interactions is a more powerful shaper of behavior. Through decades of social learning theory research in hundreds of different settings, Bandura and associates found that people will attempt to improve performance, respond well to leadership, and will accept change such as innovative ideas about work, new strategies, and new expectations if:

1. *They believe it will be worth it.*
2. *They believe others are committed, too, and*
3. *They can do what is required and have the resources necessary to do it.*[30]

---

[28] Henry Mintzberg, *The Nature of Managerial Work*, (Harper Collins, 1973) with excerpts and concepts updated in *Simply Managing*, (Berrett-Koehler, 2013).

[29] Albert Bandura, *Social Foundations of Thought and Action*, (Prentice Hall, 1985).

[30] Albert Bandura, "Evolution of Social Cognitive Theory," in K.G. Smith and M.A. Hitt (Eds.), *Great Minds in Management*, (Oxford University Press, 2005).

With these requirements in place, most employees feel engaged in the work of the organization and their performance will reflect their motivation.

Returning to the case study about Trautlein at Bethlehem Steel, it is important to point out that he did not try to convince others that his methods of leadership would require different information, knowledge, and skills to implement the changes in the organization that he thought were necessary and justified. Consequently, Bandura would have predicted Trautlein's failure as a leader.

Trautlein and Kindler's failures were complicated. They did not trust people and sometimes they were not very good at selecting the few employees that they did trust for leadership positions. Also, they were very impatient and poor communicators. Above all else, however, they were *sore losers*, which means they blamed others, did not learn lessons that could help them improve their leadership, and brooded over the "loss."

Competitive Nature: Winners and Losers

It is important to recognize that Trautlein and Kindler were sore losers because that is symptomatic of narcissism and a lack leadership acumen. Most leaders have a competitive nature that can be a strength that motivates them and pushes them to motivate others. It can be a good trait. It's part of their success. On the negative side, very competitive people with inflated egos and a disregard for the well-being of employees and other stakeholders do not know how to lose, or more importantly, how to learn from losing.

Leaders like Trautlein and Kindler simply hate to lose. To them, almost everything was competition – with the board, employees, clients, etc. They were extremely competitive and they took everything personally. Not only did they hate to lose, they were incredibly sore losers who blamed others and rationalized their failures. No leader and most people do not like to lose, but they know how to manage loss and learn from losing. However, the sore loser mentality with leaders that insist on always winning seems to be a common denominator with leaders who rely on intimidation and domination. They are always keeping score.

Rosabeth Moss Kanter, author of *Confidence: How Winning Streaks and Losing Streaks Begin and End*, describes the sore loser.

Being a sore loser is usually blamed on the person. But when people are sore losers, it is often because they have been wounded; they are sore in the sense of being in pain, covered with aches and bruises... An ailing system inflicts wounds. [31]

And this, she added, can start or escalate a losing streak for an organization because it is self-defeating with collateral damage that spreads throughout the organization.

The organization that Trautlein came into was ailing, but that same organization when he left was declining quicker and more completely. Like many such leaders, he probably felt the bitterness of wounds, even though many were self-inflicted because of his coarse personality. And because of his leadership style, he kept losing. He trusted only a few and then he found out that a couple of them were working behind his back so they could be in good standing with some board members. He took that personally, and he characterized that betrayal as another loss. He took all rebuttals personally. Any suggestion to improve on or modify one of his ideas was not viewed as constructive feedback; instead, it was considered a challenge. A more effective leader would have encouraged feedback without personalizing the feedback. But leaders like Trautlein are constantly keeping score. He like Kindler wanted what was best for the organization - no doubt his motivation was sincere, but he also wanted all the credit and no criticism. He wanted total control and all the glory. All the elements necessary to start a losing streak were in place. While this was obvious to others, Trautlein either could not or would not accept the fact that his methods were not effective and were driving the company toward insolvency.

Kanter's Nine Pathologies

The failure of Donald Trautlein, Jeff Kindler and other leaders like them follow Kanter's nine "pathologies"[32] that start the chain reaction leading to their removal from the job and disruption in the organization.

1. *Communication decreases*: The once outspoken, media-loving, and overall verbose leader begins to withdraw from making public comments, schedules fewer meetings with large groups of employees, and noticeably reduces the number of internal communication messages.

---

[31] Rosabeth Moss Kanter, *Confidence: How Winning Streaks and Losing Streaks Begin and End,* (Crown Publishing, 2006).
[32] Ibid.

2. *Criticism and blame increase*: The leader who seemed impervious to any type of criticism and who deflected complaints now responds to all criticism and complaints, no matter how trivial, by blaming the complainants and employees.

3. *Respect for others decreases*: While the leader's respect for others was based on how they could help him the confidants are increasingly ignored and their influence downplayed by the leader. The leader takes on the "who-needs-them" attitude.

4. *Isolation increases*: The leader who previously visited all facilities, offices, and made the media rounds now more often remains in his office and increasingly stays there during the work day.

5. *Their focus turns inward*: The leader becomes more introspective and even somewhat paranoid. His focus shifts from an external focus to internal control and survival – protecting his destiny and legacy become his primary motivation.

6. *Rifts/disagreements widen and inequities grow*: The submergence of the leader creates a leadership vacuum among frontline managers who were trained to rely on the leader for major decisions and now are asked to fill the void of leadership. Inconsistencies coupled with inequities increase throughout the organization at significant levels of disruption. Internal bickering increases.

7. *Initiatives decrease*: Innovation and creativity come to a standstill. The implementation of change shifts to the protection of the status quo and self-preservation. The shift of priorities extends through all segments of the organization.

8. *Aspirations diminish*: The leader no longer aspires for greatness and the next leap upwards in his career. He instead shifts into a managed decline and works on the development of a reputation-saving exit strategy.

9. *Negativity spreads*: Whatever positive messages and initiatives that the leader promoted are now in jeopardy. Work is replaced with gossip. Innovation and optimism are replaced with skepticism and negativism. Productivity grinds to a halt.[33]

Using the conceptual framework of Kanter's pathologies, I suggest a tenth pathology: *Paranoid tendencies escalate*: After failures, the leader is now in the full grip of paranoia–firmly holding on to the belief that everyone is out to get him from the first day he arrived at the organization and that several sinister people contrived to sabotage him at every turn. The self-rationalization shifts to debilitating paranoia.

---

[33] Ibid.

In an article by Sara Weaver and George Yancey, *The Impact of Dark Leadership on Organizational Commitment*, the authors describe the behavior of the *"paranoid leader"* as the loss of touch with the purpose of the organization and his role in the health of the organization.[34] The paranoid leader's focus shifts from what is best for the organization to what is best for him and what he can do to find supporters and fight off the critics in order to salvage his reputation. There is never a good ending when a leader becomes paranoid.

A paranoid leader's relationship with the board will deteriorate, also. The board that selected him because of his energy level, his intellect, his no-nonsense demeanor, his willingness to take risks, his innovative ideas, and his toughness will realize that those traits sometimes have a dark side.

Instead of working through the differences of opinion and challenges, the leader becomes defensive, which compromises almost all efficiencies and effective organizational changes. In most organizations when the relationship of the board and the leader reaches this stage the board is less interested in and therefore less inclined to work with the leader in a constructive manner. Before the crisis in leadership, board members dismissed complaints about the leader as natural resistance to change. The board now listens to every complaint about the leader. The negativity spreads rapidly. The confrontations with the board become more frequent, intense, and combative.

In his long-term study of successful companies, Jim Collins found that most successful businesses were not headed by a flamboyant, outspoken leader. They were led by thoughtful, intelligent, team-building leaders who had a clear vision and strategy and were able to implement them while motivating employees. The effective leaders, according to Collins, unquestionably understood the value of *servant leadership* and communications, while businesses that were led by tyrants were not successful.[35]

Antidotes: There are several types of leadership styles and much of the difference is based on a leader's perception of forms of power and how they

---

[34] Sara G. Weaver and George B. Yancy, "The Impact of Dark Leadership on Organizational Commitment and Turnover," Kravis Leadership Institute, *Leadership Review*, Vol. 10, summer 2010.

[35] James Collins, *Good to Great: Why Some Companies Make the Leap and Others Don't*, (Harper Business, 2001); James Collins and Jerry Porras, *Built to Last 3rd Edition*, (Harper Business, 2004); James Collins and Morten Hansen, *Great by Choice*, (Harper Business, 2011); James Collins, *Good to Great: Why Some Companies Make the Leap and Others Don't*, (Harper Business, 2001).

apply to interactions with the board, employees, and other stakeholders. According to French and Raven, there are five forms of power.[36]

1. *Legitimate power*: Comes from the position in the organization.
2. *Reward power:* Comes from the leader's ability to control rewards to employees.
3. *Coercive power*: Comes from the leader's ability and inclination to intimidate or punish employees.
4. *Expert power*: Comes from skills, experience, or knowledge.
5. *Referent power*: Comes from the leader's ability to charm, communicate with, and support employees, the board, and clients.

A leader that depends solely on *legitimate power* will lose influence if the organization's goals are not met. Without positive results, the power of position only lasts a fleeting period of time.

The *rewards-based leader* typically loses influence as soon as the rewards diminish; otherwise, he has no influence beyond rewards.

A leader that relies on *intimidation for power* will find success sometimes from sheer fear and a controlled negative work climate, but this leadership style does not maintain results and the controlling nature of the leader creates conditions that eventually reduce his power.

Expertise and/or referent power can be maintained and be effective because they are both based on a foundation of trust and respect. The expert power leader may not be personable but that is frequently dismissed because of the respect for his expertise. The referent power leader may make mistakes but she will typically learn from those mistakes and ask others for advice. She will engage several people in developing and implementing change.

Boards should look for leadership traits and styles that have been found to be effective. In his book, *The Enemies of Leadership*, Grady Bogue[37] found, as did Collins that a successful leader has traits related to what Robert Greenleaf coined the *servant leader*.[38] Bogue said that boards should actively look for servant leaders and groom leaders within the organization to be servant leaders. The servant leader's work climate increases morale and helps the organization focus on its purpose. The servant leader also promotes the sustainability of excellence.

---

[36] John French and Bertram Raven, "The Bases for Social Power," in *Studies in Social Power*, ed. Dorwin Cartwright, (University of Michigan Press, 3rd Edition, 1990).

[37] Grady Bogue, *The Enemies of Leadership*, (Phi Delta Kappa, 1985).

[38] Robert Greenleaf, *Servant Leadership: A Journey into the Nature of Legitimate Power*, (Paulist Press, 2002).

The servant leader is not a stranger to power. He simply realizes that power is an instrument awaiting the engagement of more important questions: For what end, for what purpose, for what meaning will power be employed? Growth, approval, mobility, activity, power–all these can be appropriate indicators of leadership achievement. However, the servant leader keeps these indicators in balance and holds a more complete vision of leadership effectiveness: a compassion for all employees and their challenges; a willingness to support staff in the face of criticism; finding opportunities in interruptions and setbacks; being devoted to principles beyond self; and understanding the use of authority.[39]

In their seminal work on leadership, *In Search of Excellence*, Thomas Peter and Robert Waterman discussed the importance of a leader's genuine concern for and an ability and willingness to communicate with employees, boards, and stakeholders.

Treat people as adults. Treat them as partners; treat them with dignity; treat them with respect.[40]

All leaders and all boards are selected by someone who has the authority to make such selections or by a public that has the power of the vote. Those able to make these decisions, no matter the type of organization, must give attention to the future of the organization and base selections of leaders on their ability to hold the future in mind while developing short and long-term strategies. That is not possible in the minds and actions of dominating, self-absorbed leaders. Therefore, leaders with those traits and that style of managing must be avoided at all levels, from the CEO to the lowest level manager. That type of leader cannot be effective long-term and should not be selected for leadership positions.

According to the Society for Industrial and Organizational Psychology, in an article by Silverman, Johnson, McConnell, and Carr, an organization can be damaged by an arrogant, tyrannical leader, which is clearly illustrated by their description of the former leader at American International Group (AIG), Joe Cassano.

Cassano was the president of AIG's financial products unit and is credited by some as single-handedly bringing about the downfall of AIG. Many accounts

---

[39] Grady Bogue, *The Enemies of Leadership*, (Phi Delta Kappa, 1985).
[40] Thomas Peters and Robert Waterman, *In Search of Excellence*, (Grand Central Publishing, 1982).

describe Cassano as a quintessential arrogant leader. Former coworkers report that in stark contrast to his predecessors, Cassano had penchants for yelling, cursing, bad-mouthing others, and belittling colleagues, as well as little tolerance for opposing viewpoints. In the absence of Cassano's persistent arrogant behavior (and unwillingness to tolerate dissent regarding his management practices), it is possible that AIG's crisis would have been considerably less severe or altogether avoided. However, despite the fact that it was the practices he sanctioned that led AIG to be regarded as one of the most notable examples of excess associated with Wall Street, Cassano remains unapologetic about his role and blames others for the crisis. [41]

The authors reviewed research on arrogance in the workplace and found ample evidence that tyrannical arrogance is a destructive force.[42]

But what if the leader has noteworthy talent? Can arrogance be "corrected?" Can it be tolerated or managed? There is some evidence that arrogant leaders can be redirected.

It is clearly in the best interest of an organization to redirect arrogant behavior in its leaders. This can be accomplished by the organizational encouragement of (a) continuing leadership development intended to ensure adequate efficacy for job-related skills, (b) encouraging healthy levels of humility and what that means, and (c) installing a learning-oriented climate. In taking steps to reduce arrogance in the workplace, an organization provides itself with the competitive advantages associated with effective leadership and productive social interaction of employees. [43]

Can an arrogant leader really change? Robert Greenleaf opines in his book *Servant Leadership* that leaders can be taught-they can be redirected, but only those where arrogance and disrespect for others are not embedded in their personality.[44] In other words, for leaders with these negative traits who are acting on what they learned or what they think is expected of them they can be redirected; they can change.

---

[41] Stanley B. Silverman, Russell E. Johnson, Nicole McConnell, and Alison Carr, "Arrogance: A formula for leadership failure," *The Society for Organizational and Industrial Psychology*, September 2011.
[42] Ibid.
[43] Ibid.
[44] Robert Greenleaf. *Servant Leadership*, (Paulist Press, 1977 and 2002).

Learned Leadership

In an article for *Inc. Magazine*, Max Chafkin and Leigh Buchanan compiled leadership guidelines from experts that were categorized into several components that can be used in leadership training that focuses on leadership traits and styles.[45]

1. *Set a good example for others*–A leader's attitude is contagious. Communication is a key to making members of the organization feel included in major decisions. Employees are more motivated when they feel needed, appreciated, and valued.
2. *Focus on employee happiness and work satisfaction rather than employee motivation*–Successful leaders focus on the "happiness factor" for employees and customers. For example, workplace climates that include humor are strong on camaraderie and production. Customers that feel pleased with the employees' treatment of them reinforce the positive behavior by giving positive feedback.
3. *It's important to make sure employees share in the organization's successful projects*–An employee's performance, productivity, and motivation can be linked to how invested he feels in the organization, which depends considerably on feedback and acknowledgment that his work is noticed and fits the purpose of the organization.
4. *It is important to create a culture of autonomy*–In his book *Drive: The Surprising Truth About What Motivates Us*, author Daniel H. Pink writes that the crash of Wall Street is a striking example of the perils of leaders motivating employees strictly with cash while ignoring their personal and professional needs and goals.[46] He states leaders should create conditions for employees to find joy in work itself, which means giving workers the autonomy to work with others, have a chance for feedback, and receive incentives that are meaningful. This type of leadership helps foster a desire for mastery of tasks and skill sets–and simply doing more, better.
5. *Organizational leaders should encourage workers to voice complaints*–"When Dell amassed an online 'anti-fan club,' excoriating the PC maker across the blogosphere, it not only acknowledged criticism but also actually fixed things," according to Jeff Jarvis in his book *What Would Google Do.*[47]

---

[45] Max Chafkin and Leigh Buchanan, "7 Tips for Motivating Employees," *Inc.*, (April 2010): http://www.inc.com/guides/2010/04/tips-for-motivating-employees. html.
[46] Daniel H. Pink, *The Surprising Truth About What Motivates Us*, (Riverhead Books, 2009).
[47] Jeff Jarvis, *What Would Google Do?* (Harper Business Publishing, 2009).

There are scores of reasons why employees are reluctant to offer critiques of management or their company's culture–including fear of retaliation and hesitation to appear ungrateful, particularly if the leader creates that type of work climate. But, as *Inc.*'s Leigh Buchanan writes, "When the heat is not lowered, steam escapes."[48] The climate of the workplace is critically important. It's a living, breathing entity that can be healthy or unhealthy, which is dictated or influenced by the leader.

Making Work Significant

Some effective leaders, displaying the *servant leader* trait, create opportunities for employees to have time for volunteer assignments. Leaders have found that this is a significant way to improve morale and motivation. Encouraging and then providing ways for employees to do volunteer work in the community where they live or in the community near the workplace can be a powerful incentive. This becomes even more powerful when the leader of the organization also participates in volunteer events. There are ways that the leader can encourage this activity; for example, it may be supported by compensatory work time, by public recognition of the volunteers' work during an organization's meeting, and/or by an article in the organization's newsletter. The volunteer work itself can be so rewarding that the benefit is a happier and more productive employee.

Leaders with an *engagement trait* like to appeal to the "inner start-up" spark in employees – there is a distinct energy in start-up companies that can be captured in any organization or business. Some organizational leaders operationalize this practice by periodically gathering employees in small clusters at the office. For 15-30 minutes in a very informal way, the leader encourages the flow of ideas, innovative thoughts and discussions for the purpose of creating collegiality and brainstorming ideas. The *"controlled chaos"* can energize an organization and it can provide innovative feedback to the leader.

There are negative outcomes when an organization's leader pays scant attention to the needs of the employees and organization. People will attempt to change, are willing to take risks, and will accept a leader's efforts to change if (1) they believe it will be worth it and (2) they can do what is required.

---

[48] Max Chafkin and Leigh Buchanan, "7 Tips for Motivating Employees," *Inc.*, April 2010: http://www. inc.com /guides/2010/04/tips-for-motivating-employees. html.

Employees response to change is consistent with those essential components specified in the *Three Cs of Implementing Strategy* that Scott Edinger insists are necessary for a leader's strategies to be implemented successfully.[49]

1. ***Clarify the strategy to all employees***: *All too often, strategies are expressed as high-level statements that resonate with the board members and executive level employees but fall flat with mid-level and frontline personnel. Unfortunately, if people don't understand the strategy, they are unable to connect with it. So, the first step is to clarify your strategy in a way that people in your organization can rally to support its implementation.*

2. ***Communicate the organization's strategy to all employees and stakeholders***: *Powerfully communicating the essence of your strategy at every level of the organization using multiple mediums is the key.*

3. ***Cascade the strategy so that employees and others know how the strategies are related to their daily jobs/work***: *If the strategy is 'what' you do then tactics are 'how' you do it. And if you want your strategy implemented well, you need to cascade it throughout the organization and get to the practical and tactical components of people's jobs every day. Ideally, you will involve your managers in this process, and they will help to translate the elements of the strategy for your organization to their own functional areas.*

With these in place, and with the motivation and good will of its leader, most individuals will at least try to enact the changes and innovations introduced by the leader.

There are many leadership traits and styles just like there are many personality traits. The combination of traits, styles, personalities and the needs of an organization commingle to create a complicated symphony of possibilities and outcomes. Seldom are the possibilities met or the outcomes positive when a leader has traits that are centered on dominating board members, employees, clients, and others that are important to an organization's success. Leaders that follow the tenets of *servant leadership* focus on the needs of the organization, the employees, and understand the dynamic and delicate nature of workplace climate.

Chapter Four Key Words and Concepts

Leadership Styles
Leadership Traits

---

[49] Scott Edinger, "The Three Cs of Implementing Strategy," *Forbes*, August 2012.

Laissez-Faire
Vacuum of Leadership
Tough Leader
Hersey-Blanchard Leadership Model
Fielder's Contingency Theory
$S x E (T) = R$
High Task and Low Relationship
Low Task and High Relationship
Leadership by Intimidation
Good to Great
Dictatorial Tactics
Coercive Leadership
Trickle Down Effect
Favoritism
Workplace Climate
Morale Killers
Machiavellian
Manage Change
Brevity, Variety, and Fragmentation
Social Learning Theory
Sore Losers
Nine Pathologies
Paranoid Tendencies
Servant Leader
Arrogance
Teaching Leadership
Inner Startup
Controlled Chaos
Cascade the Strategy
Legitimate Power
Reward Power
Coercive Power
Expert Power
Referent Power
Cascading Strategy
Engagement Trait

Chapter Four Discussion Items

What is Laissez-Faire leadership? Give examples of this leadership style and offer an opinion on its effectiveness.

What is a Vacuum of Leadership? How and when does it occur? What happens in an organization when it occurs?

Describe and then compare and contrast the Hersey-Blanchard Leadership Model with Fielder's Contingency Theory.

What is the significance of $S \times E\ (T) = R$ and how does it relate to High Relationship and Low Relationship leadership?

Compare and contrast Legitimate Power, Reward Power, Coercive Power, Expert Power, and Referent Power.

What is workplace climate? How can workplace climate impact organization productivity and employee retention?

Give an example of Machiavellian Leadership and how it compares with Referent Power.

Select one of the Nine Pathologies then define it and illustrate what it means by giving an example.

Chapter Four Lessons Learned

A leadership style that does not match the needs of an organization, regardless of the good intentions of the leader, usually leads to an unsuccessful experience for both the leader and the organization.

Leaders should focus on the socio-emotional dynamics that provide two-way communications, where the leader listens, facilitates, directs when necessary, clarifies goals, evaluates, and supports employees.

Employees report that a good, effective, caring, organized, and efficient leader is just as important as a good salary.

Employees that experience a coercive, abrasive leader often believe that that type of leadership is not only expected, it will be rewarded. So, at every level of the organization, it is more likely that the coercive type of leadership is emulated.

Trust comes from hiring the right employees and providing them with the vision, plan, and resources to do their jobs and then trusting them to get the job done without showing favorites that have a distinct set of expectations and standards.

The leader must be effective at communicating the strategic plan to those that will implement it at all levels.

It is clear from research that when leadership is dysfunctional and dictatorial, motivation and productivity levels plummet.

The leader that knows how to maintain a power base and develop relationships through participation and trust is much more likely to implement and manage organizations and change effectively.

CHAPTER FIVE

BUILDING A STRONG EXECUTIVE TEAM

"With a culture of individual accountability and self-reliance pervading executive suites, few senior executive groups even function as real teams."
-Jon R. Katzenback[1]

Determinants: One of the most crucial responsibilities of a leader in any organization is the development of an excellent leadership team that functions at the highest levels. No matter how talented the leader may be, there are few organizations that can be successful without a leadership team that works in tangent with the leader and that is supportive of the organization - a team that is respectful, open, and honest with each other and with the leader. A leadership team made up of sycophants will offer nothing to the organization and may cause a dysfunctional, negative, and unproductive workplace climate. Dysfunctional leadership teams can bring an organization down and jeopardize the future of the organization to such a serious degree that the team becomes destructive to the operations and purpose of the organization.

Executive Team

If the public knew what takes place in corporate executive staff meetings, in non-profit agency cabinet meetings, in higher education cabinet meetings, and other organizations, they would not know whether to be impressed, cry, or laugh. Meetings of an organization's top managers are commonly referred to simply as "cabinet" meetings.

The term *cabinet* comes from history where a cabinet was a small room that was off-limits to all except a privileged few with connections to monarchs during the 16th century. The *Oxford Dictionary* credits Sir Frances Bacon with the version of the word that extended its meaning beyond that of a small room when he used the description "Cabinet Council"[2] to describe his

---

[1] Jon R. Katzenbach, *Teams at the Top*, (Harvard Business Press, 1998).
[2] *Oxford Dictionary*: https://en.oxforddictionaries.com/ definition /cabinet. Retrieved 2014.

advisors, but it was Charles I[3] who turned the term into a functionally working entity. Over time the term cabinet meant a body of people that serve in an official capacity to advise an organization's leader.[4] If only cabinets served that purpose, it would be useful. Far too many cabinet members merely rubberstamp their leader's ideas and do not offer true advice or constructive feedback.

Cabinet meetings are varied and if dominated by a leader who does not understand operational functions, the needs of the organization, and the importance of positive human relations then the meetings are dysfunctional at worst and irrelevant at least. Most leaders schedule regular meetings with their top administrators regardless of the size of the organization. Cabinet meetings serve an essential function in any type of organization whether it is public education, non-profit, religious, higher education, or business. The cabinet provides the organization's leader the opportunity to stay in touch with the complexities of the operations at all levels, to receive reports about the various components of the organization, to troubleshoot existing or potential problems, and to plan. Also, it is the executive leadership team in large part that determines the budget, culture, workplace climate, strategic plans, and productivity of the organization. The leader typically has an agenda that includes items of importance to the organization, such as strategic planning items, budget items, challenging situations, and items that will be brought to the next board meeting, but most leaders provide time for the cabinet members to also provide department updates and input on operational issues and planning. At least that is how cabinet meetings should operate, more or less. Too often, however, the cabinet agenda is dominated by whatever is on the leader's mind. It is obviously very important to know what is pressuring the leader, but not at the expense of addressing and resolving operational issues and challenges facing the organization.

I worked for a leader who started each cabinet meeting with a light conversation about sports, theater, etc., and he always shared a story, sometimes humorous stories. I did not realize until much later in my career that this was a deliberate effort on his part to get the cabinet members to relax and join in the discussion before getting down to business. It was also a shrewd way for him to learn who on the cabinet read, kept up with events,

---

[3] Charles I of England: Charles I was born in Fife on 19 November 1600, the second son of James VI of Scotland (from 1603 also James I of England) and Anne of Denmark: https://www.royal.uk/charles-i-r-1625-1649.
[4] *The Cambridge Dictionary* http://dictionary.cambridge.org/us/dictionary/ English/ cabinet.

and who was thoughtful, insightful, creative, and articulate. He never used the cabinet meetings to embarrass anyone – never. He always reminded his staff that people may forget what you say to them or do to them but they will never forget how you make them feel, and being embarrassed in front of others is an unforgettable memory. It is noteworthy that he did not interrupt a cabinet member engaged in a debate with another cabinet member unless the debate became personal or disrespectful. Then he would intervene with a note of humor to defuse the situation. But if it was a healthy, lively debate he enjoyed that and he thought other members of the cabinet could learn from the exchanges. He also was not offended by cabinet members that did not agree with him. He encouraged cabinet members to challenge his thinking. He would say, "Tell me where my thinking is wrong; I need to better understand. " Afterward, the cabinet would leave the room more often united than divided. He also wanted to hear from every department head and he did not want the glossy version; he wanted the truth. The cabinet meetings were long but productive. He learned many things about the operations of the organization and cabinet members learned from him and from other members of the cabinet.

Effective and Dysfunctional Meetings

If a leader wants meetings of his top managers to be effective, he can follow the purpose of meetings that was included in Patrick Lencioni's book, *Death by Meeting.*[5] He noted that meetings should and can be productive instead of being used to intimidate and frighten employees either by direct confrontation, by calculated ambiguity, and/or by misrepresentation, disrespect, and threats.

The effective leader understands the importance of trust and the value of the cabinet; therefore, she makes the effort to encourage a climate of trust. If the leader of an organization and her top employees do not trust each other to be honest and supportive, the organization will suffer and the cabinet meetings will not utilize the talents of the executive team.

The former counsel to six presidents, Clark Clifford, refers to the varying dynamics in each president's cabinet as an indication of the effectiveness of the leader and the importance of the cabinet to the leader and the organization.[6] According to Clifford, President Harry S Truman's cabinet

---

[5] Patrick Lencioni, *Death by Meeting: A Leadership Fable...About Solving the Most Painful Problem in Business*, (Josey-Bass, 2004).

[6] Clark Clifford, *Counsel to the President: A Memoir*, (Random House, 1991).

was dominated by two cabinet members; nevertheless, it was clear that Truman was in charge. Contrast that with the Dwight D. Eisenhower cabinet where there was very little structure, the president was not always engaged in the conversation, and when he was participating in a discussion the members of the cabinet listened without significant reaction to the president's thoughts and opinions. President Lyndon Johnson encouraged debate among his cabinet members, but he infrequently followed their advice.

When analyzing the intricacy of cabinet meetings and the effectiveness of cabinet engagement, it's clear that much of the interaction or lack thereof depends on the level of trust of the leader and among and between the cabinet members. The leader must take the time to understand and value the opinion of others, which encourages the development of an effective leadership team.

Stephen M.R. Covey's book, *Speed of Trust*, points out the value and necessity of developing trust.[7] According to Covey, organizations are much more productive when trust is at the heart of the enterprise and at the core of the organization's leadership team. Displaying and valuing trust is how effective leaders handle their jobs, interact with each other, employees and clients, and how they handle staff meetings with the leadership team.

Contrast the importance of trust with leaders who are either so dominated or intimidated by members of the board that they share with the cabinet only those issues that board members are focused on or who project anger toward the cabinet because of pressure and criticism from the board. Many of the board's issues are localized or so narrow that they have little or no impact on the overall organization. For example, in the cabinet meeting of a large non-profit organization, the leader was perturbed because a board member complained about how employees were dressed on Fridays. A board member did not approve of business casual dress at any time, and he had basically intimidated the organization's leader. So, at the next cabinet meeting, the leader spent almost three hours with his cabinet discussing the Friday dress code, even though the organization was trying to deal with shrinking revenues, employee retention issues, increases in healthcare costs, and many other more important and pressing issues. Additional time was then spent after the cabinet meeting working on an employee dress code that greatly displeased the employees.[8]

In another organization, according to an accrediting agency report, the hostility among the top-level administrators during cabinet meetings sometimes spilled over into other aspects of the organization and aborted

[7] Stephen M.R. Covey, *The Speed of Trust*, (Simon and Schuster, 2006).
[8] Ron Auster, *Small Non-Profit Organization Case Studies*, (Auster Publishing, 2013).

decision-making. If a department within the organization was having issues, such as failing to deliver services in a timely fashion, another administrator would state *"if that was my department, I would...."* Then the arguments started and nothing was accomplished. The true business of the organization then would not be addressed, because the leader did not use the cabinet effectively.[9]

In many organizations, cabinet members choose sides. In President Harry Truman's cabinet, for example, it was clear that two of the cabinet members aligned with each other at the expense of the others; consequently, the cabinet was disrupted by two cabinet members who had their own agendas and who showed little respect for the President and fellow cabinet members. The most notoriously difficult member of the Truman cabinet was Secretary of Defense Louis Johnson, according to the author of *Truman*,[10] David McCollough. Problems in Truman's Cabinet are chronicled in *U.S. Profiles of Presidents*.[11]

> *Truman, upon becoming president, was appalled to learn of the formlessness of the Roosevelt cabinet: Secretary of Labor Frances Perkins had lost almost all of her department's divisions and agencies, and cabinet members fought each other openly, leaking their arguments to newspaper reporters. He dismissed most of the Roosevelt appointees in the initial months of his administration. He insisted upon dealing directly with members of the cabinet, and it was their task, he said, both to show loyalty to him and to control their departments. Not all Truman cabinet appointees proved able; but in the crucial areas of military and foreign affairs, his appointments were generally excellent. Cabinet meetings became business sessions, each official taking up his problems by bringing them before the group, with the president making the decision himself.*[12]

Covey wrote about the cost of the lack of trust in an organization.

> *Trust always affects two outcomes – speed and cost. When trust goes down, speed will also go down and costs will go up. The effectiveness of the organization is compromised.*[13]

---

[9] Confidential accrediting agency notes, 2011.

[10] David McCollough, *Truman*, (Simon and Schuster, 1993).

[11] *U.S. Profiles of Presidents*: http://www.president profiles. com/ Grant-Eisenhower/Harry-S-Truman-Domestic-policies.html. Advameg, Inc.

[12] Ibid.

[13] Stephen M.R. Covey, *The Speed of Trust*, (Simon and Schuster, 2006).

Covey was not referring always to financial loss. The cost can also be lost morale and an overall negative impact on the effectiveness of the organization.

Case Study #1

A non-profit agency with a national reputation had a dynamic leader who traveled so much that he provided little leadership within the organization. He delegated almost all leadership functions to the organization's vice president. The vice president was described as a charming, skillful, and intelligent Machiavellian who did not trust anyone on the executive team because of his narcissistic belief that the organization centered around him and his opinion that no one could compete with his leadership prowess, not even the president. When he was at work, the president started each cabinet meeting with a review of his most recent travels and his impression of how the organization was thriving under his leadership. He said it was important for the team to know which influential people he was meeting with, for the benefit of the organization. The president was good at raising money for the organization, or so it seemed. About half-way through his third year as president, a cabinet member said he needed the president, vice president and members of the cabinet to see the trajectory of the budget and the services provided to clients. So, he put the discussion item on the next cabinet agenda. The president was not present at the crucial cabinet meeting and in his absence the vice president dominated the conversation throughout the cabinet meeting, talking about items and issues that were not important to the internal operations of the organization and were not germane to the purpose of the meeting. Toward the end of the cabinet meeting, the vice president turned to the cabinet member who had concerns about the direction of the budget and services and said, "Nathan here has some issues with the rest of you guys. He claims that you're not pulling your weight, so revenues are down and our services to clients are diminishing." He did not provide time for a discussion; he did not allow the concerned cabinet member to give a report on the circumstances of the budget, and he purposely embarrassed him so much that he would not bring the subject up again.

The organization's decline was somewhat insidious for several months, but then it became clear that it was in financial trouble. When the organization's president realized what was going on he immediately fired the vice president and realigned his leadership team. The once promising vice president was out and the traditionally excellent community service-based organization struggled to regain its former stature in the community. The board gave the president one year to bring the budget and services back in line. The organization is still struggling to match the services provided in previous years and secure grants and donations at the rate needed to maintain solvency and relevance.[14]

Development of an Effective Team

Cabinet meetings are critically important because they can determine how an organization operates. However, when board members, community members, or executive search firms are asked to develop questions for prospective leaders they seldom ask candidates how they plan to select their executive team and how they will utilize employees or how the executive team is expected to benefit the mission and goals of the organization. In other words, "What is the role of the cabinet?"

How leaders utilize the leadership team varies, depending on the style of the leader and the organization's needs. Many successful leaders try to build a collaborative executive team and in doing so the cabinet meetings become an open dialogue that benefits the organization. In her book, *Tough Choices*, Carly Fiorina describes this style.

Collaboration requires more consultation and agreement among peers. It requires acceptance of accountability while sharing resources. It means trusting others to do their job while knowing that others must trust you to do the same.[15]

The challenge is that it can be difficult for a leader to develop an effective team; it is a real skill and a rare skill primarily because some leaders do not see the value of the team. Consequently, many executive teams do not function effectively. Jon R. Katzenbach, author of *Teams at the Top*, wrote,

With a culture of individual accountability and self-reliance pervading executive suites, few senior executive groups even function as real teams.[16]

---

[14] Mark Levy, "Training Case Studies for Leaders," *International Trade Show Conference*, Hong Kong, 2009.
[15] Carla Fiorina, *Tough Choices*, (Portfolio, 2007).
[16] Jon R. Katzenbach, *Teams at the Top*, (Harvard Business Press, 1998).

Dysfunctional Teams

An excellent resource for understanding dysfunctional executive leadership teams is Patrick Lencioni's book, *The Five Dysfunctions of a Team: A Leadership Fable.*[17] There are lessons from the book that are important for any leader or board to understand.

The first dysfunction is the *absence of trust.* In addition to Lencioni, Stephen Covey also emphasizes the strong link between trust and effective and efficient leadership, but Lencioni adds that a lack of trust is an unwillingness to be vulnerable within the executive leadership group. The leader must address this issue by making the cabinet meeting environment safe for everyone to make comments and safe for members of the executive team to explore ideas and to even be wrong without fear of impunity. It should be like Winston Churchill once said, "Success is not final and failure is not fatal."[18]

The second dysfunction, according to Lencioni is the *fear of conflict.* Constructive conflict is essential for teamwork - that is how problems are identified and resolved; how the best ideas emerge; and how potentially disastrous decisions are prevented. In an article for *Financial Times*, Naomi Shragai wrote,

A failure to address conflicts at work is one of the main reasons executives lose respect in a team. Failing to act because of a fear of conflict is often why decisions are postponed, problems are allowed to fester, and how serious realities are ignored. The desire to be liked and not thought of badly can be so strong as to paralyze thinking and stop one from expressing dissenting opinions which can, in turn, inhibit a company's growth.[19]

The cabinet should be a place where there is no fear that conflict will spiral out of control, nor should cabinet members worry that blame and accusations will emerge from differences of opinion.

The third dysfunction is a *lack of commitment.* Lencioni states that executive team members need to know that their opinions matter; that they will be heard and seriously considered by fellow members of the cabinet. An ineffective leader wants the executive leadership team to have only opinions

---

[17] Patrick Lencioni, *Five Dysfunctions of a Team: A Leadership Fable*, (Jossey-Bass, 2002).

[18] Winston Churchill, Oxford Reference: http://www.oxfordreference.com/view/ 10.1093/acref/9780199572687. 001.0001/ q-author-00002-00334.

[19] Naomi Shragai, "The Managers Who Fear Conflict," *Financial Times*, June 2014.

that mimic his or that do not create conflict with him. If members of the cabinet do not feel their opinions are at least listened to, they will not make comments and will not be fully committed and engaged even if they were assigned to the cabinet by the leader. They will not work their hardest to ensure positive results despite their good intentions. Lencioni wrote,

When you put them together and leave them to their own devices, even the most well-intentioned people will usually deviate towards dysfunctional, unproductive behavior. [20]

The movement away from productive behavior in cabinet meetings happens when the leader is not committed to making the cabinet effective which in turn negatively impacts the executive team's commitment to the work and productivity.

The fourth dysfunction is *avoidance of accountability.* The ineffective leader will hold all executive team members accountable, but only when things do not go well. Sometimes this is displayed during cabinet meetings when the leader embarrasses certain members of the cabinet if not the entire cabinet because something did not go right. Without acknowledging that he is the leader and ultimately responsible for all decisions, he blames the executive team during cabinet meetings and when he reports to the board.

Accountability of the executive team is, of course, important. Consequently, it is essential for all members of the executive team to be accountable and for each member of the team to hold each other accountable. Otherwise, the team members will not speak up even when they see that another member of the executive team is not working in an effective manner or is being a detriment to the organization. Research by Kerry Patterson confirmed this.

According to research my colleagues and I conducted, upwards of 80 percent of leaders who work on major initiatives, projects, or programs experience some form of team failure. Team failures, wherein team members are unwilling and unable to support each other, stem from a variety of problems, but they all have one solution: team leaders and members need to speak up. Our research shows a leader's ability to speak up and address team failures effectively is one of the key ingredients behind successful project execution. However, only 14 percent of leaders are able to speak up about team failures in a way that effectively addresses the problem. The rest experience poor

---

[20] Patrick Lencioni, *Five Dysfunctions of a Team: A Leadership Fable*, (Jossey-Bass, 2002).

results. Leaders who ineffectively deal with team failure exceed their budgets on 73 percent of projects, miss 82 percent of their deadlines, and experience functionality and quality problems 77 percent of the time. What's worse, team failures damage team morale on 69 percent of these projects, creating unnecessary baggage that is carried forward well after the project's end date.[21]

The research reveals a staggering loss of efficiencies and outcomes due to team failures caused by ineffective leaders who do not know how to build, utilize, and lead their executive teams.

The fifth dysfunction is *inattention to detail.* This is when the leader shows little or no interest in details of issues that impact the organization. This inattention places the executive team in an awkward situation of stagnated decision making. The executive team gets bogged down in details because the leader does not resolve issues or provide the leadership necessary to resolve detailed issues. John Wooden, the legendary college basketball coach and leadership expert wrote,

It's the little details that are vital. Little things make big things happen. Every success is team-dependent, not individually driven.[22]

Antidotes: An organization cannot be successful or realize its full potential without effective leadership and the leader cannot be effective without a stellar executive leadership team. How important is the executive team? Yaron Nili of Harvard Business School thinks it is crucial. He wrote,

Of all the complex, sensitive, and stressful issues that confront CEOs, none consumes as much time, generates as much angst, or extracts such a high personal toll as dealing with executive team members who are just not working out. Billion-dollar acquisitions, huge strategic shifts, even decisions to eliminate thousands of jobs—all pale in comparison with the anxiety most CEOs experience when it comes to deciding the fate of their direct reports. To be sure, there are exceptions. Every once in a while, an executive fouls up so dramatically or is so woefully incompetent that the CEO's course of action is clear. However, that's rarely the case. More typically, these situations slowly escalate. Early warning signs are either dismissed or overlooked and by the time the problem starts reaching crisis proportions, the CEO has become

---

[21] Kerry Patterson, "Accountability: What Dysfunctional Teams are Missing," *Psychology Today*, January 2013.

[22] John Wooden and Andrew Hill, *Be Quick but Not Hurry*, (Simon and Schuster, 2001).

deeply invested in making things work. He or she procrastinates, grasping at one flawed excuse after another. Meanwhile, the cost of inaction mounts daily exacted in poor leadership, lack of team collaboration, and lost opportunities.[23]

When reviewing applicants for leadership positions, boards should consider many qualities that a prospective leader must possess to be selected. The list of qualities must include an exploration of how he builds teams and how he has utilized and managed leadership teams in the past. This discussion should also include an inquiry into his philosophy about the role of the executive team and what qualities he will look for in the team members.

In a study by Marie McIntyre, she studied more than 500 members of 72 management groups in both business and government.[24] The teams were surveyed using the *Team Effectiveness Assessment for Management* instrument,[25] which measures team interaction, team communications, team problem-solving, and team loyalty and interdependence. Teams rated in the top 25 percent on team effectiveness measures were compared with teams rated in the bottom 25 percent on team effectiveness. The study found five *success factors* that differentiated the most successful teams from unsuccessful ones. The factors were significant indicators that clearly separated the competent teams from the dysfunctional teams. Success factors not only heightened the likelihood of highly functional teams, they were significant also at the individual level of the team members. Individuals found satisfaction in the success of the team.

The following chart depicts the factors McIntyre found that can help determine if a team is likely to be successful. There are overlapping factors, of course. In fact, the determinants are interdependent and sequential. They build upon each other. For example, gathering critical information is unproductive if the team has not first established the purpose of their work and the goals they wish to achieve.

> ***Factor 1***: To focus activity and effort, management teams need a clear understanding of their purpose and the goals they intend to accomplish.

---

[23] Yaron Nili, "When Executives Fail: Managing Performance on the CEO's Team," *Harvard Law School Forum*, March 18, 2015: https://corpgov. law.harvard .edu/2015/03/18/when-executives-fail-managing-performance-on-the-ceos-team/.
[24] Marie McIntyre, "Building An Effective Management Team": http://www.yourofficecoach.com/topics/lessons_in_leadership/effective_leadership/bu ilding_an_effective_management _team.aspx.l.
[25] *Mindtools,* https://www.mindtools.com/pages/article.new TMM _84.htm.

Factor 2: To make informed decisions, management teams must access critical information from both inside and outside the organization.

Factor 3: To cooperate in achieving team goals, management team members must be able to develop positive, supportive relationships.

Factor 4: To make good decisions, management teams must effectively process the information available to them – the research found that the leader of a management team has more influence over this aspect of team effectiveness than any other.

Factor 5: To accomplish results, management teams must make the transition from discussion to action. A poorly implemented decision will not help the organization.

These factors can be put into practice by an effective leader and by boards. McIntyre also found that trust is the overarching element of each factor.

Trust is knowing that when a team member does push you, they're doing it because they care about the team.[26]

The level of trust required to reach levels of effectiveness that benefit the organization is almost completely determined by the leader's ability and willingness to build an effective leadership team and structure cabinet meetings in such a way to maximize the potential for dynamic discussions and effective decision making. No leader can efficiently and effectively run an organization without the assistance, honest feedback, support, and innovation that comes from executive team members.

In an article for *Fortune* magazine, Kerry Healey posits that building an effective team takes some soul-searching for the leader. He must take an honest inventory of his own strengths and weaknesses. All leaders have strengths that are reliable, dependable, and finely tuned. Also, they each have weaknesses that need work and/or support.

According to Healey,

Building an effective team begins with a brutally honest process of self-evaluation and reflection. The leader must be open to a humble assessment of his or her own strengths and weaknesses mapped against the qualities, knowledge, and experience necessary to succeed. There are numerous consultants and assessment tools available to assist in this process, but the most effective leaders I have known grasp this aspect of team building intuitively, naturally gravitating to partners and advisers who 'make them

---

[26] Ibid.

whole' and who make the team-leader appear almost super-human by placing a vast array of talents and information at their fingertips.[27]

Healey found that a leader's ability to establish a productive executive team and his corresponding willingness to engage with and listen to the team is one measure that separates the effective leaders from the mediocre or ineffective leaders.

In her book about Winston Churchill, Celia Sandys wrote that one of the most important *Churchillian Principles* is magnanimity, because "magnanimity breeds trust and loyalty among subordinates and partners."[28] The magnanimous leader wants and expects his executive team to encourage him but he also needs the team to feel free to question him when they think he can improve on an idea or if they think he is wrong. Peter Drucker, a legendary expert in leadership wrote:

The leaders who work most effectively, it seems to me, never say 'I,' which is not because they have trained themselves not to say 'I.' They don't think 'I.' They think 'we'; they think 'team.' They understand their job is to make the team function. They accept responsibility and don't sidestep it, but 'we' gets the credit. This is what creates trust, what enables you to get the task done.[29]

Leaders that do not know how to build an effective executive leadership team or how to manage what could be an effective team are detrimental to an organization. Leaders who know the value of team selection and team building and are willing to improve this aspect of their leadership can look for team building experts to learn more about the dynamic possibilities of team building. Some leaders have an intuitive ability to build effective teams while others need to learn team-building skills.

Team building training ideas are available for leaders and teams on how to build effective teams, such as:

- John Maxwell (*The 17 Indisputable Laws of Teamwork: Embrace Them and Empower Your Team*)[30]

---

[27] Kerry Healey, "The Difference between a Great Leader and a Good One," *Fortune*, August 5, 2014.
[28] Celia Sandys, *We Shall Not Fail: The Inspiring Leadership of Winston Churchill*, (Portfolio, 2003).
[29] Peter F. Drucker, *The Effective Executive: The Definitive Guide to Getting the Right Things Done,* (Harper Business, 2006 Edition).
[30] John Maxwell, *The 17 Indisputable Laws of Teamwork: Embrace Them and Empower Your Team*, (Thomas Nelson, 2013).

- Patrick Lencioni (*Five Dysfunctions of a Team*)[31]
- Arbinger Institute (*The Anatomy of Peace*)[32]
- John Newstrom (*The Big Book of Team Building Games: Trust-Building Activities, Team Spirit Exercises, and Other Activities*)[33]
- Price Pritchett (*The Team Member Handbook for Teamwork*)[34]
- Thomas Kayser (*Building Team Power: How to Unleash the Collaborative Genius of Teams for Increased Engagement, Productivity, and Results*)[35]

If a leader wants ideas on how to quickly start positive team building, with the understanding that long-term team building strategies will come from the team, Bradley Sugars' book, *Instant Team Building*,[36] is a good way to kick-start the effort to build an effective team or at least change the conversation about team-building. The book contains team-building exercises, stories, research, and experientially-based ideas for cooperative team-building, and it contains information that is fun to share with the team. Bradley Sugars is a multi-millionaire who attributes his success to building effective executive teams and other teams throughout his organizations.

Chapter Five Key Words and Concepts

Sycophants
Cabinet
Sir Frances Bacon
Cabinet Council
Charles I
Harry S Truman
Dwight D. Eisenhower

---

[31] Patrick Lencioni, *Five Dysfunctions of a Team: A Leadership Fable*, (Jossey-Bass, 2002).
[32] *The Anatomy of Peace: Resolving the Heart of Conflict – 2nd Edition*, (Arbinger Institute 2015).
[33] John Newstrom, *The Big Book of Team Building Games: Trust-Building Activities, Team Spirit Exercises, and Other Activities*, (McGraw-Hill, 1997).
[34] Price Pritchett, *The Team Member Handbook for Teamwork*, (Pritchett Publishing Company, 2006).
[35] Thomas Kayser, *Building Team Power: How to Unleash the Collaborative Genius of Teams for Increased Engagement, Productivity, and Results*, (McGraw-Hill, 2011).
[36] Bradley Sugars, *Instant Team Building - Instant Success Series*, (McGraw-Hill, 2006).

Team Dysfunction
Absence of Trust
Fear of Conflict
Lack of Commitment
Avoidance of Accountability
Inattention to Results
Honest Self-Evaluation
Team Effectiveness Assessment for Management
Team Selection and Team-Building
Churchillian Principles
Magnanimity
"I" Leadership
Effective Team-Building

Chapter Five Discussion Items

What is a sycophant and how can he effect the work of an organization?

What was the original meaning of the word "Cabinet" and how did it evolve? Describe an effective cabinet.

Compare and contrast the cabinets of President Eisenhower and President Truman.

Describe and give an example of a team dysfunction. How can the dysfunction negatively impact an organization?

What is the difference between avoidance of accountability and inattention to results?

What are the essential elements of team selection and team building? Describe one of the Churchillian Principles.

Define and explain "I" leadership in an organization and how it can impact employees.

What are the most effective team-building activities that enhance communications between and among executive management members?

Describe a team-building experience you think was effective or ineffective and explain why.

Chapter Five Lessons Learned

Dysfunctional leadership teams can bring an organization down and jeopardize the future of the organization.

If the leader of an organization and her top employees do not trust each other to be honest and supportive, the organization will suffer and the cabinet meetings will not utilize the talents of the executive team.

Many successful leaders try to build a collaborative executive team and in doing so the cabinet meetings become an open dialogue that benefits the organization.

An ineffective leader wants the executive leadership team to have only opinions that mimic his or that do not create conflict with him.

The level of trust required to reach levels of effectiveness that benefit the organization is almost completely determined by the leader's ability and willingness to build an effective leadership team.

Building an effective team takes some soul-searching for the leader. He must take an honest inventory of his own strengths and weaknesses.

Leaders that do not know how to build an effective executive leadership team or how to manage what could be an effective team are detrimental to an organization.

CHAPTER SIX

HIRING THE RIGHT PEOPLE

"All the clever strategies and advanced technologies in the world are nowhere near as effective without great people to put them to work."
-Jack Welch[1]

Determinants: Successful organizations are built on the quality of work done by its employees, and the quality of work from competent employees is not possible if a leader hires people who are more loyal to the leader than to the organization. A leader's failure to select quality employees and instead promote and select sycophants will lead inevitably to a destructive working environment that compromises the organization's mission and progress. Malcolm Forbes said, "Never hire someone who knows less than you do about what he's hired to do."[2]

Hiring

An essential component of leadership is the leader's ability and willingness to set conditions within the organization to hire good and productive employees from the executive team to line staff and everyone in between. In Stephen Covey's book, *The Speed of Trust*, he points out how important it is for a leader to select people he can trust, but he warns about blind trust.[3] Hiring people a leader can trust does not mean hiring relatives, friends, relatives of friends, or staff who will always tell the leader what she wants to hear, despite knowing that the truth may save the leader or more importantly may save the organization from problems. That is not trusting, nor is it loyalty. Trust and loyalty come from people who support the leader and managers but who also are honest at every level and who have the best

---

[1] Jack Welch, *Winning*, (Harper Collins Publishing, 2005).
[2] Malcolm Forbes, *The Sayings of Chairman Malcolm*, (Harper Collins, 1978).
[3] Stephen M.R. Covey, *The Speed of Trust*, (Free Press of Simon and Schuster, 2008 edition)

interests of the organization in mind. It does not help the organization if the *"trusted"* support staff will not warn managers about poor decisions, inconsistencies, or poor choices.

In Mrunal Belvalkar's article, *Dangers of Misplaced Loyalty*, he asks important questions:

> *Have you ever found it difficult to report on someone or report something negative to someone about him? Have you found it difficult to stand up against someone because doing that made you feel like you were betraying your relationship with that person? If the answers are yes to both questions, then yours, my friend, is misplaced loyalty. Misplaced loyalty is when you are loyal to a person...and your loyalty makes you biased so that you are defensive for all the wrong reasons.[4]*

The leader of an organization must install at all managerial levels within the organization the importance of hiring the right person for the job and then encourage them to be loyal, productive, creative, innovative, and honest about the work and the work climate.

In his book *The One Thing You Need to Know*, Mark Buckingham warns leaders and managers at all levels that the employee selection process is critical to the success of the organization. He wrote,

> *In the minds of great managers, consistently poor performance is not primarily a matter of weakness, stupidity, disobedience, or disrespect. It is a matter of miscasting.[5]*

Hiring the right person for a job sounds so obvious, but it is not practiced as if it is obvious. In his book, *Winning*, Jack Welch said,

> *Nothing matters more in winning than getting the right people on the field. All the clever strategies and advanced technologies in the world are nowhere near as effective without great people to put them to work[6]*

It is very difficult to find the right person for essential jobs in any organization. That's what a good leader knows and works on relentlessly each time a job opens, and that's the message he must convey throughout the organization. Welch says that hiring the right person is so important to an

---

[4] Mrunal Belvalkar, "Dangers of Misplaced Loyalty," *Buzzle*, 2011: http:// www.buzzle.com/ authors.asp/author=85441.
[5] Marcus Buckingham, *The One Thing You Need to Know*, (The Free Press, 2005).
[6] Jack Welch, *Winning*, (Harper Collins Publishing, 2005).

organization that during his successful career he made it a top priority. He trained his executive team and human resource directors about the importance of taking the time necessary to hire the right person. Additionally, he devised three "acid tests" for selecting the right person: *integrity, intelligence,* and *maturity.*[7]

1. *Integrity* is based on telling the truth–taking responsibility for past actions, admitting, and acknowledging mistakes, learning from mistakes, and correcting them.
2. *Intelligence*-Welch's concept of intelligence as a prerequisite for hiring is not a traditional IQ test sense of intelligence, rather it is what a good job candidate possesses that denotes his knowledge of work, of people, of how to make things work, how to motivate people, how to communicate, how to identify and solve problems, and how to learn from others, experiences, and research.
3. *Maturity*-not age, but level and type of maturity. There are some long-term employees who never mature and yet there are some young candidates for jobs that show ability and skills to handle pressure, stress, and failure. They also know how to enjoy their job and career and constantly learn and improve. The mature person also knows what is appropriate behavior; when to be a high-task and low-relationship oriented and when to be low-task and high-relationship oriented. That takes a presence of mind, awareness of the situation, and an understanding of how to work with people that only comes with a certain level and type of maturity.

Case Study #1

A non-profit organization had three critical positions to fill after a new leader of the organization was hired by the board. One of the positions became vacant when the incumbent was not selected for the top position and he left the organization. Another position opened because the new leader was told by the board to get rid of the incumbent. And the third vacant position was created when a popular and very effective employee retired. The new leader was pressed to fill these three positions because they were top level positions that had very significant operational functions. While time was of the essence in filling the positions, the new leader could have taken the time to make careful selections; instead, he used time as an excuse for quickly and hastily filling the positions. As it was revealed later, each hire was not vetted carefully and each one had connections with various members of the board.

---

[7] Ibid.

There was no implication that the board members cannot and should not help get the word out in professional circles about job openings, but the board members should not advocate for hires that are clearly not ready for, qualified for or in any way mature enough and experienced enough to handle critical jobs. In the organization, unfortunately, that is what happened. A person with a few director-level years of experience in finance was named to the chief financial officer position; his mother was a close friend of a board member. The experienced and very effective human resources officer was replaced with someone who had no human resources experience, except for hiring a few people in a small office, but his father was a friend of the organization's new leader. The person named as communications officer was a board member's relative. All three of the new hires were enthusiastic, smart and clearly over their heads from the first day.

The new chief financial officer had never prepared a comprehensive annual budget for an organization, and this organization's budget was well over $500 million. He had an idea of what needed to be done, but he did not know how to do it. He also had no operational sense of the daily strains on the budget. In less than six months, an organization that was financially solid and sustainable, but never blessed with a large endowment, started paying its bills late and was in danger of finishing the fiscal year in a deficit.

The human resources officer was smart, energetic and committed, but he could not or would not make decisions. He frequently told his staff that he would get back with them after he had time to think about the issue. Many times decisions needed to be made without delay, but he would not or could not make decisions. (Jack Welch called this type of leader the *"Last-one-out-the-door boss."*[8]) The delays repeatedly hurt the organization, because the unresolved issues begin to pile into a quagmire of unresolved problems that had a collateral effect on other decisions. His chronic indecisiveness became detrimental to the organization's effectiveness.

The communications officer was responsible for fundraising and communicating with clients and the community. He was full of great ideas, articulate, and thoughtful and in general a very delightful person. Everyone who worked for him and with him immediately liked him. That is why it became a puzzle when so many good projects and great ideas never came to fruition. He could not finish what he started. He would not complete a project. He did not have that part of maturity that helps a leader cross the finish line despite problems, issues, challenges, diversions, and obstacles. He could not cope; he could not navigate disruptions, and he could not execute a

---

[8] Ibid.

plan to complete a project by working through problems or handle distractions. Welch said,

Being able to execute is a special and distinct skill. It means a person knows how to put decisions into action and push them forward to completion, through resistance, chaos, or unexpected obstacles. [9]

The three crucial positions were filled with intelligent and energetic people but they lacked the maturity that Welch and others consider crucially important to an organization. The new hires brought chaos to the organization and the board placed the blame on the CEO. He was forced to review his hiring practices and the skill sets of the top three employees. One of his executive team members suggested that the organization hire temporary tutors for the three top level employees–former employees with the maturity and experience to help teach and guide them because they each possessed talent and skills and they were diligent people who wanted to perform at the highest level. The CEO did not listen to the good, sound advice. Instead, he said he had no patience for that nor the time to do that so the three potentially excellent leaders were reassigned and the CEO tried to handle their responsibilities. The organization faced a challenging time thereafter and soon the CEO was replaced.

The Culture of Sycophants

An article by the editors of *BusinessKnowledgeSource.com* addresses the flawed hiring process of selecting family and friends over qualified people.[10]

1. *A friend or family member may take advantage of their status, knowing that it is more difficult to fire someone who is close to the leader or member of the board.*
2. *Other employees may feel jealous when a friend or family member is hired, thinking it is favoritism, which often it is. This may especially be the case when a family member or friend is given a promotion over a non-relative/friend, or when a position is created that previously did not exist.*
3. *Personal family problems or disagreements between friends may be brought to the workplace and the leader may be tasked with trying to*

---

[9] Ibid.
[10] "Advantages and Disadvantages of Hiring Friends and Relatives," *Business Knowledge Editorial Board,* (2011): http://www.businessknowledgesource .comadvantages_and_disadvantagesof_hiring_friends_and_relatives_021 220. html.

> resolve the issues, which takes his time away from the organization. This
> may make it uncomfortable for other employees and difficult for work to
> get done.
4. *It may be more difficult to create a necessary change in the workplace
   when it might negatively affect a friend or relative that works for the
   leader.*

A leader who feels challenged may drift toward the trap of coveting
employees that are loyal to him and who never criticize or offer reasonable
and constructive criticism. This becomes the selection criteria for hiring that
can permeate and contaminate the organization.

In an article by Doug Blackie, he refers to misplaced loyalty subordinates
as *"obsequious sycophants."*

> *Blind followership is not a good thing–especially when combined with
> the fallacy of executive infallibility. The CEO told me to do this so I must do
> it. Resistance is futile. You will be assimilated. I call it the fallacy of executive
> infallibility. But let's face it, executives are fallible. They're people just like
> you and me. Effective leaders are skilled at walking the fine line between
> ensuring they have the confidence of their leaders–and being able to
> objectively assess whether the latest orders handed down from above are
> indeed wise and well thought out. I believe it's a leader's responsibility to
> ensure that executive decisions are made with the best information. If
> decisions are flawed-or simply don't make sense-there is no harm in
> respectfully seeking clarification from their leader. What was the basis for the
> decision? Have they considered the unintended consequences? Are they
> aware of this alternative approach? I have found that an executive may
> reconsider their decision when presented with better information or the risks
> of a certain course of action. Or they may not. At least you've made your
> case. Challenging an executive decision involves risk, requires a lot of
> courage and a significant amount of social capital with the executive
> leadership.* [11]

Leaders and managers that engage in padding their egos at the expense of
the organization by hiring sycophants and unqualified employees instead of
qualified employees totally lose any semblance of humility, and their actions
severely hurt the organization. It also becomes the model of hiring for the
entire organization. An organization's credibility, focus on services and staff,
morale, financial stability, ability to attract and retain competent and gifted

---

[11] Doug Blackie, "Obsequious Sycophants," http://www.dougblackie.com/
2012/03/obsequious-sycophants/.

employees, and the confidence of its clients and community can be lost for a long time.

Hire-the-Right-Person Philosophy

A widely-recognized expert in leadership studies, Warren Bennis, wrote in his book *On Becoming a Leader* that effective leaders do not dwell on making mistakes because they know they will learn from them. On the other hand, those leaders who make excuses for mistakes, or blame others for the mistakes, and who listen only to those subordinates that agree with them on all matters without offering a counterpoint do not learn from the mistakes and therefore make even more blunders, which includes hiring practices that do not match the talents of the person to the needs of the organization. It becomes a destructive cycle–questionable hiring practices, unqualified employees, and managers that are sycophants.

Many excellent leaders on the world and national stage to the best in the local communities around the nation say that one of the keys to success is selecting quality people and then letting them work and listen to them. Too many leaders and boards never seem to grasp that concept and, consequently, the organization is not positioned to select the best people for jobs. Warren Bennis referred to a leader's journey as *"the process of becoming an integrated human being."*[12] That includes all aspects of leadership, including the value of hiring the right people for the right job.

In Ira Chaleff's book *The Courageous Follower*, the author states that when an organization selects a competent person for a job, the healthy organization will expect and need that person to work in partnership with his managers and others within the organization by actively engaging in dialogue that includes honest and straightforward opinions, ideas, and innovations.

It is understandable from the leader's perspective to be cautious about surrounding herself with a cadre of employees who question and criticize almost every decision to the extent that nothing is accomplished. That is a legitimate and realistic concern. Subordinates can question the leader's decisions, but not to the point of disrespectful behavior and delaying or sabotaging decisions. But the leader sets the tone for the entire organization. A caring, strong, organized, strategic, and thoughtful leader can have such a positive and profound impact on the entire organization that no matter how large or small the organization that influence filters down through all levels and the organization ultimately benefits from the hiring-the-right-person

---

[12] Warren Bennis, *On Becoming a Leader*, (Addison-Wesley Publishing, 1989).

philosophy and expectation. There are many successful leaders who have devoted their entire career to ensuring that their organization meets the needs of their clients by first selecting the right people for the right jobs and then respecting and listening to them.

Antidotes: There are leaders at all levels within an organization who believe that their power derives from their position. They also think that their power comes not only from the position but from their personality, talents, and/or intelligence; consequently, the selection of employees must first come from loyalty to the leader instead of the organization. When an employee's talent or fit for a job is secondary to loyalty to the leader then the organization is in serious trouble. This leads to a cadre of employees who are not independent thinkers and who will never advise their supervisor when he is wrong or that another course of action would be more prudent or beneficial or that some aspect of the organization is in dire straits.

Boards must be mindful of this when selecting a leader because this mindset can quickly penetrate the organization at all levels. In fact, it behooves boards to ask the organization's leader about her philosophy and practice of hiring. It may be useful to learn how many previous subordinates ascended to leadership positions and their qualifications when they were hired. Also, a selection committee should take the time and put forth the effort to ascertain if the candidates for the leadership position have a history of hiring friends and relatives. Boards should make it clear that the organization's leadership should make certain throughout the organization that positions must be filled with quality candidates. Additionally, the leader should be expected to provide a path to success not only for those with leadership potential but for all employees. An effective leader creates a working environment that values people, creativity, independent thought, and collegial relationships between and among employees. This type of workplace climate naturally leads to loyalty to the organization because the employees feel vested in its mission and operations. There is a critical difference between loyalty to the organization and loyalty to leaders and managers within the organization. Ideally, a board wants to see both types of loyalty, and certainly not one at the expense of the other.

This is not to imply that hiring quality people for the right job is easy; it can be very difficult. And there are times when a relative or friend may be qualified for a job. Therefore, it is extraordinarily important for every organization to follow precise steps when trying to match the right person for the right job.

Entrepreneur, Inc., in an article by Mary Kaiser, suggests a progressive process starting with developing accurate job descriptions and compiling a "success profile" to indicate what skills a person would need to be successful in each job.[13] The article lists three key components to selecting the right person based on the success profile.

1. *Does the candidate have the practical experience that you want/need to grow your team and your business?* Base this on current and anticipated needs, not just immediate needs at hand. A careful review of a candidate's experience and/or qualifications requires time and patience.
2. *Does he/she have the specific strengths needed for the position? Have you assessed the strengths of your existing employees/team to know where there are gaps?* Having information about open positions from inside the organization will help the leader better leverage his team's talents and ensure that the leader remains objective throughout the hiring process. A critical and specific review of the data can reveal and uncover important information that will benefit the organization by identifying what employees are doing and what types of employees need to be hired to fill the gaps and address issues.
3. *Will the candidate fit the culture of the organization and play well with others? Do they share the same values/goals?* The interview process is an opportunity to vet top candidates. It is best to use a consistent set of questions for each interview. It's important to involve existing staff and take their feedback into consideration. It can be very beneficial to the organization and to the candidates for them to come in for a day to see how they interact and communicate with others. This may provide a sense of how the team will work together.

The board must be a role model for the leader in the selection of qualified employees. Boards who advocate for friends, business partners, relatives or those affiliated with others in any way for positions in the organization are putting the leader in a difficult situation; plus, the message is loud and clear that loyalty to people overrides loyalty to the organization and its mission.

The legendary Chief Operations Officer of General Electric, Joseph Ramano, said,

---

[13] Mary Kaiser, "How to Hire the Right Person for the Job," *Entrepreneur, Inc.*, June 3, 2015.

I am convinced that nothing we do is more important than hiring and developing people. At the end of the day, you bet on people, not on strategies.[14]

Chapter Six Key Words and Concepts

Blind Trust
Misplaced Loyalty
Miscasting
Integrity
Intelligence
Maturity
Last-One-Out-of-the-Door-Boss
Completer
Hiring Friends or Relatives
Obsequious Sycophants
Integrated Human Being
Courageous Follower
Success Profile

Chapter Six Discussion Items

What is the difference between blind trust and misplaced loyalty? Give examples of each.

Describe how integrity, intelligence, and maturity impact the effectiveness or ineffectiveness of leadership.

What is a Completer?

Describe and give an example of an Integrated Human Being. How does this type of person interact with others?
How can a Success Profile be beneficial?

What are some of the most important aspects of effective hiring practices?

---

[14] Quoted by Joseph Ramano in "How Successful Companies Identify and Hold on to Their Talent and Why It's Important," *Forbes,* October 25, 2013.

What precautions should leaders take when establishing workplace hiring practices?

What is appropriate feedback to leaders from employees?

What are the signs that an employee has crossed the line from criticism to insubordination?

Give an example of a leader that had difficulty making decisions – either from your own experiences or from a source other than this book. What were the circumstances?

Chapter Six Lessons Learned

Never hire someone who knows less than you do about what he's hired to do.

Trust and loyalty come from people who support the leader and managers but who also are honest at every level and who have the best interests of the organization in mind.

The leader of an organization must install at all managerial levels within the organization the importance of hiring the right person for the job.

Integrity is based on telling the truth – taking responsibility for past actions, admitting, and acknowledging mistakes, learning from mistakes, and correcting them.

A leader who feels challenged may drift toward the trap of coveting employees that are loyal to him and who never criticize or offer reasonable and constructive criticism.

Leaders who make excuses for mistakes, or blame others for the mistakes, and who listen only to those subordinates that agree with them on all matters without offering a counterpoint do not learn from the mistakes and therefore make even more blunders.

Subordinates can question the leader's decisions, but not to the point of disrespect behavior and delaying or sabotaging decisions.

When an employee's talent or fit for a job is secondary to loyalty to the leader then the organization is in serious trouble.

An effective leader creates a working environment that values people, creativity, independent thought, and collegial relationships between and among employees.

CHAPTER SEVEN

MOTIVATION AND CHANGE

"When people are financially invested, they want a return. When people are emotionally invested, they want to contribute."

– Simon Sinek[1]

Determinants: Part of the complexity of workplace climate is understanding what motivates employees and how to prepare employees and the organization for change because change is inevitable and ubiquitous and can either make or break morale and motivation. Both employee motivation and change management are ongoing responsibilities of the leader and the board. A leader and board must strive to understand and meet the basic needs of employees. However, many organizations do not have a plan to measure or consider employee motivation or how to manage change. Many organizations do not even consider change preparation and employee motivation as leadership or board governance priorities until something fails. Further, too many leaders do not see the link between employee motivation and change. The successful leaders understand the key to change and effective responses to change are intrinsically linked to the motivation of employees. Motivation drives and dictates almost all essential components in an organization. Change is inevitable; motivation of employees determines how change is managed.

Motivation

Case Study #1

The W.T. Grant Company built department stores throughout the United States when the concept of one-stop shopping in a convenient, well-stocked store with a variety of merchandise that was reasonably priced became popular. Started in 1902, by 1970 there were 1,200 W.T. Grant department stores with 62,000 employees. As the company grew, a decision was made by

---

[1] Simon Sinek, *Leaders Eat Last*, (Penguin Publishing, 2014).

the company's CEO and executive team to embark on a managerial motivation plan aimed to keep each store operating at the highest levels of proficiency during the company's growth. The employee motivation plan was labeled the "Steak and Beans" incentive program. It focused on motivating store managers to meet their sales and credit quotas each month. However, it was based on *negative incentives* instead of *positive motivation*. Managers that did not meet their sales and credit quotas received a visit from a regional manager who would gather all of the store employees together and in of them slam a pie in the face of the store manager for his failure to meet quotas. Other negative incentives included cutting the underperforming store manager's tie in half, requiring managers to push peanuts with their nose across a table, and making managers run backward around the store. Talented managers and other employees left the company; consequently, the condition of the stores deteriorated, service declined, and sales plummeted. However, the company's reaction to dropping sales in each store was to increase the negative incentives, which eventually drove the company into bankruptcy.

Stories of the company's focus on outrageously negative motivation seemed exaggerated, but court documents from bankruptcy hearings confirmed the stories.[2] At the time, W.T. Grant's bankruptcy was the second largest in business history.[3] While there is no suggestion that the negative incentives alone caused the bankruptcy of the company, the negative treatment led to a spiral of poor management decisions that ultimately destroyed the company. When sales started declining due to poor merchandising, inventory problems, and questionable pricing, store managers were threatened with further humiliation and ultimately their jobs if they did not increase credit applications in the stores. The negative motivation led to store managers threatening and intimidating their store employees to the point that they were giving credit to almost every customer without any effort to discern if the customer had the means to pay the credit card bill. This negative-based practice spiraled out of control and eventually put the company in debt of over $200 million in unsecured credit. The once promising company was destroyed by leaders that did not understand the importance of positive motivation and positive workplace climate. This is one of many examples that illustrate that negative motivation practices seldom work.

---

[2] *Matter of W.T. Grant Co.* 4 B.R. 53, (Southern District of New York, 1980).
[3] Ibid.

Cognitive Psychology and Motivation

A rubric from cognitive psychology highlights and measures the effectiveness of change while describing the basis for behavior, attitude, and motivation of employees.[4] The rubric is based on the status of five components: *vision, skills, incentives, resources,* and *action plan.* The rubric lists six possible outcomes of change based on the prevalence of the five components of change and how they are related to employee motivation. While this is a change and employee motivation model it can also serve as an indicator of what happens in an organization over time when the focus shifts to a reactive and negative mode rather than a positive and motivation planning mode, which typically occurs when change is not managed well or when scant attention is given to those elements that motivate employees, such as in the previous case study.

- To manage employee motivation and to manage change effectively, an organization needs to have a *vision.*
- Employees must be hired and placed in jobs matched with their skills and/or trained to possess the *skills* necessary to do their jobs.
- The organization must develop *incentives,* such as high income or bonuses, flexible work schedules, and/or employee recognition programs.
- The organization must provide the *resources* to employees to enable them to do their work at the levels expected by the organization.
- The organization must have an *action plan* that guides the work of the organization so progress or lack thereof can be assessed and to provide feedback to employees.

When vision, skills, incentive, resources and action plans are in place, there is a much greater likelihood that employees are satisfied and productive. However, if one or more of these five components of change/motivation are missing, there can be a significantly negative impact on employees and the organization.

If an organization lacks a clear *vision* or does not share that vision with the employees and stakeholders, it creates confusion inside and outside of the organization, which eventually will threaten individual and organizational effectiveness, job satisfaction, employee motivation, successful adjustment to change and possibly the future of the organization.

---

[4] Mary Lippitt, *The Managing Complex Change Model*, (Enterprise Management, Ltd., 1987).

If an organization does not recognize the *skill sets* of employees and match training to skill set needs, the employees are put in recurring situations where they are expected to produce even though they do not have the skill set necessary to be successful. Not only does this negatively impact employee motivation and morale it also jeopardizes a positive reaction to change and the quality of work suffers. This causes employee anxiety–the fear of going to work each day knowing or wondering if the lack of skills and subsequent non-productivity will result in termination. Organizations, consequently, must determine what skill sets are necessary and then provide the training or retraining. Too often an employee is demoted or terminated not because he could not do the job, but because the organization did not take the time to match the employee with a job that required his skills and failed to provide the resources necessary to do the job effectively.

If the organization ignores *incentives*, this oversight jeopardizes in insidious ways the gap closure goals set in the organization's strategic plan. The need for recognition is a basic human trait and a key to motivation. Research has shown that neither money nor threats are as powerful a motivator as many leaders believe.[5] When describing this as a significant component of an effective "influencer" as a leader, Grenny, Patterson, and Maxfield found that,

> *People with power over others often trump all other sources of motivation by relying on threats. Now that others have been warned, surely they will be motivated to do the right thing. Unfortunately, negative reinforcement yields mixed results. People who develop a change strategy based on a single extrinsic motivator typically miss the importance of creating circumstances in which intrinsic rewards carry their share of the motivational load. Savvy influencers increase their likelihood of achieving success by building in multiple sources.* [6]

Content and Process

The factors related to motivation are essential to the success of an organization because the lack of attention to motivation breeds overt or covert intentional or unintentional resistance between and among individuals

---

[5] Doug White and Polly White, "Money is Nice, But It's Not Enough to Motivate Employees," *Entrepreneur*, June 23, 2015.

[6] Joseph Grenny, Kerry Patterson, and David Maxfield, *Influencer: The New Science of Leading Change: Second Edition*, (McGraw-Hill, 2013).

within the organization. Not only does this impede the functions of the organization, it also sabotages any attempt to handle change productively.

It is important for leaders to note that research for many decades has found that motivation typically falls within two categories: *content* and *process*. The *content theory* of motivation focuses on the needs of individuals–factors that motivate people while *process theory* of motivation focuses on behavior and the identification of factors that motivate behaviors.

Szilagyi, Ivancevich, and Wallace define content and process in their widely-referenced book, *Organizational Behavior and Performance*. The also specify how these two approaches to motivation apply to organizations.[7]

1. *The content approach includes factors that start or arouse motivated behavior. The content approach refers to the motivation factors that center on satisfying employees' need for money, status, achievement, and/or working conditions. The content approach requires the leader to answer the question, "What specific things or functions motivate people?"*

2. *The process approach to motivation is concerned not only with behavior but also the choice of behaviors and factors that are most likely to increase the desired behavior on a regular and predictable basis. Process motivation recognizes that motivation comes from clarifying individual's perception of work inputs and by rewarding desired behavior through several different means other than or in addition to money or status.*

Many researchers have found that promotion, salary, recognition, fringe benefits, friendly co-workers, flexible work hours, teleworking opportunities, compensation time, covered parking spaces, compensation for commuting to work, employee recognition programs, employee birthday recognition, occasional extension of the lunch hour, etc. can be significantly effective in motivating employees in an organization because they meet the needs and motives of employees.

Nohria, Lawrence, and Wilson described four basic motivational needs[8] (based on sociobiological theory[9]) that are important for the health and

[7] Andrew Szilagyi, John Ivancevich, and Marc Wallace, *Organizational Behavior and Performance 3rd Edition*, (Goodyear Publishing, 1983).

[8] N. Nohria; P. Lawrence, and E. Wilson, *Driven: How Human Nature Shapes Our Choices*, (Jossey-Bass Inc. Publishing, 2002).

[9] E.O. Wilson, *On Human Nature*, Cambridge Press Harvard, 1978, (Note: E. O. Wilson defines sociobiology as: "The extension of population biology and evolutionary theory to social organization." Introduction, p. xi)

motivation of employees in the workplace. It is also important for leaders to understand the motivational needs of employees as part of their overall emotional and physical health.[10]

1. *Acquire objects and experiences. Receiving tangible awards are important but so is receiving unique work or learning experiences.*
2. *Long-term bonding with others. Employees spend much of their lives in the workplace. It is important for them to bond with colleagues and feel that the workplace is almost like a "second home."*
3. *Learning and understanding of the world. Employees are motivated and encouraged when they are given opportunities to enrich their lives by learning about the work of colleagues and are exposed to other learning experiences.*
4. *Defense from harm. Employees need to feel physically and emotionally safe in the workplace to be motivated and productive.*

In the process approach to motivation, the leader deliberately tries to determine the expectations of individuals and the satisfaction or dissatisfaction that accompanies those expectations. That is why it is critically important for an employee to be matched appropriately with the job based on the employee's skills and experience and the requirements of the job.

Using rewards that are content-based, plus matching outcomes with employee expectations will most likely result in a motivated working environment.

A study of Victor Vroom's *Expectancy and Valence Theory* conducted by Sheridan, Slocum, and Richards provides an informative example of the *process* approach.[11]

In a study of nursing school graduates, it was found that nurses chose hospitals that let them satisfy a variety of work-related outcomes (flexible

---

[10] C.P. Alderfer, "An empirical test of a new theory of human needs," *Organizational Behavior and Human Performance*, 4, (1969); F. Herzberg, *One More Time: How Do You Motivate People?*, (Harvard Business Press, 1968); Abraham Maslow, "A Theory of Human Motivation," *Psychological Review*, 50, 1946; D.C. McClelland, *Human Motivation*, (Cambridge University Press, 1988); R.M. Ryan and E.L. Deci, "Self-determination Theory and the Facilitation of Intrinsic Motivation, Social Development, and Will," *American Psychologist*, 55, 2000.

[11] John E. Sheridan; Max D. Richards, and John Slocum, "Comparative Analysis of Expectancy and Heuristic Models of Decision Making," *Journal of Applied Psychology*, 60, (3), June 1975.

work hours, work in specialized fields of interest, and challenging work assignments). Hospitals that gave nurses opportunities to satisfy these outcomes were chosen by the nurses more often than hospitals that did not give the nurses the opportunity to achieve these outcomes even when the salary was higher.[12]

Related to motivation are *resources*. Resources should be matched to meet the needs of the organization and the expectations of employees within the organization. The lack of resources that would help employees in the organization successfully perform their jobs is commonly viewed as an example of a leader's disregard for the employees and therefore indicates that the leader does not care about or is oblivious to the work climate. Few situations in the workplace are more frustrating to a motivated employee than not being able, for example, to have his computer problems fixed in a timely manner in order to complete a project. The pressure of completing a project can be motivating – to get the job done on time and with quality – but that motivation can be jeopardized by the lack of resources which causes high levels of employee dissatisfaction and frustration. Frustration is a morale killer, especially with a motivated employee.[13]

An effective leader will check the *resources inventory* periodically to inquire if individuals within the organization have the resources they need to be effective, productive, and satisfied. A resource inventory can often reveal surprising and useful results for leaders; for example, completion of projects on time may be tied more directly to a reduction in computer work time due to malfunctions in the software or interruptions in internet access than to employee motivation, attitude or aptitude. Leaders should conduct a resource mapping project to identify resources, the level of resource support, the gaps in resources, appropriateness and timeliness of resource allocations, and appropriateness of resources.

Even if a leader has focused on vision, skills, incentives, and resources, the absence of an *action plan* (a strategic plan that is actionable and not on a shelf or one that is more theoretical than operational) that ties everything together can jeopardize the effectiveness of the leader and organizational outcomes.

In Peter and Waterman's book *In Search of Excellence,* they note that all successful organizations have one thing in common–*a bias for action.*[14] A

---

[12] Ibid.

[13] Marylyn Wentworth, "Developing Staff Morale," *The Practitioner*, 16 (4), (1990).

[14] Thomas Peters and Robert Waterman, *In Search of Excellence*, Harper Business, Reprint 2006).

bias for action starts with an action plan that consolidates, validates, and links organizational values to the outcomes enumerated in the action plan, so that not only will employees see the value of their work, they will also see the relevancy of their work as it relates to the purpose and success of the organization. The action plan focus becomes a self-fulfilling workplace climate for individuals because they have worth and value.

Without these essential components (vision, skills, resources, incentives and an action plan) an organization will never reach its potential or goals because the elements that undergird employee motivation and solidify adaptation to change are missing.

Infrastructure

Ignoring the basic infrastructure of an organization is one of the most telling elements that generate the decline in the performance, reputation, and trust of an organization. And it decimates employee motivation. Many leaders new to organizations are surprised to learn that the basic needs of employees have been ignored, dismissed as unessential, or set aside as a future project.

According to *Forbes* magazine's review of takeovers, the majority of CEOs that were hired to turn a company around found that infrastructure problems had been ignored for several years in the struggling organization. Consequently, the most problematic challenge was the need to restore resources, replace aging equipment, adjust work schedules, revisit employee incentives and focus on employee morale and re-engage employee motivation.[15]

Antidotes: A leader must understand the dynamics that can negatively impact an organization's ability to effectively handle change and address employee motivation. The leader must also understand the relationship between leadership, change, conditions for change, and how they link to employee motivation and performance.

To illustrate these points, a researcher for *Forbes* magazine studied the insight of successful CEOs. She found that they know the importance of employee motivation for performance reasons including their ability to cope with and seamlessly handle change without feeling threatened.[16] Self-

---

[15] Jason Limkin, "What Everyone Should Know About Mergers and Acquisitions," *Forbes*, March 23, 2013.
[16] Cheryl Conner, "Six Ways to Improve Employee Morale and Performance," *Forbes*, September 11, 2014.

confident and motivated employees do not fear change in the workplace; they adapt. Motivated employees respond to change with a positive attitude. They embrace change because of the learning opportunities that come with it. Also, the study found that successful leaders use six proven strategies to improve and maintain employee motivation.[17]

1. *Give them a reason to believe. Employees are part of something bigger than themselves, but do they know it? Leaders need to understand and share in the vision of what is expected and valued in the organization. That vision alone will motivate and inspire employees and the team, down to its junior members, which comes back full circle in effectively facilitating organizational growth by helping the organization succeed, which improves the local economy and creates additional jobs. Sharing the benefits of a successful organization with employees by showing them the direct and collateral benefits to the community helps them to see the value of their work.*

2. *Show you care. Recognize employee birthdays. Send gifts for new babies and weddings. Be involved in employees' lives to let them feel acknowledged and valued not only as employees but also as "family" members and as human beings with hopes and dreams and talent. Also recognize employee accomplishments, such as completing a degree, or earning certification, etc.*

3. *Recognize the good. When someone is doing something successfully, tell them. Recognize the individuals on the team who receive good feedback from clients. It is important for employees to feel their efforts are being recognized. The recognition further perpetuates their desire to go above and beyond for clients, which positively impacts the perception of the organization as well.*

4. *Learn the value and meaning of fringe benefits. An organization may not be able to offer a competitive full benefits package or raise salaries, but leaders may be surprised how much a few small (and inexpensive) benefits or incentives mean to employees, such as teleworking, flexible work hours, etc.*

5. *Promote from within. When employees see there is room to advance their career within the organization, it speaks volumes. Find out what skills and talents the different members of the organization possess and find ways to develop those skills for future use in the organization. When a leader has stellar team members he should help invest in the training they need to advance as the organization grows.*

6. *An organization that plays together stays together. This is a common thread among the fastest growing companies. Companies such as Vivint*

---

[17] Ibid. (Based on an interview with Amelia Wilcox).

(one of Forbes' "Most Promising Companies for 2015") schedule summer parties for employees and their families and friends with horse-drawn carriages, face painting, bonfires, friendly races, and dirt bikes. Even smaller organization do things like host a summer party for staff and families, provide holiday luncheons, arrange run and walk fundraising events, etc. These celebrations acknowledge to employees that the organization supports and depends on them.

A Harvard University study found that many leaders wrongly believe that applying pressure and money are the two most successful ways to motivate employees. Walter Chen wrote about the study:

In a wide-ranging study of employee motivation, Harvard Business School professor Teresa Amabile and psychologist Steven Kramer asked hundreds of employees to maintain a diary chronicling their peaks and valleys in motivation at work. They analyzed 12,000 diary entries and talked with 600 managers about what they thought was the single most important motivator for employees at work. 95% of them got the answer wrong. It's not money or pressure that drives employees at work. The most important motivator for employees at work is what Amabile and Kramer call 'the power of small wins'-employees are highly productive and driven to do their best work when they feel as if they're making progress every day toward a meaningful goal.[18]

To improve employee motivation, it is essential to not only create conditions that provide opportunities for the employee to feel confident and proud of their work, but to also generate ways for employees to measure their success. This can be done by project completion benchmark settings so employees can measure their progress toward project completion using either timelines or project completion segment completion notations. Measuring progress can be shown in a large-scale manner that is very public and tied to a team's progress; for example, using a large matrix board with a picture of the project divided into segments that are filled in when they are completed. But measuring employee progress can be accomplished in smaller ways, too, that are more specific to the employee. Setting small goals that are measurable can have the same positive impact as the larger ones. Often employees welcome the opportunity to establish measurable goals by working with the manager. People want to be successful at work and they want to be able to "feel and see" their success and make sure others can see

---

[18] Walter Chen, "95 Percent of Managers Follow an Outdated Theory of Motivation," *The Progress Principle*, September 14, 2014: http://idonethis. com/manage-ment-maslows-hierarchy-needs/.

their success, also. The importance extends beyond employee motivation – the managers and ultimately the organization's leader can use this method as a way of enhancing communications with all employees.

Communications with employees is a powerful tool for employee motivation. David Krantz, CEO of YP, found six communication strategies that improve employee motivation by making them feel connected with other employees and more engaged in the organization.[19]

1. *Send weekly correspondence to all employees in the organization. Every Monday without fail for the last three years I have sent a personally written email to every employee in the organization about things I am thinking about and important topics that are essential to the organization. This kind of communication serves as an opportunity to connect and engage with all levels of the organization.*[20]

2. *Build comfort in talking about what is not working. Many companies have a culture of focusing on the positives but also quickly identifying problems and addressing them. Great organizations focus on what is not going well so they can dig in and get better while at the same time highlighting successes.*

3. *Hold information meetings. Whether the organization has offices in one city or nationwide, leaders should plan face-to-face conversations with employees no matter what the obstacles are to getting there. Foster a two-way candid dialog. Leaders are able to learn a great deal about what is really happening in the organization from these sessions, which can help the leadership team make better decisions regarding many aspects of the organization but especially regarding employee motivation.*

4. *Schedule an annual leadership conference for top leaders. This type of conference is a working session where every leader can hear the organization's strategy and plans so they have a deeper understanding of the internal workings of the organization. The leaders are equipped and encouraged to share the information with their teams. An equally important value is the informal network building that enables leaders to have effective communications throughout the year.*

5. *Answer every employee email within 24 hours. Always have time to communicate with employees that work hard every day to serve customers and who build the organization. Employees want to be heard and feel appreciated.*[21]

---

[19] David Krantz, "Ways to Effectively Communicate with Employees," *Entrepreneur*, July 24, 2014.
[20] Ibid.
[21] Ibid.

Simon Sinek wrote in his book *Leaders Eat Last* that employees must feel engaged in the organization to be motivated.[22] They want to be successful and they want the organization to be successful. The leader can make that possible by strategically and earnestly creating conditions to motivate employees, which facilitates a healthy response to changes in the workplace. The motivational conditions are based on vision, trust, skills, incentives, resources, and action plans; otherwise, called the "*Critical Six.*"[23]

The following Critical Six chart is a summary of motivation concepts that include the motivation elements and employee reactions when that element is missing (indicated by an "X"). The most effective use of the chart is to start with the employee reaction and select the behavior that best describes the employee's behavior and attitude. Then look at the Critical Six to identify the one that is most directly linked to the employee's behavior, which provides the leader with a strategy to improve workplace conditions, if necessary.

Organization Elements	Employee Behaviors/Reactions
Lack of Vision	Anxious
Lack of Trust	Suspicious
Insufficient Training	Defensive and/or Angry
Lack of Incentives	Unmotivated, Negative Attitude
Insufficient Resources	Frustrated
Unclear Action Plan	Confused

The matrix can be used as a guideline to "diagnose" employee behavior in general terms–not for action but for consideration when employees are not productive. The purpose of the chart is to encourage leaders and managers to consider what they are doing or not doing that could be a contributing factor to an employee's work-related problems and lack of motivation and productivity.

Chapter Seven Key Words and Concepts

Motivation
Cognitive Psychology
Vision
Skills
Incentives

---

[22] Simon Sinek, *Leaders Eat Last*, (Penguin Publishing, 2014).
[23] A term used by the author.

Resources
Resource Inventory
Resource Mapping
Action Plan
Content Motivation
Process Motivation
Sociobiological Theory
Expectancy and Valence Theory
Resource Inventory
Bias for Action
Self-fulfilling Environment
Pressure and Money
Power of Small Wins
Feel and See Success
Organizational Culture
Critical Six

Chapter Seven Discussion Items

List the main components of motivation in organizations and how they impact employee productivity.

Define the importance of cognitive psychology in understanding organizational behavior and employee motivation.

Give an example of a vision statement and how that drives an organization.

What is the difference between Content Motivation and Process Motivation?

How can Expectancy and Valence Theory be useful in organizations?

What does Bias for Action mean and what is its significance in an organization.

What is the difference between organizational culture and organizational climate?

How can the Critical Six be useful in organizational employee motivation and productivity?

Give an example of an action plan and explain how it is linked to resources and incentives.

Using your own experience, provide an example of how you or someone you know was motivated to perform or complete a task or project.

Chapter Seven Lessons Learned

Motivation drives and dictates almost all essential components in an organization.

When vision, skills, incentive, resources and action plans are in place, there is a much greater likelihood that employees are satisfied and productive.

The need for recognition is a basic human trait and a key to motivation.

Promotion, salary, recognition, fringe benefits, friendly co-workers, flexible work hours, teleworking opportunities, compensation time, covered parking spaces, compensation for commuting to work, employee recognition programs, employee birthday recognition, an occasional extension of the lunch hour, etc. can be significantly effective in motivating employees.

It is critically important for an employee to be matched appropriately with the job based on the employee's skills and experience and the requirements of the job.

The pressure of completing a project can be motivating – to get the job done on time and with quality – but that motivation can be jeopardized by the lack of resources.

The action plan focus becomes a self-fulfilling workplace climate for individuals because they have worth and value.

Self-confident and motivated employees do not fear change in the workplace; they adapt.

Employees want to be heard and feel appreciated.

People want to be successful at work and they want to be able to "feel and see" their success and make sure others can see their success, also.

CHAPTER EIGHT

SAFETY AND WORKPLACE CLIMATE

*"Bully in the workplace could cost a Fortune 500 company an astounding
$24 million in lost productivity and another $1.4 million in litigation and
settlement costs."*

-Workplace Bullying Institute[1]

Determinants: The leadership requirements of any organization are very
complicated, but a leader must never forget that each organization has basic
needs that must be met before it can excel. Too often, leaders and boards fail
to understand that each organization has a workplace climate that lives and
breathes, and must, therefore, be protected and nurtured. Leaders should
recognize that organizations must take the conditions of the workplace
climate and safety seriously. Workplace climate in an organization is an
essential responsibility of leadership and board governance and should be a
major concern of every leader and board. However, many organizations do
not have a clearly defined and fully developed safety plan or methods for
monitoring and improving workplace climate. Many organizations do not
consider safety a leadership or board governance function until something
happens that threatens the safety of employees and/or clients. Also,
workplace conditions can in many ways negatively impact employee
productivity, retention, and recruitment.

Safety

People in every part of society are acutely aware of safety and there is a
full expectation that every organization understands the importance of it and,
consequently, has plans in place that include all of the essential elements for
managing safety-building, grounds, and functions of the organizations as well
as the daily operations of the organization. Safety planning and training of

---

[1] Editors, "Estimating the Cost of Workplace Bullying," *Workplace Bullying Institute*,
April 24, 2014.

employees, as well as other elements of workplace climate, are important to employees and clients and benefit the organization.

A leader's style and priorities can impact workplace climate, including safety. One of the basic and most essential infrastructure elements is a safe and healthy working environment. Safety in every type of organization has to be the top priority, but often that aspect of infrastructure is minimized until a near or actual tragedy takes place. It often happens that the follow-up story to a workplace tragedy centers on a disregard for safety, slack security essentials, poor safety planning, insufficient staff safety training, and awareness, and/or reductions in safety related services and staff.

Due to a leader's indifference about workplace climate, some organizations have a crisis management plan that is so outdated and so seldom referenced that it has become worthless. Even more troubling is the fact that some organizations do not have a crisis management plan of any type; consequently, a thoughtful, deliberate, and appropriate response that might otherwise mitigate a disaster is not possible. This leaves an organization in a very vulnerable position when a crisis occurs.[2]

A study by the National Opinion Research Center at the University of Chicago reviewed two dozen workplace surveys over a ten-year period. The researchers found that over eight of ten workers (85 percent) rate workplace safety first in importance among labor standards. The meta-analysis found that workplace safety was rated ahead of family and maternity leave, minimum wage, paid sick days, overtime pay and the right to join a union.[3]

In surveys of employees regarding workplace climate, in both for-profit and non-profit organizations, workplace safety is always in the top three lists of priorities.

A *Campus Safety Magazine* Survey found the following.[4]

1. *35 percent either disagree somewhat or strongly with the statement: If an active shooter or bomber came onto my campus, my department and my organization would be able to respond effectively.*
2. *A significant percentage of college and university student and staff respondents indicate they receive fair to good support from campus*

[2] Mark Sanborn, "Seven Steps to Keep Employees Safe in the Workplace," *Entrepreneur*, October 24, 2013.
[3] Editors, "Public Attitudes Toward and Experiences with Workplace Safety," *Public Welfare Foundation*, 2012:
http://www.norc.uchicago.edu and http://www.publicwelfare.org.
[4] Campus Supervisor Staff, "Study Finds Many Campuses May Be Neglecting Emergency Preparedness," *Campus Security Magazine*, October 18, 2015.

administration regarding safety issues. Eighty percent say their top administrators take safety and security on campus seriously, but only 65 percent of administrators say they have enough authority to carry out their safety responsibilities appropriately.

3. *Lack of resources is another challenge. Two in five say their organizations don't dedicate enough money, resources, and personnel to safety and security efforts and technology.*

4. *Hazmat incident preparedness is a significant weakness. Nearly a third of respondents (29 percent) either disagree somewhat or strongly disagree with the statement 'My organization is adequately prepared for a hazmat incident.' One in five survey takers is not satisfied with their organization's emergency/crisis plans or weather emergency/ natural disaster preparedness.*

5. *Probably the most troubling statistic of the survey involves hospitals and their inability to respond to active shooters or bombers. Surprisingly, 40 percent of hospital respondents disagree somewhat or strongly disagree with the statement: 'If an active shooter or bomber came onto my campus, my department and my organization would be able to respond effectively.'*

6. *Staffing data also correlate with the active shooter/bomber and weapons statistics. More than two in five hospital respondents (41 percent) disagree somewhat or strongly with the statement: 'My department has enough staff to respond appropriately to incidents.'*

7. *Almost four in five (79 percent) of hospital survey takers say that their top administrators take safety and security seriously, but only 74 percent of hospital respondents say they have enough authority to do their jobs well.*

In some instances, the lack of effective leadership can have tragic results, especially if safety is not a top priority or if leadership has not been given the authority to do what is necessary to secure the work environment. No one should imply that any organization is fully safe because it is impossible to plan for and prevent every type of tragedy or crisis that can occur, but leadership at all levels, especially top leadership, in every organization must understand how seemingly unrelated series of events and decisions may compromise workplace safety and security.

Workplace Violence

Workplace violence is impossible to completely prevent, but leaders and boards must take an honest and realistic view of safety on a regular interval. No decisions that undermine safety should be tolerated, especially personnel decisions, operational decisions, facility decisions, and budget decisions. There are several examples of workplace violence where the safety of the facility, training of the employees, and/or the leadership response was called into question.

Leaders and boards typically will not have the on-site expertise necessary to take an unbiased view of safety in the workplace. Therefore, it is wise for organizations to seek outside assistance. For example, organizations can utilize workplace safety information from the Occupational Safety and Health Administration,[5] Federal Emergency Management Agency,[6] and others to develop effective workplace safety plans. Safety plans are provided for specific types of organizations that include recommendations related to unique facilities, such as hospitals.[7]

Risk assessments of the workplace are essential, also. The nature of the organization's work may create situations that increase safety risks. For example, the All-Tech Investment Company in Atlanta where a gunman walked in the door and opened fire with a 9mm and 45-caliber handguns had no security checkpoints.[8] The company's business was in a high rent business district with expensive furnishings, well-paid staff, multiple amenities, and no history of security or safety problems. However, the company's work included high financial risk and volatile day trading where off-site day traders could reap or lose large amounts of money. Some day traders had called the company to complain about their losses, so a workplace safety expert would most likely have advised the company that mounting financial losses could anger a day trader and lead to a confrontation with the staff. After the tragic events that day, the company and the building complex installed a series of safety features, including the addition of security staff and security checkpoints.

Bullying

The genesis of violence in the workplace has become a source of concern and study. Bullying and intimidation are frequently cited. It is becoming more obvious that behavior like bullying develops in a workplace where the

---

[5] Occupational Safety and Health Administration, https://www.osha. gov/dsg/InjuryIllnessPrevention Programs.html.
[6] Federal Emergency Management Agency https://training.fema.gov/is/ courseoverview.aspx?code=IS-906.
[7] OSHA Hospital Emergency Management, https://www.osha.gov/dsg/ hospitals/.
[8] Steven Mufson and Cheryl August, "Nine Dead in Atlanta Office Rampage," *Washington Post*, July 30, 1999.

workplace climate is negative. Unabated bullying can lead to workplace violence.

Bullying is a major issue in some organizations either with widespread bullying or in certain sections of an organization where bullying is taking place one-on-one. Leaders cannot ignore any type of bullying. Those that dismiss the prevalence of bullying should look at the research. A *Zogby International* survey about bullying in the workplace included several key findings.[9]

1. *Half of all workers either witnessed or had been bullied in the workplace.*
2. *Thirty-five (35) percent of workers experienced bullying firsthand.*
3. *Sixty-two (62) percent of bullies are men.*
4. *Fifty-eight (58) percent of targets are women.*
5. *Women bullies target women in 80 percent of cases.*
6. *Bullying is four times more prevalent than illegal harassment.*
7. *Sixty-eight (68) percent of bullying is same-gender harassment.*

In addition to the emotional toll and increased risk safety factors in the workplace, it is a fact that bullying in the workplace is a financial liability. The *Orlando Business Journal* cited an estimated cost of $180 million in lost time and productivity to American businesses each year due to bullying in the workplace.[10] The Workplace Bullying Institute (WBI) estimates between turnover and lost productivity that bully in the workplace could cost a *Fortune 500* company an *"astounding $24 million in lost productivity and another $1.4 million in litigation and settlement costs."*[11] WBI reported that an organization can calculate the expense of bullying in the workplace based on time.

1. *The bully's direct manager counseling the bully = 80 hours.*
2. *The bullying victim's direct manager counseling the victim = 150 hours.*
3. *Witnesses of the bullying counseled =100 hours.*
4. *Human Resources employees talking with managers, bully and victim = 10 hours.*

---

[9] "2015 Workplace Bullying Survey" conducted by *Zogby International* for the Workplace Bullying Institute: http://workplacebullying.org/multi/pdf/ WBI-2015-US-Survey.pdf.

[10] L.U. Farrell, "Workplace Bullying High Cost," http://orlandobizjournals.com/orlando/stories/2002/13/8/focus1. htlm.

[11] "Estimating the Cost of Workplace Bullying," *Workplace Bullying Institute*, April 24, 2014.

5. *Human Resources employees talking with executives about the bullying problems = 5 hours.*
6. *Human Resources recruiting and training replacement of victim employee and bully =160 hours.*
7. *Based on average salary scales, the total cost could be from $50,000 to $80,000.*[12]

The tragedies that stem from bullying are the responsibility of those that ignore it in any organization because bullying can be addressed, reduced, and prevented, which would save untold suffering. This is a leadership function and a basic responsibility. Leaders at all levels must develop a plan to prevent and discourage bullying and intervene when bullying occurs.

Social isolation has the same impact of confrontational and physical bullying when a person is socially isolated purposely. This is how that type of bullying works. The colleagues ignore the victim by not speaking or by walking away. Then they start whispers or rumors about the victim and will not let him or her participate in any activity or discussion or meeting. One of the most telling and troubling things to see is to observe a socially isolated person trying to find a place to sit in a cafeteria while holding a tray of food. At every table, he is turned away by the people sitting at the table. Imagine how that person feels every day, and furthermore, imagine how that person feels about work and himself. The social isolation is tragic enough but to be publicly humiliated adds to the sad situation. Leaders should remember that bullying is a symptom of a larger problem–a negative workplace climate.

A story covered by *ABC News* reveals a disturbing set of circumstances in the workplace related to a negative work climate on a college campus that had tragic results.

In the days before Kevin Morrissey committed suicide near the University of Virginia campus, at least two co-workers said they warned university officials about his growing despair over alleged workplace bullying at the award-winning Virginia Quarterly Review. 'I told them, I'm very concerned about Kevin; I'm afraid he might try to harm himself,' said a colleague and friend of Morrissey, who asked not to be identified. 'They asked me to clarify what I meant and I repeated that I was afraid he might harm himself. If someone had just done something.' On July 30, Morrissey, the review's 52-year-old managing editor, walked to the old coal tower near campus and shot himself in the head. Morrissey's death underscored the turmoil at the high-profile journal, according to co-workers. Maria Morrissey said her brother's phone

---

[12] Ibid.

records showed that he placed at least 18 calls to university officials in the final two weeks of his life. The phone records, obtained by ABCNews.com, showed calls to the human resources department, the ombudsman, the faculty and employee assistance center, and the university president. 'Kevin was asking for help,' said Maria Morrissey, who had been estranged from her brother in recent years, but has started looking into the circumstances of his death. Kevin Morrissey, former managing editor of Virginia Quarterly Review Morrissey's sister and co-workers acknowledged that he long suffered from depression. But they insisted that he took his life only after the university failed to respond to repeated complaints about bullying by his boss, Ted Genoways. Other employees, they said, also complained about being bullied by the journal's top editor. 'Bullying seems to make it like some sort of schoolyard thing,' said the colleague who asked not to be named. 'It's really a much more subtle kind of erasure.' I'm not going to talk to you. I'm going to come in the side office and shut the door. I will pretend you don't exist.' The university has these [human resources] people, but they don't do anything. After one of your colleagues has killed himself, it's beyond the point of mediation. They didn't protect us. We went again and again and again and they didn't protect us. [13]

According to experts on workplace climate and safety, it is imperative to take measures to ensure that everyone understands the importance of safety and the necessity of a positive workplace climate. If an organization has to make budget cuts, the employees and clients should remind the board and leadership that safety measures, safety employees, safety strategies, and the elements of a positive workplace climate are essential and, therefore, should not be compromised by budget cuts.

The basic needs of employees are safety, security, and sense of belonging. Countless numbers of employees miss work each day because of workplace safety and climate concerns. It negatively impacts productivity, retention of employees, creativity, and client services.

Antidotes: Leaders must understand the relationship between leadership, conditions for productivity and how these link to workplace climate and safety. Workplace climate and safety are basic and essential requirements of every organization, but many organizations are finding it more difficult to provide a safe, secure, and positive workplace because of continued budget cuts and because it is not a top priority to some boards and leaders. Also,

---

[13] Ray Sanchez, "Did Depression or an Alleged Bullying Boss Prompt Editor's Suicide?" *ABC News*, August 10, 2010.

organizations do not understand the relationship between change, the nature of the organization's work, and workplace climate and safety.

Most courses and books on leadership or governing, whether it is directed to schools, colleges, non-profit organizations or business environments, do not adequately or strongly address the need for a safety plan nor do they establish the link between the organization's workplace climate, leadership, and productivity. This is a major oversight. Every organization, regardless of mission and size, must take the time to develop a crisis prevention and response and safety management plan and they must manage change by understanding the impact of change on workplace climate. Organizations that understand the dynamic nature of workplace climate find that respect for the climate through actions such as safety awareness and planning create conditions for success, transitions, and change in the workplace.

Field Theory

Workplace climate as a whole is more than the sum of its parts. Kurt Lewin's work on Gestalt psychology comes from the concept of "Gestalt," which in German literally means "form, shape."[14] From his study of Gestalt, Lewin developed *Field Theory*, an approach to the study of human behavior that was the genesis of social psychology and one of the first, if not the first, scientific reference to organizational climate. He pursued the study of causal relationships between and among those things that influence human behavior across the traditional boundaries of various sciences, including a person's work environment. In his famous 1935 publication, *A Dynamic Theory of Personality*, Lewin wrote,

> *Every psychological event depends upon the state of the person and at the same time on the environment, although their relative importance is different in different cases.* [15]

Lewin developed a formula that highlighted the interaction between a person and the environment: $B=f$ *(P* and *E)*, behavior is a function of both person and environment. This is a simple and yet compelling description of the interaction and interplay between people and their environments.

---

[14] Calvin S. Hall, review of "A Dynamic Theory of Personality," by Kurt Lewin, *American Journal of Psychology*, 48, no. 2, 1936: 353-355. doi:10.2307/ 1415758.
[15] Ibid.

Schneider, Bowen, Ehrhart, and Holcombe state that Lewin's work on
social climate offered the first definition of organizational climate and its
influence on people.[16] Prior to Lewin, the relationship between the work
environment and employees was dismissed as irrelevant primarily because
there was no definition of the workplace or organizational climate. Lewin
changed that.

*Organizational climate is a Gestalt that is based on perceived patterns in the
specific experiences and behaviors of people in organizations. The sense
people make of the patterns of experiences and behaviors they have, or other
parties to the situation have, constitutes the climate of the situation.* [17]

People move each day from one climate to another. When we leave home
for work or at work from one department to another we are leaving one
climate and entering another one. Climate is so pervasive to be ubiquitous;
it's everywhere. The climate at work, school, playgrounds, restaurants, places
of worship, and other places constantly interact with our personalities,
beliefs, fears, expectations, and physical and mental health and affects our
lives in powerful ways.

So much of the importance of workplace climate is linked to human
motivation and the elements that motivate people. Motivation is what causes
people to act. It is the process that moves people to meet their needs, react to
challenges, respond to fear, and drives them to engage with others or a task or
become detached [see the chapter on motivation]. The field of organizational
psychology has for many years addressed the culture of the workplace, and
its dynamic effect on employee morale, productivity, and retention. Many of
the business turnaround models and strategies and the stories of these
successful efforts have and continue to focus on changing or improving the
workplace culture and climate, which in turn affects the behavior and
productivity of employees and others that interact with the climate.

Thompson and Luthans offer seven characteristics of culture and climate
in the workplace.[18]

[16] Benjamin Schneider, David E. Bowen, Mark G. Ehrhart, and Karen M. Holcombe,
"The Climate for Service: Evolution of a Construct," in *Handbook of Organizational
Culture and Climate,* eds. Neal M. Ashkanasy, Celeste P.M. Wilderom, and Mark F.
Peterson (Thousand Oaks: Sage Publications, 2000).
[17] Ibid.
[18] K.R. Thompson and F. Luthans, "Organizational Culture: A Behavioral
Perspective," in B. Schneider (Ed.), *Organizational Climate and Culture* (San
Francisco: Jossey-Bass, 1990).

1. *Culture equals behavior.*
2. *Culture is learned.*
3. *Culture is learned through interaction.*
4. *Subcultures form through rewards.*
5. *People shape the culture.*
6. *Culture is negotiated.*
7. *Culture is difficult to change.*

According to Thompson and Luthans, people in the workplace learn and adopt behavior that they are exposed to on a regular basis – *negative* or *positive*. How employees interact with each other is often determined by how the supervisors interact with the employees, and that interaction has the "subordinate effect"–where behavior and attitude (negative or positive) is pushed out through the ranks of the organization, creating a workplace climate that results in comradeship and mutual support in the organization or has a deleterious impact employees and eventually the organization. The negative impact on employees can be the genesis of subcultures.

Subcultures

Subcultures are present in every organization. They can be productive or destructive. According to Sackman,

> *Subcultures form when a group of people within an organization share a situation, problem, or experience that is unique to them. Areas of differentiation that can cause subcultures to form in organizations include geographical separation, departmental designations, tenure, and identity.*[19]

Organizational psychology models offer an explanation of how subcultures are created in organizations. All individuals have needs and some of the basic needs are belonging, interacting, and receiving feedback from others. If a person does not feel like he belongs and only interacts with a small number of colleagues or friends, and there is always either no feedback or negative feedback from supervisors or other colleagues, the person feels driven to find a group of like individuals. Then a subculture is born. These subcultures can over time undermine the strength of the organization if the collective attitude of the subculture becomes anti-organization. Another way of explaining this is to understand the relationship of culture and climate:

---

[19] S.A. Sackman, "Cultures and Subcultures: An Analysis of Organizational Knowledge," *Administrative Science Quarterly*, 37 (1), March 1992.

culture is the behavior of people in the organization and climate is why they behave that way. This applies to any type of organization or institution.

Reciprocal Determinism

Many of the organizational psychology components are reflective of Albert Bandura's work in social psychology. Bandura developed the *Triadic Responsibility Model* that triangulated overt behavior, personal factors, and the environment.[20] The environment component of the triad includes the physical surroundings of the individual that stimulates, stifles, or otherwise influences the behavior and attitude of individuals. Bandura's theory has been referred to as *reciprocal determinism*.[21] Lee describes the interaction of the triad components:

> *Reciprocal determinism suggests that individuals function because of a dynamic and reciprocal interaction among their behavior, environment, and personal characteristics. Personal characteristics include one's thoughts, emotions, expectations, beliefs, goals, and so forth. Behavior is conceptualized as a person's skills and actions. Lastly, the environment is a person's social and physical surroundings. All three systems interact with one another; therefore, a change in one will influence the others as well. Reciprocal determinism indicates that people do have a say in their future, because of reciprocal interactions.* [22]

Reciprocal interactions suggest that altering a person's environment can trigger significant changes in his personal characteristics and behavior.

According to Jeff Blair, based on his work on workplace climate, an organization's human resources department (HRD) must take on the role of a "*strategic climate partner*." They should assist line managers to create positive workplace climates to attract and retain employees.[23] To do this, HRD must help line managers understand three important points.[24]

> *1. There is a correlation between a negative or inconsistent climate and employees' abilities to do their jobs effectively.*

[20] Ibid.
[21] Ibid.
[22] Steven W. Lee, *Encyclopedia of School Psychology* (Thousand Oaks: SAGE Publications, Inc., 2005).
[23] Jeff Blair, "A Positive Work Climate," *TLNT*, March 23, 2012.
[24] Ibid.

2. *Managers should be trained to recognize warning signs or concerns related to changes in an employee's behaviors or attitudes that can negatively affect the climate and the productivity of employees around the person.*
3. *Managers must be capable of recognizing factors that can alter the environment in positive or negative ways.*

Workplace climate is the health and atmosphere of the workplace. Just as atmospheric conditions can affect daily activities, workplace climate can impact behavior at work. A positive workplace climate can improve the employee's work habits and a negative workplace climate can impede good work habits. A positive workplace climate leads to and sustains staff motivation, higher performance, safety, and employee retention. When people work in a positive workplace climate, they seek to produce results and they interact effectively and efficiently with their colleagues. A study of several corporations found that a positive workplace climate accounted for almost 33 percent of profits, efficiency, and revenue growth.[25]

In a study of 2,500 organizational units in 24 organizations, the importance of a positive workplace climate exceeded the effects of pay and benefits.[26] The study also found that the manager working closest to the employees had the most direct impact on the workplace climate for the employees.[27] These findings point out the importance of workplace climate. If top leaders stress the importance of workplace climate then managers throughout the organization are more likely to also focus on a positive workplace climate.

Research conducted and reported by *Management Sciences for Health* found several important factors to remember about positively influencing workplace climate.[28] These factors are instrumental when evaluating and developing workplace climate strategies.

The following provides details about each factor.

---

[25] Heather K. Laschinger, Joan Finegan, and Judith Shamian. "The Impact of Workplace Empowerment, Organizational Trust on Staff Nurses' Work Satisfaction and Organizational Commitment." *Health Care Management Review* 26 (3) 2001.
[26] Daniel Goleman, "Leadership That Gets Results." *Harvard Business Review*, March/April 2000.
[27] Marcus Buckingham and Curt Coffman, *First Break All the Rules: What the World's Greatest Managers Do Differently*, (New York: Simon and Schuster, 1999).
[28] John Donnelly, "Managers Who Lead," *Management Sciences for Health*, Cambridge Press, 2005.

Get to know the staff better: Leaders at every level of the organization
need to take the time to learn more about employees. This benefits
communications and is an early detection of morale or other
problems.

Focus on clarifying expectations and identifying challenges: Employees
work in a state of anxiety if their immediate supervisor has not
established expectations and is not cognizant of employees'
challenges.

**Align and mobilize the entire team around shared goals and
aspirations:** Leaders need to focus on a common and shared agenda
for all employees to create a sense of teamwork. Shared goals and
aspirations build stronger teams.

*Mobilize individuals by addressing their needs for power, affiliation, or
achievement:* All employees have needs that are basic to their attitude
in the workplace. Some are motivated by recognition while others
strive on increasing levels of responsibility and multiple opportunities
of affiliation with other employees.

**Inspire team members by recognizing their accomplishments and
modeling the kind of behavior you seek in others:** The leader must
always recognize that employees are watching and learning, which
means many of them will emulate the behavior and attitude of leaders
while at the same time looking for feedback and recognition for a job
well done or constructive criticism.

The same research also found that an organization can improve workplace
climate when other functions and practices invite participation, such as
planning regular meetings to exchange information on progress, shared
learning, effective management experiences, and success. When colleagues
share information on a regular basis, it promotes work efficiency and
information flow, and it advocates implementing activities that move
employees toward shared goals, monitored progress, and using mistakes as
sources for learning.[29]

An expert at improving workplace climate, Phil LaDuke, found several
strategies can positively influence workplace climate and safety.[30]

---

[29] Ibid.
[30] Phil LaDuke, "Six Ways to Improve Workplace Safety Without Going Broke,"
Entrepreneur, (June 16, 2014).

1. **Hire smarter:** *When work expands, some leader might be tempted to make a quick hire. But they would be wise to consider the risk associated with a quick hire, which is more likely to be someone who could disrupt workplace climate. Instead, leaders should carefully screen candidates to ensure that they have the skills and experience it takes to be successful even if it takes extra time.*

2. **Continue to train the staff:** *Even highly skilled and experienced workers should and need to be given instructions on how to meet the expectations of the job and how they are expected to interact with colleagues. If certain techniques make doing a job more efficient and safer and there are workplace guidelines for behavior that enhance collegiality these need to be shared with all employees. Counting on common sense to keep workers safe and in a positive frame of mind is a recipe for disaster. Common sense isn't always common practice.*

3. **Demand safe work practices:** *Begin by believing there is always time to do things safely and it is never acceptable to work unsafely, cut corners, or take workplace climate for granted. Then practice what is valued. If for example, leaders choose productivity over safety, then the wrong message is being reinforced with employees. Employees need to share the organization's vision of a safe and positive workplace climate and they should be engaged and active in making that happen. Employees will support the organization's vision, goals, and expectations for workplace climate only if they believe they are sincere and important to the organization.*

4. **Provide appropriate and adequate tools and equipment:** *Leaders and managers at all levels cannot expect employees to feel valued if their work resources are not sufficient to do the work effectively. The quality of workplace equipment is instrumental to productivity, safety, and a positive work climate. There is a very strong human drive toward expediency and some workers may take short-cuts that could compromise the safety of the workplace or disrupt the workplace climate in various ways if these points and efforts are not made clear.*

5. **Demonstrate that the organization values worker safety:** *Leaders should be cautious about inadvertently fostering a culture that devalues employee relationships, trust, integrity, and safety. Leaders should recognize employees who offer suggestions for working efficiently and safely in addition to those that perform at the highest levels and who create conditions that improve efficiencies without sacrificing workplace climate and safety.*

6. **Look for ways to improve safety.** *Just as it is desirable to find work methods to achieve faster results at less cost, it is also imperative to seek ways to eliminate risk to employees, such as overwork, too much stress, unsafe conditions, etc. Leaders should spend time with workers*

brainstorming for their ideas and soliciting their concerns about safety and workplace climate.

Building and striving to maintain a positive workplace climate is a leadership and board function that will benefit the organization, its employees, and its clients.

Chapter Eight Key Words and Concepts

Safety
Workplace Climate
Bullying
Security Essentials
Safety Planning
Staff Safety Training
Crisis Management Plan
Labor Standards
Surveys of Workplace Safety
Hazmat Preparedness
Workplace Violence
Occupational Health and Safety Administration
Federal Emergency Management Agency
Workplace Safety Plans
Survey Results on Bullying
Financial Cost of Bullying in the Workplace
Social Isolation
University of Virginia Incident
Gestalt
Field Theory
B=f (P and E)
Social Climate
Organizational Psychology
Workplace Culture
Subordinate Effect
Workplace Subcultures
Triadic Responsibility Model
Reciprocal Determinism
Strategic Climate Partner
Steps to Improve Workplace Climate

Chapter Eight Discussion Items

List five of the most serious threats to safety in the workplace and what can be done to address the threats.

Describe bullying in the workplace and provide an example of how bullying impacts organizational behavior.

What are the basic elements of Crisis Management Planning?

What should be included in Hazmat Preparedness that is often overlooked by organizations?

How should Workplace Safety Plans be developed and how should the details be shared with employees?

How does Field Theory apply to workplace climate, safety, and security?

How and why do Workplace Subcultures develop? What impact can Workplace Subcultures have on the workplace?

How can the Triadic Responsibility Model apply to the workplace? Name three of the primary Steps to Improve Workplace Climate.

Chapter Eight Lessons Learned

Workplace conditions can in many ways negatively impact employee productivity, retention, and recruitment.

One of the basic and most essential infrastructure elements is a safe and healthy working environment.

Safety in every type of organization has to be the top priority.

The researchers found that over eight of ten workers (85 percent) rate workplace safety first in importance among labor standards.

Leadership at all levels, especially top leadership, in every organization must understand how seemingly unrelated series of events and decisions may compromise workplace safety and security.

It is becoming more obvious that behavior like bullying develops in a workplace where the workplace climate is negative.

Leaders at all levels must develop a plan to prevent and discourage bullying and intervene when bullying occurs.

Leaders must understand the relationship between leadership, conditions for productivity and how these link to workplace climate and safety.

Organizations that understand the dynamic nature of workplace climate find that respect for the climate through actions such as safety awareness and planning create conditions for success, transitions, and change in the workplace.

The organization can improve workplace climate when other functions and practices invite participation, such as planning regular meetings to exchange information on progress, shared learning, effective management experiences, and success.

Counting on common sense to keep workers safe and in a positive frame of mind is a recipe for disaster. Calling on experts to help develop a safe workplace climate is essential.

CHAPTER NINE

STRATEGIC PLANNING THAT MATTERS

"Strategic planning is a disciplined effort to produce fundamental decisions and actions...."

-J. Bryson[1]

Determinant: Strategic planning can be a risky undertaking because it involves the past, present, and future. Strategic planning cannot ignore the past but it cannot dwell on the past or try to correct past mistakes or replicate past successes. Strategic planning cannot ignore the present because it is the organization's current reality and plans for the future may depend on the present. Strategic planning to many leaders is mostly about the future, which includes the risks associated with predicting the future. Strategic plans seldom *control* the effects of the future but they can *manage* the effects if they are carefully and thoughtfully crafted. Even so, it is challenging to accurately anticipate future obstacles. Therein lie the challenges with strategic planning. How should organizations develop strategic plans? Should a strategic plan be an operational plan, a theoretical plan that illustrates what is important to the organization, a futuristic plan that anticipates responses to trajectories, a combination of these, or another type of strategic plan? Some organizations develop a strategic plan only in name as a perfunctory duty with no real intentions of using the strategic plan in any meaningful way. Also, organizations should remember two elements of strategic planning that are often overlooked: the decision-making process and change theory.

Strategic Planning and Change Theory

Anticipating and managing change are major features of strategic planning. Therefore, strategic planners should consider and study *change theory* before and during the development of a strategic plan.

---

[1] J. Bryson, *Strategic Planning for Public and Nonprofit Organizations: A Guide to Strengthening and Sustaining Organizational Achievement* (3rd ed.), (Jossey-Bass 2004).

According to the Center for Theory of Change,

> *The Theory of Change is essentially a comprehensive description and illustration of how and why a desired change is expected to happen in a particular context. It is focused in particular on mapping out or filling in what has been described as the 'missing middle' between what a program or change initiative does (its activities or interventions) and how these lead to desired goals being achieved.*[2]

Some change theory models are based on *inventories of thought* that are unique to specific organizations while others are so theoretical they offer very little practical application for most organizations.

There are change theories that can be applied effectively in any type of organization.

Theory U

A change theory that offers a sound theoretical base and that also provides practical applications that can be useful in the formulation of a strategic plan is *Theory U*,[3] which was developed by Otto Scharmer at the Massachusetts Institute of Technology. The theory is based on the interactions within a social system that function from *awareness, attention*, or *consciousness* at a *central source*. When leaders within an organization move closer to the central source they develop a new awareness of what is possible by shedding old ways of thinking. This is referred to as *"presencing."*

> *Presencing carries with it ideas for meeting challenges and for bringing into being an otherwise impossible or unlikely future. Theory U shows how that capacity for presencing can be developed.*[4]

The Theory U process is a journey focusing on several leadership capacities that illustrate the journey *from* and *to* a change in thinking that can impact strategic planning.[5]

---

[2] Center for Theory of Change, 2016, *www.theoryofchange.org.*
[3] C. Otto Scharmer, *Theory U: Leading from the Future as it Emerges 2nd Edition*, (Berrett-Koehler Publishers, 2016).
[4] Ibid.
[5] Ibid.

1. *Holding the space of listening*: *The foundational capacity of the U is listening-listening to others, listening to oneself, and listening to what emerges from the collective others. Effective listening requires the creation of open space in which others can contribute to the whole.* This encourages participation and "ownership" of the change and thought processes.

2. *Observing*: *The capacity to suspend the voice of judgment is key to moving from projection to true observation. This becomes important as leaders learn to apply what they have heard.*

3. *Sensing*: *The preparation for the experience...requires the tuning of three instruments: the open mind, the open heart, and the open will. This opening process is not passive but an active sensing together as a group. While an open heart allows people to see a situation from the whole, the open will enables people to begin to act from the emerging whole. A strategic plan that begins with the "whole" in mind will reflect on the past, evaluate the present, and plan for the future in ways that link all three in a constructive and far-reaching manner.*

4. *Crystalizing*: *When a small group of key persons commits itself to the purpose and outcomes of a project, the power of their intention creates an energy field that attracts people, opportunities, and resources that make things happen. This core group functions as a vehicle for the whole to manifest. It also provides an on-going self-appraisal capability that prevents the strategic plan from bogging down or becoming perfunctory.*

5. *Prototyping*: *Theory U requires the strategic planning group to open up and deal with the resistance of thought, emotion, and will and requires the integration of thinking, feeling, and will in the context of practical applications and learning by doing. Stereotypical thinking is replaced with innovative prototypical thinking which involves creating something new from the old and encourages innovative thinking such as "lateral thinking"[6] (more in the next section on lateral thinking).*

6. *Performing*: *Organizations need to perform at the macro level: they need to convene the right sets of players (frontline people who are connected through the same value chain) and to engage a social technology that allows a multi-stakeholder gathering to shift from debating to co-creating the new. By seeking input from all segments of the organization's structure, the strategic plan truly represents the entire organization, shares in innovative thought, and therefore is more likely to be implemented and evaluated.*

---

[6] Edward DeBono, *Lateral Thinking: Creativity Step by Step*, (Harper, 2015).

Scharmer states that Theory U "encourages you to step into the emerging future."[7]

Lateral Thinking

Stepping into the emerging future requires a different way of thinking, which is what *lateral thinking* encourages. In 1967, Edward DeBono created the term and the concept of lateral thinking, which focuses on creative ways of thinking that transcend and replace traditional thinking. DeBono refers to traditional thinking as "vertical logic"–digging the same hole deeper. Lateral thinking, in effect, means digging the hole in a different place. Lateral thinking includes four types of "new" thinking.[8]

1. *Idea-generating thinking that disrupts or replaces typical thinking patterns that are based on the status quo.*
2. *Broaden thinking is intended to widen the search for new ideas and concepts.*
3. *Harvest thinking is intended to ensure that the process of generating new ideas is valued and encouraged by the organization.*
4. *Treatment thinking takes into consideration the reality of the present regarding constraints, resources, and support mechanisms, both real and possible.*

The value of lateral thinking during the conceptual stage of strategic planning is the evolution of innovation and the possibility of discovering completely new ways of approaching and resolving problems and challenges while embracing the possibilities of the future.

Strategic Planning Process

The origin of contemporary strategic planning dates back to the line of demarcation around 1930 when several organizations made a shift from daily operations to daily operations *with* strategic planning. Many organizations began to depend on professional managers to lead the organizations instead of the owner/operator. The professional manager had an operations-

---

[7] O. Gunnlaugson and C. Otto Scharmer, "Perspectives on Theory U: Insights from the Field," In *Presencing Theory U* by O. Gunnlaugson, C. Baron, and M Cayer, (IGI Global Press, 2013).

[8] Edward de Bono, *Serious Creativity: How to Be Creative under Pressure and Turn Ideas into Action*, (Random House, 2015).

management orientation that viewed long-range planning as a tool. As the complexities of managing organizations grew exponentially with the demands on budgets and outcomes, strategic planning became essential.

A strategic plan identifies and aligns organizational goals to accomplish specific outcomes that serve the purposes of the organization. A leading authority on strategic planning described it as a "disciplined effort."

> *Strategic planning is a disciplined effort to produce fundamental decisions and actions that shape and guide what an organization is, what it does, and why it does it.* [9]

The level of "discipline" varies between and among organizations. Many leaders and boards realize that the credibility, functionality, efficiency, and future of their organization depends strongly on the strength, accuracy, and thoroughness of the strategic plan. Yet, there are organizations that either lack the skills necessary to develop an effective strategic plan or lack the desire to do so because of status quo thinking. Other organizations create a strategic plan with easy targets and goals set in present-day terms so that "success" of the plan is almost guaranteed. Roger Martin calls this type of strategic planning *"The Big Lie."* [10]

> *The natural reaction is to make the challenge less daunting by turning it into a problem that can be solved with tried and tested tools. That nearly always means spending weeks or even months preparing a comprehensive strategic plan for how the company will invest in existing and new assets and capabilities in order to achieve a target—an increased share of the market, say, or a share in some new one. The plan is typically supported with detailed spreadsheets that project costs and revenue quite far into the future. By the end of the process, everyone feels a lot less scared. This is a truly terrible way to make a strategy. It may be an excellent way to cope with a fear of the unknown, but fear and discomfort are an essential part of strategy making. In fact, if you are entirely comfortable with your strategy, there's a strong chance it isn't very good.* [11]

---

[9] J. Bryson, *Strategic Planning for Public and Nonprofit Organi-zations: A Guide to Strengthening and Sustaining Organizational Achievement* (3rd ed.), (Jossey-Bass 2004).

[10] Roger Martin, "The Big Lie of Strategic Planning," *Harvard Business Review*, February 2014.

[11] Ibid.

Martin said the purpose of a strategic plan is not to reduce risks but to increase the chances for success in the face of challenges. He makes a point that applies to many strategic plans. They are often *defensive plans* instead of *offensive plans.* Defensive plans rely on the past and primarily work from the philosophy that everything has to be protected. Status quo is coveted. By contrast, offensive plans are based on a philosophy that change and challenge are the norm and status quo thinking and planning will only weaken the organization. Offensive plans embrace the concepts of change theory and lateral thinking and planning.

Case Study #1

The case study of Kodak illustrates both the power and the failure of strategic planning.[12] In 1880, George Eastman, a photographer, tried different types of paper to use in his small photography developing business. He then found that film was longer lasting than paper and he believed that if he could find a way to use film it would become the wave of the future. Development film was the key element in producing quality photographs that would not fade over time. The plates for the rollers that held the film was equally important. The development of the plates progressed with the help of another photographic expert, William Walker, who joined with Eastman to further advance Eastman's photography plates. Then, in 1887, Hannibal Goodwin, working on his own in his cramped lab at home created a transparent nitrocellulose film base. Even with the combined genius of Eastman, Walker, and Goodwin something was missing in the process. In 1888, another independent photographer, Emile Reynaud, found the secret; he put perforations into nitrocellulose film. A year later, Eastman put the inventions together and created the first mass-produced rolls of transparent photographic film. From that point, he patented his invention and the industry of photography took a giant leap forward. Eastman and his business partner, Henry Strong, chose not to use their names for the company. He thought that a short and pithy name would be easier to name brand and easier for the public to remember. For no discernable reason other than for product recognition, he made up the name "Kodak" in 1889. He later explained: "A

---

[12] Jasper Rees, "The End of our Kodak Moment". *The Telegraph*, January 20, 2012; Douglas Collins, *The Story of Kodak*, (Harry Abrams, 1990); Paul Synder, *Is This Something George Eastman Would Have Done? The Decline and Fall of the Eastman Kodak Company*, (Independent Publishing, 2013); Chunka Mui, "How Kodak Failed," *Forbes*, January 19, 2012.

trademark should be short."[13] Kodak's main office was in Rochester, New York. During most of the 20th century, Kodak dominated the photographic film industry. From 1900 to 1977, Kodak held over 90 percent of film sales and over 80 percent of cameras sales in the United States. The company's strategic plans each year for decades were energetic, creative, innovative, and filled with risks because Eastman knew that nothing would remain the same and, therefore, only by understanding risk was the company nimble enough to manage risk. It made leaps toward the future that proved beneficial to the company. Eastman took risks because he believed that technology would always change.

After Eastman retired from Kodak and later passed away, the leadership insight of the company and the strategic plan became embedded in the past, despite evidence that the future of the company could be at risk if it did not embrace change and prepare for change by developing a bold strategic plan using lateral thinking. The first sign of significant change in the technology came from within Kodak when its own lab technicians created the world's first digital camera in the late 1970s. Technicians, managers, and others within Kodak saw the future in the digital camera. They saw it as a challenge filled with possibilities that could allow Kodak to take the lead in new technologies but the leaders of the company only saw a threat to its film monopoly. The strategic plan, therefore, did not include the shift from film to digital. The leaders of Kodak told its lab technicians to keep their discovery a secret. This type of strategic planning focusing on reducing risks instead of seeking advances was contrary to the company's founder, George Eastman. Twice in his tenure as the company's leader, he developed a strategic plan based on changes in the industry. He abandoned the dry plate money maker and shifted to film and later he embraced color film when others said that he was foolish to build the company's strategic plan around a costly and less stable product. But Eastman used the strategic planning process as the vehicle for taking the company around the next turn in the road. It was not always clear what was around the bend, but he knew that staying in place would not work either. Kodak's contemporary leaders lacked the founder's insight and philosophy of strategic planning and lateral thinking.

When Fuji Film became the first threat to Kodak's monopoly of the film industry, Kodak did not respond strategically and roll out its digital camera which would set back Fuji Film; instead, the company's strategic plan was to file several lawsuits against Fuji. In the meantime, the secret was out because

---

[13] Brian Cole, *The First Hundred Years: Kodak Cameras*, (Steyning Photo Books, 2003).

other labs had prototypes of digital cameras. Kodak finally accepted the fact that its film prowess was coming to an end, so the company developed a strategic plan that over the next *ten years*, beginning in the 1990s the company would "slowly" advance toward digital cameras. In reality, the company each year thereafter dusted off the same strategic plan and made no real effort to move the company into the digital future. It was very difficult for the company to give up its bread and butter product for a technology that did not need film. During that ten-year strategic plan timeline, the digital world flew past Kodak and left the once leading and proud company on the brink of bankruptcy. To ward off bankruptcy, Kodak sold off many of its patents to other companies. However, it was too late to salvage years of bad strategic plans. Kodak filed for bankruptcy in January 2012. The famous "Kodak Moment" died.

Author Chunka Mui said that the lessons learned about strategic planning from Kodak's downfall include four major elements.[14]

1. *Top management must embrace a mindset that is open to change and the possibility of significant change. Otherwise, the decision-making process becomes distorted which then makes the strategic plan flawed.*

2. *The strategic plan must reflect the willingness to think and act holistically. Some organizations specialize too much and focus only on the specialization at the expense of a holistic and more open view of the present and future trends. Kodak's leaders after the 1980s failed to understand that they were in the technology business, not the film business.*

3. *Adapt the strategic plan to changing conditions. An organization that is unwilling to change its current practices and plan, even though they may be successful, may lose the chance to adopt an "anticipate and lead" strategic plan that could prepare the organization to both continue its success and expand or sustain success through modifications that anticipate changes. It is possible to hold the present in one hand while reaching for the future with the other hand.*

4. *Agile and successful organizations use multiple methods of interactive decision-making. Successful organizations employ a wide set of data input, data retrieval, data analysis, and data interpretation methods that aid strategic planning. The data do not drive all elements of the strategic plan but data are an invaluable decision-making aid.*

There are several reasons why strategic planning fails, like the failures found in Kodak's history. According to an article in *Forbes,* there are ten

---

[14] Chunka Mui, "How Kodak Failed," *Forbes*, January 19, 2012.

major reasons why strategic plans fail: (1) having a plan for plans sake only; (2) not understanding the environment or focusing on results; (3) only partially committed to the plan; (4) not having the right people involved; (5) writing the plan and putting it on a shelf; (6) unwillingness or inability to change; (7) having the wrong people in leadership positions; (8) ignoring reality, facts, and assumptions about conditions that impact the organization; (9) no accountability or follow-through; and (10) unrealistic goals or lack of focus and resources.[15]

Arguably, the most critical negative determinant of strategic planning is the attitude by leadership and the board that the organization is invincible and is agile and smart enough to change as necessary. Consequently, the strategic plan is not very strategic. It focuses more on maintaining the present status of the organization.

If an organization does not believe in its own vulnerability, its leaders should consider the number of business failures each year; the number of non-profits that close each year; and the number of *Fortune 500* companies that no longer exist. Even the oldest company in the world failed because it did not adapt to changes. Kongo Gumi Co., Ltd. in Japan closed its doors in 2006 after being in business for over 1,500 years.[16]

Case Study #2

Tutorspree started in 2011 out of a startup incubator and was targeted early as a new and exciting way to offer tutoring support online by linking parents with trustworthy and talented tutors for their children. By 2013, over 7,000 tutors signed up on the Tutorspree platform and the company had raised almost two million dollars to expand the company. The strategic plan was meticulously developed each year based on the organization's original model. Even though the organization was technology dependent, its strategic plan focused more on the quality and availability of tutors to work with children as their clients than on the technology. The strategic plan included methods and materials to maintain a high profile among families with school-aged children. A quality control component and a marketing strategy were added to the strategic plan. However, the strategic plan focused only what was working and it did not address what was not working primarily because the view of top management was that every aspect of the organization was

---

[15] Aileron, "10 Reasons Why Strategic Plans Fail," *Forbes*, November 30, 2011.
[16] Chosunilbo, "End of the Road for World's Oldest Firm," *Digital Chosunilbo*, English Edition, December 15, 2005.

effective. During its second year of operations, Tutorspree raised significant capital from large and stable investment companies including Sequoia Capital and Lerer Ventures. The strategic plan included a modest goal to reasonably scale the growth of the organization. Then a strategic planning failure of catastrophic proportions occurred. In March of 2013, Google changed its algorithm and Tutorspree found their traffic reduced by 80 percent overnight. Tutorspree had failed to consider in its strategic plan that the organization's total dependence on Search Engine Optimization (SEO) needed to be phased into other options to reduce the organization's exposure to rapidly changing technology within SEOs. Tutorspree closed a few months later, despite 3 years of profitable operations.[17]

Even though it is not complicated to understand what went wrong at Tutorspree (see the above-referenced comments about a poorly formed strategic plan), the founder, Aaron Harris, blogged the following comments after Tutorspree shutdown.

> *Ultimately, we learned about the challenges of willing a company into existence, of building an incredible and unique team to tackle constantly shifting challenges. And finally, we learned about how to make the toughest decision of all – to shut Tutorspree down, not because it was not a business, but because we could not make it the company we wanted.*[18]

He never acknowledged the fact that the company's strategic plan was flawed because it did not include challenges and risks. Tutorspree had a good concept, solid financial backing, a growing customer base, and yet it shut down. A good strategic plan should be a reality check. A strategic should not live in the past, be based on the success of the present, and ignore or simplify the future of changes and possible risks. Tutorspree's strategic plan was The Big Lie.

Strategic Plans

The effective strategic plan will have a *mission statement* and a *vision statement* that are purposeful. The mission statement should state in clear terms and precise language the purpose and measurable objectives of the

---

[17] Alyson Shontell, "Tutorspree Shuts Down," *Business Insider*, September 8, 2013; Kristen Winkler, "Lessons from the Tutorspree Shutdown," *EduKWest,* September 15, 2013.
[18] Aaron Harris, *Tutorspree Blog*, September 2013.

organization. The vision statement describes the purpose of the organization as well as its values. It's the vision statement that directs and motivates employee behavior and attitude.

Madison Hawthorne, writing about the critically important need for effective mission and vision statements within strategic plans said,

> *Strategic planning will likely have its successes and failures. Leaders should celebrate the little successes toward meeting objectives, which are part of the mission and vision statement. The mission statement will help measure whether the strategic plan aligns with the overall goals of the agency. The vision statement helps to provide inspiration to employees. Employees who feel invested in the organizational change are more likely to stay motivated and have higher levels of productivity.*[19]

Implementing the Strategic Plan

Implementation of a strategic plan can be more difficult than it first appears. Organizational leaders think incorrectly that the strategic work is done when the strategic plan is finalized. A strategic plan has no value unless it can be put into action. In fact, the implementation of a strategic plan should be part of the strategic plan. How will the strategic plan be applied within the organization? That is a critical question for leaders and boards.

How a strategic plan is applied varies among organizations but there are critical steps that universally apply to the implementation of the plan, beginning with a critical appraisal of the strategic plan to make sure leaders within the organization understand it. If they do not, they cannot implement it. During the critical review, leaders should look for implementation problems, such as the availability of the resources presently available or their projected availability. That leads to a critically important appraisal of the strategic plan–is the implementation of the plan realistic? Is the implementation cost within reason and is the timeline for implementation workable and realistic? Does the organization have the employee resources to adequately implement the plan? Is there technical infrastructure to appropriately and fully evaluate the implementation of the strategic plan to learn if it is effective? Does the strategic plan have a feedback mechanism to gather implementation information? If the answers are negative to these

---

[19] Madison Hawthorne, "The Importance of Mission and Vision Statements in Strategic Plans," *Chron* – (Hearst Newspapers, LLC.), 2017.

questions, then a more in-depth review of the strategic plan is essential. Otherwise, there will be a Kodak Moment and a Tutorspree result.

Antidotes

Some small organizations can function effectively without a strategic plan and some survive despite an ineffective, poorly developed strategic plan. However, those organizations seldom thrive and overtime they most likely will not survive.

There are a plethora of models and elements that can shape strategic planning. The type of strategic plan developed depends on the type and nature of the organization and the timeframe for implementation. According to Paul Mastrodonato, President of Nonprofit Works, *"timing and scope"* are critically important to a strategic plan.

> *Some plans are scoped to one year, many to three years, and some to five to ten years into the future. Some plans include only top-level information and no action plans. Some plans are five to eight pages long, while others can be considerably longer. Quite often, an organization already knows much of what will go into a strategic plan. However, development of the strategic plan greatly helps to clarify the organization's plans and ensure that key leaders are all on the same script. More important than the strategic plan document is the actual strategic planning process.* [20]

There are many types of strategic plan templates with a wide variety of scope and sequence elements; however, the most useful and effective strategic plans have five basic elements.

1. ***Create a mission statement.*** *A mission statement describes why the organization exists, i.e., identifies its basic purpose. The statement should address both the types of communities or audience that the organization serves, and the services and products it will provide. The top-level management will generally develop the mission statement. The statement should change somewhat over the years depending on how the organization is adapting to risks and challenges within and outside of the organization.* [21]

---

[20] Paul Mastrodnato, "Developing a Strategic Plan for Your Organization," *National Association of Product Producers Annual Conference*, May 2005.
[21] "Strategic Planning Models," The NCJA Center for Justice Planning, 2016:http://www.ncjp.org/program-management/strategic-planning-models.

2. *Select the organization's intermediate goals.* *Goals are general statements about what needs to be accomplished to meet the purpose or mission and addresses current issues while anticipating future challenges.[22]*

3. *Identify approaches or strategies to reach each goal. Strategies are often what change most as the organization eventually conducts more robust strategic planning, particularly as external and internal environments are examined more closely to measure the degree of risk and change and the impact on the organization.*

4. *Identify action plans to implement each strategy. Action plans should list the steps that each major function (for example, a department) must take to ensure that it is effectively implementing a strategy. Objectives should be clear enough to be assessed if they have been met or not.*

5. *Monitor and update the plan. Strategic planners regularly monitor progress towards goals and whether action plans were accurately developed and are being implemented. Perhaps the most important indicator of success is positive feedback from stakeholders and clients while negative feedback provides information for strategic planners to make adjustments.*

Carter McNamara suggests that an *issues-based strategic plan* may be better suited for organizations that have limited resources, major challenges and limited success in the past with strategic planning. He said that using conventional strategic planning in these organizations is

> *...a bit like focusing on the vision of running a marathon and on deciding the detailed route and milestones-while concurrently having heart problems, bad feet, and no running clothes.[23]*

The issues-based strategic plan model includes the following phases:

1. *Identify 5-7 of the most important current issues facing the organization now. These are issues that must be addressed because they threaten the well-being and survival of the organization. It is best to put the 5-7 issues in priority order and create an issued-based strategy based on the level of significance.*

2. *Suggest action plans to address each issue over the next 6-12 months. The focus is on "action plans," not theoretical-based strategic plans. Once the priority list is established, along with a rationale for each, the*

---

[22] Ibid.

[23] Carter McNamara, "Basic Overview of Strategic Planning Models," Management Library, © Copyright Authenticity Consulting, LLC.

> *organization must develop a plan with a timeline for each issue or develop a plan that addresses more than one issue as long as the plan does not overwhelm the employees. During difficult times, employees may need to be asked to work smarter and the organization will need to improve the resources that are available to employees and improve training.*
> 3. *Include issued-based information in the strategic plan. As the issues are addressed categorically and solutions are successful, the formation of a strategic plan can begin. Elements of the issues-based plan should be included in the first phase of the more traditional strategic plan.*

Following the successful implementation of an issues-based strategic plan and when the issues related to resources and other problems have been addressed, the organization is better prepared to develop and implement a conventional strategic plan. It is a critical mistake for leaders of a struggling organization to assume that major and potentially catastrophic pressing issues can be addressed through the development of a conventional strategic plan. Some organizations that are in dire straits must adapt a more aggressive action plan to survive. According to McNamara,

> *Many people might assert that issues-based planning is internal development planning, rather than strategic planning. Others would argue that the model is very strategic because it positions the organization for much more successful outward-looking and longer term planning later on.[24]*

Steve Tobak, an expert on strategic planning, offers information on which elements are most important when organizations develop a strategic plan.[25] He includes basic elements at the operational level that include a realistic and pragmatic way of developing an effective strategic plan.

Tobak's components may seem too simplistic to be useful to a strategic planning team, but upon a closer examination of his descriptions, it becomes apparent that the matrix can be very useful and relevant. More importantly, he uses terms and phrases that all employees can relate to and understand, which enhances the organization's efforts to explain the strategic planning process.

---

[24] Ibid.
[25] Steve Tobak, "Ten Rules for Effective Strategic Planning," *CBS MoneyWatch*, April 23, 2009.

The definition: *Strategic planning is any process meant to determine a company's future direction, including its key goals, strategies for achieving the goals, and a business plan.*

Executive owner and facilitator: *Organizations need a member of the executive staff to own the process from start to finish, plus an objective facilitator from outside the company with expertise in this sort of thing.*

The team: *The strategic planning team must be committed to participating in the entire process from start to finish. There can be additions; however, bigger equals more ideas but harder to manage.*

Rules of engagement: *The facilitator or CEO sets ground rules, i.e. attack the problem, not the person; be quiet unless you have something material to add; don't beat issues to death; silence is unacceptable; no cell phones, iPads, etc.*

The problem and process: *Develop a strategic plan for a reason. Agree on the problem statement and objectives of the process. You can also give it a name if that will help galvanize everyone.*

Situation analysis: *An analysis of conditions must be honest and objective with no sugarcoating. If you don't know where you stand and you don't have data to illustrate success or failure, the entire process is a waste of incredibly valuable time for everyone on the team.*

No sacred cows: *Leaders get too close to and emotionally wrapped up in their groups, responsibilities, and programs. The team has to get beyond all the subjectivity to achieve open and honest perspective.*

Brainstorm: *Be completely open to any ideas. When they're all listed, have each person pick their top three ideas (weighted first = 3 points, second = 2 points, third = 1 point), take the top ideas as priorities.*

Coalesce: *Several meetings to present and discuss the plan and iterations are expected, including bouncing ideas and concepts of the next level of management. Sometimes asking a controlled group of outsiders to give feedback can be helpful.*

Plan and execute: *Develop a set of plans for communicating the new direction down through the organization and externally, affecting organizational and behavioral change, product development and launch, marketing, evaluation, etc.*

After the development of a strategic plan, the next step is so critical that it can mean the difference between a successful strategic plan and a failed effort. *Communicating the strategic plan* to the board, employees, and other stakeholders cannot be taken lightly or for granted.

In an article titled *Communicating Your Strategy: The Forgotten Fundamental of Strategic Planning*,[26] the authors emphasize fundamental requirements such as (1) build the communication strategy into the strategic plan and clarify objectives–identify the message that needs to be conveyed; (2) select the appropriate communications channels and methods–it may be better to have face-to-face or small group meetings to review the strategic plan instead of a formal social media or a large group presentation method; (3) package the strategic plan in the form of a message – use the language that can be understood by avoiding acronyms, slogans, or technical language, but do not underestimate the insight or intelligence of board members, employees, and others or the communications will sound condescending.

Laban and Green found that the importance of communicating the strategic plan is critical.

> *This communications plan must recognize that organizations are made up of social, communicative human beings who can achieve great things together only after they recognize that it is to their benefit to come together as a team cooperatively and communicatively.* [27]

Devising the communications methods for sharing the strategic plan is itself a good means of measuring the strategic plan. If it is difficult to capture the message of the strategic plan so that it can be described, then the plan is possibly too complicated or disconnected. If the strategic plan does not focus on key communication messages, then it is unlikely that the plan will be understood by the board, employees, and stakeholders. Even the most detailed and technical aspects of a strategic plan need to pass the communications test: *keep the message simple but deep in meaning.*

Chapter Nine Key Words and Concepts

Operations-Manager Orientation
Organizational Goals
The Big Lie
Strategic Planning

---

[26] Jack Laban and Jack Green, "Communication Your Strategic Plan: The Forgotten Fundamental of Strategic Planning," *Graziadio Business Review*, 6 (1), 2003.
[27] Ibid.

Defensive Strategic Planning and Offensive Strategic Planning
Holistic Actions
Action Plans
Interactive Decision Making
Mission Statement
Vision Statement
Implementation of Strategic Plan
Issued-Based Strategic Plan
Situational Analysis
Communicating Strategic Plan
Challenges Developing Strategic Plan
Evaluation of Strategic Plan

Chapter Nine Discussion Items

What are the purposes of Organizational Goals and how should they be developed, tracked, measured, and revised?

What is the Big Lie and what is its importance to organizational development and operations?

What is the purpose and value of Strategic Planning? What are some of the dangers of Strategic Planning?

Define and illustrate the differences between Defensive Strategic Planning and Offensive Strategic Planning.

What is the relationship between Holistic Actions and Action Plans?

What is the difference between a Mission Statement and a Vision Statement? Write an example of both.

What are some methods and best practices for implementing a Strategic Plan and Communicating a Strategic Plan?

If you were put in charge of Communicating a Strategic Plan, what innovative methods would you use to communicate the elements of the plan with employees and other stakeholders? Be as creative and innovative as possible.

Give examples of how Strategic Plans were ineffective or poorly executed. Offer your opinion about what could have been done differently.

If an organization's Communications Plan is not effective based on feedback from employees, how would you adjust the plan to make it more effective?

After reading this chapter on Strategic Planning, what would be your first step in helping an organization construct a Strategic Plan from the beginning?

As a consultant, what would be your first recommendation to an organization that has either (1) not been effective or successful or (2) has been very successful but is worried about continuing its success? Contrast how the two scenarios would influence your advice to the organization about Strategic Planning.

Chapter Nine Lessons Learned

Organizations should remember two elements of strategic planning that are often overlooked: the decision-making process and change theory.

When leaders within an organization move closer to the central source they develop a new awareness of what is possible by shedding old ways of thinking.

While an open heart allows people to see a situation from the whole, the open will enables people to begin to act from the emerging whole.

Stereotypical thinking needs to be replaced with innovative prototypical thinking which involves creating something new from the old and encourages innovative thinking.

The value of lateral thinking during the conceptual stage of strategic planning is the evolution of innovation and the possibility of discovering completely new ways of approaching and resolving problems.

Anticipating and managing change are major features of strategic planning.

The purpose of a strategic plan is not to reduce risks but to increase the chances for success in the face of challenges.

Top management must embrace a mindset that is open to change and the possibility of significant change.

The strategic plan must reflect the willingness to think and act holistically.

Adapt the strategic plan to changing conditions. An organization that is unwilling to change its current practices and plan may lose the chance to adopt successfully.

Build the communication strategy into the strategic plan and clarify objectives.

Select appropriate and effective communications channels and methods to communicate the strategic plan. Failure to do so will jeopardize implementation of the strategic plan.

CHAPTER TEN

EXTERNAL AND INTERNAL EVALUATIONS

"There are risks and costs to a program of action. But they are far less than the long-range risks and costs of comfortable inaction."
                                                                    -John F. Kennedy[1]

Determinants: A comprehensive and relevant assessment of an organization's effectiveness is critical to the success of the organization. In many circumstances, the assessment comes from an outside source, such as the Better Business Bureau, non-profit rating institutions, bond rating service organizations, accrediting associations, popular news magazines, and others. But are these organizations held accountable for how they assess the effectiveness of organizations? Does a "good score" or "negative score" mean that an organization and thus its leadership are truly efficient or inefficient? Sometimes the results come insidiously from assessments that inflate effectiveness at the expense of identifying areas of strength and weaknesses. Fully developed and comprehensive assessments can be invaluable to an organization. An organization can be hemorrhaging money, losing competent staff, losing clients, and/or losing community influence and no one knows until problems erupt that could have been dealt with much earlier and much more effectively. Sometimes assessors give scant attention to the most salient and important organizational outcomes or fail to give credit to organizations that have overcome many obstacles that are out of its control. An organization that aims for success or continued success must contemplate how to best assess its operations and not depend solely on entities that evaluate organizations based on old standards, using outdated methods, and with a narrow focus. Organizations can develop effective internal assessment methods but they should not depend exclusively on internal assessments. An organization and its leadership can be poisoned from the determinants of false success or misleading information from assessments, whether it is external or internal. The types and quality of

---

[1] John F. Kennedy, 35th President of the United States, 1961-1963. Quote retrieved from http://en.proverbia.net/cita stema.asptematica=1038.

internal and external assessments should be considered. Leaders and boards, as well as the stakeholders in organizations, should learn more about entities that rank businesses, financial organizations, public education school districts, colleges and universities, private schools, boards, and other organizations. Sometimes their methodology is dubious, unclear, inconsistent, irrelevant, redundant, and ineffective in determining how an organization can improve.

External Evaluations

Case Study #1

U.S. News and World Report's annual ranking of colleges, both public and private, is the magazine's bestselling issue each year.[2] It is a highly-anticipated report that ranks the quality of colleges and universities. Many parents and students read the magazine's "Best Colleges and High Schools" edition to make decisions about colleges based on the rankings. Colleges and universities use the rankings to recruit top students and to solicit contributions from alumni. The *U.S. News and World Report's* rankings of colleges have been an annual event for over two decades, but during that time very little if any attention was given to exactly how the magazine calculated the rankings. No one assessed the assessors.

In a 2012 news story that spread quickly across the nation, it was revealed that *U.S. News and World Report's* college rankings were based primarily on self-reported information from colleges and universities. No one at the magazine validated the accuracy of the information submitted by colleges and universities. This was discovered when a prestigious private university, Emory University near Atlanta, was found purposely exaggerating data and submitting those false reports to *U.S. News and World Report* for the annual rankings. Emory was embellishing self-reports in order to get a more favorable ranking by the magazine. And it worked because Emory was consistently ranked high on the list of colleges.

The lack of validation of data from colleges and universities was not revealed by *U.S. News and World Report*; instead, it was discovered and reported by another news media source – *The Hechinger Report*.[3] After the

---

[2] *U.S. News and World Report* "Best Colleges and High Schools:" http://www.usnews.com/education (2016).
[3] John Marcus, "Caught Cheating: Colleges Falsify Admissions Data for Higher Rankings," *The Hechinger Report*, March 20, 2013.

Emory University story became public information, six other universities admitted to falsifying the data they sent to *U.S. News and World Report*. For example, Tulane University's Graduate School of Business provided *U.S. News and World Report* false data about its number of applicants and inflated their average scores on the university's admissions tests by 35 points. Until the Emory University story was reported everyone blithely accepted this very important annual report of colleges and universities without any questions about the assessors. Leadership at the colleges and universities annually were congratulating themselves and bragging about their excellent ratings in the magazine from an "objective external assessment." How many times did a college or university miss an opportunity to take a realistic view of its leadership while depending on the rankings by *U.S. News and World Report* that lacked validation? How many students and their families made decisions about a college or university based on the questionable rankings?

Case Study #2

In the United States, there are six regional accrediting agencies for public and private elementary schools, middle schools, high schools and colleges and universities: Middle States Association of Colleges and Schools; New England Association of Colleges and Schools; North Central Association of Colleges and Schools; Northwest Association of Colleges and Schools; Western Association of Colleges and Schools; and the Southeast Association of Colleges and Schools (SACS). [4]

SACS is the most far-reaching accrediting agency and recently it has consumed some of the other accrediting agencies. These accrediting agencies determine if schools and colleges should be accredited based on several standards, but there is a strong emphasis on the quality of leadership at the institution/school being considered or reviewed for accrediting. Students are eligible for college scholarships if the high school they attend is accredited while grant eligibility depends on the accreditation of colleges. Some of the regional accrediting agencies serve a very large area. SACS, for example, accredits public and private schools and school districts throughout the United States and overseas. It is one of the most powerful groups in the public and private education sectors, and some would argue that it is the most powerful.

---

[4] Since 2006, SACS has operated under the umbrella of AdvancED, a global accrediting group that assesses 23,000 public and private schools in 65 countries.

SACS is a voluntary, nongovernmental entity that was created not by a governmental agency at the state or federal level, but by a non-profit organization. SACS is approved by the U.S. Department of Education as an entity that enforces educational standards;[5] however, the U.S. Department of Education has no standards or assessment criteria that measure the effectiveness of SACS or any other accrediting agency. SACS has virtually no competition and participating institutions, schools, and school districts pay annual dues/fees to SACS for the privilege of being accredited by an entity that answers to and is evaluated by no one.

SACS issues findings on which schools are exemplary or need improvement based primarily on the behavior of the governing board–more than on student performance outcomes. If a local board is feuding, for example, the accreditation might be in jeopardy.

SACS accreditation is used as a banner of quality by schools and colleges. SACS can put schools and colleges on probation or remove their accreditation for failure to meet SACS standards in areas such as academic or financial stewardship and governance. In at least one state, accreditation status can determine if a local school board can be removed by the governor.[6] It is interesting to note that very few school districts and colleges have lost SACS accreditation in the last 40 years. Despite all of the problems in public education, including all of the many articles in local and national newspapers on a regular basis about local board problems, plus all of the schools that were chronically on the No Child Left Behind Needs Improvement list (some for eight years or longer) because of student academic underachievement only a few have lost accreditation and only a small percentage of school districts or private schools and colleges have been put on probation. This large organization answers to no one or any authority. In fact, several private and public schools and colleges with dismal student achievement outcomes have never been placed on probation by SACS or any other accrediting agency. Colleges with graduation rates as low as 30 percent remain accredited. School districts where 30 percent of the schools are chronically failing and graduation rates are at less than 60 percent and have been for several years remain accredited.

Primarily because subpar colleges maintain accreditation, students take on considerable debt from student loans to attend a college that is not preparing them for a career, so the students then are stuck with student debts.

---

[5] United States Department of Education – Accrediting Agencies.
[6] Section 45-10-4 of the *Official Code of Georgia Annotated, 2016 Edition.*

According to Fuller and Belken, in an article aptly titled, "The Watchdogs of College Education Rarely Ever Bite"

Accreditors hardly ever kick out the worst-performing colleges and lack uniform standards for assessing graduation rates and loan defaults. Those problems are blamed by critics for deepening the student-debt crisis as college costs soared during the past decade. [7]

How do these organizations assess the quality of leadership in those organizations that they claim to know so well? The fact of the matter is they do not because they seldom look at student academic outcomes and trajectory information. Yet, there is a public impression and belief that these assessors are evaluating leaders and the quality of organizations; further, there is a perception that each accrediting agency has the authority and positive standing from some unnamed entity that sanctions the quality of their assessments and accreditation criteria. When in fact, they were self-created. Even more troubling is the fact that organizations, both public and private, gloat over the ratings of their respective organizations by these outside assessors. Consequently, dysfunctional organizations hide behind the assessors' ratings and rankings, and equally important, many of the organizations do not take a true and authentic internal view of their own strengths and weaknesses. Instead, they focus on being compliant–compliant with the requirements of the assessor organizations–basic level compliance focused more on governance issues than student achievement outcomes.[8] How then can they improve and also why should they improve?

Case Study #3

In an article for *The Guardian*, Marc Joffe said that Moody's, Standards and Poor and other credit rating agencies like Fitch deserve a failing grade because of their failure to honestly assess the standing of many financial institutions prior to the economic collapse known as the Great Recession of

[7] Andrea Fuller and Douglas Belkin, "The Watchdogs of College Education Rarely Bite," *The Wall Street Journal*, June 17, 2015.
[8] Note: As of 2017, SACS indicates that it is considering student performance outcomes as a standard for accreditation. Some state departments of education manage accreditation and some states are studying whether accrediting agencies have any impact on improving student performance outcomes; for example, see House Bill 338 in Georgia's 2017 legislative session.

2008.[9] The same conclusion was reached in a study at Stanford University that was reported in an article in the *Stanford Social Innovation Review*.[10] The authors studied the three primary groups that rate nonprofit charities.

> *We conducted a detailed study of the agencies to determine how useful a service they provide. The results were sobering: Our review of their methodologies indicates that these [entities] individually and collectively fall well short of providing meaningful guidance for donors who want to support more efficient and effective nonprofits. Based on our study, the major weaknesses of the rating agencies are threefold: They rely too heavily on simple analysis and ratios derived from poor-quality financial data; they overemphasize financial efficiency while ignoring the question of program effectiveness; and they generally do a poor job of conducting analysis in important qualitative areas such as management strength, governance quality, or organizational transparency.* [11]

Many experts believe that credit rating agencies could have prevented the 2008 economic collapse had they provided accurate, fully vetted, and comprehensive credit rating reports. Those reports could have provided warnings and directions for numerous companies, investment houses, and individual investors. The failure of the external assessments was so complete that major companies failed, like the 100-year-old Lehman Brothers. Also, the three main credit rating agencies are still trying to recover the trust of the public and others.

> *The big three credit-rating agencies–Standard & Poor's, Moody's Investors Service, and Fitch Ratings–are still trying to repair their reputations as being a level-headed, sharp-penciled bunch following the collapse of Lehman. These agencies are roundly criticized for not only failing to warn investors of the dangers of investing in many of the mortgage-backed securities at the epicenter of the financial crisis but benefiting by not pointing out deficiencies.* [12]

In a compelling article about non-profit assessors, the authors question the methodology of the non-profit sector "watchdogs" such as the largest and

---

[9] Marc Joffe, "Moody's, S&P and Other Credit Rating Agencies Deserve a Failing Grade," *The Guardian*, February 2013.
[10] Stephanie Lowell, Brian Trelstad, and Bill Meehan, "The Ratings Game," *Stanford Social Innovation Review*, Summer 2005.
[11] Ibid.
[12] Matt Krantz, "2008 Crisis Still Hangs Over Credit Rating Firms," *USA Today*, September 13, 2013.

most frequently used and quoted assessor, Charity Navigator.[13] The article states,

> There are two fatal flaws in the Charity Navigator approach: One, it misleads the public even when purportedly accurate, and two, it is often inaccurate. The public, press, and politicians are encouraged to believe that the assessor of charities, Charity Navigator, is an impartial evaluator of publicly reported financial, accountability/transparency and results reporting that exists to guide intelligent giving and advance a more efficient and responsive philanthropic marketplace. Yet its choices of rating criteria are instead— whether intentionally or inadvertently—designed to mask rather than reveal what should be intelligent giving choices. And its public behavior is anything but impartial, intelligent or promoting efficiency. [14]

What Assessments Could Have Done

How many leaders would have been replaced if they were found to be ineffective based on reliable ratings and rankings by assessing entities? How many businesses that failed during the recession could have been saved if the bond and crediting rating companies were held accountable for their assessments and remained diligent while providing oversight to businesses? Would many colleges, universities, schools, and school districts have changed leadership and possibly improved education had accrediting agencies been more focused on student outcomes? Is it possible for an organization to conduct an effective and useful internal self-assessment and find a comprehensive and meaningful external assessor?

Antidotes: There is an old saying, "what gets measured gets done."[15] Many leaders use that phrase every year to justify the assessment of employees, programs, schools, organizations, and/or initiatives. However, it is not very likely that the U.S. Department of Education is going to conduct an in-depth study of SACS and the other school and school district accrediting agencies. It is also unlikely that SACS will change its methods. Additionally, entities such as Charity Navigator that review non-profits are not going to change

---

[13] Sean Norris, "Who Watches the Charity Watchdogs?" *Leadership Management*, April 2016: http://www.nonprofitpro.com/article/who-watches-the-charity-watchdogs-charity-navigator.

[14] Ibid.

[15] The quote has been attributed to Peter Drucker, Lord Kelvin, Tom DeMarco, Rheticus and others.

their methods either, nor is it likely that bond and credit rating agencies or even *U.S. News and World Reports* will change their method of rating colleges, universities, and high schools. Therefore, it is imperative that leaders and especially boards take the outside assessments from these organizations and others like them for what they are worth, and work to develop strong internal methods and mechanisms for assessing their organizations' health while continuing to seek meaningful external assessments.

The reasons for organizational difficulties are multifaceted. And because so many things can go wrong, or so many challenges can occur, it is highly beneficial for organizations to accurately diagnose the source(s) of their difficulties so they can quickly correct course and optimize the use of scarce resources. Even when it seems that an organization is functioning efficiently there is a need for an assessment of performance because every organization can improve.

Self-Assessments

Many organizations arrange performance assessments exclusively from external vendors, and there are times and circumstances when that is appropriate and necessary but much can be learned through an organizational self-assessment, too. In fact, an honest internal review can often reveal more than an external-based review and can prevent problems from escalating.

There are numerous self-assessment models that an organization can use, or it can develop its own. First, however, there are basic considerations. *Forbes* outlined several analytic concepts for self-assessment.[16]

1. ***Understand the difference between a measure and a metric.*** *A measure is one quantitative number that counts something (for example: We made $100,000 profit last quarter.). A metric provides more information because it compares the measure to some other baseline (e.g. "We made $100,000 profit last quarter, $50,000 more than the same quarter last year.")*

2. ***Understand the difference between an outcome metric and a performance metric.*** *An outcome metric gives the result of something. It's a "lag measure," because once it is complete the measure is done. A performance metric reveals how well work is being performed and the*

---

[16] Ruth Henderson, "What Gets Measured Gets Done: Or Does It?" *Forbes,* June 2015: http://www.forbes.com/sites/ellevate/2015/06 /08/what-gets-measured-gets-done-or-does-it/#44d85 ac78600.

impact on the outcomes. These are "lead measures," because they drive the outcomes in advance of the measurement of the outcomes (e.g. "For the last three weeks we have averaged 10 sales per week, which is above our target of eight sales calls per week. ").

3. ***Figure out what is needed before measuring things.*** *Oftentimes reports are a dumping ground for all the data that is available, whether it is useful or not. These types of reports do not contain the motivational metrics and measures that create eustress and increase performance. Nate Silver stated, "One of the pervasive risks that we face in the data age...is that even if the amount of knowledge in the world is increasing, the gap between what we know and what we think we know may be widening."[17]*

4. ***Design the assessment report to tell a relevant and useful story.*** *Once the relevant data is collected and measured, the report should include information that is most relevant to the operations of the organization. The report could adopt the SWOT format, which includes strengths, weaknesses, opportunities, and threats. Regardless of the format, the report should lead the reader to the most important points of the assessment.*

According to the Center for Non-Profit Management (CNPM), organizational self-assessment should focus on things that are changeable, that the organization can control, and that directly impact the performance of employees and the organization.[18]

A good organizational assessment will identify *cause* and *effect* relationships, helping ensure that whatever corrective actions put in place will produce meaningful change and can be measured. Organizational self-assessments have additional benefits as well.[19]

1. *Self-assessment helps bring focus to the organization's improvement efforts.*
2. *Self-assessment helps optimize the use of organizational resources.*
3. *Done correctly, self-assessment emphasizes opportunities for improvement, not 'fixing blame.'*
4. *Self-assessment looks at the total organization, not just one or two aspects.*
5. *Self-assessment is performance focused, not people focused.*

---

[17] Nate Silver, *The Signal and the Noise*, (Penguin, 2015).

[18] "Organizational Self-Assessment," *Center for Non-Profit Management*, (2015):http://www.centerfornon-profit.com /site /2015.

[19] Ibid.

6. *Most importantly, self-assessment can improve results.*
Organizational self-assessments do not need to be overly formal, heavily structured, or a painstaking process to produce highly useful information. The respected Baldrige Performance Excellence Program provides a meaningful and proven approach to meaningful organizational self-assessment through its *Criteria for Performance Excellence* instrument.[20]   The self-assessment criterion from Baldrige applies to many different types of organizations and provides effective and useful feedback. Experts of the Baldrige award offer several situations where a self-assessment is appropriate.[21]

1. *Customers/clients are driving a need to change.*
2. *The industry or environment is changing.*
3. *The organization is among the best and it wants to stay that way.*
4. *The leaders want to enhance organizational learning.*
5. *The organization sees a connection between key issues and improving organizational performance.*

The Center for Nonprofit Management[22] offers resources for organizational self-assessment, as does the Annie E. Casey Foundation.[23] These two models of self-assessment can be adapted for various types of organization. They are structured to identify the strengths and weaknesses of organizations and they discern between short and long-term challenges to the organization.

Additional self-assessment models include the following.

---

[20] The *Foundation for the Malcolm Baldrige National Quality Award*: http://www.baldrigepe.org/. The Baldrige Award is given by the President of the United States to businesses and to education, health care, and nonprofit organizations that apply and are judged to be outstanding in seven areas of performance excellence.
[21] Ibid.
[22] *Center for Non-Profit Management*: http://www.cnm. org/. An organizational assessment allows nonprofits to "take a step back, look at the big picture and determine where strengths and weaknesses lie."
[23] *Annie E. Casey Foundation*: http://www.aecf.org /work/. As a private philanthropy based in Baltimore and working across the country, the foundation grants help federal agencies, states, counties, cities and neighborhoods create more innovative, cost-effective responses to the issues that negatively affect children: poverty, unnecessary disconnection from family and communities with limited access to opportunity.

1. *Nonprofit Organization Self-Assessment* from the Nonprofit Association of Oregon includes a "360-degree" self-assessment tool.[24]
2. *Organizational Self-Assessment* (free registration required) to measure a nonprofit's organizational strengths and identify areas for improvement.[25]
3. Board member self-assessments[26]
4. *Sample Board Evaluation*[27]
5. *Sample Board Meeting Evaluation*[28]
6. *Organizational Capacity Assessment Tool* (registration required)[29]
7. *Self-Assessment Checklist*[30]
8. *Organizational Assessment and Planning Tool*[31]
9. *Infrastructure Checklist*[32]

In addition to using self-assessment instruments, organizations should also consider conducting a *comparative self-assessment* based on a review of similar organizations that have proven to be successful over time. The review could also include how other similar organizations conduct self-assessments.

A genuine improvement in every organization depends heavily on an accurate assessment of its strategies, methods, mechanisms, policies, procedures, staffing, resources, etc. to maintain success or reach success. An organization that depends solely on external assessment entities that do not carefully consider internal data may not receive a useful assessment report. Also, organizations that depend on external evaluators that do not take the time or have the expertise to conduct an effective and useful evaluation will not fully understand its strengths and weaknesses. Therefore, the organization

---

[24] *Non-Profit Association of Oregon,* https://non-profit oregon.org/sites/default /files/uploads/file/NP20Org20Self%20Assess-ment_0.pdf.

[25] *Innovation Network*: http://www.innonet.org/.

[26] *National Council of Non-Profits*: https://www.councilofnonprofits.org /tools-resources/ organizational-self-assessments.

[27] *LeadingAge Minnesota*: https://www.leadingagemn.org/providers /boards-trustees/sample-forms/.

[28] *Minnesota Council of Non-Profits*: https://sampleboard meeting –www. minnesotanonprofit-form/.

[29] *Marguerite Casey Foundation*: http://caseygrants.org/resources/org-capacity-assessment/.

[30] *Free Management Library*: http://managementhelp.org/organizational performance/nonprofits/.

[31] *Michigan Non-Profit Association*: https://mnaon line.org/principles-practices-assessment/file.

[32] *Non-Profit Association of the Mid-lands*: https://nonprofitam.org/file.

will not be able to adjust or impose significant changes that could benefit its operations at present and in the future.

There are times when trust is not high enough between the leadership and the board to allow for an internal assessment of the organization. This situation, however, should not preclude an organization from carefully and thoroughly and periodically planning an internal assessment. It can be insidiously destructive to rely on outside assessments as the sole means of feedback on effectiveness and efficiency. Likewise, using only internal self-assessments as the sole source of information may not be wise if the assessment does not include a prescriptive component that is essential for converting the findings into operational changes or adjustments or if the trust between the leader and the board is not substantial enough to allow for an internal assessment.

Chapter Ten Key Words and Concepts

Assessors
Accreditation
SACS
Moody's and Standards and Poor
Charity Navigator
External-Based Assessment
Internal Self-Assessment
Measure vs. Metric
Outcome Metric vs. Performance Metric
Lag Measure
Cause and Effect Measures
Center for Non-Profit Management
Annie E. Casey Foundation
Baldrige Performance Excellence Program
Model Similar Organizational Assessments
Identifying Organizational Assessment Methods

Chapter Ten Discussion Items

Define and explain the difference between External-Based Assessments and Internal-Based Assessments. What are the advantages and disadvantages of each? Is it appropriate to use one rather than the other? If so, under what circumstances and for what reasons? If not, explain why neither or both should be used for organizational assessment.

Other than the ones offered in this chapter, give two examples of a metric and a measure and explain the difference between the two.

Explain and illustrate the difference between an Outcome Metric and a Performance Metric.

Discuss the differences between Lag Measures and Cause and Effect Measures.

Nate Silver said, "One of the pervasive risks that we face in the data age…is that even if the amount of knowledge in the world is increasing, the gap between what we know and what we think we know may be widening." What does he mean?

If you were consulting with an organization that relied solely on either internal or external assessments, what would you advise them to do to receive more useful and constructive assessment information?

There are times when trust is not high enough between the leadership and the board to allow for an internal assessment of the organization. In that situation, is the exclusive use of external assessments appropriate?

Chapter Ten Lessons Learned

Fully developed and comprehensive assessments can be invaluable to an organization.

An organization that aims for success or continued success must contemplate how to best assess its operations.

An organization and its leadership can be poisoned from the determinants of false success or misleading information from assessments, whether it is external or internal.

It is possible for an organization to conduct an effective and useful internal self-assessment and find a comprehensive and meaningful external assessor.

Some assessments rely too heavily on simple analysis and ratios derived from poor-quality data.

Many external and internal assessment overemphasize financial efficiency while ignoring the question of program effectiveness.

An effective and useful external or internal assessment is one that conducts an analysis in important areas such as management strength, governance quality, organizational transparency, and organizational outcomes.

Leaders and boards should work to develop strong internal methods and mechanisms for assessing their organizations' health while continuing to seek meaningful external assessments.
The primary purpose of an assessment is so that an organization can accurately diagnose the source(s) of their difficulties so they can quickly correct course and optimize the use of scarce resources.

One of the pervasive risks that we face in the data age…is that even if the amount of knowledge in the world is increasing, the gap between what we know and what we think we know may be widening.

Improvement in every organization depends heavily on an accurate assessment of its strategies, methods, mechanisms, policies, procedures, staffing, resources, and outcomes.

CHAPTER ELEVEN

DATA-INFLUENCED DECISIONS

"In God we trust. All others must bring data."

-*W. Edwards Deming*[1]

Determinants: Data is the source that leaders use to make decisions in many organizations, or so it is said. The phrase *"data-driven decisions"* has moved from a catchy phrase to an expectation of leaders and boards. In many organizations, vision statements, mission statements, objectives, and operational decisions must be data-driven. Platforms for change are built on data-driven planning and data-driven strategies. But are decisions data-driven? Should they be? Leaders and boards can be misled by an emphasis on data-driven decisions. The statistician will agree that "un-scrubbed" data (scrubbed means cleaning the data set for accuracy) is unreliable; unrelated data is pointless; unmanageable data is misleading; and decisions made from un-scrubbed, unrelated, and unmanageable data can be detrimental to an organization.

Data and Decisions

Many foolish decisions have been made at the altar of data, and many organizations pick and choose data to meet their needs and thereby risk making erroneous assumptions that precede poor decisions. Boards and leaders should be very precise in how data is collected and used for planning and decision-making purposes. Data can be a very powerful element that helps leaders make critical decisions, but it should not be the only driver of decisions. Too often leaders and boards do not ask the questions, "What data is missing; what additional or different data do we need? What does the data mean? What is the data trying to tell us?"

---

[1] W. Edwards Deming, *Quality, Productivity, and Competitive Position,* (Massachusetts Institute of Technology: Center for Advanced Engineering Studies, 1982.)

If a leader states that decisions should be data-driven, that proclamation needs to be explored. What exactly does that mean for the organization? Data-influenced decisions can be powerfully effective but they can also lead to unintended negative consequences.

Case Study #1

An organization's leadership team, including the board, decided to move completely to what they called "data-driven decision-making". The organization's goals, strategies, and objectives were driven by data. It was decided that no major decisions would be made without data to guide those decisions. A problem became immediately obvious—where would the data come from? A Request for Proposals (RFP) was published for data vendors to submit development proposals for a data platform. The organization settled on a vendor that was an expert in researching, developing, and reporting data in virtually every category deemed important by the organization's leadership team. The vendor went to work and soon thereafter mountains of data became available to the leader, his top staff, and the board.

It did not take long for the leadership team to realize that the data was different from the previous data retrieval systems in sheer volume and scope of the data. Soon after the data began flowing to the organization, the board asked the leadership team for a report on the data because it was excited about the prospect of data-driven strategies and planning decisions. The leadership team recognized that the data company did not provide a blueprint for *data interpretation* nor was the data analysis tied to a strategic use of the data. The RFP addressed only data collection and data delivery. The leadership team assumed they had the expertise and experience to analyze and interpret the data. Soon, however, the leadership team recognized they did not individually or collectively have the expertise to decipher the data in any meaningful way. When they met with the data company they learned that the data company could provide analytic service for them for an additional cost but there was no budget for that. So, decisions were made from the data, as best the leadership team could understand the data until conflicting data started to appear. For example, some data showed that the service delivery model that the organization had spent a significant amount of money on was not as effective as indicated in annual reports. Instead of making changes to the delivery model, the organization only referred to the sections of the data that supported at least some component of the service delivery model. That's what the board heard about, not a full report of the broad scope of the data. The leadership team developed confidence in its ability to interpret data.

However, the data-driven decisions based on incomplete analysis of data gave the leadership team a false sense of legitimacy. Little concern was given to the impact of these decisions, the reliability of the data interpretation, and conflicting outcomes. Within two years, the data-driven decisions were causing infrastructure and service delivery problems throughout the organization. The logistics-related elements of the data were not thoroughly analyzed because of the vast amount of complex data in the statistical set. Consequently, chain-supply and infrastructure adjustments necessary to cope with changing demands on logistics were not addressed. The organization began losing clients and the costs of operations increased significantly.

Making Data Relevant

Often decisions are impacted almost immediately by incoming data without first studying longitudinal data for trends or without taking the time to consider the source of the data and discovering what it means. Data can be extremely valuable for every organization, regardless of type or size, but leaders and boards should be thoughtful and careful before they plunge into data-driven decisions and they should not be all-inclusive in the use of that term. Trying to force all decisions from a data driven application can limit an organization's insight and ability to identify the nature, scope, and depth of problems. It also cannot measure the human element that always impacts organizations and individuals.

In his book *The Signal and the Noise*, Nate Silver takes the reader through many examples of how data can be fatally flawed, overused, misinterpreted, and yet many times useful.[2] Silver finds that all data tells a story but he adds: "The story data tells us is often the one we'd like to hear, and we usually make sure it has a happy ending. "[3] He explains that data is considered wonderful by an organization's leader when it supports a leader's theory, practice or expectations and, yet, data is viewed as irrelevant or suspicious if it does not support the leader's story. Silver makes the point that data can make leaders and boards lazy, if not irresponsible, because it is so readily available and because it removes tough decision-making, or so they think. If a leader can make decisions based only on data, the thinking goes, then poor decisions are not his fault; he was relying on data. Blame the data, not the leader. To that

---

[2] Nate Silver, *The Signal and the Noise: Why So Many Predictions Fail but Some Don't*, (Penguin, 2015).
[3] Ibid.

point, Silver wrote, "Before we demand more of our data, we need to demand more of ourselves." [4]

Data can make a leader and the executive team lazy and careless, plus there is a temptation to mislead others with data, such as a board, stockholders, employees, clients, contributors, and other stakeholders. Silver made additional important points about data.[5]

The signal is the truth. The noise is what distracts us from the truth.

We can never make perfectly objective predictions. They will always be tainted by our subjective point of view.

A belief in the objective truth -and a commitment to pursuing it- is the first prerequisite of making better predictions.

Prediction is important because it connects subjective and objective reality.

We must become more comfortable with probability and uncertainty.

We must think more carefully about the assumptions and beliefs that we bring to a problem.

A certain amount of immersion in a topic will provide disproportionally more insight that an executive summary.

If you have reason to think that yesterday's forecast was wrong, there is no glory in sticking to it.

New ideas are sometimes found in the most granular details of a problem where few others bother to look.

In many cases involving predictions about human activity, the very act of prediction can alter the way that people behave.

While simplicity can be a virtue for a model, a model should at least be sophisticatedly simple.

---

[4] Ibid.
[5] Ibid.

Data-Driven or Driven-by-Data

In recent years, non-profit organizations and others followed the trend started by business leaders, to say all decisions are data-driven. Non-profit and education leaders are often pressured by the public and business leaders, in particular, to operate their organizations "like a business," even though research shows that 80 percent of new businesses fail within the first two years and most of the *Fortune 500* companies from 30 years ago do not exist today.[6] Nevertheless, non-profit leaders, educational leaders, and others often adopt some business practices, so like businesses, the move to data-driven decisions seemed logical to them.

Some leaders jumped at the chance to hire high-powered and expensive consultants to implement a data analysis and data decision-making concept called the "*Balanced Scorecard*", which was developed by Bob Kaplan and David Norton in a *Harvard Business Review* paper in 1992.[7] The original concept of the Balanced Scorecard was grounded in business financial management, but it took a turn toward data collection and cataloging data in many types of organizations as a means of determining if goals and objectives are met and to guide decision-making far beyond the original intent that focused only on financial matters.

It is interesting to note the Balanced Scorecard concept that relies on data was not the subject of any research to determine if it was effective until 2008, sixteen years after it was introduced, when Dr. Andrew Neely, a researcher at the Cranfield School of Management published a research paper, *Does the Balanced Scorecard Work: An Empirical Investigation.*[8] Neely explored the performance impact of the Balanced Scorecard by employing a quasi-experimental design. He collected three years of financial data from two separate electrical wholesale divisions within the same company. One of the divisions used the Balanced Scorecard and the other did not. Neely found that the division that implemented the Balanced Scorecard saw improvements in sales and gross profit, but so did its sister divisions. There was no difference between the divisions in the number of sales and the gross profit; thereby, the

---

[6] Dane Stangler and Sam Arbesman, "What Does Fortune 500 Turnover Mean?" *Ewing Marion Kauffman Foundation*, June 2012.

[7] R.S Kaplan and D.P. Norton, *The Balanced Scorecard: Measures that Drive Performance*, (Harvard Business Press, 1992).

[8] Andrew Neely, "Does the Balanced Scorecard work: An empirical investigation," *Cranfield CERES*, (January 2008): http://dspace.lib. cranfield. ac.uk/handle /1826/3932 .

author of the study wrote, "Hence the performance impact of the Balanced Scorecard has to be questioned." [9]

Despite this finding and others like it, businesses and many other organizations continue to use the Balanced Scorecard. Many leaders and workers, as well as board members, often feel overwhelmed with the data and populating the data cells required in the Balanced Scorecard can be painstakingly slow and laborious, especially considering the questionable usefulness of the outcomes. Nevertheless, there are proponents of the Balanced Scorecard that extoll its virtues. For example, ClearPoint Strategies reports the following on its website regarding organizations that use the Balanced Scorecard.[10]

1. *87% use the Balanced Scorecard to influence business actions.*
2. *They use the scorecard frequently: 44% use it monthly, and 33% use it quarterly.*
3. *Score carding is helping companies: 31% reported it as extremely helpful, and 42% as very helpful.*
4. *29% use software other than Microsoft Office to create their Scorecard (like BSC software).*
5. *Close to half of responding organizations have more than one Balanced Scorecard in play; the average number was 12.*
6. *The Balanced Scorecard is used by small and large organizations alike: 56% had less than 500 employees.*

A recent meta-analysis by researchers Emad Awadallah and Amir Allam found that many aspects of the Balanced Scorecard are flawed.

Despite the widespread use and benefits, the Balanced Scorecard has serious limitations both in concept and in practice. The evidence is a greater number of organizations implementing the Balanced Scorecard have either failed to achieve their intended objectives or encountered serious problems during implementation. The concept of the Balanced Scorecard has no clearly defined relationship with organization performance, the objective, and definitions of measures exclude key stakeholders, lacks the definition of key success factors necessary for identifying Key Performance Indicators, and the four categories limit the view of the organization. In practice, the Balanced Scorecard focuses resources on achieving its goals leading to underutilization of organizations' potential beyond the targets of the Balanced Scorecard;

---

[9] Ibid.

[10] *Clear Point Strategy*: https://www.clearpointstrategy.com/companies-using-the-balanced-scorecard/.

hampers inter-organizational innovation; perceives an organization has hierarchical structures, clearly delineated job responsibilities and one-way linear cause-and-effect relationships; and promotes closed innovation. These limitations hamper the effectiveness of the Balanced Scorecard and contribute to some organizations wanting to abandon the Balanced Scorecard altogether for better alternatives. [11]

In another example of the fallacy of data-driven decisions, educators followed the lead of businesses by adopting the moniker that all decisions are *data-based.* Several public schools implemented data development systems, including the *Balanced Scorecard.* Educators fell for the lure of simplifying decision making and they turned a blind eye to data that did not support what they wanted it to support.

Simple/Complicated or Complex/Chaotic

According to an article in the *Wall Street Journal,* data should be used and viewed in a decision-making context based on circumstances.

Simple and complicated contexts assume an ordered universe, where cause-and-effect relationships are perceptible, and right answers can be determined based solely on facts. Complex and chaotic contexts are unordered – there is no immediate relationship between cause and effect, and the way forward is determined based on emerging patterns. The ordered world is the world of

---

[11] Emad Awadallah and Amir Allam, "A critique of the Balanced Scorecard as a performance measure," *International Journal of Business and Social Science,* 6 (7) 2015; J. Kraaijenbrink, "Five reasons to abandon the Balanced Scorecard:" http://kraaijenbrink.com/2012/10/fivereasonstoabandonthebalancedscorecard/; J. Kraaijenbrink, "Alternative for the Balanced Scorecard: The Performance Prism," http://kraaijen brink.com/2012 /10/an-alternative-for-the-balanced-scorecard-the-per-formance-prism/; D. Parmenter, "A table without any legs: A critique of the balanced scorecard methodology," In *Implementing Winning* (KPIs whitepaper, 2011): http://david parmenter.com/how-toguides; D.S. Pessanha and V. Prochnik, "Practitioners' opinions on academics' critics on the Balanced Scorecard.": http://ssrn.com/abstract =1094308; S. Voelpel, M. Leibold, R.A. Eckhoff, and T.H. Davenport, "The Tyranny of the Balanced Scorecard in the Innovation Economy." *Proceedings of the 4thInternational Critical Management Studies Conference,* Intellectual Capital Stream Cambridge University, United Kingdom, (July 4-6, 2012).

facts-based management; the unordered world represents pattern-based management.[12]

Probably only a few leaders would describe their organization as *simple* and *complicated*. Most would select *complex* and *chaotic* to describe the challenges of managing an organization. Consequently, decisions should be based on more than just data. When data is analyzed, leaders should look for patterns within the data. What questions need to be asked to determine if the data is relevant to the organization? How can the data be analyzed to reveal what additional questions need to be asked and what other data is needed? What data is missing that might be useful and is that data available? These types of questions highlight some of the differences between *fact-based management* and *patter-based management*. The outline below denotes other major differences between fact-based management and pattern-based management.

Fact-Based Management
- *System is "simple and complicated."*
- *All data reviews are focused on cause and effect.*
- *The management type is fact-based and decisions are data-driven.*

Patten-Based Management
- *System is "complex and chaotic."*
- *All data reviews are focused on finding patterns.*
- *The management type is pattern-based and decisions are data influenced not data-driven.*

An article in *Wired* magazine by Brian Christian addresses the dangers of data-driven decisions and introduces a new term - HPPO (Highest Paid Person's Opinion).[13] The HPPO usually makes the decisions in organizations that don't know how to read data and yet they make data-driven decisions. The data-driven decisions typically start with the HPPO and move on the fast-track down the organizational chart to a hard landing on the employees

---

[12] Irving Wladawsky-Berger, "Data-driven decision making: Promises and limits," *Wall Street Journal*, September 27, 2013.
[13] Brian Christian, "The A/B Test: Inside the technology that's changing the rules of business," *Wired Magazine,* April 25, 2012: https://www.wired. com/2012/04/ffabtesting/.

who are central to the day-to-day operations. The data-driven decisions in this manner become "data-driven-as-I-see-it decisions."[14]

The staff of *Intercom* wrote that data-driven decisions are only useful when applying the right methods. They indicate that data is one perspective, and only one perspective, and therefore should not be the only driving force that guides decisions.

> *If Apple were data driven, they would release a $400 netbook or shut down their Genius Bar. If Zappos were driven by data, they would abandon their generous returns policy. Just because data is objective by definition it doesn't mean that it guides you to the right decision. Just because (data) can be precise, it doesn't follow that it's valuable. Data is a false god. You can tag every link, generate every metric, and run split tests for every decision, but no matter how deep you go, no matter how many hours you invest, you're only looking at one piece of the puzzle.* [15]

It is important for leaders and boards to understand that everything that can be counted counts but not everything that counts can be counted. There is a clear difference between *data-driven decision-making* and *data-influenced decision-making*.

Case Study #2

After three consecutive years of declining revenues, the non-profit furloughed employees for five days, delayed needed equipment purchases, and scaled back services. The board became convinced that the declining economy was not the main problem, so they discerned that the problems rested with the leader and his management style. One board member described the leader as "lackluster", meaning that the revenue declines were probably tied to his poor leadership. But another board member was convinced that the problem was not the leader but the organization's lack of respect for the power of data. He convinced the other board members that mining data would turn the organization around because nothing was better than data-driven decision making. The leader explained that the organization did not lack for data. They had mounds of data, but making all decisions based just on the data could be risky. Nonetheless, the organization converted to a "data-driven decision-making model," as one board member proudly

---

[14] Ibid.

[15] Des Traynor, "The problem with data-driven decisions." *Inside Intercom*, 2014: https://intercom. com/the-problem-with-data-driven-decisions/.

proclaimed. Data was collected from every source possible in the organization, and new data sources were developed, also. Soon dozens of charts and graphs were developed. The board was convinced that decisions could be made from the data that would bring the organization back to his past glory. The board even insisted that the organization create a "Data Wall" in every office and in the Board Room.

With the strong emphasis on data, it became increasingly difficult to separate the *signal* from the *noise* of data.[16] Data indicated, for example, that aging equipment was negatively impacting productivity, but only marginally. The board determined, contrary to the opinion of the organization's leader and his leadership team that new equipment needed to be purchased. The leader said the organization could not afford the equipment during a declining economy and the needs of the clients were changing so it would be prudent to delay the purchases until new technology was developed when the economic conditions of the nation, state, and region improved. The board said the data should drive the decisions, so the leader was forced to put the already financially challenged organization further in debt with the purchase of computer upgrades and software, as well as related purchases. Silver cautioned those that view data in that way, "Extrapolation is a very basic method of prediction – usually, much too basic."[17] A few years later, the organization filed for bankruptcy.

Data taken in isolation from other factors and influences can give a misleading impression and lead to false assumptions. After the organization went into receivership, a performance and financial audit revealed that the organization did not have sufficient strategies or skills to decipher the important and relevant elements of the data fields. Also, decisions had been based on selected data instead full-scope date; in other words, the board and the leadership team were selecting data that most closely aligned their own priorities. Consequently, the data sent the leadership decision-making in the wrong direction for the wrong reasons with the wrong expectations and ultimately with the wrong outcomes.

---

[16] Nate Silver, *The Signal and the Noise: Why So Many Predictions Fail but Some Don't*, (Penguin, 2015).
[17] Ibid.

Behavioral Economics

In an article for *Foreign Affairs*, the authors express optimism about the large amount of data available to organizations but they also found several reasons to offer many precautions.

> *Knowing the causes behind things is desirable. The problem is that causes are often extremely hard to figure out, and many times when we think we have identified them, it is nothing more than a self-congratulatory illusion. Behavioral economics has shown that humans are conditioned to see causes even where none exist. So, we need to be particularly on guard to prevent our cognitive biases from deluding us; sometimes, we just have to let the data speak. This requires a new way of thinking and will challenge institutions and identities. In the world where data shape decisions more and more, what purpose will remain for people, or for intuition, or for going against the data?*[18]

Perhaps too many leaders follow literally what leadership guru, Edwards Deming, said about data, "In God we trust. All others must bring data." [19]

Antidotes: There is no doubt that data is essential to all leaders, boards, and organizations. Without data, there are no measures of effectiveness, no indications that strategic plans and objectives are working, and no way to tie the organization's budget to initiatives. Without data, an organization is operating in the blind. However, a leader and the board need to understand the purpose, potential, and limitations of data. Data that does not provide relevant information are only numerical points. Information from data is only useful if it provides insight that can be applied to the organization in a constructive manner. Data must tell a story to be useful. Former Secretary of State, General Colin Powell said, "We have plenty of data but not enough wisdom." [20]

Atul Butte, a Stanford University professor who specializes in research on how data is created, reviewed, analyzed, and interpreted laments about the

---

[18] Kenneth Cukier and Viktor Mayer-Schoenberger, "The rise of big data," *Foreign Affairs*, June 2013: https://www.foreign affairs. com/articles/2013-04-03/rise-big-data.
[19] W. Edwards Deming, *Quality, Productivity, and Competitive Position,* (Massachusetts Institute of Technology: Center for Advanced Engineering Studies, 1982.
[20] Colin Powell, *"It Worked for Me,"* (Harper Perennial, 2012).

lack of effort to carefully mine data to discover the most important elements within the data.

According to Butte, "Hiding within those mounds of data is the knowledge that could change so many things."[21]

He said that too many organizations, however, look at the obvious data and do not ask what is missing and what other internal bits of data should the organization be looking at? To illustrate this point, Nate Silver wrote in *The Signal and the Noise* that trying to determine what data is useful and how it is useful requires recognition that data can be a lot of noise with a signal embedded in the noise. It takes skill at the data entry level, skill at the data retrieval level, skill at the data mining level, skill at the data interpretation level, and skill at the data relevancy level to make data work for an organization in an accurate and productive way.[22] Otherwise, data is only noise.

There is the temptation to cherry-pick data to support favorite strategies, products, or services. Ronald Coase, the Nobel-winning economist, said, "Torture the data, and it will confess to anything."[23]

How should a leader and board use data? Many data experts recommend that leaders develop several questions related to the vision, mission, strategies, and objectives of the organization and apply those elements to data collection, review, and use. Additionally, the leader should ask the board and other stakeholders to do the same thing. The purpose of data then becomes clear; it is to answer important questions. This method is more likely to find information from the data that is relevant to the organization and makes the data more manageable. Additionally, this method has the potential to disaggregate data so that information relevant to specific components of the organization can be reviewed for program and service delivery model effectiveness measures, based on the questions and the data.

In a study of data usefulness and how organizations are often perplexed about how to effective use data, even when they have discovered data that is important to the organization, Piyanka Jain wrote,

---

[21] Atul Butte, *Stanford Data Symposium*, June 2015. Butte is a researcher in biomedical informatics and a biotechnology entrepreneur in Silicon Valley.

[22] Nate Silver, *The Signal and the Noise: Why So Many Predictions Fail but Some Don't*, (Penguin, 2015).

[23] Ronald Coase, How Should Economists Choose? In *Ideas, Their Origins and Their Consequences: Lectures to Commemorate the Life and Work of G. Warren Nutter* (Thomas Jefferson Center Foundation ed., American Institute for Public Policy Research, Washington, DC, 1988).

Data, data everywhere, not a drop to act! Every organization is collecting data today, but very few know what to do with it. Part of the challenge is, organizations don't know what to ask of data? Where to begin?[24]

Too often organizations do not formulate questions to ask that drive the importance and usefulness of data.

The author of *Five Rules for the Data-Driven Business*, Patricio Robles, offers very practical advice and warnings for organizational leaders that want to be data-driven.[25]

1. ***Remember that you can collect too much data.*** *Collecting as much data as possible is not only distracting, it can reduce the quality of data-influenced decisions because the massive amount of data is overwhelming. When too much data is collected, there is a greater likelihood that the wrong analyses will be performed, especially if the right questions are not being asked about the data.*

2. ***Key metrics derived from data should be tied to goals.*** *Numbers alone are of limited use unless they are linked to relevant information needed by the organization. Metrics should be linked to the organization's strategic plan and associated with the goals of the organization in a format that identifies issues, possible solutions, and that can be compared to other sources of information like observations and feedback from employees and clients.*

3. ***Context helps.*** *When setting goals, context is the data reviewer's friend. Tying key metrics to goals are meaningful in evaluating and setting goals for the organization. Establishing the purpose of a goal can extend to clearly delineating the purpose of the data.*

4. ***The past and present aren't the future.*** *Data is inherently limited to yesterday and today. Predictions, no matter how sophisticated the calculations may be are still just predictions. The data-influenced organization should use data to make informed decisions and not naively believe that data is a crystal ball.*

5. ***Don't dismiss the qualitative.*** *If an organization is analyzing significant amounts of data but is not considering other sources of information, the leadership team could miss elements that are crucial to the organization. The key question has to be asked: What matters most to the*

---

[24] Piyanka Jain, "3 Analytic Questions to Ask Your Big Data," *Forbes,* August 19, 2012: http://www.forbes.com/sites/piyankajain/2012/08/19/3-key-analytics-questions-to-ask-big-data/#1fee67be68f7.

[25] Patricio Robles, "Five Rules for the Data-Driven Business," *Econsultancy,* November 22, 2010: https://econsultancy.com/6870-five-rules-for-the-data-driven-business/.

organization? That question should be asked to determine if and how data is or can be useful.

Leaders must understand that there is no data that will fully replace any of the skills that make a leader and boards more effective. There are many essential facets of leadership that cannot be found in a data spreadsheet. Difficult decisions are seldom solely driven by data. Many times data is not available. Besides, there are several aspects of every organization that depend on human dynamics and perception.

Leaders and boards that hope to simplify decision-making by depending almost exclusively on data need to recognize that they could be taking a risky path. Data will never substitute for human insight, human passion and compassion, and human motivation.

John Naisbitt, the author of the *Megatrends* books, said,

Intuition becomes increasingly valuable in the new information society precisely because there is so much data.[26]

Key Chapter Eleven Words and Concepts

Data
Data-Driven Decisions
Un-scrubbed Data
Separate Signal from Noise
Objective Predictions
Data Assumptions
Balanced Scorecard
Simple and Complicated Contexts
Complex and Chaotic Contexts
Fact-Based Management
Pattern-Based Management
HPPO
Data Wall
Extrapolation
Data-Influenced Decisions
Behavioral Economics

---

[26] John Naisbitt, *Megatrends: Ten New Directions Transforming Our Lives,* (Grand Central Publishing, 1988).

Chapter Eleven Discussion Items

What is the difference between a Data-Driven Decision and a Data-Influenced Decision? Give examples of each.

Explain what "Separating the Signal from the Noise" means in relation to studying data and the relevancy of data. Provide an example of Noise and a Signal within the Noise.

What are the advantages and disadvantages of using the Balanced Scorecard?

Explain the value of data, how data should be collected, how data should be analyzed and how data should be used.

What organizations fit the Complex and Chaotic Context? Why?

Explain the difference between Fact-Based Management and Pattern-Based Management.

Define Behavioral Economics and how the principles can apply to organizational operations.

How would you use a Data Wall? What would you include on the Data Wall and why? How would you ask your employees to use the Data Wall to improve their performance?

What does this statement mean to you: "Difficult decisions are seldom solely driven by data."?

Chapter Eleven Lessons Learned

Platforms for change are built on data-driven planning and data-driven strategies.

Boards and leaders should be very precise in how data is collected and used for planning and decision-making purposes.

Data can be a very powerful element that helps leaders make critical decisions, but it should not be the only driver of decisions.

Data can be extremely valuable for every organization, regardless of type or size, but leaders and boards should be thoughtful and careful before they plunge into data-driven decisions.

Trying to force all decisions from a data driven application can limit an organization's insight and ability to identify the nature, scope, and depth of problems.

Data can make leaders and boards lazy, if not irresponsible, because it is so readily available and because it removes tough decision-making, or so they think.

New ideas are sometimes found in the most granular details of a problem where few others bother to look.

Data should be used and viewed in a decision-making context based on circumstances.

It is critically important for leaders to ask how data can be analyzed to reveal what additional questions need to be asked and what other data is needed. The leader also needs to ask the important question: what data is missing that might be useful and is that data available?

The data-influenced organization should use data to make informed decisions and not naively believe that data is a crystal ball.

Metrics should be linked to the organization's strategic plan and associated with the goals of the organization.

CHAPTER TWELVE

LEADERSHIP AND CRITICISM

"If you can keep your head while those around you are losing theirs, perhaps you don't understand the situation."

-*Nelson Boswell[1]*

Determinants: Effective leadership includes the ability to handle criticism. Ineffective leaders consider any criticism as calculated and premeditated attempts to limit their power or persuasion. Leaders must let subordinates offer honest opinions and feedback. Also, they should be allowed to make difficult decisions, and support subordinates even when decisions may not be popular. There is a destructive belief among ineffective leaders that they must always be shielded from decisions that are incorrect, ineffective, or poorly timed; consequently, lower level managers receive only blame and not support. The consequence is that lessons are not learned, morale is negatively impacted, and the quality of the organization is compromised. Mistakes and criticism are inevitable; that's how employees and leaders learn to be better. The destructive leaders run from these situations because they generate criticism and they are quick to blame others, even when the leader is to blame. One of the true measures of leadership is how a leader responds to and reacts to criticism, whether the criticism is justified or not.

Criticism and Arrogance

Case Study #1

A small college was well known for its many innovative ideas and programs. The president was a gregarious, energetic, intelligent, and ambitious leader who enjoyed the full support of the college's board. He constantly pushed his staff to implement his new ideas, even if the employees lacked specific details and even if they were still working on the president's previous ideas. Most employees agreed that the president was very innovative

---

[1] Nelson Boswell, *Successful Living Day by Day*, (Scribner Publishing. 1973).

and many of his ideas had merit. However, trying to translate ideas into practice and paying for the cost of those practices became problematic. The president's response to staff concerns was simply, "Make it work."

It was clear to the staff that the president did not want to hear that his ideas required short– and long– term plans, and he certainly did not want to hear that the college could not afford the cost of implementing and sustaining his projects and strategies. All he wanted to hear from his staff was, "Yes, sir." Also, if one of his ideas failed, it was the fault of the staff. He made that clear to his executive team.

Developing an international center for innovation at the college was one of the president's boldest ideas. He had noble visions of what it should look like and what it should do. He hired at expert to lead the effort who had a stellar reputation for leading international projects in colleges. However, once onboard at the college, the person soon realized that there was no budget for any of the projects that had to be completed to make the concept work. The new director of the center repeatedly asked the president for a budget and expressed frustration about the lack of resources necessary to accomplish the goals of the international center. The president heard from employees, community leaders, and local politicians that the international center was not making any progress in bringing in new international businesses or promoting dialogue that might lead someday to an international business and cultural center at the college.

The president, while brilliant and innovative, was not a leader that could handle criticism well at all. He told the concerned stakeholders that his vision was perfectly suited for the needs of the community and the failure to live up to the promises made must be the fault of the new director. Also, he viewed any delay in implementing his projects as a deliberate effort to circumvent or even sabotage his ideas. He approached the director of the international center and verbally lashed out at her with aggressive accusations of incompetence and deceit.

In an article on leadership, Ron Edmondson discusses how misinformed or misdirected leaders respond to criticism.[2]

1. *Finding fault with the critic*–Anyone that criticizes the leader has an ulterior motive to embarrass the leader in order to diminish the leader's influence or power.

---

[2] Ron Edmundson. "Five Wrong Ways to Respond to Criticism," *Ron Edmundson.com*. 2016.

2. ***Blaming others***–*Criticism is never "owned" or accepted by the leader because the blame always rests with others. This type of leader will insulate himself from criticism by overtly naming employees who are to blame.*

3. ***Throwing back criticism***–*Criticizing the critic or starting a war of words with the critic diverts attention away from the leader's actions. In the classic diversion tactic of ineffective leaders, this type of leader will question the critic in order to shift the attention to the critic with the aim to make the critic defensive.*

4. ***Ignoring an opportunity to learn***–*We learn more from our mistakes than from our successes but the ineffective leader does not learn from mistakes because he never accepts blame or responsibility for decisions that failed. He owns success and others own failure.*

5. ***Appease the critic***–*The ineffective leader gives false praise to the critic in order to appease him, which distracts and diverts the criticism and is intended to disorient the critic. The leader thinks that false flattery will convert the critic to his side and thus minimize or neutralize the critics.*

In this case study, each of these five elements described the college president's response to criticism, especially as one after another of his innovative ideas failed to develop due to his lack of planning and budgeting. Instead of admitting that there were implementation challenges and issues that needed to be addressed before his idea could thrive, including those that he failed to plan for, he instead attempted to discredit his staff and any person offering criticism, with public comments like,

> *They are not realistic with their expectations. I cannot find competent staff that can handle innovation. They don't understand the complexity of the projects. They don't want it to work.* [3]

When that approach backfired, his criticism of and blaming of staff intensified. The failure of the international center reached a different level of intensity when he publicly criticized the director. He said the person did not possess the wherewithal to handle the job. In fact, at one point he said the director did not handle the budget well. He failed to admit that there was no budget for the director to mishandle.[4]

---

[3] Public comments at a college forum interview conducted at Georgia Perimeter College, (2011).

[4] Maureen Downey, "Georgia Perimeter College: What is the rest of the story on the financial meltdown?" *Atlanta Journal Constitution*, June 10, 2013.

As is often the case with this type of leader, a leader who blames employees from a dictatorial mindset and fails to handle criticism makes the situation worse. The president contaminated the workplace climate with his reaction to criticism, which made any hope of salvaging the project or any of his other projects unlikely. The criticism shifted from the international center's failure to meet expectations to the president's reaction to the criticism. In similar situations where his ideas were rich in verbosity and creativity and poor in execution and practicality, he also blamed others, found fault with the critics and in almost every situation failed to learn in order to avoid the same mistakes again. Over time, his good, effective ideas were overshadowed by his egocentric, abrasive leadership style, fiscal disinterest, and his reaction to criticism. He refused to learn from his errors, refused to listen to this staff, and refused to accept responsibility for anything that failed or fell short of expectations. The morale of employees declined, and many of them left the college to take positions in other colleges. The reputation of the college was tarnished by the actions of the college president. The conceit bred his failure to accept criticism and was the determinant that led to his downfall. In a relatively short period of time, he brought the entire college to the brink of bankruptcy and lost his job because state auditors found that the college was several million.[5] To put that deficit in perspective, after the destructive leader was removed, the interim president had to terminate over 100 employees to balance the budget. When the story became headlines in local and state news, the president blamed it on the chief financial officer.[6]

Self-Destructive Leadership

In his highly respected book on leadership, *The Enemies of Leadership*, Grady Bogue, former chancellor of Louisiana State University, wrote that arrogance is one of the main enemies of leadership because it does not allow the leader to accept criticism.[7] Bogue states, "There is no place for arrogance in leadership."[8] He said that arrogance blinds a leader's ability to learn from mistakes and accept criticism that could benefit the leader's growth and the circumstances of the organization.

---

[5] Ibid.

[6] Andrew Caulthon, "Ex-President Wants His Job Back," *Champion Newspaper*, December 15, 2014.

[7] Grady Bogue, *The Enemies of Leadership*, (Phi Delta Kappa International Press, 1985).

[8] Ibid. p. 98.

In an article by Mortimer Feinberg and Jack Tarrant, *Why Smart People Do Dumb Things*, they argue that arrogance and overconfidence diminish a leader's ability to appropriately handle criticism, which can diminish a promising and effective leader.[9] They also state that when arrogance and overconfidence are combined with high intelligence a destructive element is produced. They refer to this as "Self-Destructive Intelligence Syndrome (SDIS)."[10] Leaders with SDIS, according to Fienberg and Tarrant, isolate themselves from criticism and are compromised by their own arrogance, narcissism, and a sense of entitlement. They state that this destructive combination is not only toxic for the leader; it also damages the organization.

Grady Bogue, currently a University of Tennessee professor and chancellor emeritus of LSU, recently wrote about self-defeating destructive leadership.

Four of my University of Tennessee doctoral students and two colleagues— Dr. Stephen Trachtenberg, president emeritus of George Washington University, and Dr. Gerry Kauvar, also of George Washington University— explored derailment among college presidents. The students studied 12 presidents who were shown the exit shortly after they were appointed. The presidents worked in four different organizational types—research universities, comprehensive universities, liberal arts colleges and community colleges. They found some overlap in factors associated with non-voluntary departures between corporate and collegiate leaders. These include poor interpersonal skills, inability to lead teams and key constituents, and failure to achieve goals and accept criticism. Among the distinctive factors found with college presidents were ethical breaches on the part of both presidents and trustees, difficulty in adapting to organizational cultures, and failure to view criticism as an opportunity for professional growth.[11]

The college presidents' destructive behaviors derived primarily from a complete failure to handle criticism, accept blame and learn from failure.

Case studies have found that top management and boards responsible for making decisions that ultimately prove to be wrongheaded often sink into a defensive, self-preservation mode highlighted by the most basic of desperate strategies: "It wasn't my fault." To leaders that resort to this type of reaction, someone other than themselves are to blame if something does not work or if

---

[9] Mortimer Feinberg and Jack Tarrant, *Why Smart People Do Dumb Things*, (Simon and Schuster, 1995).

[10] Ibid.

[11] Grady Bogue, "Commentary on Leadership," *KnoxNews. com*. August 2010.

something fails. Consequently, no lessons are learned and morale is negatively impacted.

Business humorists Scott Adams said sarcastically,

Informed decision-making comes from a long tradition of guessing and then blaming others for inadequate results. [12]

Case Study #2

A company with a chain of daycare centers in a large metropolitan city decided that the company needed to decentralize by putting more responsibility on the directors of each daycare center. Two years later, the company was facing a serious decline in enrollment at several of its daycare centers. Rather than taking the time to conduct an extensive study of causation, the CEO privately and later publicly blamed the company's board of directors for pressuring her into the decentralization strategy that she claimed would not work. In reality, the CEO was the driving force in the decentralization decision. Her transfer of blame created a very unstable working atmosphere and workplace climate and the company began to lose talented staff. Before the loss of talent reached a critical mass, the board ousted the CEO and promoted a senior staff member from within the company. The new CEO conducted research and found that the decline in enrollment was not unique to her company's daycare centers. Almost all daycare centers even competing daycare centers in the region were experiencing declining enrollment because of demographic changes and economic conditions. So, the company more concisely targeted its advertisement and provided more transportation options. It also made a concentrated effort to improve the workplace climate at each center by seeking input from the employees on how to spend funding and how to develop marketing strategies and support services. The company encouraged employee and customer feedback instead of viewing criticism from a defensive posture. Within two years, the organization was profitable, again.

Arrogance

Psychologists remind us that the inability to accept criticism is linked to self-importance, the lack of humility, and a dogged determination if anything

---

[12] Scott Adams, "Informed Decision-Making," Quote from the creator of the business-oriented *Dilbert Comic Strip*, United Media, 2000.

goes awry it must be due to factors other than decisions made by the person.[13] Many leaders like this do not recognize their own arrogance and quick-tempered response to criticism. They do not think others view them as arrogant either. The self-deception is the primary reason why arrogant leaders do not respond well to criticism or challenges.

Perhaps the best description of arrogance, a lack of humility, inability to accept criticism, and the destructiveness of it is captured by the famous English writer C.S. Lewis, who described arrogance in his book, *Mere Christianity*.

> *There is no fault which makes a man more unpopular, and no fault which we are more unconscious of in ourselves than arrogance. And the more we have it in ourselves, the more we dislike it in others. The vice I am talking of is pride or self-conceit. Nearly all those evils in the world which people put down to greed or selfishness are really far more the result of a lack of humility, of pride. It is pride and self-importance which has been the chief cause of misery in every nation and every family since the world began. The virtue opposite to it is called humility. If anyone would like to acquire humility, I can, I think, tell him the first step. The first step is to realize that one is proud. And a biggish step, too. At least, nothing whatever can be done before it. If you think you are not conceited, it means you are very conceited indeed and criticism will hound you.*[14]

Antidotes: One of the biggest challenges for organizational leaders and boards is handling criticism. This is linked directly to the appropriate roles of each. The failure to handle criticism in constructive ways can damage the relationship between the leader and the board, between the leader and staff, and between the organization and its clients. Leaders and members of boards can benefit from training on how to handle criticism in constructive ways. It is a major component of their respective roles and responsibilities.

Ron Edmondson, a respected expert in leadership and communications, offers ways to handle the criticism that can be an antidote to the determinants of criticism-reaction failure.[15]

> 1. **Consider the source.** *If the source of the criticism is from a person or group that seldom see anything positive about anyone or anything, that*

[13] Hendrie Weisinger, *The Power of Positive Criticism*, (AMACON Publishers, 2007).
[14] C.S. Lewis, *Mere Christianity*, (Harper Collins Press, Re-released 2001).
[15] Ron Edmundson. "Five Wrong Ways to Respond to Criticism," *Ron Edmundson.com*, 2016.

should be viewed differently than criticism from an individual or group that shares the good with the bad. Also, a criticism source that has facts, figures, etc. instead of rumors should be carefully considered and certainly should not be ignored, even if the facts and figures are painful to digest. Too often, a leader or board treats any type of criticism the same way, especially if they are arrogant and suffer from role confusion and defensiveness.

2. **Listen.** *Leaders and boards should be careful to listen to what is said and not to what they are expecting to hear or want to hear. Leaders sometimes expect the worse, especially if they have made ill-advised decisions before and if they are prone to defensive overreactions. They hear only criticism even if the critic is offering constructive criticism. The ineffective leader does not consider the possibility that the critic has effective ideas on how to remedy the situation or prevent similar poor decisions in the future.*

3. **Analyze.** *Is the criticism accurate? What is the nature of the criticism– does it require feedback or other action? Verify the purpose and target of the criticism–who is it aimed at? Some leaders may misinterpret criticism as intended for others when in fact it is directed to the leader and vice versa. Think of the ramifications if the criticism is accurate.*

4. **Common themes.** *Criticism can be widespread and vague or it can be narrow and specific. An effective leader will look for consistent criticism and thematic criticism where the same type of criticism comes from different quarters with some of the same specific information. That type of criticism cannot be ignored. Like the leader, the board should look for trends in the criticism, so information can be gathered in order for the leader to made corrections and/or help subordinates adjust accordingly to correct problems. The leader needs to share criticism trends with the board in case a policy needs to be revisited.*

5. **Give an answer.** *Criticism is best viewed as someone asking a question; therefore, oftentimes criticism deserves a response. The response should be aligned with and proportional to the criticism.*

In an article written by the editorial board at *Forbes,* six ways are suggested for leaders on how to respond to criticism.[16]

1. ***Stop your first reaction****: The natural reaction is to be defensive, angry, hurt, distraught, and either strike back or withdraw. The first reaction typically is not the one from which to respond to the criticism because it*

---

[16] The Muse, "Taking Constructive Criticism Like a Champ," *Forbes,* November 12, 2012.

is based on emotion and not on reason. Take time to absorb the criticism; walk away from it for a while to calm emotions.

2. **Remember the benefit of getting feedback**: *Successful leaders create workplace climates where feedback is routine and is an important part of the organization's self-assessment. Leaders should also consider that listening to and evaluating criticism often prevents other problems.*

3. **Listen for understanding**: *Listening to understand is very different than listening to respond or react. All criticism has a message. Sometimes the message is clear and useful; sometimes the message is unclear and lacks meaning, and sometimes the criticism message is an indirect warning that should not be ignored.*

4. **Ask questions to deconstruct the feedback**: *Trying to decipher criticism feedback requires questions to get to the real message and the real issues. Trying to deconstruct the feedback starts with asking questions that can guide a discussion.*

5. **Request time to follow-up**: *Many times people providing criticisms primarily want assurances that the leader or someone is listening. A request for time to look into a matter is typically viewed as an acknowledgment that someone is listening.*

6. **Say thank you**: *It is difficult to say thank you when someone is criticizing or giving any type of negative feedback. It is more than a courtesy; it is an acknowledgment that the organization and the leader are not afraid of feedback and can possibly benefit from it.*

Jacqueline Whitmore, in an article for *Entrepreneur* magazine, noted that leaders should not take criticism personally because most of the time the criticism is not intended to be personal.[17] Also, taking criticism personally takes a toll on the leader's confidence. Whitmore suggests that the leader asks for specific information about the criticism that can help channel the criticism into a productive review. Asking for help illustrates that the criticism is being taken seriously.

A sure-fire way to show that you're seriously interested in people's feedback is to ask their advice about how you can improve your performance. Say something like, 'I've been thinking about this myself, and really want to do better in the future. Do you have any suggestions for how I can improve?' When you candidly acknowledge possible deficiencies and solicit advice, you show your strength, and people may well respond with helpful counsel.[18]

---

[17] Jacqueline Whitmore, "Five tips for Gracefully Accepting Criticism," *Entrepreneur*, September 8, 2015.
[18] Ibid.

As an extension of the process to improve from constructive criticism, Whitmore encourages leaders to let people know that they value feedback and take feedback seriously.

How a leader handles criticism or how a leader learns to handle criticism is critical to her organization's success and her professional success.

Chapter Twelve Key Words and Concepts

Criticism and Leadership
Response to Criticism
Leadership Arrogance
Self-Destructive Intelligence Syndrome
Consider the Source of Criticism
Listen to Criticism
Analyze Criticism
Common Theme Criticism
Constructive Criticism
Personalizing Criticism
Deconstruct Criticism
Learning from Criticism
Learning to Respond to Criticism Appropriately

Chapter Twelve Discussion Items

Explain the different types of criticism of and within an organization and the circumstances that generally cause various types of criticism.

How can a leader determine if criticism is accurate or inaccurate, helpful or harmful, useful or a waste of time?

How should leaders respond to specific criticism about the leaders' abilities and effectiveness compared to non-specific criticism about how the organization is operating?

Explain the process of Deconstructing Criticism and provide an example of this process within an organizational setting.

Explain how you respond to criticism and what you have learned from criticism that proved helpful.

Explain how arrogance can impede a leader's effectiveness. Give examples of arrogant leaders and describe their behavior. If you have dealt with an arrogant boss, describe that situation and how the organization was effected.

Do you think telling someone that they are acting in an arrogant manner is wise and effective? What would you do if you had an arrogant boss whose behavior was negatively impacting workplace climate?

How do you handle criticism? Describe how you handled a situation when you were criticized.

Chapter Twelve Lessons Learned

One of the true measures of leadership is how a leader responds to and reacts to criticism, whether the criticism is justified or not.

Arrogance is one of the main enemies of leadership because it does not allow the leader to accept criticism and then learn from his mistakes.

When arrogance and overconfidence are combined with high intelligence a destructive element is produced.

Top management and boards responsible for making decisions that ultimately prove to be wrongheaded often sink into a defensive, self-preservation mode.

Many leaders do not recognize their own arrogance and quick-tempered response to criticism. They do not think others view them as arrogant either.

There is no fault which makes a man more unpopular, and no fault which we are more unconscious of in ourselves than arrogance.
If you think you are not conceited, it means you are very conceited indeed and criticism will hound you.

Leaders and members of boards can benefit from training on how to handle criticism in constructive ways.

A criticism source that has facts, figures, etc. instead of rumors should be carefully considered and certainly should not be ignored.

The leader should look for trends in the criticism, so information can be gathered in order for him to made corrections or at least to learn from the criticism.

Successful leaders create workplace climates where feedback is routine. This creates conditions where potential problems can be identified before they become a serious issue for the organization.

Criticism is a normal part of any organization. Internal and external criticism can provide beneficial insight into what may be a growing problem or provide ideas on how to improve the organization.

CHAPTER THIRTEEN

PREPARING FOR AND HANDLING BAD NEWS

"Let's find out what everyone is doing, and then stop everyone from doing it."
-A.P. Herbert[1]

Determinants: An ineffective leader hides bad news, ignores bad news, or tries to discredit the source of the bad news. The failure to address bad news typically makes matters worse, sometimes much worse than the original problem. A leader who strives to give the impression that everything is operating normally when in fact it is not has unleashed a negative determinant that will be difficult to contain and counteract. Bad things happen in every organization. Some bad outcomes are self-inflicted through poor decision-making; some are self-inflicted because circumstances were not right or a decision was implemented at the wrong time, and some bad things happen because of circumstances beyond the control of the organization. Regardless of the cause or circumstance, every organization must be prepared for bad news and have a thoughtful and considered way of receiving and managing bad news. Ignoring bad news is not strategically sound. It should also be noted that there is a difference between bad news and a crisis. Crisis situations will be discussed in the next chapter.

Bad News

Case Study #1

In Terence's *Comedies*, it is said that *"Bad news always flies faster than good."*[2] That certainly was the case when the leader of a non-profit organization heard that a major donor was withdrawing his substantial financial support of the organization because an audit finding indicated that

---

[1] Sir A.P. Herbert, *Uncommon Law*, (Methuen Publishers. 1935).
[2] Terence was a Roman playwright of comedies, 170-160 BC, Susan Raven, *Rome in Africa*, (Routledge Publishing, 1993).

the organization was mismanaging funds. The leader was shocked at the news, and he could not understand how the word of a minor audit recommendation had become public knowledge and how it could have concurrently been so exaggerated, too. There was an audit finding of a minor control weakness in an annual financial report of the small but influential non-profit organization.[3] Even the outside auditor, author of the report, said that it was not serious enough to be considered a major financial control weakness. However, the audit company did warn the organizational leadership that they needed to be more diligent when managing and controlling accounts for expenditures. The leader suddenly realized he had dismissed the audit recommendation as inconsequential when in fact it could be considered bad news. He later reflected on how poorly he handled the bad news. The leader went through the "SARA" stages in his reaction to the bad news. SARA stands for Shock, Anger, Rationalization, and Acceptance:[4]

> *Shock–The first response is shock or denial of the bad news, especially if what we hear is unexpected or contradicts our own views.*
> *Anger–Once the first shock of bad news is processed the shock can turn into anger very quickly, particularly as the realization of the consequences become clear.*
> *Resistance–If the bad news suggests the need for change this can evoke a rigid resistance because of the unknown effect or because change is viewed negatively. It is also viewed as admitting guilt.*
> *Acceptance–When bad news is accepted a healthy self-appraisal process can begin. A review of the situation is necessary to begin a problem-solving process.*

The leader was initially shocked that the auditors found anything untoward. Then he was angry that they put it in the audit report and angry that his staff "allowed" this to happen. Soon, however, he rationalized that the audit report was not that bad and that the indiscretions were not serious; besides, he thought, the auditors were being too precise and just looking for anything negative to report.

The audit report was posted on the organization's website, which was required by its internal policy. That is how the major donor learned of the audit recommendation. He did not hear about the audit problem from the

---

[3] Ronald Elde, *Using Case Studies for Non-Profit Management*, (Reveltree Publishing, 1999).
[4] Charles Rogel, *Using the SARA Model to Learn from 360-Degree Feedback.* (Decision Wise Productions, 2015).

organization's leader because the leader did not contemplate sharing the audit report with anyone except the board and even with the board he minimized the report and the finding as routine. Consequently, the donor opined that the organization was "hiding" bad news and, therefore, must have either little respect for his contributions to the organization at best or at the worst thought he was a faithful contributor who paid little attention to the organization's operations. Whichever was the case, the major contributor was so distraught about the organization's failure to talk to him that he threatened to withdraw current and future contributions. The leader contacted the donor and tried to explain the situation and the specific components of the audit recommendations, but the donor's trust in the leadership was compromised. Finally, the leader accepted the fact that he had handled the bad news ineffectively and asked the board and the donor what he could do to improve and learn from the situation.

Acknowledging Bad News

The Center for Community Engagement sponsored a dialogue entitled *Managing Bad News*, which featured Carol Love from Planned Parenthood, Jim Redmond from BlueCross BlueShield, and Rick Ammen a consultant to *Fortune 500* companies who specializes in managing bad news at the corporate level.[5] It was stated during the dialogue that managing bad news is not an issue limited to corporations; it affects all types of organizations.

> *Dealing with bad news is not limited to a Fortune 500 company. Small nonprofit organizations are just as likely as multinational corporations to appear on the front page of the local newspaper that reports allegations of misconduct, conflicts of interest or regulatory inquiries. These nonprofits may be in much greater jeopardy if the bad news is not managed effectively. Not only is the bad news embarrassing to the organization, its board of directors and employees, it may also cost the trust and support of other stakeholders and donors, which places the very survival of the organization at risk.[6]*

Citing examples from their own experiences, dialogue participants all agreed that bad news is a management issue that should not be dismissed by leaders. They stated that every organization will at some time have to manage bad news. They also revealed that many negative situations, if not most, are

---

[5] Carol Love, Jim Redmond, and Rick Ammen. "Managing Bad News." Video broadcast from *The Center for Community Engagement*, January 2010.
[6] Ibid.

caused by internal problems, as one said, "self-inflicted." That can be because of the lack of prevention and intervention planning, poor management of bad news, or poor communications.

There has been some research that's done every year by a group in Kentucky named the Institute for Crisis Management and one of the things that they point out is bad news in the public eye to see what the common denominators are. What they find, although the percentages vary slightly from year to year, it's basically two-thirds to three-fourths of bad news, regardless where they happen, were smoldering before they blew up. And 58 percent involved management. So what that says to me, and I think it says to most reasonable people, is that two-thirds to three-fourths of bad news situations are self-inflicted wounds, meaning that the organizations had some reason to believe or someone within the organization had some reason to believe that the train was coming down the track and was going to hit them and they didn't do anything to stop it. That is really significant because it says that, contrary to the kinds of things that we often think about - crisis such as fires, shootings and that sort of thing - self-inflicted wounds that really are what we need to worry about and respond to. [7]

Delivering bad news can be one of the worst parts of a leader's job. It is a triple dilemma because the leader has the bad news to contend with, he has to be concerned with how he handles the bad news, and he must judge how others will react to the bad news. Careers have been made and damaged-not so much by the bad news itself - as by how well or poorly the leader managed the bad news.

British Petroleum (BP) learned the hard way about managing bad news by delaying news of the oil spill in the Gulf of Mexico. Then to make matters even worse, BP minimized the seriousness of the oil spill. It is a commonly held belief now that had BP been more forthright and accurate, much of the damage from the oil spill could have been avoided or at least better contained.[8]

David Javitch, an organizational psychologist, said that leaders are not adept at delivering bad news.

---

[7] Ibid.

[8] Murray Bryant and Trevor Hunter, "PB and Public Issues (Mis) Management," *Ivey Business Journal*, September 2010.

Often times their intention is good, but they dig a grave for themselves when they deliver bad news. Those aren't easy topics to deal with. Unfortunately, a lot of people don't have a very good idea of how to do it and they mess it up. [9]

A serious issue in mismanaging bad news is procrastination. Seldom does delaying bad news make the bad news better. Dana Britol-Smith, the author of *Overcome Your Fear of Public Speaking*, said,

I think it just comes down to people are uncomfortable with confronting any sort of negative behavior or situation. Try to address the bad news while it's as small as it's going to get rather than let something fester for longer and longer. [10]

Trying to handle bad news is not a linear process because there are many factors that lead to circumstances that create the bad news.

Managing Bad News

In the article *Good News about Bad News* by James Lukaszewski, he states that *hesitation* in communicating bad news creates a public perception of confusion, lack of preparation, incompetence, and perhaps even callousness.[11] He also said,

Prevarication is perhaps the greatest error when managing bad news. There is no substitute for the absolute truth. [12]

In addition to hesitation and prevarication, Lukaszewski lists eight other things that leaders and boards need to consider when trying to manage bad news.[13]

1. ***Obfuscation*** *is the failure–deliberate or foolishly–to recognize that when time and understanding are critical, simplicity is a must. Otherwise, the perception is of dishonesty and insensitivity, if not downright obstruction.*

---

[9]   David Javitch, *Delivering Bad News*, (Entrepreneur, 2008).

[10] Dana Britol-Smith. *Overcome Your Fear of Public Speaking*, (Speaking for Success Publications, 2003).

[11] James Lukaszewski, "Good News About Bad News," *Security Management Magazine*, (April 2000).

[12] Ibid.

[13] Ibid.

2. **Pontification** *is dangerous. While a leader's nose is in the air, he or she gets hit in another part of the anatomy. Such a tactic is detrimental. Additionally, no one likes the attitude that pontification suggests. It is very likely that pontification will be considered a form of deception. The negative message is that the leader determines when bad news is shared or not.*

3. **Revelation** *is inevitable. If an organization is hiding bad news it can expect discovery because hiding bad news and the bad news itself will both be revealed in time, probably by a victim, employee, or news reporter. The fallout from this is certain to damage a leader's reputation, as well as that of the organization. In almost all case studies where an organization tries to hide bad news, the outcome for the organization is negative. It is very difficult for an organization to recover from this type of situation with its reputation and integrity intact.*

4. **Egos can be lethal.** *Responding to bad news based on ego almost always leads to a negative outcome. Here is an example, "I don't care what people say, we're not going to admit that we have a problem. We run this place and we have control of the messages, too." Robert Staub wrote, "The ego trap has captured executives, religious leaders, therapists, lobbyists, and politicians…it is easy to rationalize taking advantage of a person or a bad news situation when the action brings pleasure or avoids pain, and it makes [the leader] feel important or special."[14] Ryan Holiday stated, "The ego is the enemy."[15]*

5. **Downplaying the incident is misleading.** *Many times leaders have said of a bad news, "It was only an isolated incident. This is not a widespread problem. We have it contained and we are on top of it." A disturbing recent example of this were the misleading public comments made my Japanese leaders when the nuclear reactors were damaged by a tsunami.[16] The bad news was downplayed to the point of making a dangerous situation even worse. It is certainly advisable to manage expectations in response to bad news but to downplay its importance can insult clients, communities, employees, or other stakeholders. They may initially find some comfort when the situation is downplayed, more out of relief than anything else, but the full impact will eventually be revealed through some means, so ultimately there is no benefit to downplaying bad news.*

---

[14] Robert Staub, "You Should Beware the Dangers of the Ego Trap." *Triad Business Journal*, June 8, 2009.

[15] Ryan Holiday, *The Ego is the Enemy*, (Portfolio, 2016).

[16] Justin McCurry, "Naoto Kan Resigns as Japan's Prime Minister." *The Guardian*, August 26, 2011.

6. ***Arrogance is unforgivable.*** *For the most part, people are forgiving; people understand that people make mistakes, but it is also human nature to be less forgiving of leaders whose mistakes are shrouded with arrogance from defensiveness and denial. Here is an example of how an arrogant leader responds to bad news: "Why are they always looking for something to go wrong; why don't they talk about the good stuff I'm doing. It's really not their business how we run things; they don't know what we have to contend with, and we can't let our employees talk about it." Arab proverb states, "Arrogance diminishes wisdom."[17]*

7. ***Jargon doesn't fool anyone.*** *Sometimes the response to bad news is encased in jargon. Leaders that think jargon will diminish bad news can expect the following question: "So, what does that really mean?"*

8. ***Unpreparedness is not an excuse.*** *Using excuses in response to bad news is ill-advised: "We have had some problems over the last few years, but nothing that would indicate that this would happen to this degree." Being unprepared for events that no one could realistically anticipate can be excused, but being unprepared for the possible is not acceptable to anyone, regardless of what the leader or the organization's communications director say. In sharing bad news a leader must anticipate questions of preparedness; it cannot be avoided for very long.*

There is another category that can be added to the list: Blaming Others to Cover Yourself. Some leader's first response to bad news is to immediately look for someone or some entity to blame; for example, "it was not clear how we were supposed to handle the reporting." An example is when a large school district failed to report an aggravated sexual assault as required by state law to the state department of education. Instead of admitting that it was a data entry error, the school district told the news media that the incident was not reported because the state department's reporting instructions were not clear. The news media found that the school district's leadership had been provided reporting instructions, so it appeared that the school district intentionally failed to report the serious incident. Had the leaders responded appropriately and correctly that it was a data entry error, the bad news situation would have been handled swiftly and appropriately.

---

[17] Aisha Bilal. *Islamic and Arabian Quotes and Proverbs – Volume 1.* (Published by Aisha Bilal, 2013).

Case Study #3[18]

The case for sharing bad news in an efficient and thoughtful way applies to any organization. A mid-size company that manufactured tiny segments of a device that were used in telecommunications businesses received news that the raw materials essential to making the segments were no longer available.[19] The company was unprepared for this situation and top management came to the CEO panicked about the dilemma. One of the managers said to the CEO, "If our clients hear about this, we're finished and our Board of Directors will fire all of us." The CEO asked each of his managers to report their version of the bad news and what each of them thought the company should do about the situation. He encouraged everyone, even the most reluctant managers, to comment on the situation and suggest a course of action. They all encouraged the CEO to keep the situation quiet until they could figure out how to manage the bad news. One manager said,

People don't know what it takes to run this place and how complicated it is to secure the raw material and to make the segments; they don't know how difficult this can be. They won't understand. Our clients will dump us before we have the chance to do something.

The CEO noticed that one manager appeared to be thoughtfully and intensely listening to everyone but he had not offered a comment, so he asked him for a comment because he wanted to hear from everyone. The manager sheepishly looked at the others and said quietly,

This is a tough situation, but the only way to let our clients know that they can trust us is to tell them the truth and reassure them that we're doing everything we can to manage the situation. Think of it from their perspective. They depend on us and they have been loyal to us. How will they feel if we hide the bad news and cause them to possibly lose business from their point in the supply chain? I think the trust would be gone and they would dump us for the long run. It's a risk, I guess, to be honest with them; they may dump us immediately and never return. That's why I was debating with myself before saying anything. And it seems like everyone else here, and I respect everyone here, feels differently.[20]

---

[18] Howard Band, *Case Studies of Corporate Dilemmas*, (Pierpoint, 1989)
[19] Ibid.
[20] Ibid.

There was a long quiet moment before anyone said anything. Finally, the CEO told his executive team that he appreciated their thoughtful and earnest opinions about the bad news and what to do next about the situation. Then he said,

> *This is what we will do. We will continue our dialogue with our raw material supplier while looking for another source for obtaining the raw material. This will allow us to do two things, manage this situation and plan better against this happening again. I will personally call each board member and inform them of the situation – and not downplay the bad news. We need to maintain their trust, also. Immediately after that I will call our clients and let them know what is happening, including our strategies to get the raw materials, as well as our long-term strategy to keep this from happening again. They may panic and drop us and cuss me out for not informing them sooner and ridicule me for not have a backup plan. So be it. The bad news will leak out anyway and perhaps they will appreciate knowing that we informed them with the truth as soon as we learned about the dilemma. Now, let's get to work and we'll reconvene this afternoon at 2:00 to get an update from everyone. At that time, I'll let you know what our clients are saying.[21]*

It cannot be reported that all of the clients appreciated the honest and timely delivery of the bad news and did not cancel contracts with the company, for a few did. However, the core of the clients appreciated the honesty and the personal contact from the CEO and maintained their business relationship. And in a stroke of luck that derived from how the bad news was managed, one of the clients informed the CEO that he could possibly help with finding another source for the raw material. As it turned out, that company became a secondary supplier and at the same time emerged as part of the CEO's new backup plan.

Delivering Bad News

Jennifer Whitt observed many project managers deliver bad news and these are the most common methods they use.[22]

1. ***The Grenade:*** *The project manager walks into a crowded room of colleagues and other decision-makers, delivers bad news about the*

---

[21] Ibid.

[22] Jennifer Whit, "How to Deliver Bad News About Your Project," *Project Smart*, April 2, 2011.

project with its negative consequences without any prelude or closing comment and then leaves the room. Of course, this is totally unacceptable, ineffective and divisive. It is also a morale killer and fails to prepare the organization for future bad news. In fact, this method of responding to bad news is bad news.

2. ***The Silent Treatment:*** *This is when a project manager chooses NOT to deliver the message. The reasoning may be that he feels the problem will resolve itself, or he doesn't want to deal with the subsequent activity necessary to resolve the situation. This strategy seldom works effectively and in most cases, the bad news will worsen and could expand into a crisis.*

3. ***The Trial Balloon:*** *The leader meets with a couple of stakeholders at a time, laying out the facts of the situation to gauge their reaction. This strategy allows for additional options to be considered, allows time for further information to be introduced, and time for a reality check before crafting a message about the bad news.*

Antidotes: Tim Berry, an expert on leadership, wrote that a good measure of leadership can be identified by asking this question: "How quickly does the leader get bad news?"[23] If the leader is usually one of the first to hear about it, employees don't wait to tell him, employees don't tell each other first, and employees don't try to hide bad news from the leader, then the leader is someone people trust and who knows how to handle bad news.

In this chapter, some of the leaders refused to hide the bad news and refused to hide from the bad news. In fact, they made it clear to their leadership teams that no one was going to hide bad news. The leaders and the teams calmly and thoroughly identified the essential components of the bad news; developed a list of responses and resources; shared the challenge with the clients and others in an appropriate and timely manner, and ultimately implemented a plan that enabled the organization to effectively handle and respond to bad news and it allowed them to be better prepared for the future.

In an article for *CBS News Money Watch* by Steve Tobak titled, *How to Deliver Bad News*, he offered the following advice.

The method [of delivering bad news] incorporates elements of crisis management, customer service, effective communication, and even some psychology. And, if you do it with empathy and finesse, I've found that you can actually improve your relationship with the other parties in many ways. [24]

---

[23] Tim Berry, "How You Handle Bad News is the Ultimate Test of Leadership." *Business Insider*, October 17, 2011.

[24] Steve Tobak, "How to Deliver Bad News." *Money Watch*, June 26, 2011.

Additionally, Tobak advises leaders to be genuine; be empathetic; develop a plan, and deliver. It is also imperative to learn from the situation to better handle bad news in the future.

> *Be honest with yourself about the role you personally played in the outcome. This is critical because, if you played a direct role (i.e. you screwed up) you need to be straight with yourself about that or you'll end up feeling guilty and weird and that will come across negatively. In other words, you need to diffuse your appraisal and come to terms with your own emotional state and the impact of it all on the organization.* [25]

Leaders need to project how they would feel about bad news and how it was handled from the perspective of the community, employees, and other stakeholders. Leaders must try to understand what people stand to lose or how they will feel as a result of the bad news. Leaders must make sure they are clear that responsibility and accountability rest with them. In the long run, people appreciate leaders that take responsibility and show it. When leaders communicate bad news, it can be done in such a way that people believe the leader understands the situation and knows what should be done now and in the future. One of the worst things a leader can do is to focus on himself at the expense of the ones reporting the bad news and the ones most impacted by the bad news. It can be an unforgiving world for leaders who try to cover up bad news, shift blame to others, and who don't take responsibility for the bad news.

Leaders should consider all the ways they can make the situation better, understandable, or right. This may require creative, innovative ways of thinking beyond anything the leader has attempted before. During times when they have to address bad news, leaders may need to toss out existing plans and start over, or they may need to find the most effective parts of an existing plan and focus more resources on that aspect of the plan. In any case, leaders need to have a clear picture of the options at their disposal and under exactly what conditions the leader and the organization are willing to bring them to bear on the situation.

If a leader is genuine, displays empathy, and develops an appropriate plan in response to bad news, he will in most cases survive and learn from the situation. The leader's emotional state must convey a sense of care, concern, and stability. That means he will be empathetic, sympathetic, rational, but not emotionally distraught.

---

[25] Ibid.

Tobak offered a good example of how a company responded to bad news.

During the 'bad news delivery' face-to-face meeting with the customer, we held a conference call with my company's head of operations who, seemingly on the fly and under pressure from the customer, committed to an accelerated schedule that would minimize my customer's pain. That was a preplanned contingency to use if necessary. The result was a customer who felt that I would do anything to go to bat for him; my company would pull out all the stops to meet his needs, and he helped to make all that happen by the way he handled the meeting. Our relationship was stronger even in the face of bad news. [26]

One of the biggest mistakes leaders make in delivering bad news is the emotional build up and the unnecessary rush to get it over with.[27] That is an understandable human reaction and is very typical because everyone wishes for things to get back to normal as quickly as possible, which is a common recommendation when bad things happen.[28] But there are advantages, also, to contingency planning to know what can be done to make things right and under what conditions.[29]

Chapter Thirteen Key Words and Concepts

SARA: Shock, Anger, Resistance, and Acceptance
Managing Bad News
Precursors to Bad News
Prevarication
Obfuscation
Pontification
Revelation
Justification
Ego Trap
Arrogance
Jargon

---

[26] Ibid.

[27] Erika James. "Leadership as (Un)usual: How to Display Competence in Times of Crisis." *Organizational Dynamics*, Vol. 34, No. 2, 2005.

[28] Thierry Meyer and Benserik Reniers, *Engineering Risk Management*, (Delft University of Technology, 2016).

[29] Ken Sweeny. "Crisis Decision Theory." *Psychological Bulletin*, January 2008, 134(1):61-76. doi: 10.1037/0033-2909.134.1.61.

The Grenade
The Silent Treatment
The Trial Balloon
Communications Plan
Contingency Plan
Impulsive Rush to Normalcy

Chapter Thirteen Discussion Items

Give an example of each stage of SARA and how it facilitates understanding of typical responses to criticism and bad news.

Explain why arrogant responses to bad news harm the leader and the organization.

What is the dynamic process of arrogance that can jeopardize the reputation of a leader when he is responding to bad news?

Give examples of each of the following and your own experience or comment about each:
Prevarication, Obfuscation, Pontification, Revelation, and Justification.

Give examples of ill-conceived and counterproductive leadership responses and reactions to bad news.

Explain why hiding bad news is counterproductive. Give one example where a leader or organization tried to hide bad news. Describe an example from your own experience, if you have encountered this situation.

What can leaders and organizations do to prepare for bad news? How should employees be trained on how to respond to bad news?

If you were the leader of an organization, what would you do first upon hearing bad news that could jeopardize the effectiveness and/or reputation of the organization?

Chapter Thirteen Lessons Learned

Regardless of the cause or circumstance, every organization must be prepared for bad news.

Bad news always flies faster than good.

Not only is the bad news embarrassing to the organization, its board of directors and employees, it may also cost the trust and support of other stakeholders.

Many negative situations are caused by internal problems. That can be because of the lack of prevention and intervention planning, poor management of bad news, or poor communications.

Delivering bad news can be one of the worst parts of a leader's job.

If bad news suggests the need for change within the organization, this can evoke a rigid resistance from the leader and others within the organization.

Careers have been made and damaged - not so much by the bad news itself - as by how well or poorly the leader managed the bad news.

Trying to handle bad news is not a linear process because there are many factors that lead to circumstances that create the bad news.

Prevarication is perhaps the greatest error when managing bad news. There is no substitute for the absolute truth.

In almost all case studies where an organization tries to hide bad news, the outcome for the organization is negative.

Being unprepared for events that no one could realistically anticipate can be excused, but being unprepared for the possible is not acceptable to anyone.

If the leader is usually one of the first to hear about bad news that typically means that the flow of information is based on trust, which is an indication that the organization is well situated to handle bad news appropriately and effectively

CHAPTER FOURTEEN

PLANNING FOR AND RESPONDING TO A CRISIS

"If they expect us to expect the unexpected, doesn't the unexpected become the expected?"

-Diane Ackerman[1]

Determinants: Leaders must expect the unexpected. Many times, the success or failure of a leader is determined by her reaction to the unexpected. So much depends on the leader's decision-making acumen during difficult times. Some leaders are known for making quick decisions and are praised for their decisive response in difficult situations. Other leaders are more deliberate and inquisitive when a decision must be made, and are admired for taking the time to make the best decision during a crisis. Depending on the situation, a quick decision maker can make a crisis worse by not collecting and confirming all the facts, elements, and possible consequences before making a decision. Yet, there are times when a leader can be paralyzed by indecision when a timely decision is essential. It is a measure of a leader's effectiveness if he can determine which crisis situations call for which type of response.

Responding to a Crisis

Case Study #1

The news of the Tylenol poisoning deaths in 1982 reached the CEO shortly after a lunch meeting.[2] At that time, the makers of Tylenol, Johnson & Johnson, commanded 35 percent of the United States over-the-counter analgesic market, which was 15 percent of the company's profits. A million

---

[1] The quote is attributed to Diane Ackerman but other versions of the quote are attributed to various people: http://*topfamousquotes.com*/quotes-about-expect-the-unexpected/

[2] Jerry Knight, "Tylenol's Maker Shows How to Respond to Crisis", *The Washington Post*, October 11, 1982.

possibilities went through the CEO's mind at the same time – the safety issues, the public's confidence in all of the company's products, his board's reaction, the impact on the company's stock market performance and reputation, the attitude of employees, and many other thoughts.

Some observers of leadership behavior and many business analysts predicted that the CEO would take a cautious approach as he contemplated a reaction to the crisis. They were correct in the prediction that the CEO would move mountains to get the facts and determine what happened. However, they did not accurately forecast that the CEO's first thoughts were his concern and grief for the victims and the safety of consumers. To him, there could be no hesitation in removing all Tylenol products from the shelves. He let it be known around the world that his company was first and foremost concerned about the safety of the public, and his company could not and would not hesitate or respond in measured strategies. His decision was based on a basic principle that was at the heart of his company but mostly at the heart of his attitude about his company's mission. The company focused on the safety of its customers. Had he hesitated; had he taken a defensive posture; had he blamed others; had he taken a wait-and-see attitude, the safety of many customers could have been compromised, and the future of the company would have been at risk. Instead, his decision-making during the crisis and his follow-up decisions were applauded by the business world and the public.

Ambiguity during a Crisis

The CEO at Johnson & Johnson had so many choices and decisions to make he could have fallen victim to the "centipede syndrome"[3] where he did not know which foot to put down next. That is the weakness of some leaders who are efficient and effective during good times but sink into what Michael Cohen and James March in their book *Leadership and Ambiguity* call "*ambiguous decision-making*" during crisis times when tough, clear decisions have to be made.[4] Cohen and March describe leaders that try to avoid major

---

[3] In 1923, poet George Humphrey wrote the short poem *The Centipede's Dilemma*, which psychologists used to describe the "centipede effect" when automatic or unconscious reactions are interrupted to the point of inaction by awareness of the reactions or over-awareness by thinking too much instead of responding. George Humphrey, *The Story of Man's Mind*, (Small, Maynard and company, 1923).

[4] Michael Cohen and James March, *Leadership and Ambiguity 2nd Edition*, (Harvard Business Press, 1986).

decisions during a crisis by communicating ambiguous decisions which can be misinterpreted or misunderstood. *Deliberate ambiguity* may create a failsafe from criticism for the leader when his response to a crisis is evaluated but it does not help the organization in the short-term or long-term. The ambiguity will erode confidence in the leader and make a crisis more dangerous for clients, employees, and the organization.

In the article *How a Good Leader Reacts to a Crisis*, John Baldoni said that leaders have to be thoughtful about the crisis and their reaction to it. He offers advice for leaders in several areas that are important to effectively managing a crisis in a way that maintains morale, safety, integrity, and confidence.[5]

1. ***Take a moment to figure out what's going on****: In many crisis situations, the first meeting of pertinent staff is often dominated by nervous chatter, where everyone is talking at once. This seldom leads to constructive decision-making but it is a normal and typical reaction. Under these circumstances, it may be wise for the leader to get the staff to focus on what is important and eliminate the distractions by delegating responsibilities and directing the staff to reconvene in one hour. According to Baldoni, "This helps impose order on a chaotic situation."[6]*

2. ***Act promptly, not hurriedly****: A leader must provide direction and respond to the crisis in a timely fashion. But acting hurriedly instead of promptly only makes people nervous. A leader can act with deliberateness as well as speed. It is primarily how the messaging is handled, the communication style of the leader, and confidence and poise of the leader. The legendary coach John Wooden advised, "Be quick, but don't hurry."[7]*

3. ***Manage expectations****: When a crisis strikes people want it to be over very quickly so things can return to normal as soon as possible. It falls to the leader to address the size and scope of the crisis. The leader cannot be afraid to speak to the magnitude of the situation and what may be required to manage the crisis and manage expectations during and after the crisis.*

4. ***Demonstrate control****: During a crisis, many things are happening quickly. No one person may have control, but a leader must try to assume control and let everyone know that the situation is manageable. A good*

---

[5] John Baldoni, "How a Good Leader Reacts to a Crisis," *Harvard Business Review*, January 2011.

[6] Ibid.

[7] John Wooden and Andrew Hill, *Be Quick but Not Hurry*, (Simon and Schuster, 2001).

example comes from Gene Kranz, the Flight Director of Apollo 13 who said, "Let's work the problem people."[8] He also said, "Failure is not an option."[9] Leaders cannot control the crisis per se, but a good leader can control the response. An effective leader puts himself into the action and brings the people and resources to bear.[10] The leader of the organization has to show that he is leading everyone through the crisis. He is in charge. There are times during a crisis when the leader has to delegate responsibilities in order to manage the scope of a crisis; however, the delegation of responsibilities is not the same as abdicating his leadership role. It should be clear that the leader is in total control of the crisis response. Delegation of duties is not the same as capitulating responsibility to others within the organization nor is it abdicating responsibility for decisions. Delegation of duties expands the organization's ability and capability to manage a crisis by utilizing manpower but also by encouraging problem-solving across the organization.

5. ***Stay calm and illustrate calm:*** *If a leader loses his self-control, he immediately loses his effectiveness. He must control his thoughts and emotions during a crisis. A leader can never afford to lose his composure. Winston Churchill said that his best advice during a crisis is to, "Keep calm and carry on."[11] This has implications for the leader's ability to adapt rapidly while maintaining at the same time a calm demeanor. Churchill's calm during major crisis situations was legendary.[12]*

6. ***Be prepared to adapt to the fluid nature of a crisis:*** *The hallmark of a crisis is its tendency to change quickly; therefore, the leader's first response may not be his final response. In these situations, a leader cannot be wedded to a single strategy. He must continue to consider new relevant information (or revised information), listen carefully, and consult with the staff closest to the crisis.*

---

[8] William Broyles, Jr. and Al Reinert, *Apollo 13 Screenplay*, (Universal Pictures, June 30, 1995).

[9] Ibid.

[10] Ibid.

[11] This phrase was used by the British Government during World War II. The quote was from British Prime Minister Winston Churchill. It was printed on thousands of posters distributed across Great Britain to boost morale.

[12] Robert Lewis Taylor, Winston Churchill: *An Informal Study of Greatness*, (Double Day Press, 1952).

Maintaining Trust during a Crisis

Another important aspect of crisis management and decision-making that every leader must understand is the trust factor. In each and every crisis trust becomes an important part of the crisis and the response to the crisis. The importance of trust–trust between the leader and the board, trust between the leader and employees, and trust between the leader and the community and/or clients, and between the leader and other stakeholders is essential. An effective leader can ill afford to take a moment to figure out what's going on if he cannot trust the information provided by his staff. He must trust that the information is timely, accurate, and relevant. Otherwise, the decision-making window becomes very narrow. Also, a leader cannot provide directions and respond in a timely manner if trust does not exist among the leader, board, and employees. Almost everyone wants a crisis to end as soon as possible. It is human nature to desire a return to normalcy as soon as possible. Returning to normalcy is the strongest motivation for most people because there is security in normalcy, but a crisis is different than bad news. A return to normalcy that is interrupted by a crisis may take a long time, much longer than recovering from bad news.

The messages of reassurance that the crisis is being managed can be met with skepticism if trust in the leader is lacking. Without trust, the leader's ability to manage expectations is minimized, thus the crisis itself may not be contained and there may be collateral damage from an unmanaged crisis.

As reported by Markus Hasel in his study on leadership in crisis situations, he found that successful leaders know the importance of managing crisis situations in calm and measured tones. Hasel said no effective management of a crisis has occurred in situations where the leader is manic and overreacts in such a manner that the organization's response to the crisis is not well-managed. Effective management in a crisis starts with a calmness that assures others that the crisis can be managed.

Beyer and Browning's (1999)[13] report on Robert Noyce, founder of Intel, highlights the importance of particular leadership styles during a crisis. Through his engaging, involving, and emotionally intelligent leadership style, Noyce successfully led the US semiconductor industry through its most turbulent and crisis times when facing strong competition from cheaper Asian

---

[13] J. M. Beyer and L.D. Browning, "Transforming an industry in crisis: charisma, routinization, and supportive cultural leadership," *Leadership Quarterly, 10* (3), 1999.

rivals. The entire US semiconductor industry was in a crisis. This example demonstrates the importance of people-focused leadership during a crisis.[14]

Case Study #2

One of the most important requirements of a leader is the demonstration that he is in control during a crisis–truly in control; however, that can be an illusion. There is a trust calculus that determines if the leader is actually in control. If the leader is not truly in control of the crisis or at least the response to the crisis and if the public or employees do not trust the leader's comments or actions, it is very unlikely that the leader will remain calm throughout the crisis. How a leader handles a crisis can forge a strong trust bond between him and employees, between him and the board, and between him and the public. A leader that did not manage a crisis well is a leader that will be questioned and second-guessed each time a crisis has to be dealt with.

A significant example of this comes from the aftermath of the Boston Marathon terrorist bombing in 2013. Several of the deputy fire chiefs in the Boston Fire Department complained that the Boston Fire Chief did not respond well to the bombing crisis.[15] They claimed that the Fire Chief did not help coordinate the emergency response, was not available to make timely decisions, and at times could not be found. Consequently, the deputy fire chiefs stated that their leader's failure to respond to the crisis had eroded their confidence in him to lead. Thirteen of the 14 deputy chiefs signed a letter of "no confidence" in the fire chief.

At a time when the city of Boston needed every first responder to take decisive action, Chief Abraira failed to get involved in operational decision-making or show any leadership."[16] *Comments that the fire chief made during the crisis were contrary to the trust his staff had in him and his ability to respond to such a widespread and major tragedy. As the story unfolded, it became more apparent that many of the fire chief's deputies did not have trust in him before the crisis.*[17]

---

[14] Markus Hasel, "A question of context: the influence of trust on leadership effectiveness during crisis," *Management*, March 2013.
[15] Stephanie Gallman and Christina Sgueglia, "Fire Chief Resigns After Criticism of Bombing Response," *CNN*, June 4, 2013.
[16] Ibid.
[17] Ibid.

Case Study #3

It is important to understand and therefore recognize the origin of situations where trust is a factor with leadership during a crisis, such as in the Toyota crisis. Typically it is either because the leader is perceived as weak and consequently unable to make crisis decisions or the leader is arrogant and does not have a history of listening to staff or others. Helga Drummond's *Guide to Decision Making* offers a rich discussion of decision making during a crisis.[18] She states that calamity loves the overconfident. Drummond found that,

> *Our innate tendency is to overestimate our abilities so that we often see ourselves as superior to other people. We also view ourselves more positively than others see us.* [19]

Consequently, many leaders do not trust the opinions of subordinates routinely and especially during a crisis. The danger, according to Drummond, is the complacency of over-confidence. She sites Toyota's response to a deadly product failure as an example of how leaders can mismanage a crisis by doing nothing because of supreme overconfidence.

> *Toyota's leaders inflicted huge damage upon the company by refusing to recall vehicles with potentially lethal accelerator pedals. Toyota had known about the accelerator pedal crisis for months before reports began appearing in the news in late 2009, but acted only when forced to do so by mounting public pressure.* [20]

Ira Kalb in an article that studied the failure of leaders at Toyota noted how confused customers, reporters, investors, and employees were by the response to the crisis by its leadership.

> *When complaints of self-acceleration were first reported, Toyota did not know how to handle them. Rather than say that they are investigating the complaints and will issue a complete report at the conclusion of their investigation, Toyota representatives reacted to the complaints in ways that confounded marketing and crisis management experts. They confused everyone by jumping to conclusions and suggesting different causes in rapid*

---

[18] Helga Drummond, *Guide to Decision Making: Getting it More Right than Wrong*, (Wiley, 2012).
[19] Ibid.
[20] Ibid.

succession. First, they attributed the problem to operator error, which is the most frequent cause of self-acceleration problems in automobiles (the issue that nearly triggered the demise of Audi in the US market during the mid-1980s). Then, Toyota suggested the cause of the problem was floor mats that trapped the gas pedal. This was followed by the suggestion that faulty electronics caused the unintended acceleration. Instead of reassuring the marketplace, Toyota acted in a way that caused owners to fear for their safety and prospective buyers to look for other makes and models. For example, Jim Lentz, president and chief executive officer of Toyota Motor Sales, USA, went on the Today Show and looked like a "deer in headlights" in response to Matt Lauer's cross-examination. In a poll taken before Lentz spoke, 37% said they were less likely buy Toyota cars. The negative numbers jumped to 56% after he spoke. The uncertainty created by Toyota representatives triggered a series of costly recalls, lawsuits, and lost business.[21]

Case Study #4

Another example of leadership during a crisis comes from the H1N1 influenza virus pandemic in 2009. In the spring of that year, the H1N1 influenza virus shocked the world, especially in the United States and more specifically the Centers for Disease Control (CDC) and state health departments. Years of planning for a virus such as the more lethal H5N1 (bird flu) had taken place at the national, state, and local levels, but the main premise of the planning was flawed because the basic assumption was that a virus, such as the H5N1, would evolve in some other part of the world and the United States would not be impacted until three or more weeks later. By then CDC and/or the World Health Organization (WHO) scientists, epidemiologists, and virologists would know the severity of the virus and could react accordingly to the crisis. In other words, the United States would know what to do depending on the mortality rate, how quickly the virus spreads, and what age groups were most vulnerable. There were no plans if a serious virus appeared in the United States from a closer source that would require a more immediate response. In addition to the failure of planning for a different point of origin for a virus, the leaders also had crisis blind spots. One of which was the impact on schools and daycare centers.

During the crisis there was considerable debate centered on whether or not to close schools if a pandemic broke out in the United States. CDC, state, and local public health experts did not have a realistic view of the impact of

---

[21] Ira Kalb, "How Toyota's Crisis Management Failure Added to Billion Dollar Settlement, *Business Insider*, December 2012.

closing schools and daycare centers. Many of the public health experts thought it was rather simple: close schools to avoid the spread of a virus. However, as the debate matured it became more apparent that the public health impact, the economic impact, the psychological impact, and the educational impact of closing schools were very significant. In fact, the Brookings Institute estimated that closing all public schools in the United States for four weeks would cost over a billion dollars and reduce the Gross National Product (GNP) by a significant amount. When the Brookings Institute released the economic statistics from a financial impact study regarding closing schools during a pandemic crisis, it shocked many experts who had underestimated the impact public schools have on the United States economy (adding private school closures to the calculations would increase the loss considerably).

We find that closing all schools in the U.S. for four weeks could cost between $10 and $47 billion dollars (0.1-0.3% of GDP).[22]

When the H1N1 virus appeared suddenly in Mexico that spring and rapidly spread, CDC and other Health and Human Services agencies were shocked that this type of virus began so close to the United States; nevertheless, they all sprang into action. They reviewed the crisis plans and scripts developed for a virus like H5N1 and soon realized that those plans would not apply to other types of virus situation. State public health agencies found the same. They did not know enough about the virus to make carefully considered decisions so a controlled panic set in among and between public health experts and leaders.

The issue of closing schools moved very quickly to the forefront, particularly since the virus came to the United States so quickly. At a National Institute of Health pandemic public health conference that was hastily scheduled six months into the H1N1 pandemic, a large number of the public health officials identified the most complicated situation and what was causing them the most angst was the decision whether or not to close schools during the crisis.[23] Up to that point, the opinion from educators about closing schools was not sought by public health officials either at the federal level or

---

[22] Howard Lempel, Ross Hammond, and Joshua Epstein, "Economic Cost and Healthcare Workforce Effects of School Closures in the United States," *Brookings Institute*, September 30, 2009.
[23] National Institutes of Health, http://www.hhs.gov/asl/testify/2009/07/t 20090729b.html.

at state levels. The public health officials reacted to the crisis in an arrogant, narrow-minded, condescending manner.

This type of response to a virus-based crisis was a point of concern at a National Governors Association (NGA) meeting about pandemic planning two years before the H1N1 pandemic. Thirteen states were represented. The facilitators of the meeting asked how many educators were on the state teams. Only two states had the education community represented on their pandemic planning team. The NGA was very concerned that public health had left education off of the planning teams and reported to governors across the United States that education should be included in all public health emergency crisis planning.[24] NGA made the same recommendation to the United States Department of Human Services, but the reaction was mixed. Some states took notice and followed the NGA recommendations most did not; therefore, a major decision component during a crisis was purposely omitted by public health leaders.

When the H1N1 virus spread to the United States, CDC and the World Health Organization were still trying to determine if the virus was dangerously lethal. They never planned to make that crisis decision while a virus was newly found in the United States. They had counted on advanced warning. Without a grasp of the severity of the virus, CDC leaders overreacted and issued guidance to school districts across the nation to close school even if only one student became ill with H1N1- like symptoms, and to close the entire school district if one student in more than one school became infected. The leaders did not (1) take a moment to figure out what was going on; (2) they acted hurriedly; (3) they did not manage expectations; (4) they did not demonstrate control, and (5) they did not stay calm and illustrate calm.

The education community, employers, and parents were caught in the middle of a crisis situation where leaders were not communicating effectively. They were asking, "*What type of crisis decision-making is this?*" How could they justify closing thousands of schools when little was known about the virus; yet, how could they respond if a student or several students became gravely ill because they kept the schools open against the advice of public health? In the communities where the virus spread, schools were closed, which released thousands of students into the malls, stores, and streets. That did not seem like a good example of social distancing (limiting social contact to prevent the spread of the virus), which was the purpose of

---

[24] National Governors Association:
http://www.nga.org/files/live/sites /NGA/files/pdf/0607PANDEMIC PRIMER. PDF.

school closures in the first place. Some school districts remained closed for up to a week or longer, and some schools reopened after closing for only a couple of days. It was a chaotic time and trust in leadership was threatened. Fortunately, CDC, NIH, and the World Health Organization found that the severity of the virus was no worse than seasonal flu, so they recanted the guidance to close schools.

> *In other words, the leaders in those organizations trusted their respective employees and the community leaders to be honest and forthright with them. The leaders were at the center of the decision-making process and made timely and thoughtful, albeit tough, decisions during a major crisis, which quickly shifted the mistrust to trust.*[25]

Public health officials around the country finally understood how important public schools were to the fabric of social existence and daily life in the United States and, therefore, the decision to close schools should be taken more seriously and be part of the crisis decision-making process. The leaders acknowledged and learned from their mistakes during the crisis; consequently, future crisis responses will be better.

Failed Leadership in a Crisis

Michael Hyatt, head of Intentional Leadership, wrote in an article titled *When Leadership Fails* that leadership failures during a crisis are often the result of several elements: poor planning, inexperience, stubbornness, lack of vision, naiveté, and/or pride. These elements impact an organization's ability to effectively respond to a crisis.[26] Hyatt makes a very important point for all who work in organizations.

> *Failed leadership in a crisis happens more often than we would like to admit. When we are the victims, though, we notice it all the time. We see ourselves as being stuck in our circumstances. We complain. We gossip. We throw our hands up in the air and ask, 'What if?' That is not necessarily a bad question. But instead of asking, 'What if those leading me were better,' we should ask, 'What if I had responded to poor leadership better [during a crisis]?'*[27]

---

[25] Garry W. McGiboney, *Crisis Planning for Schools and Centers*, (Einstar Publishing, 2016).

[26] Michael Hyatt, "When Leadership Fails," *MH* 2015: https://michael hyatt.com/when-leadership-fails.html.

[27] Ibid.

Hyatt says that a common response to poor leadership during a crisis is to retreat. Instead, he suggests, encourage each person to continue to work hard on the tasks before them and learn from the mistakes that are made during the crisis because there will be other crises. Poor leadership during a crisis is bad enough, but the failure to learn from a crisis is unforgivable and poison for any type of organization.

Case Study #5

The Buffalo Creek Disaster was one of the most tragic incidents in United States history and is an illustration of neglectful leadership during a crisis that was followed by an unconscionable failure to respond appropriately to a leadership-caused tragedy.[28]

On February 26, 1972, coal impoundment dam #3 breached and collapsed sending a cascade down through West Virginia's Buffalo Creek hollow, completely destroying every part of the town and community and killing 125 people. The flood also left 4,000 people not only without homes but without a community. The flood of 130 million gallons of water, coal waste products, sludge, dirt, and debris was 25 feet high and caused destruction that was brutally complete, laying everything in its path annihilated. The Monday before the flood, the superintendent of the Buffalo Mining Company, which was owned by the Pittston Coal Company, was concerned about dam #3, a dam built to hold waste debris from coal mining, a common practice in the coal mining process. The superintendent knew that the dam did not have a runoff that would safely drain excess water build up to avoid a breach of the dam. That concern was shared by the director of Buffalo Mining Company operations, who was responsible for the day-to-day running of the coal mining. They were both concerned because of the continuing heavy rain and the rise of the water behind the dam. The concerned was even shared with the president of the Pittston Coal Company. The president flew to the area with

---

[28] Gerald Stern, *The Buffalo Creek Disaster: How the Survivors of One of the Worst Disasters in Coal Mining History Brought Suit Against the Coal Company and Won*, (Vintage, 2008); http://www.wvculture.org/history/buffalocreek /bctitle. html; *Buffalo Creek Disaster: Environmental Case Study:*, University of Michigan Environmental Studies (2008): http://umich. edu/~snre492/ Jones/buffalo. html; Dennis Deitz and Carlene, *Buffalo Creek: Valley of Death*, (Mountain Memory Books, 1992); Tom Nugent, *Death at Buffalo Creek: The 1972 West Virginia Flood Disaster*, (W. W. Norton & Company, 1973); Kai T. Erikson, *Everything in Its Path: Destruction of Community in the Buffalo Creek Flood*, (Simon and Schuster, 1976).

some of his top executives but inexplicably they never went to the dam. Even though it continued to rain all week, and despite knowing on Thursday of the same week that the water in the dam continued to rise, no warning was raised for the people living downstream from the dam. By Friday, the director of operations found the water was dangerously close to breaching the dam. Even after receiving these reports, the president and his staff left to go home by helicopter which could have easily and quickly flown over the dam to observe its condition. They didn't. They showed a callous disregard for the crisis.

Friday night the rain intensified and some citizens in the community were growing uneasy about the rain and the dam. In fact, the sheriff's office was contacted at 3:30 Saturday morning of the same week by citizens who thought everyone in the community should be warned. Calls also went to the Buffalo Mining Company about their concerns, and there was a suggestion that the National Guard should be called to warn or evacuate the community. Everyone was assured by the director of operations that there was nothing to worry about. Nevertheless, some citizens left their homes and went to the local school building for shelter, and for what they thought would be a safe haven in case the dam failed. It was not a safe place to be.

Just a few hours before the dam collapsed, the superintendent of the Buffalo Mining Company was worried but the director of operations was not as concerned, and when the president of Pittston was informed of the continuing rising water, he made no call to warn people nor did he send the company's chief engineer or any engineer to the dam to inspect it and make a risk assessment. At 7:30 Saturday morning, the director of operations called the sheriff's department to reassure the sheriff and his deputies that there was nothing to worry about and there was no need to call the National Guard. Only 30 minutes later, the dam collapsed and unleashed a tidal wave of destruction and death.

Soon after the tragedy, a lawyer for Pittston made a statement that the responsibility for the disaster was Pittston's. However, when the top executives in New York, the site of the corporate offices, heard this they made the lawyer "clarify" and retract his statement. That was the first clue that neither the Buffalo Mining Company nor its parent company Pittston and none of the leaders were going to accept any blame for the disaster and the loss of life and property. In fact, to prepare for any possible litigation, Pittston claimed that Buffalo Mining Company was a separate company and if there was going to be any litigation it would have to be at the state level and levied against Buffalo Mining Company and not Pittston. This was a strategic position because West Virginia laws favored the coal companies by limiting wrongful death claims to an incredibly meager amount of $10,000. If the family could somehow show that the death of a loved one was even more tragic, such as the loss of a father who was the only provider of support for his family, the ceiling for claims was $110,000.

When Pittston learned that individual and family survivors of the flood were seeking legal counsel in order to rebuild their lives, Pittston executives sent settlement counselors to the area to offer the survivors immediate money to settle. Some took the money, accepting as little as $4,000 and others no more than $10,000.

The number of plaintiffs that would be part of the lawsuit reached 450. Later, an additional 150 plaintiffs were added to the lawsuit. Experts estimated that the psychological damage to the plaintiffs would total $20 million, roughly $50,000 each while the property damage was $11 million. Because the claim alleged wrongful and knowing neglect and disregard for safety, the victims also sought $21 million in punitive damages. The punitive damage claim amount was to make the lawsuit "materially" damaging since Pittston was valued at $42 million. The victim's families wanted to send a message to other coal companies in West Virginia that coal companies had to change their operations procedures so that miners and their families would be safer and well protected. The psychological (called "psychic") claim, the property damage claim and the punitive damage claim altogether totaled $52 million. However, two years later another 25 plaintiffs were added to the plaintiff list, for a total of 625 which then raised the claim to $64 million. When divided among 625 individuals it equals $102,400 for each person. As the case dragged on, the survivors received nothing for over two years, and in the end, the victims settled for $15 million, which was only $25,000 per person, on the average. That is just an average because some received a little more for property claims and 600 received $13,000 for psychic claims, including $8,849 for each of the 226 children suffering from psychological damage. Some of whom have life-long psychological issues that require long-term treatment.

Pittston stated publicly that it had won the case proving that the company was not responsible for acts of nature. During the litigation, Pittston fought access to records, such as records of the Grand Jury and Ad Hoc Committee. The Ad Hoc Committee studied the disaster and pointed blame at the company's executive decision-making before, during, and after the crisis. Also, Pittston would not allow victim's attorney to look at the details of the company's insurance policy that had mysteriously been changed just two days before the disaster because of the insurer's concerns about Pittston's history of dam structure failures and the failure of other dams in coal mining history.

Unlike the CEO and other top executives at Johnson & Johnson during the Tylenol crisis, the leadership at Pittston responded by avoiding all manner of responsibility for the tragedy at Buffalo Creek. They also released incomplete if not inaccurate information, showed no remorse or sympathy for the victims and their families, made no effort to restore the lives of the victims and took almost no steps to prevent future tragedies of this type.

Antidote: Erika James and Lynn Wooten in their article *Leadership as (Un)usual: How to Display Competence in Times of Crisis*, suggests that there are two types of crisis: (1) *Sudden Crisis* and (2) *Smoldering Crisis*.[29] Sudden crises occur without any warning and are beyond the organization's control; consequently, leaders are judged completely on how they respond to the crisis within what was possible and what was controllable, given the circumstances. Smoldering crises are different from sudden because they begin as minor and escalate into a significant crisis.

James and Wooten recommend that all leaders create a crisis preparation mentality and modality by starting with a signal detection strategy or plan. This can be accomplished at least in part by encouraging employees to inform leadership when something happens or is happening that may smolder and become a crisis. Many crises can be prevented, but leaders must grow situational skills that include the ability to sift through a lot of information and determine what is important, what can be delayed, and what needs to be addressed rapidly.

Leaders must develop trust with employees and the board before a crisis strikes. Many crises can be averted or controlled if employees have the trust that leadership will listen and respond to potential crisis situations when the employee reports them. In many crisis situations, someone within the organization had information or knowledge that could have been used to avoid or minimize a crisis had they trusted the leadership.

Trust is essential before and during a crisis. In fact, the lack of trust is perhaps the most compelling obstacle during a crisis. The underlying mistrust can be detrimental to an organization during a crisis and impede its timely and appropriate response. A "bunker mentality" response to a crisis is not uncommon when the leader, employees, and board do not trust each other and no good decisions can come from that environment.

---

[29] Ericka James and Lynn Wooten, "Leadership as (Un)usual: How to display competence in times of crisis." *Organizational Dynamics*, 34(2), 2005.

People need, want, and expect leadership during a crisis. A few weeks after Hurricane Katrina flooded New Orleans, an editorial cartoon appeared in *Time* magazine that showed a man standing in waist-deep water holding a sign that pleaded, *"Leadership Please."*[30]

During and after Hurricane Katrina hit New Orleans, the lack of trust between local leadership and state leadership led to a disastrous leadership response to the crisis. Dan Bobinski described what happened and the lessons learned.

> *The lessons learned? If you're going to have plans, write them before you want to use them, and make sure everyone knows their roles them before you have to implement them. And make sure all issues are addressed. People need time to be trained and know what is expected of them before a crisis plan is invoked. Also, if someone offers genuine help, swallow your pride and accept it. No sin exists in admitting you can't run everything all by yourself during a crisis. The third failure I'd like to examine is the lack of communication amongst the various leaders during a crisis. Think of it this way: If both sides of your brain want to do different things but don't communicate with each other on how to get it all done, your body is going to suffer. Such was the case in this disaster. At the same time that New Orleans mayor C. Ray Nagin was on TV demanding to know the location of emergency food and water, Louisiana's state officials were denying the Red Cross access to New Orleans.*[31]

In his book *Crisis Leadership*, Gene Klann wrote that very few situations define the perception of a leader more than the leader's response to a crisis.

> *Nothing tests a leader like a crisis. The highly charged, dramatic events surrounding a crisis profoundly affect the people in an organization and can even threaten the organization's survival. But there are actions a leader can take before, during, and after a crisis to effectively reduce the duration and impact of these extremely difficult situations. At its center, effective crisis leadership is comprised of three things - communication, clarity of vision and values, and caring relationships. Leaders who develop, pay attention to and*

---

[30] *Time,* http://ideas.time.com/category/cartoons-of-the-week/

[31] Dan Bobinski, "Leadership Lessons from Katrina," *Management Issue*, September 2005.

practice these qualities go a long way toward handling the human dimension of a crisis. In the end, it's all about the people and the plan.[32]

In an article on *crisis decision theory*, Kate Sweeny looked at coping theory and decision-making.[33] Her study of crisis response focused on three steps of crisis decision-making theory:

1. **Assessing the severity of the crisis.** *An effective leader will immediately search for all means available to determine the size and scope of the crisis without relying on one source of information.*
2. **Determining response options.** *An effective leader and his staff will have a working crisis preparation and response plan but there is a tendency to depend too much on preplanned decision making if a crisis does not match all of the components of the organization's crisis plan (i.e., the above-referenced case study on the H1N1 pandemic). The effective leader will be agile enough to recognize and adapt to unique features of the crisis and not be overly dependent on what may have worked in the past if it is not appropriate for the current crisis.*
3. **Evaluating response options.** *Sweeny found that "Some crises have more consequences than others, but crisis decisions theory recognizes that not all crisis situations require the same set of responses."*[34]

There are no precise and exact crisis decision-making protocols that will be appropriate for every type of crisis events. However, at the very least, every organization should build a crisis response protocol based on the three primary elements of Sweeny's work in crisis response theory.[35]

1. *How serious is the crisis?*
2. *What are the response options?*
3. *What are the pros and cons of each response option?*

Organizations that are familiar with, and especially those that use the SWOT (Strengths, Weaknesses, Opportunities, and Threats)[36] analysis can

---

[32] Gene Klann, *Crisis Leadership*, (Center for Creative Leadership, 2003).

[33] Kate Sweeny, "Crisis decision theory: Decisions in the face of negative events," *Psychological Bulletin*, 134 (1), 2008.

[34] Ibid.

[35] Ibid.

[36] Martin Blade and Shehan Wijetilaka, "5 tips to grow your start-up using SWOT analysis". *Sydney* December 2015; Albert Humphrey, "SWOT Analysis for Management Consulting," *SRI Alumni Newsletter. SRI International*, December

use SWOT in crisis situations to assess the severity of the event and evaluate the response options.

1. *What are the strengths of each response option?*
2. *What are the weaknesses of each response option?*
3. *Does a response option have opportunities for making a crisis situation a valuable learning experience?*
4. *Can the decision response possibly strengthen the organization's standing by illustrating its ability to respond effectively to a crisis?*

The *Management Study Guides for Non-Profits* provides an excellent summary of SWOT and how it can support organizations. This is a summary of each element:[37]

1. **Strengths**-*Strengths are the qualities that enable organizations to accomplish its mission and respond to crises. These are the elements on which continued success can be made and continued/sustained. Strengths can be either tangible or intangible. These are what leaders are well-versed in or what they have expertise in, the traits and qualities employees possess (individually and as a team) and the distinct features that give the organization its consistency and ability to pivot and respond to many types of crises. Strengths are the beneficial aspects of the organization or the capabilities of an organization, which includes critical components.*

2. **Weaknesses**-*Weaknesses are the qualities that prevent the organization from accomplishing its mission and responding appropriately to a crisis. These weaknesses deteriorate influences on the organizational success and growth from a crisis. Weaknesses are the factors which do not meet the standards they should meet. Weaknesses in an organization may be insufficient research and development facilities, poor decision-making, etc. Weaknesses are controllable. They must be minimized and eliminated or the organization will not be prepared to respond to a crisis.*

3. **Opportunities**-*Opportunities are presented by the environment within which our organization operates. These arise when an organization can take benefit of conditions in its environment to plan and execute strategies*

2011; Ahmad Ommani, "SWOT analysis for business manage-ment," *African Journal of Business Management*, 5 (22), September 2011; Christian Osita, Idoko Onyebuchi, and Nzekwe Justina, Nzekwe, "Organization's stability and productivity: the role of SWOT analysis, " *International Journal of Innovative and Applied Research*, January 2014.
[37]*Management Study Guides for Non-Profits*: http://www.Manage-mentstudy guide.com/swot-analysis.htm. (April 2016).

that enable it to respond to a crisis. Organizations can better manage a crisis by making use of opportunities. Organizations should be careful and recognize the opportunities and grasp them whenever they arise and plan for their usefulness during a crisis.

4. ***Threats**-Threats arise when conditions in external environment jeopardize the reliability of the organization's functions and when possible crisis conditions are ignored internally. They compound the vulnerability when they relate to the weaknesses. Threats are uncontrollable but can be manageable. When a threat comes, the stability and survival of the organization can be at stake; therefore, the organization's response to the threat must be appropriate in order to manage the crisis. The identification of possible threats can help an organization prepare and respond to a crisis.*

The SWOT process can inform an organization before, during, and after a crisis. It can be an effective tool for any organization. It is one of many ways a leader can create an expectation for the organization to be prepared for and respond to a crisis. It is not foolproof, of course, and it does not mitigate other problems such as a lack of trust, but it can help an organization take a serious and accurate assessment of its readiness for a crisis and how people in key positions should respond to a crisis. It can be an action review plan and template with the agility that is necessary to respond to a crisis.

Basic Elements of Crisis Planning

There are two fundamental types of crisis situations. The previous section addressed how organizations react to crisis situations that require management decisions at the leadership level to prevent the crisis from damaging the organization and harming others that depend on it. The second type of crisis is a physical threat to the organization and its employees. This section covers the physical threat crisis.

The basic elements of crisis planning include a comprehensive approach to crisis management that places a strong emphasis on prevention. Beyond the basic crisis plan, the plan should be developed with the understanding that a more fully developed crisis plan is necessary to match the needs of each organization. Some organizations have unique situations that mandate specific crisis management strategies. However, each crisis plan should at the very least include the following.[38]

---

[38] Garry W. McGiboney, *Crisis Management Planning*, (Einstar Publishing, 2016).

1. *Strategies that establish communication procedures with local emergency management.*
2. *A review of the organization's building(s) design and use of space.*
3. *The development of personnel management policies.*
4. *The creation of plans for training of employees.*

Effective crisis management planning anticipates potential problems and establishes a coordinated response to minimize threats to the safety of clients and employees and manages stress and disruption in the organization. A crisis management plan should also be developed with the goal to prevent a crisis from escalating. While it is not possible to anticipate all events, at the basic level there are elements that should be included in every crisis management plan.[39]

1. *Employee and local emergency management participation in crisis planning.*
2. *Planning for a wide range of potential crisis events.*
3. *Establishing a communication and information network with local emergency responders and other local points of communications and resources.*
4. *Establishing a coordinated response within the organization and with the local emergency responders while also identifying in-house resources that need to be stored for ready use.*
5. *Organizing and conducting debriefing sessions after a crisis for the purpose of reviewing and if necessary revising the crisis plan.*

Crisis management is a time-sensitive and a focused intervention designed to identify, respond to and manage a crisis, restore order, restore equilibrium, restore safety, and restore operations. The chances of successfully managing a crisis are increased if there are policies and procedures that function within the framework of best crisis management and response practices and are tailored to conditions requiring a specific set of responses and resources but that also include the agility necessary to respond to unexpected events within a crisis.

The development of policies and procedures that are appropriate and relevant for a crisis environment may need to deviate from traditional policy and procedure templates, because of the unique circumstances of crisis situations. Policies and procedures that are specific to crisis conditions provide an organized, systematic method for preparing employees for a crisis

---

[39] Ibid.

because they know should know how to respond to an impending or possible crisis and an active crisis.

If employees are trained on how to operate collaboratively within specified guidelines to make decisions and respond appropriately to crisis situations they are more likely to make appropriate decisions. The training also provides important preparation for employees so they know under what circumstances and how to seek resources, report problems, make decisions, and work together to respond to rapidly evolving situations. It is also important to have contact on a regular basis with local emergency responders and those agencies and entities with crisis response assets.

The Federal Emergency Management Agency (FEMA) strongly recommends that each organization develop a Continuity of Operations Plans (COOP). A COOP is defined by FEMA.

Continuity of Operations, as defined in the National Security Presidential Directive-51/Homeland Security Presidential Directive-20 (NSPD-51/HSPD-20) and the National Continuity Policy Implementation Plan, is an effort within individual executive departments, organizations, businesses, and agencies to ensure that Primary Mission Essential Functions continue to be performed during a wide range of emergencies, including localized acts of nature, accidents and technological or attack-related.[40]

According to FEMA, each COOP should be developed with these purposes in mind.[41]

1. *Ensuring that an organization can perform its essential functions under all conditions.*
2. *Reducing the loss of life and minimizing property damage and loss.*
3. *Executing an order of succession with accompanying authorities in the event a disruption renders that organization's leadership unable, unavailable, or incapable of assuming and performing their authorities and responsibilities of office.*
4. *Reducing or mitigating disruptions to operations.*
5. *Ensuring there are facilities from where organizations can perform essential functions.*

---

[40] *Continuity of Operations Planning*, Federal Emergency Management Agency, 2016: https://www.fema.gov/ continuity-operations.

[41] *Continuity of Operations Planning Assumptions*, Federal Emergency Manage-ment Agency, 2016: https://www.fema.gov/media-library-data/Non_Federal_ Continuity_ Plan_Template_and_ Instructions.pdf.

6. *Protecting personnel, facilities, equipment, records, and other assets critical to the performance of essential functions in the event of a disruption.*
7. *Achieving the organization's timely and orderly recovery and reconstitution from an emergency.*
8. *Ensuring and validating continuity readiness through a dynamic and integrated continuity Test, Training, and Exercise program and operational capability.*

The COOP should include several elements that are essential during a crisis:[42]

1. *Emergency Calling Directory*
2. *Emergency Relocation Group Checklist*
3. *Essential Functions Checklist*
4. *Continuity Site Acquisition Checklist*
5. *Emergency Operating Records*
6. *IT Checklist*
7. *Emergency Equipment Checklist*
8. *Delegations of Authority*
9. *Orders of Succession*
10. *Maps and directions to the Continuity facility and seating chart*

An organization's COOP should also consider *recovery strategies* that will help the organization recover from the crisis. This includes a plan to check the conditions of the workplace structure inside and out; a plan to communicate with employees to determine their health and conditions and when they are able to return to work; ensuring that all building utilities are back online; and providing for the possibility that employees may need counseling or other forms of support when they return to work to cope with possible post-traumatic stress disorders.

Rahm Emanuel, the former chief of staff for President Obama, said,

You never let a serious crisis go to waste. And what I mean by that it's an opportunity to do things you think you could not do before. [43]

---

[42] Ibid.
[43] Quote is attributed to Rahm Emanuel in 2008 during the financial crisis when he was President Barack Obama's Chief of Staff. A similar quote was noted by Charles Doyle, Wolfgang Mieder, and Fred Shapiro, coauthors of *Dictionary of Modern Proverbs* (Yale University Press, 2012) who traced the quote to 1976 when the author

What is missing in his message is a declarative statement on the importance of crisis planning and leadership during a crisis.

There is more at stake during a crisis than some leaders understand. Jacqueline Whitmore, writing for *Entrepreneur*, addressed this in a poignant article about crisis response.

When a crisis arises at work, your first instinct may be to panic. Unfortunately, severe anxiety and stress can result in a complete meltdown. This response can cause long-term damage to your health and lower your ability to perform optimally.[44]

Whitmore found that a leader's effectiveness during a crisis is largely dependent on his ability to remain calm because even the most effective crisis plan has to be executed and a crisis of leadership during a crisis will certainly jeopardize an organization's response to a crisis. Whitmore offers several recommendations for leaders during a crisis.[45]

1. ***Slow down.*** *See yourself as an active participant, try to view yourself as a representative of your company. This perspective will help you remain less emotional and improve your ability to make decisions.*
2. ***Stay positive.*** *Stop yourself from beginning to imagine the worst-case scenario. Instead, let go of negative thoughts and refocus your mind on something positive, no matter how small.*
3. ***Never ask "what if?"*** *This worst question you could ask yourself or others in the middle of a crisis begins with "what if." This line of questioning induces sheer panic and forces you to process situations that have not occurred and may never happen.*
4. ***Limit caffeine intake and remain hydrated.*** *Caffeine may trigger a release of adrenaline, giving you a quick burst of energy and physical strength, only to be followed by a crash marked by fatigue and irritability in some cases. Instead of reaching for that cup of coffee, soda or an energy drink, hydrate yourself with water.*
5. ***Call a trusted friend or mentor.*** *Use your support system and don't be afraid to ask for advice with a stressful situation. Someone who isn't*

M.F. Weiner wrote an article in *Medical Economics* entitled "Don't Waste a Crisis — Your Patient's or Your Own." Weiner meant that a medical crisis can be used to improve aspects of personality, mental health, or lifestyle.

[44] Jacqueline Whitmore, "Ways to Stay Calm during a Crisis," *Entrepreneur*, October 7, 2014.
[45] Ibid.

emotionally invested in the situation will be able to see the crisis from a different perspective.

The management of crisis situations has either made or damaged the reputation of leaders in different types of organizations. There are few ways to ensure that a leader can cope with and respond effectively to a crisis. However, leaders who anticipate that a crisis is always possible are better prepared to respond more appropriately than those that are not prepared.

Chapter Fourteen Key Words and Concepts

Centipede Syndrome
Ambiguous Decision-Making
Deliberate Ambiguity
Delegate Responsibilities
Manage Expectations
Crisis Management
Collateral Damage
Trust Calculus
Complacency of Overconfidence
Pandemic
Centers for Disease Control
World Health Organization
National Governors Association
Retreat from Decision Making
Buffalo Creek Disaster
Sudden Crisis
Smoldering Crisis
Crisis Decision Theory
Crisis Response Basic Protocol
SWOT: (Strengths, Weaknesses, Opportunities, and Threats)
Time-Sensitive and Focused-Intervention
Continuity of Operations Plans (COOP)
Leadership Self-preparation and Response

Chapter Fourteen Discussion Items

What is the Centipede Syndrome and how does it apply to decision-making during a crisis?

Discuss the importance of Crisis Management Planning. Identify the most important elements in planning for a crisis and explain why they are so important.

What did the CEO of Tylenol do that helped the company respond effectively to the crisis compared to how leaders responded to the Buffalo Creek disaster?

How can the elements of SWOT be utilized in Crisis Management Planning and when debriefing after a crisis? Give examples.

How would you explain to an organization the value of a COOP?

What points would you make about the importance of a COOP to the health and future of the organization?

How should an organization's Crisis Management Plan be communicated to its employees?

What are the most important leadership functions during a crisis and which functions are the most critical to an appropriate response to a crisis?

What are some of the most common problems during a crisis situation that cause a crisis to spiral out of control?

Give an example from your own experience or from what you read or heard about where a crisis was either handled well or was not responded to effectively.

Chapter Fourteen Lessons Learned

It is a measure of a leader's effectiveness if he can determine which crisis situations call for which type of response.

Leaders should not ever avoid major decisions during a crisis by communicating ambiguous decisions because they can be misinterpreted or misunderstood, which only deepens the crisis.

A leader must provide direction and respond to the crisis in a timely fashion.

Leaders cannot control the crisis per se, but a good leader can control the response.

There are times during a crisis when the leader has to delegate responsibilities in order to manage the scope of a crisis; however, the delegation of responsibilities is not the same as abdicating his leadership role.

If a leader loses his self-control, he immediately loses his effectiveness.

In each and every crisis trust becomes an important part of the crisis and the response to the crisis.

Without trust, the leader's ability to manage expectations is minimized, thus the crisis itself may not be contained.

Returning to normalcy is the strongest motivation for most people because there is security in normalcy.

Leadership failures during a crisis are often the result of poor crisis preparation and planning, lack of experience in crisis situations, stubbornness, lack of vision, naiveté, defensiveness, failure to listen to advice, and/or pride.

Poor leadership during a crisis is bad enough, but the failure to learn from a crisis is unforgivable and poison for any type of organization.

The effective leader will be agile enough to recognize and adapt to unique features of the crisis.

The basic elements of crisis planning include a comprehensive approach to crisis management that places a strong emphasis on prevention.

Establishing a communication and information network with local emergency responders and other local points of communications and resources is an essential crisis function.

The chances of successfully managing a crisis are increased if there are policies and procedures that function within the framework of best crisis management and response practices.

A leader's effectiveness during a crisis is largely dependent on his ability to remain calm because even the most effective crisis plan has to be executed and a crisis of leadership will certainly jeopardize an organization's response to a crisis.

CHAPTER FIFTEEN

RUMORS MANAGEMENT AND CONTROL

"Life is simple; it's just not easy."

-Steve Maraboli[1]

Determinants: There is no doubt that rumors and unbridled gossip are impediments to employees and organizational productivity and can contaminant any organization because the organization's workplace climate and stability are compromised. Workplace climate can be an incubator for rumors to grow if employees do not feel important, informed, and respected. The lack of communications is one of the most significant fuel for rumors, which is a sign of weak leadership. Also, a vacuum of leadership will almost always be filled with rumors. Employees will use rumors to fill the gaps of information – they fill in the blanks. This becomes even more serious during times of change. Rumors and change are linked if a leader does not manage both well.

Rumors

There are many definitions of rumors, but the definition used in this context is the one most commonly used in sociological research of rumors: an account or explanation of events, persons, places or things circulating from person to person that are not based on fact or accuracy.[2]

Interestingly, arrogance at the leadership level can actually fuel rumors because communication with employees is not deemed important. Arrogance can impact decisions by encouraging the *directional motivation*[3] of leaders so

---

[1] Steve Maraboli, "Unapologetically You," *A Better Today*, 2013: http://www.goodreads. com/work/ quotes/2508 6973-unapologetically-reflections-on-life-and-the-human-experience.

[2] *Rumor and Gossip Research*, American Psychological Association, *Psychological Science*, 2005: http://www.apa.org/science/about/psa/2005/04/ gossip. aspx.

[3] Georgia Kernal and Kevin Mullinax, "The Scope of the Partisan Perceptual Screen," *Institute for Policy Research, Northwestern University* WP 13-15, July 2013:

that a leader ignores sound advice, data, and probabilities and then makes decisions based more on arrogance and in response to rumors than on what is best for the organization. In some instances, rumors are started at the leadership level. Rumors can be a fast-spreading negative determinant that permeates an organization before the leader can do damage control.

Rumors can result in lawsuits[4] and can be costly in many other ways, such as lost productivity time from employees spreading the rumors, employees distracted by the rumors, and employees directly impacted by the rumors.

A study by the Huffington Post found that rumors extract a significant financial cost to organizations.

> *If a company has 200 employees and each employee spent one hour a day trading gossip that would result in $160,000 of lost productivity each month. That's a loss of $1.92 million a year (based on $40 per hour, salary & benefits).[5]*

There are elements that together form rumors. It's important to know and understand those elements in detail. Dr. Vivencio Ballano, a sociology professor and consultant to numerous organizations about rumors and how to manage them, defines the elements of rumors.

> *A rumor is a piece of information gathered informally that is used to interpret an ambiguous situation (Schaefer, 2005). It is unsubstantiated 'news' about a subject that is spread informally by people. Like gossip, a rumor is also an unverified piece of information or story. Thus, if the release of salary for the employees on a specified date is delayed without prior notice from the company, rumors are expected to circulate to explain why this incident occurred.[6]*

Fueling Rumors

The behavior and attitude of a leader can be the fuel that feeds rumors in the workplace. Typically, when a leader loses his or her humility rumors are

---

Directional motivation is when an individual's goal is to reach a desired conclusion, such as an opinion consistent with prior belief.

[4] Ken Hardin, "False Workplace Gossip Can Result in Company Liability," *Tech Republic*, March 3, 2003: http://www.techrepublic.com/article/false-workplace-gossip-can-result-in-company-liability/.

[5] Janice Celeste, "5 Steps to Stop Gossip in the Workplace," *Huffington Post*, September 8, 2015.

[6] Dr. Vivencio Ballano, "How to Handle Rumors or Gossip in Business or Public Life," *Linkedin Company Culture*, August 25, 2014.

inevitable. In his book *What Got You Here Won't Get You There*, Marshall Goldsmith discusses several weaknesses that can doom a leader.[7] But the root cause of all of the weaknesses is ego issues. The ego that tells the leader that he knows everything and is always right and, therefore, there is no need to listen, learn, or communicate effectively. The ego that tells the leader he is better than all others and is especially smarter and wiser than any subordinates or board leaders. The ego that tells the leader that any and all rules do not apply to him and that his role is not defined by anyone or any limitations. Alone, however, it is difficult for the leader to sustain this state of ego; therefore, he will occasionally recruit "co-ego" conspirators referred to as *enablers* to re-inflate his ego and reassure him that his ego and leadership style are healthy while all those around him are either incompetent or are well-meaning stooges who need their leader to tell them what to do. Sometimes the sycophants will start well-placed rumors to discredit members of the leadership team who do not always agree with the leader. Then the leader can use those rumors to justify his decisions. This is just one of many situations in organizations that create a culture of rumors that starts with the leader.

Unfortunately, rumors are a part of any organization; however, some rumors are simply the nature of people while others, as previously stated, are part of a deliberate effort to undermine members of a leadership team or even a board.

In his book *Manager's Guide to Understanding and Combating Rumors*, Allan Kimmel writes:[8]

> *Rumor. Think about this word. Say it out loud. Rumor. It has such ugly connotations, doesn't it? A statement that cannot be proved or disproved. Rumor. 'Rhymes with the word tumor.'* [9] *Rumors that spread rapidly are difficult to control and nearly impossible to ignore and can have damaging and even deadly consequences.*[10]

---

[7] Marshall Goldsmith, *What Got You Here Won't Get You There: How Successful People Become Even More Successful*, (Hachette, 2007).

[8] Allan J. Kimmel, *Manager's Guide to Understanding and Combating Rumors*, (Prentice Hall, 1995).

[9] Quoting P.R. La Monica, "On the Wings of Rumors," *Smart Money*, September 17, 1999a in Allan Kimmel's *Manager's Guide to Understanding and Managing Rumors*.

[10] Allan Kimmel, *Manager's Guide to Understanding and Managing Rumors*, (Prentice Hall, 2004).

Motives for Rumors

The impact of rumors and the motive for rumors vary. Rumors about colleagues can damage reputations. Rumors started by board members to discredit a leader can be devastating and usually damage the workplace climate for everyone. Rumors about a non-profit organization can impact donations. Rumors about a business can impact sales. Rumors about inappropriate use of funds can have political implications for community leaders. Rumors that a new learning program in another school district increased test scores can lead a school district to spend money on an untested product. Rumors that a chief financial officer may have personal financial problems may cause a board to non-renew his contract. Rumors can be devastating.

Rumors can create behaviors and reactions that are not based on facts, and a well-placed rumor can lead to ill-fated decisions within any organization. Therefore, rumor prevention and control are significant leadership functions.

Anybody who works in any organization for any length of time will soon learn that rumors are a regular part of working with people. Yet, very few if any leaders are ever trained on rumor control. And certainly board members are not trained in rumor control. Too often even leaders succumb to rumors, especially if the rumors reinforce what they want to believe. This can create a dangerous situation for the leadership and the organization.

In his article for *Small Business*, Alex Saez wrote about rumors.

Rumors in the workplace are a serious problem. They can hurt the organization's reputation, decrease morale and damage productivity. There are many reasons employees may spread rumors, such as fear of reprisal, burnout, resentment or personal issues among them -- to name a few. Regardless of the cause, it is the management's duty to provide a safe, healthy and productive work environment.[11]

There is danger for a leader that encourages rumors in the mistaken belief that he will somehow benefit from the rumors and he can control the rumors, because once rumors start they can rage out of control.

Stephen Leigh, the author of *Speaking Stones*, said,

---

[11] Alex Saez, "How Should Supervisors Handle Rumors?" *Small Business*, 2011: http://smallbusiness.chron.com/howshould-supervisors-handle-rumors-55036.html.

Rumors are like lightning on summer tinder, producing flames that dance in flickering brilliance from person to person, sometimes flaring in great conflagrations of exaggeration.[12]

Another dangerous mistake a leader can make is listening to and believing rumors without validation. Leaders who are struggling in their role, particularly ones who are under fire from the board or others, are very susceptible to the temptation to believe and encourage certain rumors. It's a dangerous game. Over time a leader that listens to and starts believing rumors will eventually become a source of rumors and eventually the target of rumors. The tragedy is that some good ideas, strategies, and programs are damaged because of rumors.

It is a reality that leaders in any organization will have to address issues related to rumors, but they must understand that they may be intentionally or unintentionally feeding rumors by encouraging them, ignoring them, or reacting to them in a manner that perpetuates the rumors.

The worst rumors are those that seem to be valid, based on the messenger, the content, and/or the timing of the rumor. These "seemingly valid" rumors often spread very quickly and are therefore difficult for a leader to manage or respond to in an effective manner.

Types of Rumors and How They Begin

According to research by Susan Pendleton, rumors originate primarily due to one of three circumstances: *wish fulfillment rumors*, *boogie man* or *fear rumors*, and *malicious intent rumors*.[13]

W*ish fulfillment rumors* reflect what people want to happen–what they want to hear. For example, employees may be under the leadership of a tyrannical boss who rules by intimidation and fear. An employee tells colleagues that he wishes the boss would find another job. In the course of this conversation, the evolution of a rumor begins with a statement that the boss is *"most likely"* looking for another job and that *"most likely"* to the next person changes to the boss is *"probably"* looking to move. It then becomes shortened during a brief conversation to,

---

[12] Stephen Leigh, *Speaking Stones*, (Phoenix Pick, 2009).
[13] Susan Coppess Pendleton, "Rumor research revisited and expanded, *"Language & Communication*, Vol 18(1), January 1998: http://dx. doi.org/ 10.1016/ S0271-5309(97)00024-4.

Have you heard that the boss is looking for another job? Well, no, I haven't heard that; where is he going? I don't know, but wouldn't you think it would be another state since no one likes him around here? Yea, probably another state.

Not too long after the rumor starts, the leader hears about it but ignores it. The leader soon gets a phone call from a board member, asking, *"Why are you looking for another job and why didn't you tell us?"* To which the leader is completely puzzled, but the stammering denial only fuels the board member's perception. Before the befuddled leader can contemplate how such a rumor was started, the rumor has spread to all parts of the organization; thus, disrupting the operations of the organization.

The second type of rumor Pendleton describes is the *boogie man or fear rumors* that reflect feared outcomes, either motivated by a need to prepare for the worse or portray the situation as helpless or hopeless. Sometimes these types of rumors accompany bad news or a negative event, making the situation worse. An example of this type of rumor is illustrated in this case study.

Case Study #1[14]

The leader of a non-profit organization looked at the budget challenges and determined that the budget needed to be scaled down, so he announced to the executive team that projected financial statements indicate that organizational changes may be necessary sometime in the future, but layoffs would be the last resort. He simply said that the budget for each department needed to be carefully watched and some budget decisions may be necessary for the future if the financial trends continue. The leader mentioned layoffs or furlough days (unpaid days off) as an unlikely last resort. A department head called a meeting to relay the leader's message about being frugal, and he added, "I hope this doesn't mean layoffs in the future." Then the rumor spread that the organization was in such serious financial trouble that layoffs might be considered. As rumors circulated, they became more succinct and incorrect, so this rumor became, "We're going to have layoffs." But that is not where it ends. It's only natural to ask, "When? When we will have layoffs?" At this point, the rumor had energy and substance to move rapidly across the organization in this form: "We're in such bad shape it's only a

---

[14] Elde, Ronald, *Using Case Studies for Non-Profit Management*, (Reveltree Publishing, 1999).

matter of time before they start laying off employees." The rumor may seem innocuous, but rumors can spread so quickly and have the emotional force to take employees' concentration away from their jobs. The leader, upon hearing the rumor, tried to reassure employees that layoffs were not part of the solution, "yet." He did not intend to add the word *"yet"* at the end of his statement, but he did because he did not want to box himself in the future if that decision had to be made. Thereafter, all efforts to stem the rumor were compromised.

Leaders need to remember that any effort to control or counteract a rumor must be carefully planned and executed. A wrong word in the wrong place at the wrong time can change an interpretation of the meaning of the message to make it worse or it spins off into another series of rumors.

The third type of rumor, according to Pendleton, is the *malicious intent rumor*. Divisive rumors are often by design, so that a staff member can, for example, cut off competition for a promotion or drive a wedge between and among employees in order to manipulate social messaging and workplace interaction, perhaps to one's advantage at the expense of another employee. An employee, for example, determines that another employee is his competition for any future promotion in the organization. Consequently, the manipulative employee, Zach, asks a staff member if he has heard anything about another employee, Joe, suggesting that he was unhappy and might consider giving up his job to go back to college. Of course, the rumor starts and Joe initially is oblivious to the rumor. One day someone asks Joe if it was true that he was leaving the organization to go back to school. Joe, again unaware of the rumor and quick to dismiss the rumor without being cautious of his words said, "No, I have to work, even though I would like to go back to college and finish my MBA.*"* Joe has just inadvertently confirmed the contents of the rumor by acknowledging in an off-handed manner that he would like to go back to college. That innocent spark is all that is needed to enable Zach to spread the rumor throughout the organization that Joe is leaving to go back to college. Joe, consequently, moves to quell the rumor but enough fragments of the rumor remain to dog him for months, and who is to say the unfounded rumors did not play a role in Joe coming in second for a promotion opportunity?

Intentional and Malicious Rumors

The malicious rumor is often used by organizations in competition with other organizations. Some organizations seem to use rumors as standard operating procedures with competitors. Two organizations, for example, in competition for the same grant may depend on receiving the grant to maintain prestige and/or programs. One of the organizations resorts to rumors about fiscal mismanagement at the other organization to scare off the grantors. More often this use of malicious rumors is found in businesses.

An example of this type of rumor victimized McDonald's restaurants when a competitor started a rumor in the mid-1970s that McDonald's hamburgers were made with worm meat in order to save money.[15] The rumors were dismissed by the executive leadership at McDonald's so there was no communications effort to quell the rumor. What appeared at first to be a silly rumor found traction and negatively affected sales in Atlanta, Georgia stores. In fact, this particular rumor resurfaced as recently as 2016.[16] When the rumor resurfaced, McDonald's launched an immediate aggressive denial, unlike its slow and unclear response earlier. In 1989, over seven million people heard a rumor that Coca-Cola contained carcinogens; a rumor that was supposedly started by a Coca-Cola competitor.[17]

The use of rumors is not limited to just a few examples. Numerous times businesses, organizations, or individuals started rumors to intentionally damage the reputation of others. Note the number, type, and consequences of rumors enumerated by DiFonzo and Bordia:

Rumor effects may be classified as behavioral or attitudinal. In business settings, behavioral effects of rumor include those that affect purchase behaviors. The false rumor that Tropical Fantasy Soda Pop was owned by the Ku Klux Klan and made black men sterile reportedly caused sales to drop by 70% and incited attacks on delivery trucks (Freedman, 1991). Unger (1979) reported similar losses in sales due to false product rumors: Bubble Yum bubble gum is contaminated with spider eggs, and Pop Rocks candy, ingested with soda pop, explodes in your stomach. Rumors have also affected stock purchase behaviors—and thus stock values. For example, prior to publication of takeover rumors published in the "Heard on The Street" column of The Wall Street Journal, price run-ups occurred, indicating that the takeover rumors pushed prices up as they diffused through the financial sector.[18]

---

[15] H. Unger, "Business Rumors and How to Counteract Them," *Canadian Business,* 49, 1979.

[16] Kate Taylor, "A viral rumor that McDonald's uses ground worm filler in burgers has been debunked," *Business Insider*, January 2016.

[17] Nicholas DiFonzo and Prashant Bordia, *Rumor Psychology: Social and Organizational Approaches*, (American Psychological Association, 2007).

[18] Ibid.

Ambiguity and Negative Rumors

Rumors often arise in situations that are ambiguous. Many employees feel threatened by ambiguity because it threatens their job security. Ambiguous situations in organizations include primarily leadership issues, either from the organization's leader or from the board.

E.K. Fiske reports in *Research on Gossip: Taxonomy, Methods, and Future Directions* [19] that it is natural for people to react to unsettled or unsettling situations because of a core need to understand and to act in some manner when a situation is chaotic, unorganized, or rifled with a lack of trust, particularly when the leader of an organization is ineffective. He further noted that as rumors spread, the information in the rumor is truncated so the message becomes more precise and therefore spreads more rapidly among and through more people. According to Fiske,

> *About 70 percent of details in a rumor are lost in the first five to six person-to-person (verbal to verbal) transmissions and it spreads rapidly thereafter.* [20]

He cited the research of William Stern who set up experiments on the chain of rumors and the subjects of rumors. Stern found that rumors are shortened and change significantly by the time they reach the end of a line of people. By the time the rumor reached the end of the line, it was more succinct and yet more inflammatory. [21]

Gordon Allport, a student of Stern, discovered that negative rumors are much more likely to be disseminated to others than positive rumors; concluding that it is only human nature to more quickly pass along a negative rumor than it is a positive rumor. [22]

In their book *Switch: How to Change Things When Change is Hard,* Dan Heath and Chip Heath note a study that found people are much more likely to share and remember negative information, pictures, and images than positive ones. [23] There is, therefore, a natural tendency to quickly adhere to negative

---

[19] E.K. Fiske, "Research on Gossip: Taxonomy, Methods and Future Directions," *Review of General Psychology*, Vol. 8, No. 2, 2004: doi: 10. 1037/1089-2680.8.2.78.
[20] Ibid.
[21] Ibid.
[22] Gordon W. Allport and Leo Postman, "An analysis of rumors," *Public Opinion Quarterly*, Oxford Journals, 10 (4), 1946: doi:10.1093/poq/10.4.501.
[23] Dan Heath and Chip Heath, *Switch: How to Change Things When Change is Hard,* (Crown Publishing, 2010).

stories and negative rumors and, consequently, share the negative information with others without verification.

Leaders of any organization must understand the dynamic nature of rumors and become familiar with this human behavior phenomenon instead of dismissing rumors as a paltry nuance that should be ignored. The mistaken belief that rumors are inevitable and will eventually go away is misdirected and can be dangerous to individuals and the organization. That is a naïve and risky attitude.

As previously noted, there are many examples of how a rumor raged out of control while the organization ignored the rumor or downplayed its importance or significance.

Out-of-Control Rumors

One of the most powerful examples of a rumor that spiraled out of control because of benign neglect by the CEO, executive team, and the board is the case of Proctor & Gamble's "Man-in-the-Moon" rumor.

This is a study of how a seemingly absurd and insignificant rumor can move rapidly and grow into a major situation for an organization, especially when the organization ignores the reactions and downplays the impact of the rumor.

It is a case study that clearly shows how important rumor management and control are to an organization.

Case Study #2

In 1979, the symbol on Proctor & Gamble (P&G) products represented by a long-haired wizard-type man in the moon with stars became the focal point for a rumor that at first seemed insignificant and localized; consequently, the incident became a classic example of how not to handle a rumor.

horn

horn

ᴜInverted 666!

The devil's two horns and Antichrist's number 666

The rumor stated that P&G was secretly controlled by Satan worshippers and the product symbol, which is admittedly strange, was representative of Satan. The company fairly ignored the rumors even though it did release a brief press statement denying the rumors. People who believed the rumor maintained that the "proof" was found in P&G's "Man-in-the-Moon" logo that revealed the company's link to Satan. They pointed to the curlicues of 666 (the number in the Book of Revelations 13:18 refers to 666 as the mark of the "Beast" – the devil) in the moon man's hair and beard and the horns on each side of the moon man's profile. P&G continued to deny the rumor but the company did not make an all-out press to quell the rumor, so it persisted and grew.

The rumor began to affect P&G's employees because the rumors that were external turned into internal rumors that spread rapidly because P&G's leadership did not communicate with its employees. P&G finally realized in the early 1990s that the rumor was out of control and must be managed because there were widespread rumors inside and outside of the company that the company's CEO appeared on the then-popular Phil Donahue show and admitted that a percentage of the company's profits went to Satanic-based organizations. This rumor, not based in fact on anything the CEO had ever said publicly or privately, spread quickly. Finally, P&G took up an aggressive campaign to dispel the rumor. The company asks Phil Donahue to inform the public that no such interview ever took place; in fact, the CEO nor any other member of P&G leadership had ever appeared on the show.

In 1991, P&G replaced the moon man trademark with a "P&G" emblem. When the rumor resurfaced in 1998, P&G immediately and publicly refuted the rumor in the news media and internally with its employees. The rumor died quickly because the company managed and controlled the rumor.

Rumors Fill Communications Gaps

Prashant Borida and Nicholas DiFonzo published an article in *Social Psychology Quarterly* that describes *rumor transmission* as a *"collective explanation process."*[24] Rumor transmission is a means of explaining why dysfunctional organizations are rife with rumors, especially when leadership has drifted away from the organization's vision, mission, objectives, and initiatives and when problems and issues go unresolved without explanation. Then employees create and find their own explanations. Rumors fill the communications gaps and create links between speculation and inaction. Additionally, rumors can become such a controlling factor that it can be difficult for a leader or board to manage them or counter them.

Some researchers have found that rumors are more likely to arise in circumstances where there is a lack of formal communications or reliable communications. This is most likely to occur during periods of organizational change because the need for information is not being met.[25] Leaders can make this situation worse by focusing so much on the change that the communication of the change and the purposes and goals of change are not shared with employees that are hungry for information and a modicum of reassurance. The ineffective leader ignores an essential component of leadership with the intended or unintended message that he does not owe anything to any of them and he will let them know only what he thinks they should know and when. This type of workplace climate becomes an incubator for rumors.

---

[24] Prashant Borida and Nicholas DiFonzo, "Problem Solving in Social Interactions on the Internet: Rumor as Social Cognition," *Social Psychology Quarterly,* 67 (1), 2004: URL: http://www. jstor.org /stable/3649102.
[25] E.K. Fiske, "Research on Gossip: Taxonomy, Methods and Future Directions," *Review of General Psychology*, Vol. 8, No. 2, 2004: doi: 10.1037/ 1089-2680.8.2.78.

Case Study #3

The new executive of a small private foundation roared into his new job with change on his mind. During every meeting with employees and executive staff, the new leader reminded them that he was hired to make changes in the organization, but when he was asked about the changes he demurred. He refused to offer any indication of what the changes might include and who they might affect. He once told his executive staff, "I'll tell you what you need to know when I decide that you need to know it."

Employees cannot function in that type of work environment by quietly going about their work as if nothing is wrong; it's not normal human behavior to act as if everything is the same when the threat of vague change is being tossed around recklessly by an organization's leader. So, there was fertile ground for dissent and therefore rumors. A rumor started that the new leader was going to dismiss several employees, so out of fear some of them started slipping anonymous notes to the new leader disparaging other employees. At the same time, competent employees started looking for other jobs. The situation reached a critical stage when the leader heard a rumor that his top two executives were undermining each other and were both trying to sabotage the new leader. The leader was in a difficult situation, though most of it was due to his lack of control and communications because he realized over time that he really needed both talented employees. But what should he do about the rumors that they were plotting his downfall? Where they true, fully or partially? How accurate were the rumors that two of his top employees were at each other throats and yet after him, too?

The leader was faced with a situation where, being new on the job, he had to sort out the facts from rumor while trying to acclimate to his new job. Wisely, he called upon his former mentor. The mentor listened patiently while the leader discussed his dilemma with the rumors and how he was perplexed because he did not know if the rumors were true, including rumors that at least one of the talented and knowledgeable top executives was plotting his overthrow, if not both of them. His mentor listened very carefully but offered no comment. The leader became very frustrated with his mentor's silence. Finally, he said, "Well, what should I do?" The mentor walked around the leader's office with his hands folded behind his back in a thoughtful pose. Then the mentor stopped and said,

In ancient Greece, Socrates was considered the wisest of his wise peers. One day Socrates was called upon suddenly by a friend who ran up to him excitedly and said, 'Socrates, my teacher, do you know what I just heard

about one of your students?' 'Wait a minute,' Socrates replied. 'Before you tell me about the rumor I'd like you to pass a little test. It's called the Triple Filter Test.' Socrates continued despite an impatient and puzzled look from the messenger, and said, 'That's right; it's called the Triple Filter Test, and before you talk to me about my student let's take a moment to filter what you're going to tell me. First, have you made absolutely sure that what you are about to tell me is true?' 'No,' the man said. 'Actually, I just heard about it and...' 'All right,' said Socrates. 'So you don't really know if it's true or not. Now let's try the second filter. Is what you are going to tell me about my student something good?' 'Well, no,' the man said, 'on the contrary.' 'So,' Socrates said interrupting the messenger again, 'you want to tell me something bad about him, even though you're not certain it's true?' The embarrassed man shrugged his shoulders. Socrates continued, 'You may still pass the test because there is a third filter–the filter of usefulness. Is what you want to tell me about my student going to be useful to me?' The man said, 'Ah, not really, no.' 'Well,' Socrates concluded, 'if what you want to tell me is not true, good or useful why tell me at all?' [26]

The leader seemed puzzled and said to his mentor that he did not understand the relevance of that story and his own situation because he was hearing the rumors from more than one person. The mentor said simply,

Why do you listen to the rumors and why would you react negatively to the rumors? You don't know if they are true; you know they are negative; and how are they useful to you? Be the leader; look at what you're doing that fosters an atmosphere that is ripe for rumors. How much of this are you responsible for?

Then the mentor moved closer to the leader and asked, "And have you spread the rumors, too?" Taken aback, the leader first said he had not, but the mentor suspected differently. So, he pressed him. Finally, the leader said to his mentor,

Well, yes, I did share the rumors with a couple of board members, but only because I wasn't sure what to make of the rumors. Don't worry, I'll go back to those board members and tell them what I heard was probably not true. I can fix this.

---

[26] McKinney Ellington, *Socrates Fables*, (Maxter Publishing, 1921): updated at http://www.inspirationpeak.com/cgi-bin/stories.cgi.record=150.

The mentor said, "Read the Parable of the Feathers." The leader asked about the parable, but the mentor told him to find it on his own. They parted ways and the leader went back to work. He tried to concentrate on his work, but the *Parable of the Feathers* haunted him, so finally, he pushed his work aside and searched for the parable. This is what he found.

> *Once upon a time, a villager went to the town monk. "Monk," he confessed, "I have been slandering you to my neighbors. I have thought about and I regret doing it. I am truly sorry for what I've said and how I've treated you and talked about you behind your back, spreading rumors. I take back all the bad I have said. How may I find penance?" The monk nods then sagely offer these instructions: "Go pluck 3 chickens. Stuff a bag with the feathers then place one feather on every doorstep where you have slandered me. Return to me when you complete your task." Scurrying away, the village man meticulously complies. He returns to the monk the next day. "Monk," he said, "I have completed your instruction. I put a feather on the doorstep of every citizen that I told a false rumor about you. What should I do now?" "Now," said the monk, "go collect back every feather that you placed on the doorsteps." "But, but," the village man said, "that's impossible; it has been an entire night and the wind has blown the feathers in all directions." The monk nods in agreement. He then turns and walks away.*[27]

After reading the parable, he leaned back in his chair and felt the pang of guilt and remorse. He understood the *Parable of the Feather*–one cannot so easily take back the harmful words of rumors. He made a decision that he later said probably saved his career. In fact, he said he grew as a person and a leader that day because he took a different and honest view of himself. He didn't like what he saw. The leader called the two top executives into his office and told them about the rumors he had heard, but he focused primarily on their skills and how much he will depend on them in their respective leadership roles. He admitted that the rumors distracted him and even troubled him until he realized that he was part of the problem; his failure to communicate and interact with his staff had created conditions for rumors. He said the organization will only survive and thrive if they all work together.

Thereafter, as a team, they worked on an organizational plan and vision and shared that with all employees and the board the same week it was concluded. The organizational plan was successfully implemented and the

---

[27] The origin of the parable is unknown but it was first attributed to a rural Rabbi in the 18th century by a traveler from Japan who returned from a visit to central Europe. 羽のたとえ Hane no tatoe

organization grew steadily for several years. The leader became a mentor to both top executives, and he is now grooming someone to take his place. He has already told his successor the *Parable of the Feather* and about Socrates' *Three Filters Test*.

Rumors as a Mode of Communications

Leaders and board members should be acutely aware of the power of rumors to disrupt the organization. They must anticipate that rumors will fill any communication vacuum. The potential danger of rumors is especially heightened before, during, and after a leadership change.

In research by Colleen Mills, she examined how employees made sense of the formal and informal communication that was associated with the anticipated change of leadership.[28] The study focused on what communication was encountered, what messages were embedded consistently in the communication, and how the messages were created. She discovered three phases of communications, as noted below.[29]

1. *The CEO's disengagement period, which started when the leader reduced or ignored communications within the organization.*
2. *The recruitment and selection phase, which is the period during which recruitment activity and selection processes occurred and corresponded with the period when an acting CEO was at the helm of the organization.*
3. *The engagement period of the new CEO, which commenced on her arrival and ended when she faced her first major crisis.*

The findings indicate that rumors focused on why the CEO was leaving–the "pushed" versus "willing departure" rumor and the track record of the prospective new CEO candidates. Mills wrote:

The succession-related rumors centered primarily on known and likely candidates and their suitability and potential impact on the organization if chosen as the next CEO. Rumors about who had applied were often coupled with stories about these rumored candidates' performance in their previous and current roles that allowed judgments of suitability to be made. Those participants who had personally experienced working with any of these

---

[28] Colleen Mills, "Experiencing gossip: The foundations for a theory of embedded organizational gossip," *Group and Organizational Management*, 35 (2) April 2010, doi: 10.1177/1059 601109360392.
[29] Ibid.

people were often among those actively sharing their experiences and assessments. One participant (referred to as PPT) explained to the author (CM) why there were rumors about the composition of the shortlist. PPT: 'Oh certainly, there was a lot of rumor around about who was possibly on the short list, and certainly particular individuals.' CM: 'Right, so what do you put down that rumor and interest to?' PPT: 'Concern for the direction the organization might go in if certain known individuals got the job. You know, certainly, I probably shared some of those concerns as well for some of the names being thrown around.' A few people did remain interested in the succession process and kept it in the front of others consciousness by adding any gossip and rumor-type information they were in possession of into their formal and informal exchanges. This behavior was explained in terms of 'being involved,' 'staying informed,' and 'something to talk about.' Employees who had shown little interest in the succession process previously became more receptive and in some cases active participants in rumor activities. This was attributed variously to interest, wanting to know what the future held, curiosity, the lack of communications and concern about possible impacts. As time passed and the paucity of information about the new CEO's style and priorities began to take its toll on employee's desire for certainty about the future, the scant rumors took an evaluative turn. Individuals reported becoming critical of the CEO's invisibility and in some cases, they remembered the immediately departed CEO's profile to make comparisons that they considered justified the criticism. [30]

Overall, the researcher concluded that rumors were strongly contingent on the type and use of communication within the organization and the attitude and competency of the leader, as well as how the search for a new leader was perceived by employees.

Antidotes: Rumors fill a trust and communications void caused by leaders that do not communicate effectively with employees because they lack effective communication skills or they have not fully considered the importance of communications. Rumors fill a trust void caused when leaders do not understand and do not make any effort to understand the needs of employees, which has the effect of eroding trustful communications between the leader and employees. Employees view the lack of communications as a message that organizational leadership does not trust employees; thereafter, employees have no hesitations about starting or sharing rumors.

Robert Whipple, stated in *The Trust Factor*,

---

[30] Ibid.

Trust and rumors are incompatible. It there is low trust, it is easy for someone to project something negative for the future. When trust is low, these sparks create a roaring blaze of rumors.[31]

There are times when a leader has to address rumors, regardless of whether he wants to or not, but there are also situations when a leader inherits a workplace climate that is filled with rumors. Whipple offers possible antidotes for the poison of rumors:[32]

1. *Intervene quickly when there is a rumor and provide solid, believable, truthful information about what is really going to happen. It is best to plan this type of intervention before the rumor even starts by communicating with employees on a regular basis and by encouraging employees to talk to leadership staff. The consistent communications up and down the organizational chart allow an immediate response across the organization if rumors start. In many organizations, this type of regular communications with employees prevents rumors from starting. It is also wise to check with key employees periodically to make sure the communications information from the leader has actually been received by employees. This is also a key moment for the leader in another regard. The leader must take the time to make an honest self-assessment. Has the leader indirectly or directly spread rumors and gossip? Has the leader intentionally or unintentionally encouraged gossip and ignored rumors? Did the leader create conditions that fueled rumors? Has the leader quickly quashed some rumors but allowed others to fester?*

2. *Coach the worst rumor offenders to stop. Usually, it is not difficult to identify the employees who like to stir up trouble by starting or embellishing rumors. They are easy to spot in the break room, in the hallway, and other places where work does not take place. Take these people aside and ask them to tone down the speculation. One interesting way to mitigate a group of gossipers is to get to know them better-go and sit at the lunch table with them, for example. This may feel uncomfortable at first, but it can be very helpful at detecting harmful rumors early, and it gives the staff the opportunity to talk to the leader, which can quell rumors. Just as in fighting a disease, the sooner some treatment can be applied, the easier the problem is to control. If the same employees continue to be the genesis of rumors, a more direct approach to them may be in order to quell the behavior. They must come to understand that rumors negatively affect the work of the organization and will not be tolerated.*

---

[31] Robert Whipple, *The Trust Factor*, (Productivity Publications, 2003).
[32] Ibid.

3. **Double the communication in times of uncertainty.** *There are times when the genesis of a rumor is easy to identify. Suppose all the top managers have a long closed-door meeting with the shades pulled. People are going to wonder what is being discussed. Suppose the financial reports indicate that continuing on the present path is impossible-that operational changes will have to be made? What if there are strangers walking around the organization with tape measures? What if all travel has been canceled and purchase orders limited? What if a consultant is going around asking all kinds of probing questions? All these things and numerous others are bound to fuel speculation on what may be happening, and from that rumors are born. When this happens, smart leaders get out of the office and interface more with employees. They also communicate with employees about anything that seems out of the ordinary. If not, employees will find or create an explanation. Unfortunately, when there are unusual circumstances too many leaders like to hide in their offices or in meetings to avoid having to deal with pointed questions. That is exactly the opposite of what is needed to prevent rumors from taking control and contaminating the workplace climate.*

4. **Find multiple ways to communicate the truth.** *People need to hear something more than once to start believing it. In a national survey, nearly 60 percent of people indicated they need to hear the organizational news (good or bad) at least three to five times before they believe it.[33] It is important to utilize all available means of communicating with employees–in small or large group meetings, through memorandums, emails, conference calls, webinars, etc. and keep the communications flowing.*

5. **Reinforce open dialog.** *Leaders can find themselves in a precarious situation when engaging in dialog with employees. Leaders should always encourage questions to make sure all of the areas fertile for rumors are addressed. One of the most counterproductive reactions by a leader to questions and comments is to be defensive, condescending, or critical of the person asking questions. Criticizing and discouraging questions is a quick way to fuel the rumor mill. It is critically important to remember that increasing the trust level is the best way to subdue the rumor agents.*

6. **Model a no-gossip policy.** *People pick up on the tactics of a leader and mimic the leader's behavior throughout the organization, especially at the managerial level. If the leader is intentionally leaking out bits of unsubstantiated speculation, then others in the organization are likely to do the same thing. Conversely, if a leader refuses to discuss information that is incorrect then he models the kind of attitude that will be picked up*

---

[33] Ibid.

*by many employees. The key to modeling a no-gossip workplace climate is
to develop a no-gossip expectation-not just a policy, but an expectation,
which can be encouraged and clarified through guidelines of what to do
when employees hear a rumor. This may include a definition of rumors
and advice on how to respond to rumors (e.g., Ask one's immediate
supervisor about rumors, gossip, or other information that may be
misinformation).*

7. **Extinguish gossip behavior.** *This may mean breaking up a clique of
employees or at least adding new managers to the group. It may get to the
point that employees who are consistently and persistently at the center of
rumors are too destructive to continue employment. Rumors are that
serious. If rumors continue one after the other because of the behavior
and attitude of the same employees then they need to be warned, then
reassigned, and then terminated if it continues.*

It is also important to watch for patterns of rumors, which can help the
leader narrow down the source of the rumors as well as the possible causes.

Leaders should routinely audit their own behavior and model that for
employees by encouraging senior staff to do the same. As stated in an article
by *Mindtools,*

*If everyone holds themselves a more accountable for rumors in the workplace,
their frequency–and their negative consequences – will drop.*[34]

The management of rumors requires a multifaceted approach. Dr.
Vivencio Ballano recommends the following steps to manage rumors.[35]

1. **Don't remain silent:** *Speak, reach out to the discontented, or say you're
sorry if needed. To do nothing only makes matters worse.*
2. **Take gossip as constructive feedback:** *To improve one's self a leader has
to take an honest look at feedback. Turning away from feedback can be
instrumental in flaming rumors.*
3. **Provide frequent, clear and convincing information:** *There is no
substitute for on-going communications and sharing information
throughout the organization, but be mindful and deliberate in how
communication is shared. Slipshod and incomplete information will not
be effective and can create rumors.*

---

[34] "Rumors in the workplace: Managing and preventing them," Editorial Staff,
Mindtools, 2016: https://www.mindtools. com/pages /article/new TMM_25.htm.
[35] Dr. Vivencio Ballano, "How to Handle Rumors or Gossip in Business or Public
Life," *Linkedin Company Culture*, August 25, 2014.

4. ***Reshuffle people to minimize the influence of power cliques and create a culture of candor:*** *There are times when the leader has to take charge of the rumor culture and minimize its impact and ongoing growth by dividing the culprits or confronting them. However, there is a caution here. Samuel Goldwyn tried to quell rumors after a series of his movies failed by telling his employees, "I need your honest feedback on what's wrong with me; you're telling everyone else so tell me, even if it means losing your job."[36]*

It is clear that rumors in the workplace can compromise the climate, reduce productivity, spur lawsuits, threaten careers, and create animosity between and among employees. An important leadership function is to prevent and control rumors, but more importantly, it is imperative for leaders to identify and correct those elements that make rumors more likely to occur and spread.

Chapter Fifteen Key Words and Concepts

Rumors
Directional Motivation
Ego and Rumor
Rumor Control
Wish Fulfillment Rumors
Boogie Man or Fear Rumors
Malicious Intent Rumors
Behavioral Rumors
Attitudinal Rumors
Truncated Information and Rumors
Chain of Rumors
Negative Rumors versus Positive Rumors
Collective Explanation Process
Socrates' Triple Filter Test
Parable of the Feathers
Disengagement Period
No Gossip Policy
Rumor Management
Communications and Feedback

---

[36] James O'Toole and Warren Bennis, "A Culture of Candor," *Harvard Business Review*, June 2009.

Chapter Fifteen Discussion Items

Define the term Rumor and how it applies to organizational settings. Give three examples of rumors from your own experience that had a negative impact on an organization, person, or project.

Name the different types of rumors and how they each effect people and organizations.

What are some of the most effective means to prevent rumors, control rumors, and counteract rumors?

If you were leading an organization, what methods and practices would you utilize to prevent and respond to rumors? Include any methods and practices that are not in this book that you think would be effective and explain why.

What language should be included in a No Gossip Policy? How would you communicate a No Gossip Policy to employees?

What are the most critical factors in Rumor Management?

Chapter Fifteen Lessons Learned

Workplace climate can be an incubator for rumors to grow if employees do not feel important, informed, and respected.

Rumors can be a fast-spreading negative determinant that permeates an organization before the leader can do damage control.

The behavior and attitude of a leader can be the fuel that feeds rumors in the workplace.

Rumor prevention and control are significant leadership functions.

Too often even leaders succumb to rumors, especially if the rumors reinforce what they want to believe. This can create a dangerous situation for the leadership and the organization.
Over time a leader that listens to and starts believing rumors will eventually become a source of rumors and eventually the target of rumors.

Rumors often arise in situations that are ambiguous. Many employees feel threatened by ambiguity because it threatens their job security.

As rumors spread, the information in the rumor is truncated so the message becomes more precise and therefore spreads more rapidly among and through more people.

The mistaken belief that rumors are inevitable and will eventually go away is misdirected and can be dangerous to individuals and the organization.

Rumors will fill any communication vacuum.

Employees view the lack of communications as a message that organizational leadership does not trust employees; thereafter, employees have no hesitations about starting or sharing rumors.

Consistent communications up and down the organizational chart allow an immediate response across the organization if rumors start. In many organizations, this type of regular communications with employees prevents rumors from starting.

It is important to utilize all available means of communicating with employees– in small or large group meetings, through memorandums, emails, conference calls, webinars, etc. and keep the communications flowing.

The key to modeling a no-gossip workplace climate is to develop a no-gossip expectation - not just a policy, but an expectation, which can be encouraged and clarified through guidelines of what to do when employees hear a rumor.

NOTES ON THEORIES AND MODELS

This section provides details about leadership, change, and response theories and models that can be applied to the psychology of leadership principles, practices, and priorities. The information is constructed to address both the academic and theoretical aspects as well as elements related to practical use of the theories and models.

Cognitive Dissonance

Content Theories of Motivation

Contingency Theory

Crisis Decision-Making Theory

Expectancy Motivation Theory

Field Theory

Hawthorne Effect

Attribution Theory

Hersey-Blanchard Situational Leadership Theory

Theory U

Epidemiological Model

Cognitive Dissonance Theory

Leon Festinger

In 1957, Leon Festinger proposed *cognitive dissonance theory*. Festinger was born in New York City in 1919. He studied under the legendary psychologist Kurt Lewin who was a pioneer in social psychology at the University of Iowa. Festinger developed the theory of *cognitive dissonance* when he worked at the Massachusetts Institute of Technology.

Cognitive dissonance is based on the theory that people possess an internal mechanism and a psychological need to hold all thoughts, beliefs, and values in harmony to avoid dissonance (disharmony).[1] A major component of dissonance is the principle of *cognitive consistency* which controls all efforts to find the balance or the harmony between beliefs and behaviors. When there is dissonance people react in ways to counteract the disharmony. This moves people to look for actions and explanations to justify the dissonance.

The origin of Festinger's research and theory development came from his earlier study of a religious-based cult group that believed the world was destined for destruction by a Biblical-type worldwide flood. The cult members gave up their careers, lives, friendships, and homes to prepare for the end of the world. What fascinated Festinger was the cult members' reaction when the end-of-days did not take place. They compensated for the dissonance by stating that the destruction did not take place only because of the cult members' faithfulness. In their collective minds, their belief that the world was going to end in a catastrophic way was accurate and their strong beliefs saved the world. That was the message and "rationale" for their continuing faith in the work and beliefs of the cult.

Festinger studied other groups and individuals and postulated that there are three ways people reduce dissonance. Typically, a person will choose one of the three but it is not unusual for people to move between and among the three ways.

1. *A person can change his attitude.*
2. *A person can obtain more information.*

---

[1] Leon Festinger, *A Theory of Cognitive Dissonance,* (Stanford University Press, 1957).

3. *A person can reduce in his own mind the importance of the belief or attitude.*[2]

First, changing a person's attitude is the most difficult, such as choosing a learned and reinforced behavior like smoking or drinking alcohol in which the behavior is an expression, for example, of independence. The second way of reducing dissonance is by acquiring more information or more accurate or updated information which causes more dissonance - to the point that the belief, attitude, or behavior changes; for example, a heavy drinker who is shown research about liver damage due to excessive alcohol usage. But it only takes one other piece of information that challenges that research to remove the dissonance, such as research that one glass of wine each day "may" be healthy.

The most common example of the third way to reduce dissonance is rationalizations like "live for today" and not for the long term because no one knows how long anyone will live. The person rationalizes the dissonance away.

Cognitive dissonance in the workplace is common and can negatively impact morale. If, for example, an organization has printed rules and training sessions that focus on the importance of being on time for work but no leader within the organization enforces the rule it can create cognitive dissonance in employees who see colleagues routinely coming in late while they rush to get to work on time. The difference between what an organization says it values and what diligent employees accept as a valued behavior are compromised by the organization's failure to act. Employees who respect the organization's rule are suffering from cognitive dissonance, so they can either come in late, change how they view and value the rule, or rationalize that most of the late arrivers probably work late, and, therefore, have an acceptable reason for being late.

Content Theories of Motivation

The most widely recognized *content* theorists are Abraham Maslow, David McClelland, and Frederick Herzberg. *Content Theory* focuses on the specific motivating needs of people–what motivates them to action.

---

[2] Leon Festinger, "Cognitive Dissonance," *Scientific American,* 207(4), 1962.

Abraham Maslow

Probably the most well-known *content theory* derives from Maslow's Need Hierarchy, where the basic needs have to be met at different levels before a person can reach the higher order thinking and personal reward of *self-actualization*.[3]

1. *Physiological–These needs must be met in order for a person to survive, such as food, water, and shelter.*
2. *Security–Includes personal safety, financial stability, and good physical health and well-being.*
3. *Social Needs–The need for friendships, other positive social interactions, and positive family relationships.*
4. *Esteem–The need to feel confident in abilities, motivation, outlook, and feel respected by others.*
5. *Self-Actualization–The state of mind where self-satisfaction, confidence, acquiring long-sought goals, and contentment lead to ease of mind and comfort.*

Content theory organizations use reinforcements, such as various types of rewards to spur motivation at the basic level. Organizations find that morale and motivation can be negatively impacted if employees feel unsafe. However, it seems to be a static measure because providing a safe work environment does not necessarily ensure higher morale without considering other workplace climate factors such as verbal encouragement, consistent feedback on work quality, opportunities for advancement, or other types of recognition. The additional factors were part of David McClelland's work. He added several elements to the basic understanding of motivational needs.

David McClelland

David McClelland' famous book *The Achieving Society* launched his career.[4] In the book, he theorized about motivation in three spectrums: *achievement motivation; authority/power motivation,* and *affiliation*

---

[3] Abraham Maslow, "A theory of human motivation," *Psychological Review,* 50 (4) 1943: *doi:10.1037/h0054346*

[4] David McClelland, *The Achieving Society*, (Harvard University Press, 1961); David McClelland, "Managing motivation to expand human freedom," *American Psychologist*, 33 (3)1978; McClelland, D.C.(1965). "Toward a theory of motive acquisition," *American Psychologist*, 2, 1965.

motivation. Each of these types of motivation can drive morale and productivity as well as employee job satisfaction.

1. ***Achievement:*** *Employees need and desire a sense of achievement. This can only be accomplished when they have completed a task, project, or in some measurable way achieved a goal.*
2. ***Authority/Power:*** *Employees have the need for some authority, either over other people, over a project, over planning, etc. A basic need for authority exists at all levels of an organization.*
3. ***Affiliation:*** *Employees have a strong need for affiliation. One of the basic human needs is to be with and a part of something with other people, which meets the social need of affiliation and the accomplishment need of completing a task.*

Each of these three motivational components can be applied to the workplace. McClelland said the most productive organizations with the most productive and satisfied employees are those that employ strategies that use all three types of motivation.

Frederick Herzberg

Frederick Herzberg's landmark book *The Motivation to Work* introduced the concepts of *hygiene motivation* and *job enrichment* as motivation factors.[5] The concepts were derived from his study of 200 engineers in Pittsburgh, Pennsylvania. Herzberg was a meticulous researcher, which was illustrated in the level of sophistication of the study design and the amount of rich data he gathered from his research. His fundamental finding, which was groundbreaking at the time, was that *satisfaction* and *dissatisfaction* at work were not based on two responses to the same factors but were instead reactions to different factors of the work and the workplace. Herzberg expresses the concept this way:

> *We can expand by stating that the 'job satisfiers' deal with the factors involved in doing the job, whereas the 'job dissatisfiers' deal with the factors which define the job context.*[6]

The best way to distinguish between the *hygiene factors* (expectations) and the *motivation factors* (enrichment) is to list examples of each.

---

[5] Frederick Herzberg, *The Motivation to Work,* (Wiley Books, 1959).
[6] Ibid.

Hygiene factors: work conditions; benefits; salary; status; workspace; security; relationship with colleagues; relationship with supervisor; organizational policies, etc.

Motivation factors: measurable achievement; recognition; increasing trust and responsibility; advancement; selection for special projects or assignments, etc.

If organizations do not discern the difference between hygiene factors and motivation factors it is likely that its workforce will be less productive than it could be and with high turnover rates. Hertzberg's article in *Harvard Business Review* in 1978, *One More Time: How Do You Motivate Employees*[7] is the magazine's most requested reprint article with over 1.2 million copies sold.

Herzberg's theories of categories can be compared with Maslow's need hierarchy. Most of the hygiene factors are at the lower levels of the need hierarchy and motivational factors are at the higher levels.

Maslow's Need Hierarchy	Herzberg's Motivation Levels
Self-actualization, fulfillment, Self-realization	Achievement, personal growth, responsibility, intrinsic value of work
Esteem and status	Advancement, recognition, status
Social activity	Interpersonal relations with colleagues peer group
Security and safety	Organizational policies, processes, Stable work climate, job security
Physiological needs	Work conditions, salary, work hours

Contingency Theory

Contingency theory[8] is based on the concept that there is no best way to develop an organization or manage an organization because of situations, timing, needs, risks, etc. are different and vary from time and place. Therefore, the type of organizational structure is contingent upon internal and

---

[7] Frederick Hertzberg, "One More Time: How Do You Motivate Employees," *Harvard Business Review*, September-October 1978.

[8] Fred Fiedler, "The contribution of cognitive resources to leadership performance," *Journal of Applied Social Psychology*, vol. 16, 1986.

external factors. This theory applies to leadership style and organizational decision-making–it depends on the situation and the status of the organization as well as the pressures and dynamics influencing the organization.

The genesis of contingency theory derived from three separate studies at major universities: Ohio State University, University of Michigan, and the University of Chicago. Surveys conducted by the universities found that the prevailing theories of management, such as Taylor's *Scientific Management*,[9] did not adequately account for the value of an organization's ability to adapt to changes and interruptions nor did it consider the necessary versatility of an organization's leadership to handle both the daily management of an organization, the motivation of employees, and interruptions. Furthermore, the studies found that there is a distinction between *task-oriented leadership* and *relationship-oriented leadership*. The selection of leadership style is contingent on the situation. Prior to these studies, most business leaders and production managers were task-oriented.

In some instances, the work schedule and the demands on work outcomes require an "all-hands-on-deck" approach to management, which would be high-task and low-relationship. On the other hand, if there are indications, for example, that morale is declining the leader may shift to a high-relationship and a low-task orientation of leadership to focus more on the needs of the employees to reduce staff turnover. This shift does not sacrifice production because improved morale increases production.

The work of Fred Fiedler[10] and Robert Blake and Jane Mouton[11] produced the most original and sustaining descriptions and uses of contingency theory in the workplace.

---

[9] Fredrick Taylor, Taylor, Frederick Winslow, *Shop Management*, (American Society of Mechanical Engineers, 1903). The publication was first printed as a pamphlet from the American Society of Mechanical Engineers after Taylor made a presentation at a conference. Taylor's *Scientific Management* derived from his belief that production could improve if managers used scientific principles in the workplace. His methods focused on production processes and not motivation or any other needs of workers.

[10] Fred Fiedler, "A theory of leadership effectiveness." In L. Berkowitz (Ed.), *Advances in Experimental Social Psychology*. (Academic Press, 1964).

[11] Robert Blake and Jane Mouton, *The Managerial Grid: The Key to Leadership Excellence*, (Gulf Publishing Co., 1964); *The Managerial Grid III: The Key to Leadership Excellence*, (Gulf Publishing Co., 1987).

Fred Fiedler

Fiedler said that the effectiveness of motivational strategies is dependent on the style of leadership and control over situations. According to Fiedler,

> *There need to be good leader-member relations, a task with clear goals and procedures, and the ability for the leader to mete out rewards and punishments. Lacking these three in the right combination and context will result in leadership failure.*[12]

Fiedler created the *least preferred co-worker* (LPC) scale to measure the perspective and insight of leaders as well as their attitude and perception of co-workers, particularly the ones they supervise. On the LPC scale, a leader is asked what traits can be ascribed to employees that the leader likes the least based on performance, social interaction with others and personality characteristics and skills that some professionals would refer to as "people skills."

The LPC scale uses four dimensions on a scale of 1 to 8 with 1 representing the lower end of the dimension and 8 representing the highest level of the dimension.

Uncooperative 1-8	Cooperative 1-8
Unfriendly 1-8	Friendly 1-8
Hostile 1-8	Supportive 1-8
Guarded 1-8	Open 1-8

High LPC leaders have a positive relationship with employees and communicate in a supportive manner. Low LPC leaders always put the task first, even at the risk of sacrificing a positive relationship with employees which can negatively impact future projects.

Robert Blake and Jane Mouton

Blake and Mouton created a theory that illustrated the potential and the danger of selecting leadership management practices based on high-relationship and low-task or low-relationship and high-task. According to Blake and Mouton, the leader must make difficult decisions based on the

---

[12] Fred Fiedler, "A theory of leadership effectiveness." In L. Berkowitz (Ed.), *Advances in Experimental Social Psychology*. (Academic Press, 1964).

294 Notes on Theories and Models

situation and cannot force decisions that are not compatible with the circumstances even if those decisions are standard operational procedures. Inappropriate management decisions can cost the organization in less productivity and damaged morale if the contingent conditions are not appropriate. Blake and Mouton focus on two primary elements.

> ***Concern for People:*** Based on how much a leader is concerned about his team members' needs, personal and professional development, and creative and professional needs when determining how to accomplish a task.
> ***Concern for Results:*** Based on how much a leader focuses on goals and objectives, organizational efficiency, and quality productivity when determining how to accomplish a task.

Working from these two constructs, Blake and Mouton defined five leadership styles that are based on circumstances. Sometimes situations dictate the shift from high-relationship to high-task or high-task to low-relationship. Effective leaders study the needs at the time to determine the appropriate focus and priority.

1. ***Country Club Management:*** *high relationship and low task – the leader relies on reward power to motivate employees but is not capable of employing any type of negative feedback or place demands on employees. This is "management by charming employees."*
2. ***Team Management:*** *high relationship and high task – the leader focuses on and is adept at building a team spirit and motivating employees to accomplish almost any task. The entire team focuses on the collective power and productivity of the team.*
3. ***Impoverished Management:*** *low relationship and low task – the leader does not have the commitment to relationships or tasks. Consequently, the leader shows very little interest in the organization, employees, or tasks. This is "absence management."*
4. ***Authoritarian:*** *low relationship and high task –the leader, as the label implies, is a task master with little regard for employees or concern for employees. He is only results-driven even if it is at the expense of employees.*
5. ***Middle of the Road:*** *unclear which is the most important, relationship or task –the leader is indecisive, which may work but only if the employees are skillful, self-directed, self-motivated, and self-confident.*

Blake and Mouton advocate for a leader that is team-oriented because balancing the needs of employees with the needs and productivity of the organization produces positive results for both.

Crisis Decision-Making Theory

Karen Sweeney

Based primarily on the seminal work by Karen Sweeney, *crisis decision-making theory* studies how people respond to negative events, including how leaders respond in times of crises. According to Sweeney,

> *Crisis decision theory combines the strengths of coping theories with research on decision making to predict the responses people choose under negative circumstances. The theory integrates literature on coping, health behavior, and decision making, among others, into three stages that describe the process of responding to negative events: (a) assessing the severity of the negative event, (b) determining response options, and (c) evaluating response options.*[13]

Understanding these three stages is critical because it can enable leaders and organizations to respond to negative events in a successful manner.

Assessing the severity of a negative event requires an honest approach and an attitude of absolute truth-seeking. There is no time for defensiveness or paranoia; otherwise, the negative event could become worse and the leader and organization will not learn from the event. The effectiveness of assessing a negative event can be enhanced by developing an assessment plan protocol instead of hastily and ineffectively developing a plan only at the time of a crisis.

Determining response options to a negative event is almost completely dependent on accurate information and updated information throughout the negative event. In most situations, the leader and the organization will have both short-term and long-term response options. There is a temptation to make quick, short-term decisions that could without forethought create long-term problems for the organization.

At times, a leader must make a prompt decision, such as what we read about earlier with the Tylenol poisoning crisis that required an immediate response, but even that quick decision was made with the long-term interests of the organization in mind and was based on how the company planned for events that challenged the safety of its products–the leader's philosophy of putting customer safety first was a premeditated response plan.

---

[13] Karen Sweeney, "Crisis decision theory: decisions in the face of negative events, *Psychological Bulletin.* January 2008:134(1) doi: 10.1037/0033-2909.134.1.61.

The evaluation of negative events response options is a difficult process for organizations because oftentimes the options come with some measure of sacrifice. The organization, for example, may have to invest a significant amount of money to respond quickly to a negative event instead of budgeting for the expenses over several months.

All of these factors are only a small part of the complexity of evaluating responses to negative events, but the dialogue that can be generated by internal discussions about crisis decision-making theory can lead to an organizational philosophy and set of beliefs that can drive and direct the organization's response to a crisis.

Expectancy Motivation Theory

Victor Vroom

Victor Vroom first postulated *expectancy motivation theory* because his study of how individuals make decisions found that outcomes expected from the decisions are matched with the person's desires or needs.[14] Thus, an employee's motivation is based substantially on the person's expectations. Vroom put the theory into a thought-action formula.[15]

> *The cognitive process evaluates the motivational force (MF) of the different behavioral options based on the individual's own perception of the probability of attaining his desired outcome. Thus, the motivational force can be summarized by the following equation:*

$$MF = \text{Expectancy} \times \text{Instrumentality} \times \sum (\text{Valence(s)})$$

Expectancy (E)
Expectancy refers to the "effort-performance" relation. Thus, the perception of the individual is that the effort that he or she will put forward will actually result in the attainment of the "performance". This cognitive evaluation is heavily weighted by an individual's past experiences, personality, self-confidence and emotional state.

---

[14] Victor Vroom, *Work and Motivation*, (Wiley, 1964)
[15] *The Expectancy Theory of Motivation*, Victor Vroom, as reported in Leadership-Central, 2015, citing the work of Vroom from Porter, L. W., and Lawler, E. E. 1968. *Managerial Attitudes and Performance*. Homewood, IL: Richard D. Irwin, Inc

The Instrumentality (I)
Instrumentality refers to the "performance-reward" relation. The individual evaluates the likelihood or probability that achieving the performance level will actually result in the attainment of a reward.

Valance (V)
Valance is the value that the individual associates with the outcome (reward). A positive valance indicates that the individual has a preference for getting the reward as opposed to a negative valance that is indicative that the individual, based on his perception determined that the reward doesn't fill a need or personal goal, thus he or she doesn't place any value towards its attainment. As the Motivational Force (MF) is the multiplication of the expectancy by the instrumentality it is then by the valence that any of the perception having a value of zero or the individual's feeling that "it's not going to happen", will result in a motivational force of zero.

The theory has been criticized because of its alleged failure to account for the importance of emotion, both rational and irrational, in determining the expectation employees have in the workplace, which also includes the biases and prejudices of expectations and the collateral effects of expectations. An example of the latter is the expectation of a promotion at work. The promotion comes through but it requires the employee to relocate to another city, which his wife and children do not want to do. The motivating expectation then has the reverse effect on the employee and creates an additional level of stress for the employee.

It can be difficult for leaders and organizations to match or meet the expectations of employees in the workplace. However, it is worth the effort to explore what motivates employees because the failure to do so will almost certainly result in "a motivational force of zero."[16] To this point, Lunenburg stated,

> Vroom's expectancy theory differs from the content theories of Maslow, Alderfer, Herzberg, and McClelland in that Vroom's expectancy theory does not provide specific suggestions on what motivates organization members. Instead, Vroom's theory provides a process of cognitive variables that reflects individual differences in work motivation. From a management standpoint, the expectancy theory has some important implications for motivating employees. It identifies several important things that can be done to motivate employees by altering the person's effort-to-performance expectancy,

---

[16] L. W. Porter and E.E. Lawler, *Managerial Attitudes and Performance*, (Richard D. Irwin, Inc., 1968).

performance-to-reward expectancy, and reward valences. Some employees may value a promotion or a pay raise, whereas others may prefer additional vacation days, improved insurance benefits, day care, or elder-care facilities. Many companies have introduced cafeteria-style benefits plans—incentive systems that allow employees to select their fringe benefits from a menu of available alternatives.[17]

Field Theory

Kurt Lewin

There are two types of *field theory*–one in physics and the other is in psychology. Field theory in psychology studies the relationship between individuals and their environment. Kurt Lewin was the first to apply the physics concept of field to psychology when in 1940 he postulated the formula that derived from his theory:

B = f (p and e), meaning that behavior (B) is a function of the person (p) and his/her environment (e) [18]

Lewin's theory was related to his work in Gestalt psychology.[19] The environment that Lewin ties to the theory is not limited to the physical surrounding of a person but also to the beliefs and attitudes that comingle with a person's environment in such a way that the blending impacts and drives behavior. Organizations can use the concept of field theory by viewing the entire organization as a system that is held together by a delicate balance of factors that motivate employees within the physical workplace surroundings and how all of the factors in this workplace "field" interact and react. A change in one component of the field can impact other components–sometimes in unexpected ways. Field theory in organizations reminds leaders that collateral effects should be considered when changes are made that are

[17] Fred Lunenburg, "Expectancy Theory of Motivation: Motivating by Altering Expectations," *International Journal of Management, Business, and Administration*, 15 (1) 2011.

[18] Kurt Lewin, "Defining 'Field at a Given Time.'" *Psychological Review.* 50: 292-310. Republished in *Resolving Social Conflicts & Field Theory in Social Science,* Washington, D.C.: American Psychological Association, 1997.

[19] Kurt Lewin, *"Der Begriff der Genese in Physik, Biologie,"* *Entwicklungsgeschichte* 1922, (Lewin's Habilitationsschrift).

only intended for one segment of the organization. He also discusses the importance of *life space*.

Behavior exists in a totality of interacting facts which comprise a dynamic field. The circumstances or conditions in any part of the field are influenced by and depend on every other part of the field. This psychological field is otherwise known as the life space which comprises the individual and his psychological or behavioral environment also known as facts that affect the behavior or thoughts of the individual at a certain point in time. Life space is most frequently determined by the physical and social environment that the individual finds himself in. It may include places where he goes, events that occur, feelings about places and people encountered, what he sees on TV or reads in books, how he interacts with colleagues at work, his imagined thoughts, and goals.[20]

Lewin is also known for his characterization of organizational leadership styles and the resulting cultures created by the leaders, including coining the term *laissez-faire* management/culture. The others were *authoritarian* and *democratic*.[21]

Hawthorne Effect

Henry Landsberger

In 1950, psychologist Henry Landsberger published research that was later referred to as the *Hawthorne Effect* because a series of social psychology experiments were conducted at the Western Electric factory in Hawthorne, Chicago.[22]

The original purpose of the study was to determine what motivates employees. Researchers theorized that employees were motivated by different effects of *"reinforcers"* that depended on individual needs and expectations. However, after months of observations and meticulous notations of employee behavior, what the researchers found was a tendency

---

[20] Editors, "Kurt Lewin's Psychology of Field Theory," *Psychology Notes*, September 29, 2013: http://www.psycho-logynoteshq. com/psychological-field-theory/.

[21] Kurt Lewin, "Frontiers in Group Dynamics: Concept, Method and Reality in Social Science: Social Equilibria and Social Change". *Human Relations Journal*, June 1947, doi:10.1177/00 1872674700100103.

[22] Henry A. Landsberger, *Hawthorne Revisited*, (Ithaca, 1958). [Note: The experiments were conducted under the supervision of Elton Mayo, a sociologist who became a professor of industrial psychological research at Harvard University.]

for employees to work harder and perform at higher levels when they were *being observed* by the researchers. When the researchers made this discovery, they manipulated the physical surroundings of the factory, such as the lighting, temperature, length of breaks, working hours, and sound levels to see if any of those manipulations affected employee motivation. The researchers found that no combination of physical factory changes reached the level of motivation that being observed reached.[23]

Unfortunately, the Hawthorne Effect has been misrepresented at times as "proof" that employees on their own will not work hard or perform well unless a supervisor is constantly watching them. That is not representative of the Hawthorne Effect and does not accurately represent the findings of the research project. Instead, the Hawthorne Effect should be viewed as employees' need to be recognized, need to be relevant to the purpose and mission of the organization, and the need to be appreciated.

Fritz Roethlisberger, a leading member of the Hawthorne research team, wrote:

> The Hawthorne researchers became more and more interested in the informal employee groups, which tend to form within the formal organization of the company.[24]

This points out another aspect of the Hawthorne Effect: the importance of how an individual employee interacts with and feels a part of the work team. The "*observational effect*" that was attributed to being observed by the research team also applied to being observed by colleagues. Mayo noted,

> The working group as a whole actually determined the output of individual workers by reference to a standard that represented the group conception of a fair day's work.[25]

---

[23] Roethlisberger, F.J. and Dickson, W.J., *Management and the Worker: An Account of a Research Program Conducted by the Western Electric Company, Hawthorne Works, Chicago*, (Harvard University Press, 1939).

[24] G. Gillespie, *Manufacturing Knowledge, A History of the Hawthorne Experiments*, (Cambridge University Press, 1991).

[25] E. Mayo, *Human Problems of an Industrial Civilization 2nd Edition*, (1st Edition, Macmillan, 1936; 2nd Edition, Harvard University, 1946).

Attribution Theory

The basic premise of *attribution theory* is that people react to the behavior of others based on their perception of the motivation (cause) for the behavior more than the behavior itself. If a person assigns the cause of another person's behavior to something negative and internal, such as the person's personality, dishonesty, etc. then that person is more prone to react in a negative way to the behavior than if they attribute the person's behavior to external factors, such as factors that the person cannot control (i.e., "He was in the wrong place at the wrong time.")

Bernard Weiner

Bernard Weiner developed the *Three-Dimensional Theory of Attribution* that is based on the assumption that most people want to know more about why they react to others in a certain way in order to better understand their own motivation and behavior.[26] Weiner believed that the characteristics of a person's attribution tendencies are very important to understanding behavior and future reactions. Weiner found three important attribution factors that can be linked to behavior in the workplace.

1. ***Stability***–*How stable is the attribution? If an employee believes that he does have the ability to do a project, this is a stable factor. An unstable factor is less permanent, such as an injury from an accident. Stable attributions for achievements, like successfully completing a project at work, can lead to positive expectations and thus higher motivation for success with future projects while negative attributions can hinder future performance at work.*
2. ***Locus of control***–*Is the behavior caused by an internal or an external factor? If an employee believes his own lack of skills or ability led to his failure to complete a project at work, he may be less motivated in the future because of his attribution. If on the other hand, the employee feels like his failure is due to outside factors such as poor equipment, unclear instructions, or the lack of support, he may not feel as negative about future projects if he thinks future projects will be better coordinated and equipped. Attributing cause to internal factors versus external factors is a major component of attribution theory applied to the workplace and is*

---

[26] Bernard Weiner, "Attribution theory, achievement motivation, and the educational process," *Review of Educational Research*, 42(2), 1972.

> *important for a leader to discern which factor is motivating or negatively impacting employees.*

3. ***Controllability*–**How controllable are the circumstances? If an individual believes he has control of circumstances that are necessary for success at work he is motivated. If he feels he has no control of conditions necessary for his success, his motivation will diminish. Attribution based on the perception of control is one of the strongest components of employee motivation.

Hersey-Blanchard Situational Leadership Theory

Situational Leadership Theory is based on the premise that no single leadership style applies best to any and all types of situations in an organization. Factors and tasks vary and the conditions within and outside of the organization also vary and are constantly changing; consequently, leadership has to adapt to the conditions and match the organization's capacity to cope with and respond to the conditions. Sometimes this requires pivoting to meet the needs of the changing conditions inside and outside of the organization. A leader's effectiveness is based on her leadership style and ability or maturity to identify and address critical factors, as well as employees' level of ability and maturity.

Paul Hersey and Kenneth Blanchard

Hersey and Blanchard conceptualized the Situational Leadership concepts that are necessary for a leader to effectively manage a wide variety of situations, referred to as "S" for situations.[27]

> ***S-1 Telling***: The flow of information from the leader to the employees and from the employees to the leader must be constantly in motion and encouraged by the leader. If the bilateral flow of information ceases, the organization will not be prepared to adapt to changing circumstances and requirements.

---

[27] Paul Hersey and Kenneth Blanchard, *Management of Organizational Behavior – Utilizing Human Resources*, (New Jersey/Prentice Hall, 1969); "Life cycle theory of leadership," *Training and Development Journal.* 23 (5) 1969; *Management of Organizational Behavior 3rd Edition– Utilizing Human Resources*, (Prentice Hall, 1977).

S-2 Selling: The leader provides the social and emotional support necessary to convince the employees that the leader can and should lead the organization through any type of situation.

S-3 Participating: The leader always shares decision-making responsibilities with employees and encourages a team spirit and common agenda. The leader listens to, considers, and when appropriate incorporates ideas and concepts from employees.

S-4 Delegating: The leader identifies individuals and groups to handle essential tasks and empowers them to make decisions and take responsibility for those decisions.

Four maturity (**M**) levels of the group are suggested by Hersey and Blanchard with the following letter designations that can be matched with the situations (**S**). However, these levels are not the same for each employee and each task. For a task (or situation) an employee may be at **M-4** but for another task, the same employee may be at **M-1**. It's important for the leader with input from employees to make that distinction.

M-1: An employee that lacks the maturity to complete the task due to incompetence or unwillingness to do the work because of lack of skills, lack of motivation, lack of interest, and/or inability to work with a team.

M-2: An employee that does not have the level of ability to complete the work but who is willing to try and will work hard.

M-3: An employee who either because of internal forces or negative external experiences is competent to do the task but lacks self-confidence.

M-4: An employee who is ready, willing, and able to do the work

An employee's developmental (**D**) level is based on his level of competence, aptitude, and commitment to the job. Competence is illustrated by the knowledge and skills from education, training, and experience and commitment.

D1 - Low competence and low commitment
D2 - Low competence and high commitment
D3 - High competence and low or variable commitment
D4 - High competence and high commitment

Effective leaders will learn about their employees at a deep enough level to discern their ability level and their level of maturity, which is a form of leadership based on understanding the situation of the task at hand and the ability and maturity level of employees so that assignments are developmentally appropriate not only to the situation but also for the employees. This provides the leader with another method of matching the task situation with the appropriate employees.

The permutations derived from *Situation, Maturity,* and *Development,* according to Hersey and Blanchard, can provide an analysis of the situation and, consequently, a complete understanding of what the leader needs to do to prepare for and manage any type of situation.

Theory U

A theory that addresses how individuals and organizations move from status quo to successful change by identifying inner "blind spots."

C. Otto Scharmer

Scharmer is a Senior Lecturer at the Massachusetts Institute of Technology (MIT), Professor at Tsinghua University, and co-found of the Presencing Institute.

After studying some of the world's most accomplished and influential leaders and innovators, Scharmer identified leadership traits that are essential to embrace and drive change. His work evolved from the question of why so many attempts to address challenges fail. Where do leaders, executive teams, groups, and organizations go wrong when trying to plan and then resolve or solve problems?

We are blind to the deeper dimension of leadership and transformational change. This blind spot exists not only in our collective leadership but also in our everyday social interactions.[28]

According to Scharmer, when leaders look beyond their blind spot, they are more future-oriented and can pull the veil of uncertainty and hesitation back to reveal what is not only possible but also what is necessary. He calls this experience *"presencing."*

Leadership in its essence is the capacity to shift the inner place from which we operate. Once they understand how, leaders can build the capacity of their systems to operate differently and to release themselves from the exterior determination of the outer circle. As long as we are mired in the viewpoint of the outer two circles, we are trapped in a victim mind-set ("the system is

---

[28] Otto Scharmer, *Theory U: Leading from the Future as It Emerges,* (Society for Organizational Learning, 2007).

doing something to me"). As soon as we shift to the viewpoint of the inner two circles, we see how we can make a difference.[29]

Theory U has one *process* with five *movements.*

We move down one side of the U (connecting us to the world that is outside of our institutional bubble) to the bottom of the U (connecting us to the world that emerges from within) and go up the other side of the U (bringing forth the new into the world). On that journey, at the bottom of the U, lies an inner gate that requires us to drop everything that isn't essential. This process of letting-go and letting-come establishes a subtle connection to a deeper source of knowing. The essence of presencing is that these two selves—our current self and our best future self—meet at the bottom of the U and begin to listen and resonate with each other. All people effect change, regardless of their formal positions or titles. Leadership in this century means shifting the structure of collective attention at all levels.[30]

The value of taking the U learning journey is the seven essential leadership capacities that emerge. They not only allow change but also drive and influence change—manageable and energetic change.[31]

1. ***Holding the space:*** *Listen to what calls you to listen (self, others, experience, will, hope, insight, imagination). Link the consciousness of your own insight with the results of your collective innovations and work.*
2. ***Observing:*** *Observe with your mind wide open, not an observation based on judgment, biases, experience, or expectation. Visualize decision-making.*
3. ***Sensing:*** *Connect with your heart. It's okay to look for connections that touch the heart; that feel right; that feel relevant but new. Develop conscious principles that connect change with vision and integration of processes and policies.*
4. ***Presencing:*** *Recognize the emerging self and how innovative ideas emerge in a parallel way. Connect the emerging self with change and innovation. Explicitly connect practices and change to manage the emerging future of innovations that matter.*
5. ***Crystalizing:*** *Access the power of intention. Intentional change and not reactionary change is the most engaging and energizing. Find others that*

---

[29] Ibid.

[30] Ibid.

[31] Peter Senge, Joseph Jaworski, Otto Scharmer, and Betty Flowers, *Presence: Exploring Profound Change in People, Organizations, and Society*, (Nicholas Brealey Publishing, 2005).

are committed to intentional change not reactionary or bureaucratic change.

6. ***Prototyping****: Integrate the head, the heart, the will, and the hand, which means that we should act and not let paralysis of action by over-analyzes stifle innovative change.*
7. ***Performing****: Find the right leaders to do the right things for the right reasons in the right way that embrace and drive collective change and results through individual and collective action and social technology.*

The seven elements that emerge within the U as a leader or organization transitions through the five movements provide a framework for managing and even provoking significant organizational change.

Epidemiological Model[32]

The word epidemiology comes from the Greek words *epi*, which means on or upon, and *demos*, which refers to people while *logos* refers to the study of. The word epidemiology has its roots in the study of what impacts a population; it's a population-based term.

The following definition includes the underlying principles and public health aspects of epidemiology.

Epidemiology is the study of the distribution and determinants of health-related states or events in specified-populations and the application of this study to the control of health problems.[33]

Epidemiology is a scientific discipline that focuses on methods of scientific inquiry at its foundation. Epidemiology is data-driven and relies on a systematic and reliable approach to the collection, analysis, and interpretation of data without bias. Basic epidemiologic methods depend on careful observation and use of valid comparison groups to studied trends and impacts, such as the number of cases of a disease in a particular region during a specified time period or the level of exposure among persons with disease. However, epidemiology also draws on methods from other scientific fields, including biostatistics, social, economic, and behavioral sciences.

---

[32] Applied Epidemiology and Biostatistics, Section One-Concepts in *Principles of Epidemiology in Public Health*, Centers for Disease Control (CDC); (CDC Publications 2002).

[33] J.M. Last, *Dictionary of Epidemiology 4th Edition*. p. 61, (New York: Oxford University Press; 2001).

Epidemiology is the basic science of public health because it is a quantitative discipline that relies on expertise in the fields of probability, statistics, and sound research methods. Also, epidemiology is a method of causation study and reasoning based on developing and testing hypotheses grounded scientific fields that include biology, behavioral sciences, physics, and ergonomics to explain health-related behaviors, states, and events that produce certain outcomes. Epidemiology does not, however, rely solely on research activity; it depends on an integral component of public health, providing the foundation for directing practical and appropriate public health action based on this science and causal reasoning.

Epidemiology studies the frequency and patterns of health events in populations based on foundational principles *distribution* and *determinants*.

Distribution

Frequency *refers not only to the number of health events such as the number of cases of meningitis or diabetes in a population, but also to the relationship of that number to the size of the population. The resulting rate allows epidemiologists to compare disease occurrence across different populations.*[34]

Pattern *refers to the occurrence of health-related events by time, place, and person. Time patterns may be annual, seasonal, weekly, daily, hourly, weekday versus weekend, or any other breakdown of time that may influence disease or injury occurrence. Place patterns include geographic variation, urban/rural differences, and location of work sites or schools. Personal characteristics include demographic factors which may be related to risk of illness, injury, or disability such as age, sex, marital status, and socioeconomic status, as well as behaviors and environmental exposures.*[35]

Determinants

Epidemiology is also used to search for determinants, which are the causes that influence the occurrence of disease and other health-related events. Epidemiologists start their studies with the assumption that diseases

---

[34] Applied Epidemiology and Biostatistics, Section One-Concepts in *Principles of Epidemiology in Public Health*, Centers for Disease Control (CDC); (CDC Publications 2002).

[35] Ibid.

or illnesses do not occur randomly in a population, but happen only when determinants exist. To search for these determinants, epidemiologists use epidemiologic study methods to provide the "Why," "Where," and "How" of such events. Epidemiologists assess whether groups differ in their demographic characteristics, genetic or immunologic make-up, social or individual behaviors, environmental climate exposures, or other potential risk factors. Hopefully, the analytical study provides evidence to determine prompt public health control and prevention measures.

IDENTIFYING LEADERSHIP STYLE
BY SELF-EVALUATION

Many leaders are interested in their own leadership style and how it impacts others in the organization. There are thousands of articles and hundreds of books on leadership. They are evenly divided between what works and what does not work. However, there can be no doubt that organizational improvement always begins with leadership. Leaders who are looking for principles, practices, and methods to identify priorities to improve themselves are more likely to be successful in their work because constant changes inside and outside of organizations demand it.

There are no failsafe or foolproof methods of self-appraisal for leaders to determine how well they are performing or to identify their leadership style but some have found that self-appraisals provide insight that gives pause for them to consider areas they need to improve on or be aware of in order to grow as a leader. Theory U notes that understanding the self through *presencing* has the potential to reveal untapped resources and innovation in leaders.

The following are examples of leadership style assessments that are being used widely used by leaders seeking self-appraisals. Of course, no self-assessment is expected to be completely accurate and certainly will not identify with certainty all of the strengths and weaknesses of leaders. However, it is possible for leaders to glean some insight from self-assessments of their leadership style and tendencies.

The follow examples of leadership style self-assessments are not intended to be all-inclusive. There are many other types of leadership style self-assessment instruments.

Instinctive Leadership Style Assessment
Blake and Mouton Managerial Grid Leadership Self-Assessment Questionnaire
Sage Leadership Style Assessment
Gestalt Leadership Style Evaluation

Instinctive Leadership Style Assessment

Robert Galford and Reginald Fazio Maruca developed a survey that addresses many of the components that identify leadership style in relation to a leader's *interaction* with and *influence* on others in the organization. There are thirty questions in the survey on *"instinctive leadership style."*[1]

Below is a list of questions. The questions focus on how others interact with the leader. The questions also include values, priorities, and perceptions.

Instructions: Read each question carefully and circle either "yes" or "no" after each question. For best results, answer as truthfully as possible.

1. *Do you have a reputation for breaking new ground, and do you like to do it without breaking the glass?*
   Yes   No
2. *Do you tend to rally for a cause at work?*
   Yes   No
3. *Do people rely on you for career advice, even after they've left the company or their division?*
   Yes   No
4. *Do you have a strong sense of justice that is not directed by politics?*
   Yes   No
5. *Are you happiest and most driven at the start of things?*
   Yes   No
6. *Are you an excellent listener, able to put yourself in another's shoes?*
   Yes   No
7. *Do you act as the go-between when others are in conflict, or during negotiations?*
   Yes   No
8. *Are you known for being relentless about pursuing initiatives?*
   Yes   No
9. *Do you have a very large contact list, and are you good at keeping in touch with people?*
   Yes   No
10. *Are you regarded as being methodical about collecting facts before making a decision?*
    Yes   No

---

[1] Robert Galford and Regina Fazio Maruca, *Your Legacy Leadership*, http://www.yourleadershiplegacy.com/assessment. html

11. *Are you often the "idea person" and the driver of new initiatives?*
Yes   No

12. *Are you a natural "therapist"?*
Yes   No

13. *Are you an instinctive problem solver?*
Yes   No

14. *Have you been called a perfectionist (sometimes in a negative way)?*
Yes   No

15. *Do you introduce new people to new ideas and new paths?*
Yes   No

16. *Is being fair really important to you, to the extent that you will solicit input from a wide variety of people to ensure everyone's voice is heard?*
Yes   No

17. *Do you frequently see opportunities for new products and markets?*
Yes   No

18. *Do others count on your supply of information and wisdom?*
Yes   No

19. *Are you the one holding the spotlight, rather than standing in its beam?*
Yes   No

20. *When something doesn't seem quite right are you compelled to do something about it?*
Yes   No

21. *Do you often chat with your employees about their lives outside work?*
Yes   No

22. *Are you ever accused of being too rational?*
Yes   No

23. *Do you tend to juggle a lot of different projects, both at work and at home?*
Yes   No

24. *Are you often the one people turn to for guidance during or after a particularly stressful situation?*
Yes   No

25. *Of the last 10 people to come into your office, how many were asking you to get involved to fix something?*
Yes   No

26. *Of the last 10 people to come into your office, how many were there to discuss something you thought needed improving?*
Yes   No

27. *Of the last 10 people to come into your office, how many were there to discuss career or personal issues?*
Yes   No

28. *Of the last ten people to come into your office, how many left with a greater understanding of some pivotal issues or the root cause of a problem?*
Yes   No

29. *Of the last 10 people to come into your office, how many were there to discuss something new that is exciting to you?*
Yes   No

30. *Of the last 10 people to come into your office, how many were there purely to ask for your advice or counsel?*
Yes   No

After completing the survey, participants may go to this website: *http://www.yourleadershiplegacy.com/assessment.html.* The website will provide specific feedback from the survey to determine rankings and ratings in the following categories of leadership style.[2]

> ***Ambassador:*** *Ambassadors instinctively know how to handle a variety of situations with grace. They tend to be the people diffusing nasty situations. The ones getting involved in conflicts on behalf of broad constituencies, as opposed to their own benefit. They are apt to be persistent in a gentle way.*
>
> ***Advocate:*** *Advocates instinctively act as the spokesperson for a group. They tend to be articulate, rational, logical, and persuasive. They also tend to be relentless, championing ideas or strategic positions. Advocates tend to use both linear and non-linear approaches when they argue a point.*
>
> ***People Mover:*** *People Movers instinctively take the lead in building teams. They're also instinctive mentors. They generally have large contact lists; they are always introducing new people to new ideas and new paths. They're also generally mindful of their employees' lives outside of work; they view performance through the larger lens of potential.*
>
> ***Truth-Seeker:*** *Truth-Seekers are unfailingly competent in their field; their competence is unquestioned. Truth-Seekers instinctively level the playing field for those in need. They also help people understand new rules and policies. They act to preserve the integrity of processes. They try to identify the root-cause issues or pivotal issues.*

---

[2] Ibid.

Creative builder: *They instinctively see new opportunities for new products, new companies and take ideas and make them real. They're also often "serial entrepreneurs" over time, even if they remain in one leadership post. Creative Builders instinctively understand that building is not necessarily about invention, but about the process of making an invention real. Builders are constantly energized by new ideas, yet they have the staying power to see them through to fruition.*

Experienced guide: They have a way of helping people think through their own problems; they are natural therapists. Often, they are seemingly bottomless wells of information on a diverse range of topics. These are the people who can always be counted on to supply the right quotation or the right historical connection. They are not necessarily mediators, yet the experienced guide is often the person who finds him or herself 'in the middle,' with people on both sides of a conflict seeking advice.[3]

The Blake and Mouton Managerial Grid Leadership Self-Assessment Questionnaire[4]

The *Situational Leadership Theory* of Blake and Mouton focuses on the ability of the leader to recognize and adapt to changing situations inside and outside of the organization.

Instructions: Read each of the following statements carefully. Using the 0 to 5 scale, decide the extent to which the statement applies to you. For best results, answer as truthfully as possible.

Never		Sometimes		Always	
0	1	2	3	4	5

1. __I encourage my team to participate when it comes decision-making time and I try to implement their ideas and suggestions.
2. __Nothing is more important than accomplishing a goal or task.
3. __I closely monitor the schedule to ensure a task or project will be completed in time.
4. __I enjoy coaching people on new tasks and procedures.
5. __The more challenging a task is the more I enjoy it.
6. __I encourage my employees to be creative about their job.

---

[3] Ibid.
[4] Robert Blake and Jane Mouton, *The New Managerial Grid 4th Edition*, (Gulf Publishing Company, 1981b).

7. __When seeing a complex task through to completion, I ensure that every detail is accounted for._

8. __I find it easy to carry out several complicated tasks at the same time._

9. __I enjoy reading articles, books, and journals about training, leadership, and psychology; and then putting what I have read into action._

10. __When correcting mistakes, I do not worry about jeopardizing relationships._

11. __I manage my time very efficiently._

12. __I enjoy explaining the intricacies and details of a complex task or project to my employees._

13. __Breaking large projects into small manageable tasks is second nature to me._

14. __Nothing is more important than building a great team._

15. __I enjoy analyzing problems._

16. __I honor other people's boundaries._

17. __Counseling my employees to improve their performance or behavior is second nature to me._

18. __I enjoy reading articles, books, and trade journals about my profession; and then implementing the new procedures I have learned._

After completing the questions, transfer answers to the spaces in the following matrix for scoring.

People Questions	Task Questions
1__	2__
4__	3__
6__	5__
9__	7__
10__	8__
12__	11__
14__	13__
16__	15__
17__	19__
Total __ x 0.2=__	Total__ x 0.2=__

Take the total score from the *People Questions* section and the total score from the *Task Questions* section and plot them as intersecting lines on the matrix below. The intersection of the two plot lines will indicate which leadership style the participant typically operates from. If the intersection of the plot lines is at 5, this means that the participant is an *uncertain* leader.

Blake and Mouton developed the Managerial Grid to depict leadership style based on the behaviors of the leader. Although there are several variations of leadership style and behavior, Blake and Mouton found that most, if not all, leadership styles fall within four categories on a scale with some overlap. The following descriptions of the four-leadership style provide more information about the tendencies of each style of leadership.[5]

> ***Country Club Style Leader (focus on low task, high relationship)***: *This person uses predominantly reward power to maintain discipline and to encourage the team to accomplish its goals. Conversely, they are almost incapable of employing the more punitive coercive and legitimate powers. This inability results from fear that using such powers could jeopardize relationships with the other team members.*
>
> ***Team Style Leader (focus on high task, high relationship)***: *This type of person leads by positive example and endeavors to foster a team environment in which all team members can reach their highest potential, both as team members and as people. They encourage the team to reach team goals as effectively as possible, while also working tirelessly to strengthen the bonds among the various members. They normally form and lead some of the most productive teams.*
>
> ***Impoverished Style Leader (focus on low task, low relationship)***: *A leader who uses a "delegate and disappear" management style. Since they are not committed to either task accomplishment or maintenance; they essentially allow their team to do whatever it wishes and prefer to detach themselves from the team process by allowing the team to suffer from a series of power struggles.*
>
> ***Authoritarian Style Leader (high task, low relationship)***: *People who get this rating are very much task oriented and are strict with their workers (autocratic). There is little or no allowance for cooperation or collaboration.*

According to Blake and Mouton, the most desirable place for a leader is to be a 9 on *task* and a 9 on *people*, - a *Team Leader*, which is a leader who knows how to create and build a team that is supportive, talented, collegial, persistent but patient, and goal-oriented. The leader is a team leader who motivates the team and lets the creativity and ingenuity of the team flow.

---

[5] Robert Blake and Jane Mouton, *The New Managerial Grid 4th Edition*, (Gulf Publishing Company, 1981b).

9	Country Club Leader	Team Leader
8		
7		
6		
5	Uncertain Leader	Uncertain Leader
4	Impoverished Leader	Authoritarian Leader
3		
2		
1		
	1 2 3 4 5	6 7 8 9

Sage Leadership Style Assessment[6]

The purpose of the Sage Leadership Style Assessment is to identify the participant's style of leadership and to examine how the participant's leadership style relates to other styles of leadership

Instructions: For each of the statements below, circle the number that indicates the degree to which you agree or disagree. Give your immediate impressions. There are no right or wrong answers.

Statements

Strongly Disagree, Disagree, Neutral, Agree, Strongly Agree

1. *Employees need to be supervised closely or they are not likely to do their work.* **1 2 3 4 5**

---

[6] Sage Leadership Style Assessment: https://www.cdph. ca.gov/programs/.

2. *Employees want to be a part of the decision-making process.* **1 2 3 4 5**
3. *In complex situations, leaders should let subordinates work problems out on their own.* **1 2 3 4 5**
4. *It is fair to say that most employees in the general population are lazy.* **1 2 3 4 5**
5. *Providing guidance without pressure is the key to being a good leader.* **1 2 3 4 5**
6. *Leadership requires staying out of the way of subordinates as they do their work.* **1 2 3 4 5**
7. *As a rule, employees must be given rewards or punishments in order to motivate them to achieve organization objectives.* **1 2 3 4 5**
8. *Most workers want frequent and supportive communication from their leaders.* **1 2 3 4 5**
9. *As a rule, leaders should allow subordinates to appraise their own work.* **1 2 3 4 5**
10. *Most employees feel insecure about their work and need direction.* **1 2 3 4 5**
11. *Leaders need to help subordinates accept responsibility for completing their work.* **1 2 3 4 5**
12. *Leaders should give subordinates complete freedom to solve problems on their own.* **1 2 3 4 5**
13. *The leader is the chief judge of the achievements of the members of the group.* **1 2 3 4 5**
14. *It is the leader's job to help subordinates find their "passion."* **1 2 3 4 5**
15. *In most situations, workers prefer little input from the leader.* **1 2 3 4 5**
16. *Effective leaders give clear orders and clarify processes and procedures.* **1 2 3 4 5**
17. *People are basically competent and if given a task will do a good job.* **1 2 3 4 5**
18. *In general, it is best to leave subordinates alone to let them do their work.* **1 2 3 4 5**

Scoring

- Sum the responses on items 1, 4, 7, 10, 13, and 16 (*Authoritarian leadership*): Total _____
- Sum the responses on items 2, 5, 8, 11, 14, and 17 (*Democratic leadership*): Total _____

- Sum the responses on items 3, 6, 9, 12, 15, and 18
  (*Laissez-faire leadership*): Total ____

Scoring Interpretation

The questionnaire is designed to measure three common styles of leadership: *authoritarian, democratic,* and *laissez-faire.* By comparing scores, the participant can determine which styles are most dominant and least dominant within the participant's style of leadership.[7]

- If the score is **26–30**, the participant is in the very high range.
- If the score is **21–25**, the participant is in the high range.
- If the score is **16–20**, the participant is in the moderate range.
- If the score is **11–15**, the participant is in the low range.
- If the score is **6–10**, the participant is in the very low range.

Gestalt Leadership Style Evaluation[8]

Based on the work of Kurt Lewin, the Gestalt Leadership Style Evaluation assist participates in understanding the styles of leadership and which qualities are manifest in their leadership style. More importantly, the evaluation can be assistive in pointing out leadership qualities that may need to be reconsidered and the importance of leadership elements that are essential to effective leadership.

Gestalt refers to creating perceptions by our interaction with the outside world through experiences that combined with our insight help us understand how the experiences have impacted our thoughts and actions. How we derive meaning from perceptions and experiences in large part drives what we can and or willing to do to reach success.

Instructions: In the following chart, select A, B, C, or D in each category and place your answer in the first column on the left in each section.

---

[7] Ibid.

[8] Kurt Lewin, "Defining the Field at a Given Time," *Psychological Review.* 50: 292-310, 1943. Republished in *Resolving Social Conflicts & Field Theory in Social Science,* Washington, D.C.: American Psychological Association, 1997.
http: //www.first practice management.co.uk /posts/quiz-test-your-leadership-style/.

It is essential that you circle the answers that most accurately reveal your leadership decisions.

Decisions and Changes
A-I make quick decisions-there is no need to confer
B-I welcome ideas/suggestions from my team
C-Team members are encouraged to be part of decisions
D-Decisions are based solely on policies and procedures

Feedback
A-I don't expect staff to criticize processes and methods
B-I will listen to feedback from the team
C-I encourage feedback from the team
D-Feedback is brought to my attention based on procedures

Communications
A-I tell my team what they need to know
B-I share what is going on with the team
C-I consult with the team regularly
D-I release updates based on a schedule

Performance
A-I ensure that tasks get done myself
B-I encourage team members to work style for performance
C-We agree on targets and objectives that support the work
D-I expect employees to work and I reward following rules

Supervision
A-I supervise all aspects of my team's roles and work
B-I trust my team to perform
C-Employees are guided on how to perform
D- Policies, rules, and procedures adhered to and policed

Behavior
A-Poor conduct is quickly and strictly managed
B-I trust my team to be professional and do their work
C-We agree on expectations and I address them when they fail
D-I use policies to decide who does or does not meet standards

Scoring

Mostly A's – *Autocratic*
Strengths: Quick at making decisions and productive.
Weaknesses: Poor morale with team; high sickness and turnover of staff; lack of team creativity.

Mostly B's - *Laissez Faire*
Strengths: Great with skilled, loyal, intellectual and experienced employees and fosters good working relationships.
Weaknesses: Style can result in a lack of focus or results within the team; behavior can easily become a problem in less professional and creative environments.

Mostly C's - *Democratic/Participative*
Strengths: Encourages development of skills; encourages creative ideas; high team morale and motivation.
Weaknesses: This style of management can be time-consuming.

Mostly D's – *Bureaucratic*
Strengths: Ensures safety and quality is focused on and is good with routines.
Weaknesses: Discourages creativity and independence and does not promote flexibility/engagement.

ADDITIONAL LEADERSHIP
SELF-ASSESSMENT INSTRUMENTS

- *Evaluation of Leadership Effectiveness - Mindtools*:
  https://www.mindtools.com/pages/article/newLDR _50.htm.

- *Leadership Style Test – Psychology*:
  http://psychologytoday.tests.psychtests.com/take_test.php?idRegTest
  =3205.

- *Situational Leadership Style Assessment – Motivation*:
  http://www.learninganddevelopment.org/www_learninganddevelopm
  ent_org/media/Documents/Leadership/Situational-Leadership-Self-
  Assessment.pdf.

- *Leadership Behavior Description Questionnaire -– Form XII Self*:
  Ohio State University:
  https://cyfar.org/sites/default/files/BDQ_1962_Self_Assessment.pdf.

- *Isabel Briggs Myers' Personality Type Assessment*:
  http://www. humanmetrics.com/cgi-win/jtypes2.asp.

- *From Manager to Breakthrough Leader*:
  https://membershipsite.s3.amazonaws.com/quizzes/mgr-to-brkthru-
  leader.pdf.

- *Keirsey Leadership Temperament Assessment*:
  http://www.keirsey. com/sorter/register. aspx.

- *Managerial Leadership Tendencies*:
  http://highered.mheducation.com/sites/007040187x/student_view0/ch
  apter12/self-assessment_12_5.html.
- *The Trusted Leader Assessment*:
  http://www.thetrustedleader.com/self-assess-1.html.

- *Assessment: What's Your Leadership Style – Harvard Business:* http: //hbr.org/2015/06/assessment

- *MMDI Personality Questionnaire*: http://wwmetarasa.com

- *Global Executive Leadership Inventory:* http://www.ketsdevries.com

REFERENCES

Adams, Scott, "Informed Decision-Making," Quote from the creator of the business-oriented *Dilbert Comic Strip*, United Media, 2000).

AdvanceEd (SACS) Accreditation Guidelines, (2015).

Advantages and Disadvantages of Hiring Friends and Relatives, 2011: http://www.businessknowledgesource.com/blog/advant-ages_and_ disadvantages_of_hiring_friends_ and_relatives _021220. html.

Alderfer, C.P., "An empirical test of a new theory of human needs," *Organizational Behavior and Human Performance*, 4, 1969.

Allport, Gordon W. and Leo Postman, "An analysis of rumors," *Public Opinion Quarterly*, Oxford Journals, 10 (4), 1946: doi:10.1093/ poq/10.4.501.

American Psychological Association, Psychological Science, *Rumor and Gossip Research*, 2005: http://www. apa.org/science/about/psa /2005/04/gossip.aspx.

Anandalingam, G. and Henry C. Lucas, Jr., *Beware the Winner's Curse,* (Oxford University Press, 2004).

Andromedon, Titus, from "Unbreakable Kimmy Schmidt," Reference to the philosopher's quotes and treatises referenced by Stephen Thrasher, *The Guardian*, 2015.

Annie E. Casey Foundation: http://www.aecf.org/work/. A private philanthropy based in Baltimore, Maryland.

Applied Epidemiology and Biostatistics, Section One-Concepts in *Principles of Epidemiology in Public Health*, Centers for Disease Control (CDC); (CDC Publications 2002).

Asbury, T.L., "Superintendent and School Board Member Turnover: Political versus Apolitical Turnover as a Critical Variable in the Application of the Dissatisfaction Theory," *Education Administration Quarterly*, 39 (5), 2003.

Auster, Ron, *Small Non-Profit Organization Case Studies*, (Auster Publishing, 2013).

Awadallah, Emad and Amir Allam, "A critique of the Balanced Scorecard as a performance measure," *International Journal of Business and Social Science*, 6 (7) 2015.

Axelrod, Alan, *Elizabeth I, CEO: Strategic Lessons from the CEO who Built an Empire*, (Prentice Hall Press, 2000).

Axelrod, Alan, *Patton on Leadership*, (Palgrave MacMillan Books, 2007).

Baldoni, John, "How a Good Leader Reacts to a Crisis," *Harvard Business Review*, January 2011.

Ballano, Vivencio, "How to Handle Rumors or Gossip in Business or Public Life," *Linkedin Company Culture*, August 25, 2014.

Bandura, Albert, *Social Foundations of Thought and Action*, (Prentice Hall, 1985).

—. "Evolution of Social Cognitive Theory," in K.G. Smith and M.A. Hitt (Eds.), *Great Minds in Management*, (Oxford University Press, 2005).

Belvalkar, Murnal, "Dangers of Misplaced Loyalty," *Buzzle*, 2011: http://www.buzzle.com/authors= 85441.

Bennis, Warren, *On Becoming a Leader*, (Addison-Wesley Publishing, 1989).

Berry, Tim, "How You Handle Bad News is the Ultimate Test of Leadership." *Business Insider*, (October 17, 2011).

Beyer, J. M., and Browning, L. D. "Transforming an industry in crisis: charisma, routinization, and supportive cultural leadership." *Leadership Quarterly,* 10 (3), 1999.

Bilal, Aisha, *Islamic and Arabian Quotes and Proverbs – Volume 1.* (Published by Aisha Bilal, 2013).

Blackie, Doug, "Obsequious Sycophants," 2003: http://www.dougblackie.com/2012/03/ obsequious-sycophants/.

Blade, Martin and Shehan Wijetilaka, "5 tips to grow your start-up using SWOT analysis", *Sydney*, December 2015.

Blair, Jeff, "A Positive Work Climate," *TLNT*, March 23, 2012.

Blanchard, Kenneth, *One Minute Manager*, (Harper Collins, 1982).

—. *The Servant Leader*, (Thomas Nelson Publishing, 2003).

Board Composition and Succession Planning, *National Directors of Corporate Directors*, 2012.

Bobinski, Dan, "Leadership lessons from Katrina," *Management Issue*, September 2005.

Bogue, Grady, "Commentary on Leadership," *KnoxNews.com*, 2012.

—. *The Enemies of Leadership*, (Phi Delta Kappa International Press, 1985).

Borida, Prashant and Nicholas DiFonzo, "Problem Solving in Social Interactions on the Internet: Rumor as Social Cognition," *Social Psychology Quarterly,* 67 (1) 2004: URL: http://www.jstor.org /stable /3649102.

Boswell, Nelson, *Successful Living Day by Day*, (Scribner Publishing. 1973).

Britol-Smith, Dana, *Overcome Your Fear of Public Speaking*, (Speaking for Success Publications, 2003).

Brooks, Chad, "Few Companies Prepared to Replace CEO," *Business News Daily*, March 7, 2014.

Brown, Erica, Leadership in the Wilderness, (Maggid Press, 2013.)

Bryant, Murray and Trevor Hunter, "PB and Public Issues (Mis) Management," *Ivey Business Journal*, September 2010.

Bryson, J., *Strategic Planning for Public and Nonprofit Organizations: A Guide to Strengthening and Sustaining Organizational Achievement* (3rd ed.), (Jossey-Bass 2004).

Buckingham, Marcus, *The One Thing You Need to Know*, (The Free Press, 2005).

Burnison, Gary, *The Twelve Absolutes of Leadership*, (McGraw-Hill Education Publishing, 2012).

Butte, Atul, Stanford Data Symposium, California, June 2015.

Cambridge Dictionary, http://dictionary.cambridge.org/us/ diction-ary /English/cabinet.

Campus Security Editors, "Study Finds Many Campuses May Be Neglecting Emergency Preparedness," *Campus Security Magazine*, October 18, 2015.

Carter, Ellis, "Top Ten Non-Profit Governance Mistakes." *Charity Lawyer,* (September 12, 2009) charity lawyerblog.com/2009/ 09/12/top-ten-non-profit-governance-mistakes/#ixzz 4K9x8oqJc.

Casey, Patti, "Sembler Property Offer Considered." *GoDeKalb.com*, 2004.

Caulthon, Andrew, "Ex-President Wants His Job Back," *Champion Newspaper*, December 15, 2014.

Celeste, Janice, "5 Steps to Stop Gossip in the Work-place," *Huffington Post*, September 8, 2015.

Center for Non-Profit Management, Organizational Self-Assessment, 2015: http://www. centerfornon-profit.com/site/2015.

Center for Theory of Change, 2016, *www.theoryof change. org.*

Chafkin, Max and Leigh Buchanan, "7 Tips for Motivating Employees," *Inc.*, April 2010: http://www.inc.com/guides /2010/04/tips-for-motivating-employees.html.

Charles I of England: Charles I was born in Fife on 19 November 1600, the second son of James VI of Scotland (from 1603 also James I of England) and Anne of Denmark: https://www.royal.uk/charles-i-r-1625-1649.

Chen, Walter, "95 Percent of Managers Follow an Outdated Theory of Motivation," *The Progress Principle*, September 14, 2014: http:// idonethis.com/ manage-ment-maslows-hierarchy-needs.

Christian, Brian, "The A/B Test: Inside the technology that's changing the rules of business, *Wired Magazine,* April 25, 2012: https://www.wired.com/2012/04/ ffabtesting.

Churchill, Winston, Oxford Reference: http://www.oxfordreference.com/view/10.1093/acref/978019957 2687.001.0001/q-author-00002-00000334.

Ciampa, D., and Watkins, M. *Right from the Start: Taking Charge in a New Leadership Role*, (Harvard Business School Press, 2005).

Citrin, James and Julie Hembrock, *You Need a CEO – Now What?* (Crown Business, 2012).

Clemens, John and Douglas Meyer, *The Classic Touch*, (McGraw-Hill Publishing, 1999).

Coase, Ronald, "How Should Economists Choose?" In *Ideas, Their Origins and Their Consequences: Lectures to Commemorate the Life and Work of G. Warren Nutter* 63 (Thomas Jefferson Center Foundation, American Institute for Public Policy Research, Washington, DC, 1988).

Cohen, Allan and David Bradford, *Influencing Up*, (Wiley Publishing, 2012).

Cohen, Michael and James March, *Leadership and Ambiguity 2nd Edition*, (Harvard Business, 1986).

Cohen, Steven, *Sustainability Management*, (Columbia University Press, 2011).

Collins, Douglas, *The Story of Kodak*, (Harry Abrams, 1990)

Collins, James and Jerry Porras, *Built to Last 3rd Edition*, (Harper Business, 2004).

Collins, James and Morten Hansen, *Great by Choice*, (Harper Business, 2011).

Collins, James, *Good to Great: Why Some Companies Make the Leap and Others Don't*, (Harper Business, 2001).

Collins, Jim, *Built to Last*, (Harper Business Essentials, 1994).

Cheryl Conner, "Six Ways to Improve Employee Morale and Performance," *Forbes,* September 11, 2014.

Continuity of Operations Planning, Federal Emergency Management Agency, 2016: https://www.fema.gov/ continuity-operations.

Cooper, B.S., L.D. Fusarelli, and V.A. Carella, "Career Crisis in the Superintendency? National Survey Results," *The American Association of School Administrators*, 2002.

Corsi, Carlo, Guilherme Dale, Julie Hembrock Daum, John Mumm, and Willi Schoppen, *Five Things Board Directors Should Be Thinking About*, (Point of View, 2010).

Covey, Stephen M.R., *The Speed of Trust*, (Free Press of Simon and Schuster, 2008 edition).

Crisis Management and Communications, *Institute of Public Relations*, Updated 2014: http://www.institute forpr.org/crisis-management-communications/.

Crisis Response Team Training, *Crisis Prevention Institute*: http://www.crisisprevention.com/ Resources/Know-ledge-Base/ Crisis-Response-Team-Training.

Cukier, Kenneth and Viktor Mayer-Schoenberger, "The Rise of Big Data," *Foreign Affairs*, June 2013: https://www.foreign affairs.com/articles/2013-04-03/rise-big-data.

Curry, Pat, "Ten Lethal Mistakes." *Bankrate.com.*, 2014.

Danzberger, Jacquelyn, *Facing the Challenge: the Report of the Twentieth Century Task Force on School Governance,* (Brookings Institute, 2002).

Davenport, Geoffrey, Ian McDonald, and Caroline Moss-Gibbons (Editors). *The Royal College of Physicians and its Collections*, p. 48. (Royal College of Physicians. 2001).

Davenport, Thomas, Brook Manville, and Laurence Prusak, *Judgment Call: Twelve Stories of Big Decisions and the Teams That Got Them Right*, (Harvard Business Press Books, 2012).

DeBono, Edward, *Lateral Thinking: Creativity Step by Step*, (Harper, 2015).

—. *Serious Creativity: How to Be Creative Under Pressure and Turn Ideas into Action*, (Random House, 2015).

Deitz, Dennis and Carlene Deitz, *Buffalo Creek: Valley of Death*, (Mountain Memory Books, 1992).

Deming, W. Edward, *Quality, Productivity, and Competitive Position,* (Massachusetts Institute of Technology: Center for Advanced Engineering Studies, 1982.)

Denning, Steve, "Seven Lessons Every CFO Must Learn," *Forbes*, January 2013.

DiFonzo, Nicholas and Prashant Bordia, *Rumor Psychology: Social and Organizational Approaches*, (American Psychological Association, 2007).

Doss, Henry, "Status Quo Leadership is the Biggest Impediment to Innovation*," Forbes*, March 28, 2015.

Downey, Maureen, "Georgia Perimeter College: What is the rest of the story on the financial meltdown?" *Atlanta Journal-Constitution*, June 10, 2013.

Doyle, Charles, Wolfgang Mieder, and Fred Shapiro, *Dictionary of Modern Proverbs*, (Cambridge University Press, 2000).

Drucker, Peter, *The Effective Executive: The Definitive Guide to Getting the Right Things Done,* (Harper Business, 2006 Edition).

Drummond, Helga, *Guide to Decision Making: Getting it More Right than Wrong,* (Wiley, 2012).

Dupree, Max, *Leadership is An Art,* (Crown Business Publisher, 2004).

Edinger, Scott, "Three Cs of Implementing Strategy," *Forbes,* August 2012.

Editorial Staff, Rumors in the workplace: Managing and preventing them," *Mindtools,* 2016: https://www.mind-tools.com/pages/article/newTMM_25.htm.

Edmundson, Ron, "Five Wrong Ways to Respond to Criticism." *Ron Edmundson.com.* 2016.

Edwards, Greg, "Truman Bank Board Member Resigns Cites Interference." *St. Louis Business Journal,* September 28, 2011.

Ehrenkrantz, Dan, "Why You Should Run Your Business Like a Non-Profit," *Forbes,* September 2014.

Elde, Ronald, *Using Case Studies for Non-Profit Manage-ment,* (Reveltree Publishing, 1999).

Ellington, McKinney, *Socrates Fables,* (Maxter Publishing, 1921): updated at http://www. inspiration peak.com /cgi-bin/stories.cgi? record=150.

Environmental Case Study: Buffalo Creek Disaster, University of Michigan Environmental Studies: 1977, http://umich.edu/~snre 492/Jones/buffalo.html.

Erikson, Kai T., *Everything in Its Path: Destruction of Community in the Buffalo Creek Flood,* (Simon and Schuster, 1976).

Estimating the Cost of Workplace Bullying, *Workplace Bullying Institute,* April 24, 2014.

Facuette, Joey, "Are You Your Employee's Morale Problem?" *Entrepreneur,* August 2011.

Farrell, L.U., "Workplace Bullying High Cost," http://orlandobizjournals.com/orlando/stories/2002/13/8/ focus1.htlm.

Federal Emergency Management Agency: https://www.fema.gov /disaster/4085/updates /2012/developing-emergency-plan-workplace.

Feinberg, Mortimer and Jack Tarrant, *Why Smart People Do Dumb Things,* (Simon and Schuster, 1995).

FEMA Continuity of Operation Preparedness: https://training. fema.gov/programs/coop/.

Festinger, Leon, *A Theory of Cognitive Dissonance,* (Stanford University Press, 1962).

Fiedler, F.E. and Garcia, J. E. Garcia, *New Approaches to Leadership, Cognitive Resources, and Organizational Performance*, (John Wiley and Sons, 1987).

Fiorina, Carla, *Tough Choices*, (Portfolio, 2007).

Fischer, Peter, *The New Boss: How to Survive the First 100 Days*, (Kogan Page, 2008).

Fiske, E.K., "Research on Gossip: Taxonomy, Methods and Future Directions," *Review of General Psychology*, 2004, Vol. 8, No. 2, 78–99 1089-2680/04/DOI: 10.1037/ 1089-2680.8.2.78.

Flagerty, Malcolm, *Once Upon a Failed Success*, (Provider Independent Press, 1981).

Forbes, Malcolm, *The Sayings of Chairman Malcolm*, (Harper Collins, 1978). Foundation for the Malcolm Baldrige National Quality Award: http://www. baldrigepe.org/.

Frampton, Will, "DeKalb County Schools Face Even Deeper Cuts." *CBS46 News*, [written transcript], July 11, 2012.

Free Management Library: http://managementhelp.org/*organizational performance* /nonprofits.

Fuller, Andrea and Douglas Belkin, "The Watchdogs of College Education Rarely Bite," *The Wall Street Journal*, June 17, 2015.

Gallman, Stephanie and Christina Sgueglia, "Fire Chief Resigns After Criticism of Bombing Response," *CNN*, June 4, 2013.

Georgia Department of Education Criterion-Referenced Competency Tests, *gadoe.org* (2004).

Georgia Department of Education Discipline Records, *gadoe.org* (2005-2006).

Georgia School Boards Association application form for superintendent candidates, Georgia School Boards Association website, *gsba.org.*, 2016.

Gerstner, Edward, *Elephants Can Dance*, (Harper Collins, 2003).

Gilmore, A. "In With the New: Leader Dos and Don'ts," *Talent Management*, 2008.

Gkorezis, Panagiotis; Eugenia Petridou, and Theodora Krouklidou, Monitoring Editor: Vlad Glăveanu, "The Detrimental Effect of Machiavellian Leadership on Employees' Emotional Exhaustion: Organizational Cynicism as a Mediator," *European Journal of Psychology*, November 2015; 11(4): Published online 2015 November 27. doi: 10.5964/ ejop.v11i4.988

Glass, Thomas, Lars Bjork, and Cryss Brunner, *The 2000 Study of the American Public School Superintendent,* (American Association of School Administrators, 2000).

Goldman, Alan, "A Toxic CEO Manifesto," *Psychology Today*, (July 2011).

Goldsmith, Marshall, *What Got You Here Won't Get You There: How Successful People Become Even More Successful*, (Hachette, 2007).

Goleman, Daniel, "Leadership That Gets Results," *Harvard Business Review*, March 2000.

Goleman, Daniel, Richard Boyatzis, and Annie McKee, *Primal Leadership: Unleashing the Power of Emotional Intelligence*, (Harvard Business Review Press, 2013).

Goodyear, Martha and Cynthia Golder, *Leadership Transitions*, (Professional Development Publishing, 2008).

Greenleaf, Robert, *Servant Leadership*, (Paulist Press, 1977).

—. *Servant Leadership: A Journey into the Nature of Legitimate Power and Greatness*, (Paulist Publishing. 2002).

Gregoire, Crispin, "The Role of Boards in Fostering Accountability." *The International Journal of Not for Profit Law*, Volume 2, Issue 3, March (2000).

Grenny, Joseph, Kerry Patterson, and David Maxfield, *Influencer: The New Science of Leading Change: Second Edition*, (McGraw-Hill, 2013).

Griffin, Nicholas, Editor, *The Cambridge Companion to Bertrand Russell*, (Cambridge University Press. 2003).

Grissom, Jason, "The determinants of conflict on boards in public organizations," *The Journal of Public Administration Theory and Research*, 2009: doi: 10.1093 /jopart/mup043.

Gunnlaugson, O. and Otto Scharmer, "Perspectives on Theory U: Insights from the Field," In *Presencing Theory U* by O. Gunnlaugson, C. Baron, and M Cayer, (IGI Global Press, 2013).

Hakala, D., "Promoting from Within," *HR World,* October 2011

Hall, Holly, "Feasibility Studies for Capital Campaigns Are a Waste of Money." *The Chronicle of Philanthropy*, March 17, 2015.

Hall, Jay, "To achieve or not: the manager's choice," *California Management Review*, Haas School of Business, University of California Berkeley, 18/4 summer 1976: http://cmr.berkeley.edu/search/ article Detail.aspx article=5114.

Hannum, Kelly, Jennifer W. Martineau, and Claire Reinelt. *The Handbook of Leadership Development Evaluation*, (Jossey-Bass Publishers, 2006).

Hardin, Ken, "False Workplace Gossip Can Result in Company Liability," *Tech Republic*, March 3, 2003: http://www.techrepublic. com/article/ false-workplace-gossip-can-result-in-company-liability.

Harris, Sidney J., AZQuotes.com. *The Wind and Fly* LTD, 2016.

http://www.azquotes.com/author/6311-Sydney_J_Harris,   accessed
September 25, 2016.

Harrison, K.R., *Victors and Victims*, (Authentic Publishers, 2014).

Hasel, Marcus, "A question of context: the influence of trust on leadership
effectiveness during a crisis," *Management*, March 2013.

Hayar, Vincent, "Managing Three Types of Bad Bosses." *Harvard Business
Review*, December 1, 2014.

Healey, Kerry, "The Difference between a Great Leader and a Good One,"
Fortune, August 5, 2014.

Heath, Chip and David Heath, *Made to Stick*, (Random House, 2007).

Heath, Dan and Chip Heath, *Switch: How to Change Things When Change is
Hard,* (Crown Publishing, 2010).

Henderson, Ruth, "What Gets Measured Gets Done: Or Does It?" *Forbes,*
June 2015: http://www.forbes.com/sites/ellevate/2015/ 06/08/what-gets-
measured-gets-done-or-does-it/#44d85 ac78600.

Henneberger, Melinda, "Gang Membership Grows in Middle-Class
Suburbs," *The New York Times*, (July 24, 1993).

Herbert, A.P., *Uncommon Law*, (Methuen Publishers. 1935).

Hernandez, Oscar, "Medi-Quote," *The Edinburgh Medic*, April 27, 2009.

Hersey, Paul and Ken Blanchard, *Management of Organizational Behavior:
Utilizing Human Resources 3rd Edition*, (Prentice Hall, 1977).

Herzberg, Frederick, *One More Time: How Do You Motivate People?*
(Harvard Business Review, 1968).

Hess, Fredrick, "The Role of the Local Board," *Center for Public
Governance*, 2002.

Holiday, Ryan, *Ego is the Enemy*, (Portfolio, 2016).

Hume, David, https://www.leader-values.com/word press/ David-hume-
philosopher-extraordinaire-quotes/.

Humphrey, Albert, "SWOT Analysis for Management Consulting," *SRI
Alumni Newsletter. SRI International*, December 2011.

Humphrey, George, *The Story of Man's Mind*, (Small, Maynard, and
Company, 1923).

Hyatt, Michael, "When Leadership Fails," *MH* 2015: https://michael
hyatt.com/when-leadership-fails. html.

Iannucci, Lisa, *Dealing With Difficult Board Members*, (The Cooperator,
2008).

Innovation Network: http://www.innonet.org/.

Issurdatt, Sharon, "Gangs: A Growing Problem in Schools," *Practice
Perspectives*, National Association of Social Workers, September 2011.

Jackson, Eric, "Sun Tzu's 31 Best Pieces of Leadership Advice," *Forbes*, May 23, 2014.

James, Erica, "Leadership as (Un)usual: How to Display Competence in Times of Crisis." *Organizational Dynamics*, Vol. 34, No. 2, 2005.

Jantsch, John, *The Commitment Engine*. (Penguin Group, 2012).

Jarvis, Jeff, *What Would Google Do?* (Harper Business Publishing, 2009).

Javitch, David, *Delivering Bad News*, Entrepreneur, January, 2008.

Jay, Anthony, *Management and Machiavelli: A Prescription for Success*, (Prentice-Hall, 1996).

Joffe, Marc, "Moody's, S&P and Other Credit Rating Agencies Deserve a Failing Grade," *The Guardian*, February 2013.

Kaiser, Mary, "How to Hire the Right Person for the Job," *Entrepreneur, Inc.*, June 3, 2015.

Kalb, Ira, "How Toyota's Crisis Management Failure Added to the Billion Dollar Settlement, *Business Insider*, December 2012: http://www.business insider.com/ toyota-paying-billions-because-of-marketing-failures-2012-12.

Kanter, Rosabeth Moss, *Confidence: How Winning Streaks and Losing Streaks Begin and End*, (Crown Publishing, 2006).

Katz, David A., Wachtell, Lipton, Rosen & Katz, "Advice for Boards in CEO Selection and Succession Planning," *Harvard Law Forum on Corporate Governance and Financial Regulation*, June 11, 2012: corpgov.law. harvard.edu/2012/06/11/advice-for-boards-in-ceo-selection - and-succession-planning/.

Kayser, Thomas, *Building Team Power: How to Unleash the Collaborative Genius of Teams for Increased Engagement, Productivity, and Results*, (McGraw-Hill, 2011).

Kellerman, Barbara, *Bad Leadership*, (Harvard Business Review Press, 2014).

Kennedy, John F., 35th President of the United States, 1961-1963. The quote was retrieved from http://en.proverbia.net/citastema. asp? tematica=1038.

Kent, Emerson, "Henry Adams," *History for the Historian*, 2012: http://www.emersonkent.com/history_notes/ henry_adams.htm.

Klann, Gene, *Crisis Leadership*, (Center for Creative Leadership, 2003).

Knight, Jerry, "Tylenol's Maker Shows How to Respond to Crisis", *The Washington Post*, October 11, 1982.

Koeppel, David, "Executive Life; A Tough Transition: Friend to Supervisor" *New York Times* March 16, 2003.

Kowalski, Theodore, *Effective Communication for District and School Administrators 2nd Edition*, (Rowman and Littlefield, 2015).

Kraaijenbrink, J., "Alternative for the Balanced Scorecard: The Performance Prism.": http:// kraaijen brink.com/2012/10/*an-alternative-for-the-balanced-scorecard-the-performance-prism/*.

—. "Five reasons to abandon the Balanced Scorecard: http://kraaijenbrink.com /2012 /10/*fivereasonstoabandonthebalancedscorecard/*.

Kraft, Cindy, "Executives Transitions Market Study:" http://www.cfo-coach.com/2008/06/executive-transitions-market-study.html.

Krantz, David, "Ways to Effectively Communicate with Employees," *Entrepreneur,* July 24, 2014.

Krantz, Matt, "2008 Crisis Still Hangs Over Credit Rating Firms," *USA Today*, September 13, 2013.

Kruse, Kevin, "100 Best Quotes on Leadership," *Forbes*, October 16, 2012.

LaBelle, Antoinette, "Transition to new leadership: The first 1,000 days," *The Bridgespan Group,* September 2011.

LaBelle, Antoinette, *Transition to New Leadership*, (The Bridgespan Group, 2012).

LaDuke, Phil, "Six Ways to Improve Workplace Safety Without Going Broke," *Entrepreneur,* June 16, 2014.

La Monica, P.R., "On the Wings of Rumors," *Smart Money*, September 17, 1999a.

Larson, Randall, *The Bloch Companion: Collected Interviews 1969–1986*, (Starmont House, 1989).

Laschinger, Heather, Joan Finegan, and Judith Shamian. "Impact of Workplace Empowerment, Organizational Trust on Staff Nurses' Work Satisfaction and Organizational Commitment." *Health Care Management Review* vol. 26, no. 3, 2001.

Last, J.M., *Dictionary of Epidemiology 4th Edition.* p. 61, (New York: Oxford University Press; 2001).

Leadership on Organizational Commitment and Turnover," Kravis Leadership Institute, *Leadership Review*, Vol. 10, summer 2010.

LeadingAge Minnesota: https://www.leadin gagemn.org/providers /boards-trustees/sample-forms/.

Leblebici, Demet, "Impact of Workplace Quality on Employees Productivity," *Journal of Business, Economics and Finance Survey*, Volume 1, Issue 1, 2012.

Lee, Steven, *Encyclopedia of School Psychology* (Thousand Oaks: SAGE Publications, Inc., 2005).

Leigh, Stephen, *Speaking Stones*, (Phoenix Pick, 2009).

Lempel, Howard, Ross Hammond, and Joshua Epstein, "Economic Cost and Healthcare Workforce Effects of School Closures in the United States," *Brookings Institute*, September 30, 2009.

Lencioni, Patrick, *Death by Meeting: A Leadership Fable About Solving the Most Painful Problem in Business*, (Josey-Bass, 2004).

Lencioni, Patrick, *Five Dysfunctions of a Team: A Leadership Fable*, (Jossey-Bass, 2002).

Leon, Derrick, *Ruskin - The Great Victorian*, (Routledge Imprint of Taylor and Francis Publishing, 2015).

Letters to the Editor. *Champion Newspaper*, October 1, 2004.

Lewin, Kurt, Ronald Lippitt, and Ralph White, "Patterns of Aggressive Behavior," *Journal of Social Psychology*, Vol. 10 (2), 1939.

Lewis, C.S., *Mere Christianity*, (Harper Collins Press, Re-released 2001).

Likert, Robert, *The Human Organization: Its Management and Value*, (McGraw-Hill, 1967).

Limkin, Jason, "What Everyone Should Know About Mergers and Acquisitions," *Forbes*, March 23, 2013.

Lipman, Victor, "5 Easy Ways to Motivate and Demotivate Employees," *Forbes*, March 2013.

Lipman-Blumen, Jean, *The Allure of Toxic CEOs*, (Oxford University Press, 2006).

Lippitt, Mary, *The Managing Complex Change Model*, Enterprise Management, Ltd., 1987.

List of Hewlett-Packard Executive Leadership, Wiki-pedia, 2015: https://en.wikipedia.org/ wiki/Listof_Hewlett-Packardexecutive_ leadership.

Llopis, Glenn, "The Most Successful CEOs Do 15 Things," *Forbes*, February 8, 2014.

Local Board Voter Participation Survey, Iowa School Boards Association, 2007.

Love, Carol, Jim Redmond, and Rick Ammen. "Managing Bad News." Video broadcast from *The Center for Community Engagement*, January 2010.

Lowell, Stephanie, Brian Trelstad, and Bill Meehan, "The Ratings Game," *Stanford Social Innovation Review*, Summer 2005.

Lukaszewski, James, "Good News about Bad News," *Security Management Magazine*, April 2000.

Management Study Guides for Non-Profits: http://www.*Managementstudy guide.com*/swot-analysis.htm.

Manderscheid, S. V. "New Leader Assimilation: An Intervention for Leaders in Transition." *Advances in Developing Human Resources,* 2008.

Maraboli, Steve, "Unapologetically You": http:// www. goodreads. com/work/quotes/25086973-unapologet-ically-your-reflections-on-life-and-the-human-experience.

Marcus, John, "Caught Cheating: Colleges Falsify Admissions Data for Higher Rankings," *The Hechinger Report,* March 20, 2013.

Marguerite Casey Foundation: http://caseygrants.org /resources/org-capacity-assessment.

Martin, Roger, "The Big Lie of Strategic Planning," *Harvard Business Review*, February 2014.

Maslow, Abraham, "A Theory of Human Motivation," *Psychological Review*, 50, 1946.

Matteucci, Megan, "Superintendent's Contract is Terminated," *Atlanta Journal and Constitution*, April 16, 2010.

Maxwell, John, *Everyone Communicates but Few Connect*, (Thomas Nelson, 2010).

—. *The 17 Indisputable Laws of Teamwork: Embrace Them and Empower Your Team*, (Thomas Nelson, 2013).

Michigan Non-Profit Association: https://mnaonline.org/ principles-practices-assessment/file.

Minnesota Council of Non-Profits: https://sample board-meeting – www.minnesotanonprofit-form/.

Mintzberg, Henry, *The Nature of Managerial Work*, (Harper Collins, 1973) with excerpts and concepts updated in *Simply Managing*, (Berrett-Koehler, 2013).

McClelland, David, *Human Motivation*, (Cambridge University Press, 1988).

McCullough, David, *Truman*, (Simon and Schuster, 1993).

McCurry, Justin, "Naoto Kan Resigns as Japan's Prime Minister." *The Guardian,* (August 26, 2011).

McGiboney, Garry W., *Crisis Management Planning for Schools and Centers*, (Einstar Publishing, 2016).

McIntyre, Marie, "Building an effective management team": http://www.yourofficecoach.com/topics/lessons_in_leadership /effective _ leadership/building_ an_ effective_management_team. aspx.l.

Mendels, Pamela, "The Real Cost of Firing a CEO," *Chief Executive*, April 1, 2013.

Meyers, Chris, "Why Bullies Make Bad Leaders." *Forbes*, April 1, 2016.

Mills, Colleen, "Experiencing gossip: The foundations for a theory of embedded organizational gossip," *Group and Organizational Management*, April 2010, 35 (2): 10.1177/1059601109360392.

Morgan Johnson, Eileen, "Succession Planning for Non-Profit Leaders," (*The Center for Association Leader-ship*, 2007.)

Morgeson, Frederick, "Leadership in Teams: A Functional Approach to Understanding Leadership Structures and Processes," *Journal of Management*, 36, 2010.

Mui, Chunka, "How Kodak Failed," *Forbes*, January 19, 2012.

Myatt, Michael, "*15 Ways to Identify Bad Leaders*," *Forbes*, October 2012.

Naisbitt, John, *Megatrends: Ten New Directions Transforming Our Lives*, (Grand Central Publishing, 1988).

National Council of Non-Profits: https://www.council ofnonprofits.org /tools-resources/organizational-self-assessments.

National Governors Association: http://www.nga.org/ files/live/sites/ NGA/files/pdf/0607PANDEMIC PRIMER.PDF.

National Institute for Occupational Safety and Health, *Publication #99-101*, (1999).

National Institutes of Health, http://www.hhs.gov/asl/testify /2009 /07/t20090729b.html.

Neely, Andrew, "Does the Balanced Scorecard work: An empirical investigation," *Cranfield CERES*, January 2008:http://dspace. lib. Cranfield.ac.uk /handle/1826/ 3932.

Newstrom, John, *The Big Book of Team Building Games: Trust-Building Activities, Team Spirit Exercises, and Other Activities*, (McGraw-Hill, 1997).

Nili, Yaron, "When executives fail: Managing performance on the CEO's team," Harvard Law School Forum, March 18, 2015: https://corpgov. law. harvard.edu/2015/03/18/when-executives-fail-managing-performance-on-the-ceos-team/.

Nohria, N., P., Lawrence, and E. Wilson, *Driven: How Human Nature Shapes Our Choices*, Jossey-Bass Inc. Publishing, 2002).

Non-Profit Association of Midlands: https:// nonprofit am.org/file.

Non-Profit Association of Oregon, https://nonprofit oregon.org/sites/ default/files/uploads/file/NP%20Org%20Self%20Assessment_0.pdf.

Norris, Sean, "Who Watches the Charity Watchdogs?" *Leadership Management*, April 2016: http://www. nonprofitpro.com/article/ who-watches-the-charity-watchdogs-charity-navigator/.

Nugent, Tom, *Death at Buffalo Creek: The 1972 West Virginia Flood Disaster*, (W. W. Norton & Company, 1973).

Nussbaum, Debra, "Calling All Superintendents," *New York Times*, September 4, 2007.

Office of Juvenile Justice Delinquency Prevention, *"Gangs-OJJDP,"* 2014:https://www.ojjdp.gov/jjbulletin /9804/gangs.html.

Ogden, Dayton and John Wood, "Succession Planning: A Board Imperative," *Bloomberg Business Week*, March 2008.

Ommani, Ahmad, "Using a SWOT analysis for business management". 5 (22), *African Journal of Business Manage-ment*, September 2011.

Opportunity Knocks, Inc. Opportunity Knocks, Inc. is a non-profit organization dedicated to enhancing the capacity of individuals with disabilities to live, work and participates as active members of their communities. http://www.idealist. org/view /nonprofit /SJd tnsn6t pw4/.

Osita, Christain, Idoko Onyebuchi, and Nzekwe Justina, Nzekwe, "Organization's stability and productivity: the role of SWOT analysis," *International Journal of Innovative and Applied Research*, January 2014.

Oxford Dictionary: https://en.oxford dictionaries.com/definitions /cabinet.

Parker, Carla, "School District Officials Discuss What to Do with Briarcliff Property." *The Champion Newspaper*, September 27, 2013.

Parmenter, D., "A table without any legs: A critique of the balanced scorecard methodology." *In implementing Winning KPIs*: http:// davidparmenter.com/how-to-guides, 2012.

Patterson, Kerry, "Accountability: What dysfunctional teams are missing," *Psychology Today*, January 2013.

Patterson, Kerry, Joseph Grenny, David Maxfield, Ron McMillian, and Al Switzler, *Influencer: The Power to Change Anything*, (McGraw-Hill, 1987).

Pendleton, Susan Coppess, "Rumor research revisited and expanded," *Language & Communication*, Vol 18(1), January 1998: http://dx.doi.org/10.1016/S0271-5309 (97) 00024-4.

Pessanha, D. S., and V. Prochnik, "Practitioners' opinions on academics' critics on the Balanced Scorecard": http://ssrn. com/abstract=1094308.

Peters, Thomas and Robert Waterman, *In Search of Excellence*, (Grand Central Publishing, 1982).

—. *In Search of Excellence*, (Harper Business, Reprint 2006).

Pink, Daniel H., *The Surprising Truth About What Motivates Us*, (Riverhead Books, 2009).

Piraino, Rick, "Leadership and Favoritism," *Ezine Articles*, December 2008: http://ezinearticles.com/?Leadershipand-Favori tism&id =1768 715.

Powell, Colin, *It Worked for Me: In Life and Leadership*, (Harper Perennial, 2014).

Pritchett, Price, *The Team Member Handbook for Teamwork*, (Pritchett Publishing Company, 2006).

Public comments at a college forum interview conducted at Georgia Perimeter College, 2011.

Ramano, Joseph - in "How Successful Companies Identify and Hold on to Their Talent and Why It's Important," *Forbes,* October 25, 2013.

Raven, Susan - Terence was a Roman playwright of comedies, 170-160 BC, *Rome in Africa*, (Routledge Publishing, 1993).

Rees, Jasper, "The End of our Kodak Moment". *The Telegraph*, January 20, 2012.

Robles, Patricio, "Five Rules for the Data-Driven Business," *Econsultancy,* November 22, 2010: https:// econsultancy.com/6870-five-rules-for-the-data-driven-business/.

Rogel, Charles, *Using the SARA Model to Learn from 360-Degree Feedback.* (Decision Wise Productions, 2015).

Ryan, R.M. and E.L. Deci, "Self-determination Theory and the Facilitation of Intrinsic Motivation, Social Development, and Will," *American Psychologist*, 55, 2000.

Sackman, S.A., "Cultures and Subcultures: An Analysis of Organizational Knowledge," *Administrative Science Quarterly*, 37 (1), March 1992.

Saez, Alex, "How Should Supervisors Handle Rumors?" *Small Business*, 2011: http://smallbusiness.chron.com/should-supervisors-handle-rumors-550 36.html.

Sanborn, Mark, "Seven Steps to Keep Employees Safe in the Workplace," *Entrepreneur*, October 24, 2013.

Sanchez, Ray, "Did Depression or an Alleged Bullying Boss Prompt Editor's Suicide?" *ABC News*, August 10, 2010.

Sandys Celia, *We Shall Not Fail: The Inspiring Leadership of Winston Churchill*, (Portfolio, 2003).

Scharmer, C. Otto, *Theory U: Leading from the Future as It Emerges*, (Society for Organizational Learning, 2007).

—. *Theory U: Leading from the Future as it Emerges 2nd Edition*, (Berrett-Koehler Publishers, 2016).

Schneider, Benjamin, David E. Bowen, Mark G. Ehrhart, and Karen M. Holcombe, "The Climate for Service: Evolution of a Construct," in *Handbook of Organizational Culture and Climate,* Eds. Neal M. Ashkanasy, Celeste P.M. Wilderom, and Mark F. Peterson (Thousand Oaks: Sage Publications, 2000), 21-36.

Schwerdt, Guido and Martin R. West, "The Impact of Alternative Grade Configurations on Student Outcomes through Middle and High School," *IZA DP No. 6208*, December 2011.

Section 45-10-4 of the *Official Code of Georgia Annotated*.

Senge, Peter, Joseph Jaworski, C. Otto Scharmer, and Betty Flowers, *Presence: Exploring Profound Change in People, Organizations, and Society*, (Nicholas Brealey Publishing, 2005).

Sheridan, John E., Max D. Richards, and John Slocum, "Comparative Analysis of Expectancy and Heuristic Models of Decision Making," *Journal of Applied Psychology*, 60, (3), June 1975.

Shragai, Naomi, "The managers who fear conflict: Leaving a conflict unresolved can harm your career and colleagues," *Financial Times*, June 2014.

SHRM Workplace Forecast, The Top Trends of HR Professionals, *Society of Human Resources Management*, May 2013.

Silver, Nate, *The Signal and the Noise: Why So Many Predictions Fail But Some Don't*, (Penguin, 2015).

Silverman, Stanley, Russell E. Johnson, Nicole McConnell, and Alison Carr, "Arrogance: A formula for leadership failure," *The Society for Organizational and Industrial Psychology*, 2011.

Simon Sinek, *Leaders Eat Last*, (Penguin Publishing, 2014).

Sivaloganathan, Mohan, "Why and How You Should Run Your Non-Profit Like a For-Profit Organization," *FC Leadership*, January (2015).

Skogstad, Anders, Stale Einarsen, Torbjorn Torsheim, Merethe Aasland, and Hilde Hetland, "The destructiveness of laissez-faire leadership behavior," *Journal of Occupational Health Psychology*, Vol 12(1), Jan 2007: http://dx.doi.org/10.1037/1076-8998.12. 1.80.

Smith, Jacquelyn, "10 Reasons Why Humor is a Key to Success at Work," *Forbes*, May 3, 2013.

—. "Commons Reasons Half of All New Executives Fail," *Business Insider,* March 2, 2015.

Sowell, Thomas, Rose and Milton Friedman Senior Fellow on Public Policy, Hoover Institution: http://www.hoover.org/ profiles/thomas-sowell.

Stangler, Diane and Sam Arbesman, "What Does Fortune 500 Turnover Mean?" *Kaufman Foundation*, 2012.

Staub, Robert, "You Should Beware the Dangers of the Ego Trap." *Triad Business Journal*, June 8, 2009.

Stephenson, Carol, "The Role of Leadership in Managing Risk," *The Ivey Business Journal*, December 2010.

Stern, Gerald, *The Buffalo Creek Disaster: How the Survivors of One of the Worst Disasters in Coal-Mining History Brought Suit Against the Coal Company and Won*, (Vintage, 2008).

Succession Planning With Your Board. *Society for Human Resource Management,* (Guideline Series 2014).

Sugars, Bradley, *Instant Team Building - Instant Success Series*, (McGraw-Hill, 2006).

Sweeny, Kate, "Crisis decision theory: Decisions in the face of negative events," *Psychological Bulletin*, 134 (1), 2008.

Sweeny, Kenneth, "Crisis Decision Theory." *Psychological Bulletin*, January, 2008, 134(1): doi: 10.1037/0033-2909.134.1.61.

Synder, Paul, *Is This Something George Eastman Would Have Done? The Decline and Fall of the Eastman Kodak Company*, (Independent Publishing, 2013)

Szilagyi, Andrew, John Ivancevich, and Marc Wallace, *Organizational Behavior and Performance 3rd Edition*, (Goodyear Publishing, 1983).

Taylor, Kate, "A viral rumor that McDonald's uses ground worm filler in burgers has been debunked," *Business Insider*, January 2016.

Thompson, K.R. and F. Luthans, "Organizational Culture: A Behavioral Perspective," in B. Schneider (Ed.), *Organizational Climate and Culture* (San Francisco: Jossey-Bass, 1990).

The Anatomy of Peace: Resolving the Heart of Conflict–2nd Edition, Arbinger Institute, 2015.

The Critical Role of the Board in Effective Risk Oversight, Ernest & Young, 2015.

The Great City Schools Survey of Superintendents, (*Great City Schools Council*, 2003).

Tobak, Steve, "How to Deliver Bad News." *Money Watch*, (June 26, 2011).

Traylor, Agatha, "Church Leadership Declines," *Christian Notes and Legacies*, March 2000.

Traynor, Des, "The problem with data-driven decisions." *Inside Intercom*, https://blog.intercom. com/the-problem-with-data-driven-decisions/.

U.S. News and World Report "Best Colleges and High Schools:" http://www.usnews.com /education (annual editions).

U.S. Profiles of Presidents: http://www.president profiles.com/ Grant-Eisenhower/Harry-S-Truman-Domestic-policies.html. *Advameg, Inc.*

United States Bureau of Labor Statistics, Annual Report – 2014. *United States Government*.

United States Office of Personnel Management:

https://www. opm.gov/policy-data-oversight/worklife/reference-materials/
workplaceviolence.pdf.
Voelpel, S., M. Leibold, R.A. Eckhoff, and T.H. Davenport, "The Tyranny of
the Balanced Scorecard in the Innovation Economy." *Proceedings of the
4th International Critical Management Studies Conference*, Intellectual
Capital Stream Cambridge University, United Kingdom, July, 4-6.
Wainert, Tom and Stephen A. Miles, "Advice to the New CEO: How to
Handle Your Board," *Forbes*, November 12, 2009.
Wagner, Eric T., "Five Reasons Eight Out of 10 Businesses Fail," *Forbes,*
September 2013.
Walton, Alice G., "The Dark Side of Leadership." *Forbes*, February 7, 2013.
Watkins, M., *What Should a New Leader Do When Entering Into an Existing
Team*? The First 90 Days, (Harvard Business School Publishing, 2003).
Watkins, Michael, "Advice for Vikram Pandit, the New CEO of Citigroup,"
Harvard Business Review, October 2010.
—. *The First 90 Days: Proven Strategies for Getting Up to Speed Faster and
Smarter, Updated, and Expanded*, (Harvard Business, 2013).
Watson, Jr., Thomas, *Father, Son, and Company*, (Bantam Books, 1991.)
Weaver, Sara G. and George B. Yancy, "The Impact of Dark Leadership on
Organizational Commitment and Turnover," Kravis Leadership Institute,
Leadership Review, Vol. 10, summer 2010.
Weeks, Kent, *Boards: Duties, Responsibilities, Decision-Making, and Legal
Basis for Local Board Powers*, (State University Press, 2000).
Weisinger, Hendrie, *The Power of Positive Criticism*, (AMACON Publishers,
2007).
Welch, Jack and Susy, "5 Types of Directors Who Don't Deliver,"
Linkedin.com.
Welch, Jack, *Winning*, (Harper Collins Publishing, 2005).
Wentworth, Marilyn, "Developing Staff Morale," *The Practitioner*, 16 (4),
1990.
Whipple, Robert, *The Trust Factor*, (Productivity Publications, 2003).
White, Doug and Polly White, "Money is Nice, But It's Not Enough to
Motivate Employees," *Entrepreneur*, June 23, 2015.
Whiting, Jim, *The Life and Times of Plato*, (Mitchel Lane Publishing, 2006.)
Whitt, Jennifer, "How Do You Deliver Bad News About Your Project?"
ProjectSmart, April 2, 2011.
Whitmore, Jacqueline, "8 Ways to Stay Calm during a Crisis," *Entrepreneur*,
October 7, 2014.
—. "Five Tips for Gracefully Accepting Criticism," *Entrepreneur*, September
8, 2015.

Wilson, E.O., *On Human Nature*, (Cambridge Press Harvard, 1978).

Wladawsky-Berger, Irving, "Data-driven decision making: Promises and limits," *Wall Street Journal*, September 27, 2013.

Wooden, John and Andrew Hill, *Be Quick but Not Hurry*, (Simon and Schuster, 2001).

Workplace Bullying Survey conducted by Zogby International for the Workplace Bullying Institute:
http://workplacebullying.org /multi/pdf/WBI-2015-US-Survey.pdf.

Young, Michelle, George J. Petersen, and Paula Scott, "The Complexity of Substantive Reform: A Call for Interdependence among Key Stakeholders," *Educational Administration Quarterly*, April 2002, vol. 38 no. 2: doi: 10.1177/ 0013161X02382003.

BIOGRAPHY

Leadership

Effective leadership does not occur by chance. Leaders must be trained and groomed for the daunting responsibility of leading organizations. Research shows that half of the people currently in leadership positions will fail. Why they fail and what can be done to prevent failure are the main subjects of this book. The author shows that effective leadership is possible and he illustrates why and how. This book offers examples of leadership and governance from the non-profit sector, businesses, public and private education, higher education, and other organizations. The author highlights over 50 case studies to illustrate concepts about leadership. Also, there are over 530 references and numerous theories and concepts about many aspects of leadership. Key concepts, discussion items, and lessons learned are provided at the end of each chapter.

Author

Garry W. McGiboney, is a nationally recognized leadership and psychology expert. He is the author of eight books and over 40 professional journal publications. Dr. McGiboney has appeared as an expert on *CNN*, *The Discovery Channel*, *National Public Radio*, *Nickelodeon Network* and many other media channels. He has been quoted in *Time Magazine*, *USA Today*, and other major news outlets. Dr. McGiboney is a frequent speaker at state and national conferences. He has received numerous state and national awards. Recently, he was inducted into the University System of Georgia's Hall of Fame for his efforts to help children.

INDEX

absence of trust, 120
active shooter, 159
AdvancED, 197
Alan Axelrod, 38, 49
Alan Goldman, 8
Albert Bandura, 99, 167, 344
Alexcel Group, 77
ambiguous decision, 255
American Association of School
    Administrators, 43, 47, 52, 348,
    352
American International Group
    (AIG), 105
avoidance of accountability, 122

Balanced Scorecard, 214, 215, 216,
    344, 357, 362, 364, 369
Baldrige Performance Excellence
    Program, 204, 224
benchmark settings, 152
benevolent leader, 38, 40, 41, 42,
    56, 57, 60, 61
Better Business Bureau, 195
bias for action, 79, 149
Big Data, 220
Bloomberg, 27, 72, 363
BlueCross BlueShield, 240
British Petroleum, 241
Buffalo Creek Disaster, 264, 277,
    350, 367
Buffalo Mining Company, 265, 266
bullying, 8, 9, 21, 97, 161, 162, 163,
    173
C.S. Lewis, 232
Cabinet Council, 114
Caesar, 94

Carlo Corsi, 30
Carly Fiorina, 120
Center for Community Engagement,
    240, 359
Center for Creative Leadership, 93,
    269, 357
Center for Non-Profit Management,
    204, 205, 346
Centers for Disease Control, 260
chain-supply, 212
Charity Navigator, 201, 202
Charles I, 114, 347
Chip Heath, 290, 354
Civic Index, 15, 16, 44
Clark Clifford, 116
ClearPoint Strategies, 215
Coca-Cola, 288
cognitive dissonance, 10
cognitive psychology, 144
Colin Powell, 47, 221
collateral damage, 100, 257
collective explanation process, 292
content theory, 146
crisis decision theory, 269

Daniel Goleman, 92, 169
data-driven, 210, 211, 212, 214,
    216, 217, 218, 219, 222, 223,
    225, 365, 368
determinants, 7, 9, 11, 12, 14, 25,
    48, 233, 298, 353
Dwight Eisenhower, 46

Edmund Burke, 58
Edward Gerstner, 45, 46, 59, 63, 80,
    87

Edwards Deming, 210, 220
ego, 7, 8, 243, 283
Emory University, 196
epidemiology, 7, 12
Everyone Communicates Few
    Connect, 75
Expectancy and Valence Theory,
    148
Extrapolation, 219

fear of conflict, 121
fear rumors, 286, 302
Federal Emergency Management
    Agency, 160, 351
Field Theory, 165
Fredrick Hess, 16

Gary Burnison, 29, 44, 45
George Patton, 37
Georgia School Boards Association,
    352
Gestalt psychology, 164
Global CEO turnover, 77
Good to Great, 91, 92, 103, 348
Great Recession, 200

H1N1, 260
H5N1, 260
Harry S Truman, 116
Hay Group, 67
Hazmat, 159
Henry Mintzberg, 98
Hersey-Blanchard Leadership
    Model, 89
hesitation, 108, 242, 243, 254
Hewlett-Packard, 50, 359
Holiday, 7, 243, 355
HPPO, 217

IBM, 45, 59, 62, 64, 79, 87, 98
In Search of Excellence, 105, 149,
    364
inattention to results, 122

Influencer, 57, 64, 145, 353, 364
Institute for Crisis Management,
    241
Institute for Executive
    Development, 77
Iowa Governing Boards
    Association, 16, 17, 359

Jack Welch, 8, 38, 86, 130, 131, 133
Jim Collins, 33, 91, 103
John Jantsch, 23
John Maxwell, 55, 75, 126
John Naisbitt, 223
John Wooden, 123, 255
Johnson & Johnson, 253, 267

Kellerman, 7, 8, 356
Ken Blanchard, 63, 89, 355
Kurt Lewin, 61, 63, 164, 165

lack of commitment, 121
laissez-faire leader, 37, 62, 63, 64,
    86, 96
Lipman-Blumen, 9, 359
Lisa Iannucci, 26
Louis Johnson, 117
Louisiana State University, 229
Lyndon Johnson, 116

Machiavellian, 94, 95, 118, 352
malicious intent rumor, 287
Management Sciences for Health,
    169
Marcus Buckingham, 42, 54, 81,
    131, 169
McDonald's, 288, 368
Megatrends, 223, 362
Mere Christianity, 232, 359
Michael Watkins, 65, 74
Military Leadership, 37
military model, 7
Moody's, 200, 356

Nate Silver, 212, 219, 221
National Association of Corporate
  Directors, 73
National Governors Association,
  262, 277, 362
National Institute of Health, 262
National Opinion Research Center,
  158
No Child Left Behind, 198
Nonprofit Association of the
  Midlands, 206

Obfuscation, 243
Occupational Safety and Health
  Administration, 160
One Minute Manager, 63, 345
Opportunity Knocks, 52, 363
organizational psychology, 166, 167
Oxford Dictionary, 113, 114, 363

Parable of the Feathers, 295
paranoid leader, 102, 103
Peter Drucker, 126, 202
Pittston Coal Company, 265
Planned Parenthood, 240
Plato, 370
Pontification, 243
Prevarication, 242, 252
process theory, 146

reciprocal determinism, 168
resources inventory, 148
Revelation, 243, 250, 251
Robert Greenleaf, 12, 37, 39, 41,
  104, 106
Ronald Coase, 221
Rosabeth Moss Kanter, 80, 100

SARA, 239, 365
Self Destructive Intelligence
  Syndrome, 230
Servant Leadership, 12, 37, 41, 106,
  353

Signal and the Noise, 212, 219, 221,
  366
Sir Frances Bacon, 113
Smoldering Crisis, 268
social learning theory, 99
Society for Human Resource
  Management, 73, 367
Society for Industrial and
  Organizational Psychology, 105
Socrates, 294, 296, 350
sore loser, 100
Southeast Association of Colleges
  and Schools, 197
Southern Association of Colleges
  and Schools, 17
Speed of Trust, 29, 60, 91, 94, 116,
  118, 130, 348
St. Louis Business Journal, 20, 350
Standards and Poor, 200
Stanford University, 10, 78, 200,
  221, 351
Stephen Covey, 29, 94, 130
Steve Denning, 43
success profile, 138
succession plan, 28, 73, 74, 75, 77,
  78, 79, 83
Sudden Crisis, 267, 277
SWOT, 270, 272, 345, 355, 363
sycophants, 113, 130, 135, 136, 283,
  344

Team Effectiveness Assessment for
  Management, 124, 139, 140
Terence, 238, 365
The Center for Association
  Leadership, 43, 361
The Classic Touch, 58, 61, 94, 347
The Commitment Engine, 23, 356
The First 90 Days, 64, 74, 369
The Institute of Executive
  Development, 78
Thomas Peters, 105, 149
Thomas Watson, Jr, 45, 46

Three Cs of Implementing Strategy, 109, 350
totalitarian, 9, 37, 38, 39
Toyota, 259, 260, 356
Triadic Responsibility Model, 167
Triple Filter Test, 294
Tylenol, 253, 267, 357

U.S. Department of Education, 198, 202
United States Office of Personnel Management, 368
University of Tennessee, 230

Victor Vroom, 148

Warren Bennis, 136
Winston Churchill, 120, 126, 256, 365
wish fulfillment rumors, 285, 302
Workplace Bullying Institute, 157, 161, 162, 351, 370
World Health Organization, 12, 261

Zappos, 218